RUNNING AT THE EDGE OF THEIR WORLD

THE SUSPECT DEVICE FANZINE STORY

BY
TONY SUSPECT + GAZ SUSPECT

Published by Earth Island Books

Pickforde Lodge

Pickforde Lane

Ticehurst

East Sussex

TN5 7BN

www.earthislandbooks.com

ISBN 978-1-916864-22-1

Printed and bound by Solopress, Southend

For everyone who supports the DIY Punk Scene.
Co-operation not competition.

Foreword

GET OFF YOUR ASS AND DO SOMETHING

I've long thought it ironic that the outside view of Punk tends to be a negative one, concentrated on violence, nihilism, etc. Sure, there's always been elements of that. But from the inside, my overriding Punk experience has been of its extreme creativity.

Its's a well-worn analogy now, but Punk was a movement that in so many ways carved out a highly functioning 'network' long before technological advancements made the term something otherworldly all together. Back then, it involved being in a band purely for the fun of it. Tape trading and exchanging info and ideas by post (don't forget to Soap your Stamps!) Making flyers. Buying records distributed from people's bedrooms. Booking gigs, and even whole tours, by phone (and on trust). Releasing records on small labels, where breaking even was a great success. Binding it all together were fanzines; sometimes crude, but always lovingly assembled publications that allowed its writers the freedom to cover music and issues they were passionate about. Spreading the word. For a period in the mid-Eighties there were tons of 'zines being produced all round the world; it was extraordinary how this under-the-radar movement galvanised so many kids into participating. For a vast majority of them it was an exciting but relatively short-lived phase before other priorities came into play. Getting on with Life, and all that.

Which is why – and I know they will be cringing at the adulation - it's so impressive that, 40 years on from assembling their first issue of Suspect Device at Gary's parents' house in Southampton, he and Tony are still at it. As you will read, in the stories recollected in these pages, this pair of teenage Punks-in-Arms have grown up, gotten responsibilities, ridden out whatever adversities Life has thrown at them, and stuck at it, with a resolute spirit that's solidified their friendship.

For me, it's been a real honour contributing to Suspect Device over the years. Much of my respect for Tony and Gary is down to the way they go about their business in such an unassuming way. The commitment and devotion to keep the 'zine going for so long is incredible, but there's little song or dance about their illustrious past. It's barely worth a mention. The focus is to keep moving forward, sharing what's new 'n interesting to them, and having likeminded mates involved. Some have been part of the S.D. Family for decades, which speaks volumes itself about the primary importance placed on friendship, participation, and cooperation. You will find many of these valued comrades supplying content to this book. It's the S.D. way.

Suspect Device has never been about just Tony and Gary, but You and Me too. It's not about competing in a great credibility race. That would never even enter their consciousness. And, whilst this book is a wonderful celebration of their 'zines remarkable longevity... you can guarantee that behind the scenes, the kettle is on and the gears are already turning, with thoughts on the next issue. Contributions Welcomed.

Pete 'Zonked' Craven

"Enthusiasm the only reason. Continuation is our dedication"

(Heresy – 'Network of Friends')

Introduction To The Opposites

This is a book about our zine, but it also about the punks who came together to create a scene based on the principles of DIY, Friendship and co-operation.

There are countless documentaries and films about punk rock, and generally they never get past 1979, which is a shame because when those doors were kicked open by the original punk bands, kids from all over the world stormed through them. The floodgates were open, and although the early 1980s did bring in something of a punk uniform, there was much more going on than that, and the biggest, most influential evolution was the reaction to Crass. Some of the original London punks often disparage what came next, and when they do they sound like the sort of out of touch old people they initially stood against, the very attitudes that fuelled the anger and frustration that allowed punk rock to explode the way it did. They quickly became what they (supposedly) hated, the elitism and snobbery is disappointing to see in people who should be applauded for heralding in a new era of opportunity and creativity. Those early bands may have spoken about doing it yourself and being an alternative to the music industry, but a lot of the bands jumped at the chance to join the mainstream as soon as they could, played the game and joined the industry. I am not denying their influence and the impact they had on youth culture, and more specifically me, but a lot of them lost sight of their initial ideals. When Crass came along, they showed that you didn't need the mainstream, and leading by example they proved that it was possible to do everything yourself; and so we did. Punk really did become more than music, and more that just a phase.

Gaz and me loved the early punk bands, but we also liked the next generation just as much, and we wanted to be part of this thing, not just consumers, so we started a fanzine, without really knowing what we were doing. Luckily for us a local punk scene sprung up at just the right time, kids from the outskirts of Southampton who were our age came together and decided to make things happen, starting bands, puttting on gigs and starting fanzines. We got involved, and were inspired and energised by this new scene and, although our fanzine journey had already started, the support we felt, and the acceptance and inclusion into a DIY punk scene was inspiring. The inflammable material had been planted in our heads and the explosion was a catalyst for creativity.

Neither of us are particularly comfortable writing about ourselves, Suspect Device has never been about us, it's always been about the bands and people we've featured. But this is the story of our zine, and also of the local scene, and the friends we've made along the way, both of which did so much to help and encourage us and inspire us to continue doing a punk rock fanzine.
(Tony)

Disclaimer!

I guess most disclaimers in a book are not in the introduction, but mine is, and from the outset I wish to make it clear that Suspect Device Punk Fanzine, (There have been others!) but our version, is only here today because of my old mate Tony 'Bones' Suspect. His dedication and sheer enthusiasm for all things Punk is why I'm sitting here typing this! I can claim nothing other than being along for the ride!
(Gaz)

Tony Suspect - Back when I was younger...

I was born in March 1966 in a top floor flat of a converted house on the edge of Millbrook Estate in Southampton. Not long after that we moved to a flat in a block on the estate itself, where my sister was born. Dad was an electrician, working shifts, and mum ran Keep Fit classes. Not long after that, now there were two young children around, dad changed jobs. He moved to the Oil Refinery on Southampton Water, still as an electrician, but no longer working shifts. To be a bit nearer his work we moved to a small terraced house in Hounsdown about three miles west, towards the New Forest. The house cost £3000 and my parents had trouble convincing the bank to give them a mortgage.

We didn't have much money, but I don't remember feeling like we were going without anything. There were plenty of other kids around and we had the run of the streets. I mainly played football out on the road, but there was an older kid, Chris, the son of a friend of my dad who was into music. He wasn't the most academic of kids, but when it came to music he was a genius. To keep him out of trouble his dad had built a practise room in their back garden, it was all sound proofed and my dad had done the the the electrics, and I remember being sat in the rafters while he ran wires around. Once completed most of the room was taken up with a drum kit and I'd go and watch him drum. He'd put headphones on and drum along to records by Genesis, Queen and ELP while I sat under a table watching. It was mesmerising, I couldn't hear what music he was listening to, but just his drumming was enough. After a while he decided he was bored with just playing the drums, and as Phil Collins was left handed, he taught himself to pay left handed, and practised until he was just as good. Then he decided to learn guitar and because he'd read that Brian May had built his own guitars, he decided to build one himself. Soon he became an excellent guitarist. He did play in at least one band, but playing covers in pubs was never going to satisfy him, and when I knew him he only really played on his own. At some point he gave me a pair of drum sticks which I kept for years and years, and they were what I used as I mimed drumming along to my favourite records in years to come.

I liked music from an early age, it had always been on in our house. Mum played a lot of instrumental music as she arranged her Keep Fit classes, and I remember liking a tune called 'Popcorn' by Hot Butter. My dad liked Country, and I can still remember a Roger Millar album being played on the stereo system in our house, but I couldn't tell you any of the songs. Dad also played Willie Nelson and Johnny Cash a lot. The other song I liked in my early childhood was 'Monster Mash' by Bobby Pickett, but by the mid 1970s my favourites were Slade, The Sweet, T-Rex, Suzi Quatro and, er, Gary Glitter. But apart from those Top Of The Pops compilation albums, and the 'Funky Gibbon 7" by The Goodies, which were all presents, I hadn't bought any records of my own, I just contented myself with watching Top Of The Pops and listening to the radio. I remember once telling my drumming friend that I liked 'Tiger Feet' by Mud, and him scoffing that it wasn't proper music, I didn't know then that I'd be hearing that quite a bit more in the years to come when it came to my music of choice. I wasn't so concerned with lyrics then, I wasn't aware of any song being subversive, political or having any sort of social commentary, but then maybe the songs I liked just had throwaway lyrics. However, maybe subconsciously, hearing The Sweet saying "We just haven't got a clue what to do" resonated somehow, maybe it was the anxiety I felt, something that was particularly strong when I lay in bed at the end of the Xmas holidays, not being able to see a light at the end of the dark tunnel that the New Year seemed to have plunged me into.

At that time none of the bands I liked made me feel I could make music and be in a band, that was a different world, and not one the likes of me could enter. My main love was football, I'd been playing and watching it for as long as I remember, and music definitely came second to that.

Gaz Suspect – Nobody's Hero

I'm not entirely sure as I sit here that I want to be in this book! I know that may sound really ungrateful as our backers are fine people and I'm beyond flattered by their offer, so after much deliberation and procrastination I've finally decided to make a start. Where my contribution will end up is anyone's guess, so I'll start at the beginning as everything has to start somewhere, even outer space apparently had a beginning?! Give yourself a meltdown trying to think of what was there before that!

I've taken months to even begin typing this sentence as the fanzine was always designed in my mind at least, to be about what other people were doing and to highlight their efforts and results, in turn this would hopefully pass on my enthusiasm for others to read about. I just like being part of a scene I feel I have an affinity with and the people I've met along the way have for the most part been a credit to Humanity and stayed in touch. It's been one big social really, although being a political creature it does have its serious side.

I've decided not to read what the others have written so far and it's going to be interesting to read when we're done!

Having just written the last paragraph I will give you a short history, as Tony has done about how I arrived at an old Barn in Norfolk aged 57 typing this though! It's nothing remarkable, just how life has gone!

I was born in Lyndhurst in the New Forest on 11th November 1965 at 4am (Checked with Mother for that fact! Only the time – I do know the date you comedians out there). My Dad only had a motorbike at the time and my Uncle Bill had to come and bring my Mum and me home from the small Cottage Hospital according to my Dad. I grew up in Eling (near the much lauded Totton), not to be confused with Ealing in London and it allegedly gets a mention in the Doomsday Book, although I've not read it to prove that fact. Anyway, fast forward to age five and Tony's mother and mine turn up together at the school gates and drop us off for our first day of education. One thing that will become apparent during my contribution to this book is that my memory is to put it mildly – fuggin' awful. I think I've spent most of my waking hours over the last 57 years wondering why I've just walked upstairs to get something, get there and can't remember what the fuck I went upstairs for! Even more worryingly it does not come back to me either! Mind you its kept me reasonably fit over the years. OK! I've digressed. Push the fast forward button again to Hounsdown Secondary School where Tony and me arrive at about 12 years old and a year or so in we find our mutual interest besides football is Punk! Just rewinding a bit, I'm not entirely sure how much Tony and me knocked about together between starting school and getting up to Secondary School, but he may know more about those years than me?

Now I will not claim to have been into Punk since '76' as the most significant thing that year for me was Southampton's stunning win over Manchester United in the FA Cup Final as a then second division club. Ironically the 83rd minute winner was scored by a bloke from Pompey called Bobby Stokes! Tony even got to go to the final, but as my parents had no interest in any sport I had to wait until January 1977 to get to my first Saints game. My Uncle Bill again stepped in and took me – he is nearly 90 now and still goes to games. My interest in Punk and starting to become aware of bands was probably 78/79 time with the Ruts, Public Image and the Angelic Upstarts being in the vanguard for me. Although thinking about it – I had a mate called Dougie Wilson and his sister Jackie was well into Punk from the off and even had the first Crass single, but she was about three years older and like a lot of early Punks had largely lost interest by 78/79 time.

To briefly answer Gaz's question, although we weren't constantly round each other's houses in our pre-teenage lives, we did sit together in one class at junior school, getting into trouble when we carved our names in the old wooden desk we sat at, and there were the odd occasion when he'd come to my house for tea after school, and I'd do the same at his house. I'd also go over to his house and we'd go out on the streets with all the other kids in the area and play huge games of "it" running though the cut-ways and around the garages, or kicking a ball about over the rec. But we lived a mile or so apart, we were very young, so we weren't together as much as we would be in the years to come.
(Tony)

Tony Suspect - Here comes the new punk

The first ten years of my life were dominated by football, I was brought up going to watch my dad play and was eventually the mascot (back then a mascot wasn't someone in an oversized animal costume, it was someone who went with the captain to the ref and toss the coin to decide which team would take the kick off), I'd also collect the tracksuit tops from the players to take back to the dugout. Occasionally I would sit in the dugout with the substitute (at this point dad was the player manager), but mainly I would be kicking a ball about behind the goal while the game was going on. When I was 7 I was taken to an evening game at The Dell. My grandad was a steward there so I was able to stand right at the front with a perfect view and was mesmerised by the look of the pitch under the floodlights and amazed by the noise of the crowd. That was the point I became a Southampton fan.

This meant that, three years later, during Punk Rock's ground zero in 1976, the highlight of my year was going to the FA Cup Final at Wembley to see Southampton win.

But things were starting to change, even if I wasn't consciously aware of it. Later that year I sold my bike, I got £15 for it and I spent half the money on a second hand record player (I bought a Saints FA Cup Final kit with the other half).

The other hint that things were about to really change for me came when my older cousin started wearing straight leg jeans. I couldn't believe it, I was even more shocked when he told me I'd be wearing them soon.

As 1976 turned into 1977 I started to see headlines and shock reports about these punk rockers in my parents' Daily Mirror. I didn't know what it was all about, but the pictures of the strange clothes and safety pins piercing their faces fascinated me. Obviously these people were from big cities, far away from where I was living, on the edge of the New Forest, so although I was interested in these reports, I didn't think anything like that would ever affect my life.

We moved to a new house in 1977, when my grandad came to live with us, it wasn't really that far from our old house, but it felt like we'd moved to the other end of the country. Gaz lived a full two and a half miles away now. I remember, not long after we'd moved in, sitting in the middle of the garden, in the sun feeling a bit cut off and alone and it was only the song of a Blackbird that seemed to offer any comfort. I needed something.

At some point that summer I was in my room tuning in a new radio when I came across Radio 1, it was their Newsbeat show and the first words I heard were something like "We will be speaking to Johnny Rotten and Sid Vicious from the Sex Pistols." I was immediately interested as I recognised those two funny names from the Newspaper scare stories. Then they played 'Pretty Vacant'.

There's a scene in the film Good Vibrations, about Terri Hooley, where he discovers punk at a Rudi gig in Belfast, that does a good job of capturing the thrill and amazement of hearing this music for the first time. I imagine my face looked somewhat similar as the now so familiar 'Pretty Vacant' intro started up, making way for an unbelievably exciting thunderous noise. That opening guitar, the pounding drums and then the sneering vocals, I'd never heard anything quite like it, and it seemed like the best thing ever, like a shining light entering the room and illuminating the grey world around me. I was 11, and I somehow knew I'd found that something.

It would be another year before I started buying records, but punk bands were starting to be played on the radio and appearing on Top Of The Pops. My cousin not only had straight leg jeans, but also records by bands like The Stranglers and Elvis Costello and he would tape them for me. I don't think he ever thought of himself as a punk, but he also introduced me to Ian Dury, Tubeway Army, Boomtown Rats and The Tubes. I was eager to hear as many of these new bands as possible and through the TV and radio I was soon getting acquainted with X-Ray Spex, Blondie, The Clash, Generation X, Penetration and loads more.

A big moment came in 1978 when I went into a record shop and purchased a record with my own money for the first time. It was 'Jilted John' by Jilted John, it had sounded so great on Top Of The Pops, it was basic, snotty and simple, it my have appalled grown ups, and would be sniffed at by some older punks, but it appealed to me straight away.

The shop was called Abbey Music, just a small chart shop that had an upstairs room full of instruments for sale. The downstairs had a rack of LPs, a wall at the back full of cassettes, with the singles over near the counter. On the back wall of the shop there was a bank to TVs for sale. One our school friend's mum worked there, which in years to come proved handy as I could pre-order singles and my friend would bring them to school on the morning of release. There were always unexpected gems to be found in the album racks, I managed to get both Channel 3 albums and the first 'Punk & Disorderly' album from that shop and Gaz got the first Exploited album from there. Although we would do most of our shopping in the years that followed in Southampton, we were still regular visitors to this shop. One Saturday afternoon we were in there as I wanted to buy the new Ruts 7", 'Something That I Said", while we were in there the heavens opened and it chucked it down with rain, so we stayed in the shop. Our friend's mum was working so we chatted to her, persuaded her to play the Ruts single several times, and watched Grandstand, which was on all the TVs with the sound down, to see football scores coming in. It pleases me that although the record shop has long gone, the Chinese take away which now occupies that shop is called Hong Kong Garden. However, that meant that when I once went in there the name of the shop obviously set the Banshees song playing in my head and when I went to order a mushroom chow mein I actually asked for chicken chow mein!I don't go there any more, just in case.

There was another record shop in Totton, Apple Records, which was over the train tracks. We didn't go there as much, but it was more of a proper record shop. I remember buying 'Plastic Letters' the second Blondie album just after Xmas in 1978, the first album I bought with my own money. I also got Sham 69, Cockney Rejects and Angelic Upstarts singles from there in 1979, and Killing Joke's 'Follow The Leaders' 10", it didn't have a proper sleeve and I cannot comment either way on the rumours that a price tag was switched before purchase.

Once I walked the three miles or so from my house to Apple Records just to get a Sex Pistols poster. I remember it being a warm day, I had just broken my arm playing football, and it was still painful which meant with less movement in my hand and having a plaster cast from fingers to elbow, I wasn't able to properly grip the handlebars or breaks on my bike, so I decided to walk down the country lanes instead, just to get a poster.

After that first single was purchased, I'd save my pocket money up until I had enough to buy singles by The Clash, The Damned, Ian Dury, Buzzcocks and the singles , credited to the Sex Pistols, from the 'Great Rock n Roll Swindle'. The early albums I got, along with 'Plastic Letters', were Blondie's 'Parallel Lines', 'A Tonic For The

Troops' by Boomtown Rats (both for Xmas in 1978), The Clash's 'Give 'em Enough Rope', 'Replicas' by Tubeway Army and then 'Never Mind The Bollocks'.

As much as I was absorbing all this new music, I was pretty obsessed with the Sex Pistols and, for a while Sid Vicious. My cousin lent me the Swindle LP and although these weren't really Sex Pistols records, I loved them all the same. When someone at school let me borrow the 'God Save The Queen' 7" It really did feel exciting, and naughty going home and playing this record in my bedroom.

I also remember asking my mum to lend me the money to buy the 'Never Mind The Bollocks' LP, an album I would play so much I had to replace the vinyl after a couple of years.

Once, when I went with my dad to one of his football matches, a team mate was driving and dad asked him if he'd pull over near a record shop so I could run in to buy a particular record. It was the 'Great Rock n Roll Swindle' 7", when dad's friend asked what it was and I said it was by Sex Pistols he said "And I thought you were a nice boy."

I wasn't aware of anyone else liking this music, I don't even know if I was aware that Gaz was also into it at this point. When we went to Secondary School, there were others there who were into punk, and they had records that I could tape. I borrowed a compilation album called '20 Of Another Kind' which introduced me to more bands, like The Lurkers, The Cure, The Boys and one song that had a particular impact on me, 'Suspect Device' by Stiff Little Fingers.

I wanted more by Stiff Little Fingers, so I asked Abbey Records to order the 7", along with their second single, 'Alternative Ulster'. Initially they couldn't find one of them on their order list, because they were looking for 'Suspect Of Ice'.

Very soon it was obvious Gaz was into punk too, and while there were others at school also into it, I would borrow their records and tape them and build up my list of favourite bands and developed a lengthening wants list.

One day I was round a mate's house who's older step brother was into punk, he was out so we went into his room to see what new records he had. This particular day he had two new singles, 'Reality Asylum' by Crass and 'Into The Valley' by Skids. I had heard the Skids one on the radio and it was on my wants list, so we played that, then we played the Crass one, the side we put on was 'Shaved Women' and I hated it. Little did I know the impact Crass would have on my life, or that in time I would come to view 'Shaved Women' as one of my favourite Crass songs. But, at that point, I was 13 and my own politics hadn't yet evolved past being left of centre, so I wasn't ready for what Crass had to say or the way they said it, what I wanted was the punch the air anthems like those provided by the Skids. As soon as I could I went out and bought the Skids 7". It was 1979. Thatcher was elected as Prime Minister, and I would soon be getting myself much more acquainted with politics.

1979 was also the year I got my first pair of Dr Martin boots, a faux leather jacket and a Sid Vicious t-shirt. I was now identifying as a punk.

At some point around this time I got a paper round, so I had some more money of my own. I didn't really like getting up so early and cycling round the village in all weathers, running the gauntlet of angry geese (much more of an issue than dogs where I lived), but it gave me money for records so I put up with it. I still played and watched football, but punk was definitely now the thing I was most interested in, and with this extra money I was buying more records, and releases by bands like The Ruts, Siouxsie & The Banshees, X-Ray Spex and Adam & The Ants were bolstering my collection.

As much as I loved bands like Siouxsie & The Banshees, Buzzcocks and The Ruts, bands who's songs have stayed with me through all these years, there were a few songs that were maybe less sophisticated, but appealed to the teenage angst in me more directly at that time. Songs that were simple, to the point and perfect for a teenage school boy. Angelic Upstarts released their 'I'm An Upstart' 7", a song with a shouty chorus and lyrics that got to the heart of feeling like a punk rebel but having no real outlet for it. The B-Side, 'Leave Me Alone' was great to sing along to when teenage frustrations were strong. Sham 69's, 'If The Kids Are United', 'Hersham Boys' and 'Hurry Up Harry' may not have spoken to me in the same way, but they were great, simple, sing along songs, and when I listen to them now I am taken back to my bedroom and can see the record turning on my turntable. The same can be said of the Cockney Rejects' early singles.

However, those songs may have been great for a wannabe teenage rebel, but it was 'At The Edge' by Stiff Little Fingers that really hit home. I was already a fan of SLF, of course, and I'd managed to get hold of a copy of their third 7", 'Gotta Gettaway', again by ordering it from the local record shop, and I'd bought 'Straw Dogs' from Virgin Records in Southampton, but 'At The Edge', was a real eye opener. At weekends, after my paper round I would often go back to bed and lay there with headphones on listening to my precious records. When this 7" came out I was listening to it one morning and was struck at how much the lyrics spoke to me. These were words that I could relate to, they echoed some of the thoughts that were swirling round my head. It was really the first time where I felt punk was more than just and exciting soundtrack, the first time I was aware of it relating directly to my life, it seemed somehow different than that Angelic Upstarts single; that gave me an outlet for my frustrations, 'At The Edge' was more personal, it seemed to explain where those frustrations came from. I mean as much as I loved the songs that had got me into punk, I didn't really know then what 'Anarchy In The UK' meant, and there was never going to be a 'White Riot' where I lived (unless the cows broke out of their field, which they did from time to time) but talking about teenage frustration and the alienation I felt with the world, and the expectations I thought people had for me was pretty powerful. The way I looked at punk changed then.

Compilation albums were invaluable during these early years, after borrowing, taping and eventually buying, '20 Of Another Kind' (and then a little later '20 Of Another Kind 2'), I also picked up a cassette version of 'Live At The Roxy' and 'The Rare Stuff' LP, both giving me my first vinyl versions of songs by Wire, Johnny Moped, Eater, The Flys, The Saints and Rich Kids . I was desperate to hear as many bands as possible, so a compilation only had to have one band, or even one particular song that I didn't already own, or hadn't yet heard, for me to buy a compilation. The other good thing about these early punk compilations is that they were available in mainstream shops, so I was able to get the 'Back Stage Pass' LP in WH Smiths in 1980, which was the first time I heard Cyanide, and at that time I didn't have the Angelic Upstarts 'Police Oppression', Anti-Pasti 'Four Sore Points' or Cockney Rejects 'Flares & Slippers' singles, and even better it had the combined version of 'Emotional Blackmail' by UK Subs. I bought the 'Jubilee' soundtrack LP just for 'Plastic Surgery' by Adam & The Ants and on a school trip to London, where for some reason they took us into Harrods, I bought a cassette version of 'We Do 'em Our Way' for Devo' version of 'Satisfaction' and the Slits doing 'Heard It Through The Grapevine'. I also liked the fact that I went into Harrods and while everyone else was marvelling at the riches on show, I bought a punk tape. Many more compilations were purchased into the 1980s, and all of them fuelled my love for, and knowledge of, this music.

Two other important stages in my education were when I discovered John Peel's radio show, and when, in 1980, I went to my first gig.

John Peel's show was on Monday to Thursday from 10pm until midnight, and would introduce me to so many great new bands over the years, ones that you wouldn't hear on day time radio or on Top Of The Pops. One of the earliest discoveries was Dead Kennedys when he played 'California Uber Alles', that was a real eye opener, but there were many more to come.

Gaz wasn't able to go to see Adam & The Ants at Southampton's Gaumont in November 1980, so I went to my first gig with two school friends. I'm not really sure why either of them wanted to come with me, neither were into punk, I guess they just wanted to see live music. My dad dropped us off outside the venue, and we stepped out into this throng of punks. I was both excited and totally terrified at the same time, I'd never seen so many punks gathered in one place, I wanted to be part of this, but also I was scared stiff. One girl looked fantastic in her studded jacket and dark Siouxsie style make-up and although it was a cold November night her t-shirt was fashionably ripped, I only realised that I had been staring at her when she scowled at me and I crapped myself and scurried off. Who knows what my companions thought of all this, I was too caught up in what was going on around me to ask.

I feel bad that I didn't take too much notice of support band Gods Toys, in fact I don't remember too much about anything before the lights went out and there was a sound of a stampede as people rushed to the front. We moved to the back of the now standing crowd just before bright lights blinded us and the thunderous sound of two drum kits filled the air and the Ants started their set in an explosion of noise and colour. It was captivating, exciting and they blew my mind. It all seemed to go by in a blur, with old songs still in the set alongside the new, more tribal stuff. I loved it all.

I walked out into the cold night afterwards, dripping in sweat, ears ringing, rolled up poster in my hand and a huge smile on my face.

When 'Dog Eat Dog' was on Top Of The Pops I got a lot of stick at school for liking the Ants. But a few months later, Adam & The Ants were the biggest band in the country and everyone liked them. I enjoyed the fact that I had seen them, and all these new "fans" hadn't.

By now I was getting Sounds delivered each week, and would periodically buy NME and Melody Maker too, the three weekly national music papers. 1981 saw an explosion of new records that Gaz and me couldn't get enough of. We'd regularly get the train into Southampton, walk up the hill and through the bus station to Subway Records, a small packed shop with the singles upstairs. We went in so often that the guy who worked there got to know us and would often let us look through any new releases before they went out on the shelves. After Subway we'd walk down to Virgin Records by the Bargate (the castle-like building in the middle of Southampton, that was originally the northern entrance to the city), and from there over to HMV which was then a tiny shop the other side of the Bargate. Here the singles were downstairs. We'd then go through the parks to St Mary Street, there we'd go to Underground Records, a second hand shop, and then on to Henry's, a shop that my dad used to go to when he was younger. Underground was a great shop, by the early 1980s people were getting rid of the punk records they bought in the late 1970s as they'd moved on to the latest thing, so Gaz and me were able to get those early records we were too young to pick up originally, and they were pretty cheap too, none of this record collector nonsense you get now. There was a joy in flicking through the racks and finding real gems that you could actually afford. I was able to pick up copies of singles by The Vibrators, Chelsea, Generation X, Ramones, Eater, Radiators From Space and Crass' 'Feeding Of The 5000' on Small Wonder records.

New records we were buying during this period were by new bands like Blitz, Peter & The Test Tube Babies, Adicts, Discharge, Chron Gen, Action Pact, Flux Of Pink Indians, and more importantly Subhumans.

In April 1981 Gaz went to his first gig, and this time we went together. It was Stiff Little Fingers and The Wall at the Southampton Gaumont.

We went to lots more gigs together from this point on, including Siouxsie & The Banshees, Bauhaus, Newtown Neurotics, Atilla The Stockbroker, New Model Army, The Alarm, Big Country, Killing Joke and Dead Kennedys with MDC and Peter & The Test Tube Babies.

By this time pretty much everyone else at school who'd previously shown an interest in punk had moved on to other stuff.

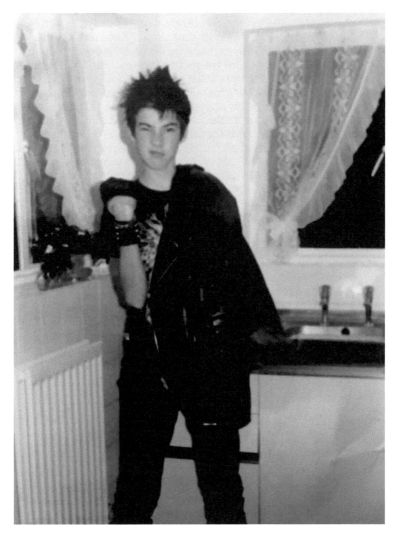

Gaz Suspect - Closed Groove

I never really had any interest in music before Punk! The first record I think I ever brought was either 'Never Mind The Bollocks' or 'Hanx' by Stiff Little Fingers?! I liked a bit of Glam Rock, but can't claim anything like a lot of others I've read books by. I do remember hating Abba and Leo Sayer and let's face it that's enough to make anyone turn Punk for the alternative to that shite! I still feel roughly the same now, although my diatribes have mellowed a bit! But only a bit!

As Tony and me progressed through our Secondary education it became apparent that we were really the only kids who liked Punk to any great extent in the entire school. As the 1970's ended and the 1980's started, so did a new wave of well documented Punk bands.

We were starting to go to a few gigs and apart from a few quid going on a rail excursion or two, (Trainspotter alert! Still am!!) all of my available cash was going on Punk vinyl as was Tony's. We left school in 1982 and spent that summer playing Punk records. Southampton as a City seemed quite a poor relation to other places as far as Punk went in the early 1980's – most of our Punk heroes successfully managed to give the place a wide berth with the exception of the Dead Kennedys and the idea of going further afield to us was not on our radar at that time. Bands like Discharge, The Exploited, Blitz, you name them, never made it! We had the records though and for a while that sufficed! Like everyone else we scoured the columns of Sounds for our Punk fix and of course the man who did more than anyone to put Punk bands of this era on the map – 10pm to Midnight the late great John Peel. Me and my old radio drifting in and out of tune and sleep listening for anything and all things Punk.

We both did a year at Southampton Technical College and both left in the summer of 1983 where upon I started an Apprenticeship as a Radio & TV Engineer off the back of my finest exam result ever! A City and Guilds in 'Electronic Servicing'. I can't say I had that much enthusiasm for that sort of thing, but after avoiding one of Thatcher's Youth Opportunity Scheme's that was better than the alternative and my Dad suggested the future was technology! I still wanted to be a train driver, but the railway seemed a closed shop and rife with nepotism. I actually left school without knowing what I wanted to do and performed poorly in most of my exams due to being unable to motivate myself to revise my entire education and recount it during two and a half hours sat in the school gymnasium. I think Tony did Business Studies! I'll let him explain what that was.

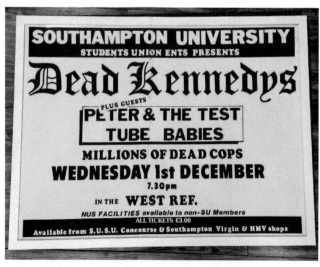

Tony Suspect - Think of something that you want to do with your life

I didn't know what I wanted to do when I left school, the careers advice was either work in a bank, or join the army, and I didn't want to do either. The dream my younger self had of becoming a footballer was obviously not going to happen, and although I had some sort of interest in working with animals I really didn't know what that meant. The only other thing I was interested in was music. What I didn't realise then was that doing something like Sound Engineering would have interested me, but I didn't really know that was a thing then. I went to an open day at the local Tech College and when I said I wanted to do something with music, they suggested drama. I didn't want to do drama. Somehow I ended up on a business studies course, just because I didn't know what else to do. My first day at college saw me turn up with my arm in a plaster cast after breaking it (for the third time) playing football, I had big Doc Martins on with skin tight jeans and a GBH t-shirt. This look got me the nickname Golf Club, because I was skinny as a rake and wore these big boots. It was such a feature of me that when I damaged ankle ligaments (again playing football) and couldn't get my boots on, the sight of me in trainers caused a bit of shocked reaction from the people on my course.

On that first day at college I'd made sure I got into town early enough to go to Henry's records to buy the new Exploited single, the Attack/Alternative 7". Gaz was at the same college, but doing a different course, and there were no other punks on my course, but some interesting characters. There was one guy who seemed to be a bit older, even though he was the same age as me, he thought he was a bit suave but he was actually an ok guy, and we got on pretty well. Another used to say "never refuse a cup of tea, it could be your last" which endeared me to him somewhat, but he was the sort who would probably have ended up working in the city, or a bank at the very least, we had nothing in common apart from a liking for tea. Another just used to say to me "You're such a cliche punk" which I didn't take seriously from a guy who wore a suede jacket and a Doors t-shirt. The girls were much more down to earth and I got on particularly well with two of them. One was a fan of U2, and as I had the first two U2 albums we had something to talk about. The other girl I don't remember being into music much, but she was funny and somehow shared my excitement when I found out the Dead Kennedys were playing Southampton, even though she didn't know who they were. They were both genuine friends for the year I spent at college, the U2 fan and her boyfriend were in a horrible car crash and spent a lot of time in hospital towards the end of my time there.

A lot of people on my course would go to the pub in dinner breaks, but I went record shopping, I was always more interested in records than alcohol. I remember getting back for one afternoon session with the first Blitz album and my class mates not being able to believe how many songs were on the record!

I left after a year and found myself on one of Thatcher's YTS schemes, but again, only because I didn't know what else to do. All I was interested in was buying records and going to gigs, thinking about a future of working wasn't something I was fully able to get my head around.

In 1983 Subhumans released their 4th 7", the 'Evolution' EP. I had discovered the Subhumans back in 1981 after reading a short write up in Sounds which made me want to check them out, it wasn't a completely complimentary piece, but something about it seemed to indicate that they were a band I'd like. I remember going to buy the 'Demolition War' 7", and as was usual back then I asked for two copies, one for Gaz.

But they only had the one copy in stock. Gaz did get the record soon after and we were both instantly fans. The first three EPs, and the album 'The Day The Country Died' have remained favourites to this day, but, for me, the 'Evolution' EP proved to be a really important release. This wasn't just because it features more great songs, but it really opened my eyes to Animal Rights, and the cruelty us humans inflict on animals. I had always viewed myself as an "animal lover", but I'd never really thought too much about eating them or the fact that they were used in cruel experiments. This record made me reevaluate my life and although I didn't actually become vegetarian for a little while, I did begin to question myself, and it became harder and harder to justify eating meat and wearing leather. Also, there was an insert that listed the companies who's products were not tested on animals (as it was easier than listing those that did animal tests). That really had an impact on me, the fact that even if I couldn't directly stop the tests, I could choose to not to give my money to those companies that profited from these cruel and unnecessary tests. I realised that boycotting was something that I could easily do. It's fair to say that buying this record was the first step on my journey to veganism.

By this point, punk was already influencing and informing my political outlook, and now I could add a growing awareness of animal rights too.

In July of 1983, Killing Joke released their fourth album, 'Fire Dances'. I bought it on cassette as I then had a personal cassette player. Not a Sony Walkman, I couldn't afford one of those, mine was a cheaper Sanyo version, and was the size of a brick. But I took it everywhere, even strapping it to the rack on my bike when I rode anywhere. It explains why I bought quite a few albums from that time on cassette.

That summer we had a family trip to France, towing an old caravan that dad had bought and had done up. It was an eventful trip that included a car accident (we were hit after about an hour in France, wrecking the caravan), which meant we aborted the planned extended trip down to Italy and and meant we eventually found ourselves on a campsite in the South of France. I started sleep walking, I also managed to kick a car park hard enough to put a hole in my trainers, sock and big toe, then passed out from the pain. Mum lost jewellery, I played in a football tournament with a French team I didn't know, who's English wasn't great (I didn't speak French), but they'd come to ask me to play after seeing me kick a ball about outside the battered but patched up caravan. The tournament was in a big stadium and our first game was at midnight. The holiday was abandoned a week early, and we got a puncture on the way back and missed the ferry. But during all this, dad had said that the four of us could bring two cassettes each to play on the long drives, and we'd alternate. My choices were the 'Fire Dances" cassette and The Damned's 'Machine Gun Etiquette', so both albums remind me of being sat in a hot car, stuck in traffic on long, straight French roads. I also bought myself a Sex Pistols t-shirt from a market stall near the camp site, and got dad to drive around looking for a record shop as I wanted to buy Plastic Bertrand's 'Ca Plane Pour Moi' in France (I didn't realise then that Plastic Bertrand was from Belgium).

It wasn't a great trip, but it gave me a lot of stories and I had punk rock to get me though it.

Tony Suspect - Collect up the ideas and duplicate

I'm not sure what initially made me want to do a zine, other than wanting to be more than just a consumer. I would have been aware of Sniffin' Glue and Ripped & Torn, but hadn't seen a copy of either at this point.

Punk was evolving, the older, bigger bands were changing, and those from the early 1980s were looking at those bigger bands and a lot of them were diluting their sound in an attempt to "appeal to a wider audience", some were actively looking for major label deals. But, with Crass showing the way, there was a move to really put the "anyone can do it" message at the forefront of what punk was about, and that was what appealed to me, and doing a fanzine was a way of being part of that.

I can't remember the first fanzine I saw, but it was probably something like Raising Hell or Concrete Jungle, certainly I would have sent off for zines after seeing a mention or a small ad in the music press, and by 1983 I wanted to do a zine. However, I wasn't the most confident, outgoing person, and my nervousness meant there was no way I was going to do it on my own. It seemed obvious, to me, that I'd do a zine with Gaz, we were doing most things together, always round each other's houses or going record shopping or to football. Sadly, Gaz wasn't in to it, so I put the idea on the back burner.

Pete Zonked!

"The first 'zine I bought was issue one of Kill Your Pet Puppy, in early 1980. I've no clear recollection how I came to know of its existence, but we got the NME every week in the school library (which I'd spend my Wednesday mornings studying) so it could be there was mention of KYPP in the classifieds. Wherever I did read about it, the inclusion of Adam and The Ants + Crass got me interested enough to send off a postal order for the requested funds (25p + postage). In all honesty, being new to this game, I wasn't sure exactly what it was I was sending off for, with some vague notion it might be a flexi disk, and a booklet? Who knows! What arrived was a colourful thin A5 size magazine. The page layouts were very different to the regimented look of the weekly music broadsheets I was used to, but the more time I spent poring thru it, the more I came to appreciate the raw cut 'n paste aesthetic, which encouraged me to experiment with my own artwork and collages. Was another key moment in my Punk Education. Shame I lost that issue along the way though (doh)."

I did find another way to satisfy my creative urges. I had been listening to Attila The Stockbroker who had opened my ears to other ranters, Seething Wells, Porky The Poet (Phil Jupitus) etc and I had written few poems. These were inspired by the early 1980s punk bands, and my growing political understanding, and were my attempt to unleash my frustrations at the crumbling state of Thatcher's Britain. I even put these poems together in a booklet. Gaz and me made a cover and to try and make it properly represent "Burning Britain" we singed the edges of the cover, leaving burn marks on it and tried to age the paper with tea. I called it Great What? after the Conflict song. I guess you could call it a prototype fanzine, although I only did one copy. My desire to do a punk zine hadn't dimmed though.

For years I was convinced that I picked up a copy of issue 4 of Dorset zine Damaged at a West Indian Club gig. However, it appears that by the time gigs started at the West

Indian Club we had already started the zine, so I must have picked up the zine from somewhere else, probably a small ad in Sounds.

The issue had a 4-Skins interview on one page and on the facing page was a Crass interview, and seeing these two bands from supposedly rival factions of punk featured in a zine next to each other really resonated. Gaz and me had never been interested in picking sides, we liked the bands we liked and didn't care which label the music press had given them. So seeing the 4-Skins and Crass in one zine was inspiring and reignited my desire to do a zine.

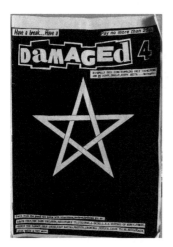
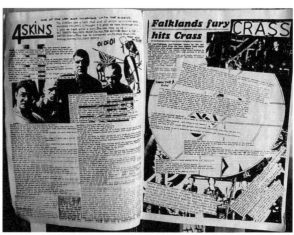

Wherever I got it from, that issue of Damaged really inspired me and I was now more than ever determined to do a zine. I suggested it again to Gaz as I still had my fears of doing it alone, and happily he was more into it this time and we started writing to bands and reviewing records and gigs straight away.

The name of the zine was easy to come up with. We had flirted with the idea of doing a band, and being huge Stiff Little Fingers fans, we were going to call this band Suspect Device. However, we didn't really know anyone else who'd want to join us, and although Gaz had a guitar, and I had a bass and a drum kit, we never got as far as writing any songs, so when we decided that our creative collaboration should be a zine rather than a band, we just kept the name.

When it came to content for our first issue, I had already been in contact with both Gaz Stoker from Red London, and Gaz Naylor the original drummer of Resistance 77 for some time. I'd initially sent off for practise/demo tapes from both of them, and our correspondence had continued, so they were were obvious choices to be interviewed. Also, at the time both of us were into the ToyDolls, their silliness and fast songs had struck a chord, so we also sent them a few questions.

We went to see the Toydolls in Portsmouth, from memory Rob Callen and Bod (from Southampton - there was another Bod, from Winchester) came with us. By the time the Toydolls hit the stage we'd already missed our last train home. It was February and cold, with freezing fog clinging to the night air as we left the venue after the gig, our leather jackets and t-shirts weren't keeping the cold out. So we just wandered the streets. We tried to squeeze in a phone box to keep warm, but that didn't work. Rob had enough money to get a tea, but the rest of us didn't, and the low point of the night was being down at the waterfront and being so cold we'd forgotten how much we had enjoyed the gig. In the end we found a block of flats and sat in the lobby, it was the warmest place we'd found. I'm not sure how long we'd been in there, but when someone emerged from he lift as they made their way to work and looked horrified at the four punks sprawled on the floor that they ran out of the building, we thought it was time to leave the building and head back to the station. We got on the first train back to Southampton, and I can still remember how welcome the train's heaters were. Funny enough, we were back in Portsmouth soon after, this time to see The Damned. We made the last train home that night, and got back to Gaz's house some time in the early hours. But Gaz had forgotten his keys, and didn't want to wake his parents up as his dad had to be up and off to work early. Luckily his dad's car was unlocked in the garage, so we got in there to keep warm and to grab what sleep we could. When his dad got up we went into the house and explained what had happened. His parents laughed and said "You should have knocked on the door."

When it came to putting the zine together, it has to be said we didn't really know what we were doing, or what to ask bands, but we bashed on regardless.
At this point we hadn't really been exposed to any sort of DIY scene, and my tastes we still quite focused on the bigger, more established bands and, to my shame, I was very sniffy of some of the new, hardcore bands, especially ones from North America, even though I loved the Dead Kennedys, DOA, Kraut, Youth Brigade and Channel 3. I'd heard them all on John Peel and had bought their records, but hadn't, at that point investigated too many more bands. For example, when MDC played with the Dead Kennedys and Peter & The Test Tube Babies in Southampton, in December 1982, I couldn't get my head around what they were doing at all. It was like nothing I'd experienced before and to say I wasn't impressed is something of an understatement. In time I would, of course, come round to what they were doing, and learn to love those early songs.
So our first issue included a lot of coverage of bands like SLF, The Damned, Ramones, Peter & The Test Tube Babies, Neurotics, Angelic Upstarts and New Model Army, but we did have reviews of Cult Maniax, DOA, Rubella Ballet and The Oppressed. We also included way too many playlists, but as I said we didn't know what we were doing, we were just doing it. I did notice that as well as Damaged zine, Concrete Jungle also got a mention, and we included poems, and the back page was a collage of anti-vivisection leaflets.
Initially, most of the zine was typed and laid out at Gaz's house, because at that point he was the only one with access to a typewriter. We'd sit around the dining table at his house with this huge typewriter, Pritt Sticks and scissors and made our first zine. My dad had bought himself one of those Amstrad home computers and a cheap printer, so I could type out reviews on that, then take the bits of paper to Gaz's to be stuck in.
Despite my enjoyment of doing the zine and excitement at actually doing something more than just buy records, I was still worried about exposing myself to ridicule, and the reviews in the early issues are not credited to either of us.
Although my dad was still working at the same place, he now had a more supervisory role, which meant he had a desk in an office, and that office had a photocopier. So when we had finished the first issue, he would stay late to print off copies for us. I would then lay all the pages out on the floor at home, collate them and then staple the pages together.

One thing that has become obvious now we have delved into the beginnings of our fanzine, is that although we started writing the zine in 1984 and did a lot of the work on it through the latter part of that year, the first issue didn't actually come out until mid 1985. But you'd never date a band's formation from their first gig, you'd go from the point they got together ask started making a racket together, and it was 1984 when we started writing, typing, sticking and reviewing.

SD#1 is not a great issue, but it was a start and definitely a DIY publication, we were full of enthusiasm and using the tools and knowledge available to us at that time. However, it is interesting that in the intro we said that we didn't know if we'd do another one.

But, something was stirring, and the origins of a local scene were forming. We'd already met up with a couple of other local punks by this point. Gaz had met another punk at night school, while I had been writing to someone who lived in Totton, who'd got in contact via a ToyDolls newsletter, and it turned out that this was the same person, Rob Callen. Not long after we realised we were both talking to the same person, we found out about a gig in Southampton. This was a gig in a pub, not a concert, and so we arranged to go with Rob. We met Rob near Totton train station, and Rob had a mate with him, someone called Rut. Funny enough, before getting on the train we'd met up outside a pub called the Red Lion, and that night there was a band playing there called The Yah Yahs, their guitarist would end up playing football with Gaz and me, and we'd feature his next band on our first comp tape. At this point we didn't really know Rut, but had often seen the name of his band, Suburban Filth, sprayed on the railway bridge in Totton, and had even seen an ad for their demo on the noticeboard of Bondage In General, a shop in Southampton that sold punk clothes (I'd bought an SLF t-shirt there and later on bondage trousers and a leather jacket).

Bondage In General has long gone, the building has been replaced by Student Halls. Rob, Rut, Gaz and me took the train into Southampton and made our way to The Joiners, it was the first of hundreds of gigs I would see at this venue. The bands playing were I am 7, The Sack and another I cannot remember, but also at the gig were people who would become friends, in fact most of them I still see to this day. I bought an Anarka & Poppy demo from a friendly guy holding a carrier bag full of tapes, this was Craig Burton who did the first Southampton DIY punk zine.

Before long we were going to more small gigs and it wasn't long before we got our hands on other local zines, and these smaller, more intimate and ultimately more interesting and exciting gigs were starting to happen more often. As well as Craig Burton's Beercan, there was Mike Fox's Another Krummy Zine and Rob Callen's Bouquet Of Barbed Wire.

So, despite what we said in the first one, it wasn't long before we were doing another issue.

Gaz:

(A resume of the issues of Suspect Device, without looking at what Tony or anyone else has written!)

Issue #1 – As I type this I'm not actually in possession of a copy and can't actually remember what I did for that issue? (Not much if memory serves me correctly!) I don't think I interviewed any bands, but I think the bands were Resistance 77 who released the excellent 'Thoroughbred Men' LP just a few months before Tony interviewed them. The Toy Dolls were in there too, along with Red London. Had the pleasure of seeing Red London at Rebellion a couple of years ago and had forgotten how good they were.

Tony: I remember us collaborating on the interviews for this one. I certainly had contacts in Resistance 77 and Red London, but my memory is of us writing the majority of this issue at Gaz's house and both having input for the interviews.

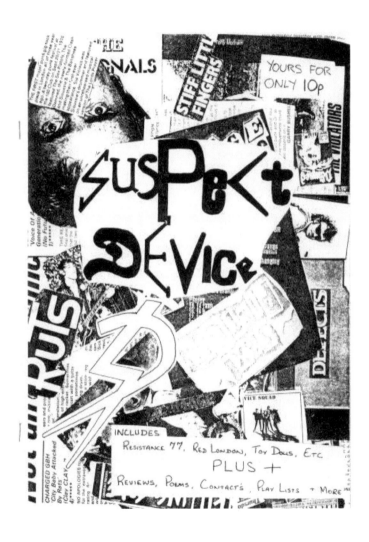

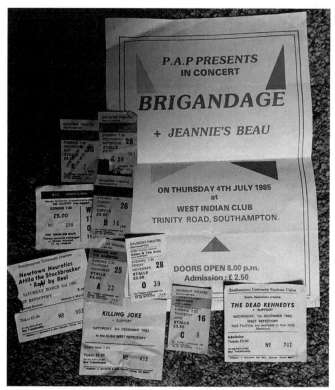

Some early gig tickets and Poster for Brigandage gig

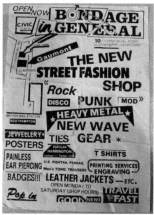

Advert for Bondage In General shop
(Image supplied by Garran Green)

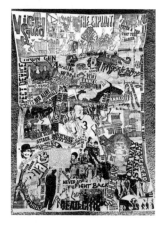

A1 collage created by Gaz, mid 1980s

Gaz Suspect - DIY Punk

I'm not sure when the real awakening to real DIY Punk came about, but Tony was on it quicker than me that's for sure. He wanted to start writing Suspect Device long before me and if I'd have sorted myself out, the first issue could easily have been out a year earlier! Once again, we were quite prolific at taking a punt on bands we'd read about and used to pushbike into Southampton to save on the train fare to find the 'Pay No More Than' records in Subway or Henry's Records. I didn't even realise that a lot of the bands I was buying records by actually organised their own gigs etc. I was even sending off to Dick Lucas of the Subhumans for tapes from his Bluurg distro and another great tape label – BBP Tapes and still didn't really have the 'sus' on what was going on! Naïve I think is the word as you can't use words like a bit 'thick' or 'dim' these days!

Three blokes and a Dutch lady walk into a pub! One used to sing in a band called Crass; one is a History Professor; one is a semi-retired Telephone Engineer, who helps write a Punk Fanzine that's been around for a few years; and the Dutch lady is married to the bloke who used to sing for Crass! (Are you following this?) Collectively they call it 'The Office'. The regular venue is 'The Jubilee' in Norwich and within its walls many a random subject is discussed – and as the beer sinks in, a lot of the discussions are not remembered in any great detail! However, on this occasion, a digital tape recorder is on the table. Two of the blokes, let's call them Steve and Matt, think it'd be a good idea to interview the other bloke called Gaz about his fanzine Suspect Device. The Dutch lady, Jona, decides she'd rather go shopping. So, on the afternoon of Friday 30th June 2023, the ales are going down well and the following was recorded and transcribed thereafter by a fine fellow by the name of Richard.

Matt - Why and when did you start a fanzine Gaz? **Gaz** - We started the fanzine in the year 1984. We should have started earlier, but due to my own apathy and not matching my friend Tony's enthusiasm, the first issue appeared in early 1985.

Matt - How did you decide who was in it? And how much did it cost? **Gaz** - The bands in it, and I only know this because I looked it up recently, were Resistance 77, The Toy Dolls, and a band called Last Rough Cause (It was Red London in issue number 1, Last Rough Cause appeared in issue 2 - Tony). We had a contact at a very large petrochemical company (Tony's Dad) who used to take our originals to his office photocopier on the night shift and print them out for us. If that isn't DIY I don't know what is. A huge multinational footing the bill! The cover price was only 10p.

Matt - With the first copies being from Xerox photocopying machines, how many lasted like that before you looked elsewhere? **Gaz** - I did know some girls in the office at work and they knocked out loads for us.

Steve - Was it easy to get in touch with bands? The Toy Dolls, for example. Did you find when you were doing interviews with people, they took you as seriously as they would have done with someone like Jon Savage or whoever? **Gaz** - That's a good question. At the time, I think all the addresses came either off the back of a record cover or out of a music magazine. It was the only way then. No internet, nothing.

Steve - Who was the most famous? **Gaz** - Initially we came off the back of the early-1980s era bands, so we focused on them. But then we got a bit more sussed and thought 'let's do bands that don't get coverage or would like more coverage'. We learnt as we went along and it got more DIY over time. Outside of poncing off other people's photocopiers, we started going for bigger bands, but then we got into bands that were even less well-known! – particularly into the late 1980s.

Matt - Was a lot of it done through the post or did you do some live interviews? **Gaz** – Famously, we did a band from Portsmouth called Red Letter Day who were really good. We sat in a situation like this in a pub and recorded an interview; we did that a few times. Most of it, though, was literally writing questions on a piece of paper, sending it to the band, then they'd send them back on another sheet of paper and we'd type them up on an old manual typewriter, which my dad had pinched from work!

Matt - Other than interviews what other kinds of things do you do? **Gaz** - Gig reviews, record reviews, all the fun of the fanzine fair. We got sent an awful lot of stuff to review, but we also reviewed the records that we bought. Once the fanzine got more established, we did get sent a hell of a lot to review.

Matt - So how many did you do in 1985? **Gaz** - It would have run into hundreds, but we never kept count of them. The earlier fanzines from the 1980s going into the '90s, just before the advent of the internet, were easily the best sellers.

Steve - Do you think the internet killed off fanzines or had they had their day anyway? Sounds packed it in around this time. **Gaz** – Well, that possibly marked the start of the decline, but we were never good at selling them. We used to hawk them around gigs and so on, but we were never good salesmen. If somebody didn't want to buy something we'd leave them alone.

Matt - Did you ever try getting into the fanzine networks that started for local distribution? **Gaz** - When we started the zine a lot of the gigs we went to were all part of the South Hants Fanzine Collective. A lot of people in the mid-1980s who wrote fanzines used to get together and put on gigs. It was good DIY stuff really. But everything has its day and once the internet began to ramp up some people moved on.

Matt - There seems to have been a bit of a comeback of fanzines though? **Steve** - I've been given things at gigs, fanzines and so on, and they tend to be like comics: cartoons and so on. I really miss the old typeface, the clickety click of the typewriter. There's something about looking at some of the old fanzines done on typewriters and Xeroxed.

Gaz - A lot of fanzines tried to overlay type onto picture backgrounds and, depending on where they were printed, I found them hard to read. I don't think fanzines have truly had their day, otherwise we wouldn't persevere with what we've been doing for the last 40 years. We only sell a couple hundred now, but people do like to have a physical copy and don't always want to look at a screen.

Steve - I never had problems doing interviews with fanzines at all. I always found it really easy. If I was doing an interview with Sounds or somebody, then I'd know loads of people would be reading it and I'd think to myself that I have to be careful. While doing a fanzine I can let loose a lot more. I was personally never a great fan of Maximum Rocknroll. Was it a fanzine or what was it? I also found it too overwhelming to read through. I did an Interview with the guy who ran it, really nice geezer and everything, but that was the end of fanzines as I knew it. **Gaz** - Fair comment. I used to read MRR, but not all the time because as you say there was a lot to it and the Americans have a slightly different slant on stuff don't they?

Matt - I'm writing a book about fanzines and when MRR came out in mid-1982, you can begin to see British fanzines covering more American bands. You can really see its influence. **Gaz** - We tried not to divide punk into different genres like Anarcho-Punk, Oi, Street Punk, Garage Punk, whatever subcategory. If we liked a band and they had something to say, we'd interview them. We tried to be all-encompassing.

Matt -Did anybody not want to be interviewed? **Gaz** - Never had that actually, although people might not reply for whatever reason. But nobody actually said 'no, we don't want to be in your fanzine'. We've had a lot of questions not returned for whatever reason.

Matt - Did anybody respond to any of the reviews you wrote? **Gaz** - Loads of people and generally good. The only own goal, which was down to me really, was I interviewed the Oi band Condemned 84 from Ipswich, who apparently had dodgy links; or one or two of them did. I did this in the same issue of the fanzine as Attila the Stockbroker. Now, he did object to that and looking back it was a bit of an own goal by me ... but you live and learn. Can't make any apologies, because we didn't do it deliberately.

Steve - I think that's the difference with Maximum Rocknroll and the American thing. They would refer to 'the scene' and to me punk was never 'a scene'. **Matt** - MRR always seemed to have a 'line' didn't they, about what they believed punk was and who was part of it? **Steve** - It would be interesting to see if a suburb of Chicago had their own fanzine. **Gaz** - They all had their own scenes. There was the New York Hardcore bands. When Minor Threat came out and Ian MacKaye started Dischord Records, there was the DC scene and all sorts of stuff like that. They just put their own spin on it really and I think a lot of it has been copied over here too. Many people, myself included, were looking for something a bit different as the early 80s punk scene ran out of steam over here. A lot of the bands split up and many of us were just looking for something different to get into. The American bands filled the void really.

Matt - What about other countries, because you'd have big punk scenes happening in Scandinavia and places like that? **Gaz** - We did some stuff with those bands. South American bands as well. **Matt** -During my research, I found some really odd things like somebody had a punk report from Poland from around the year 1981. What's the furthest you got to? **Gaz** - Oh we've been to all of those places interviewing bands, especially in recent issues. A lot of them are young as well.

Matt – So did the type of the people you're interviewing change over time then? **Gaz** - When Suspect Device first came out, everybody was in the same age range really . We were all more or less in our late-teens going into our early-twenties and we got older together. Nowadays, we really try to focus on finding new bands from all over the world, and we've found some bloody good ones. You speak to any touring band now, for example Peter and the Test Tube Babies, and they do four-or-so dates in four different South American countries. By all accounts, they go absolutely mad for it over there. It's not until this day and age that people have the opportunity to see bands they'd only ever previously heard of.

Matt – Are you getting younger bands sending you stuff? **Gaz** - There are a lot of people who are my age, in their 50s, that starting bands and still wanting to be in bands, which is great. Many are experienced musicians now. They've done a lot of gigs in other bands and bring out new stuff. But personally, and I know Tony who does the fanzine with me thinks this, we are always looking for people at least half-our age to get their take on it all.

Matt - Do you still type it up on a typewriter? **Gaz** - It's all on Microsoft now. Bill Gates and his cronies have finally got us. There's no way around it. They've added to their billions by selling us a software package. However, what we do try to do by way of computers is try to make it look like it was put together on an old typewriter. **Steve** - That's so weird, because I was in the studio doing something with Sotos and he showed me something and I thought 'that sounds authentic!' There's an actual program you can put it though that makes it sound like an old audio cassette. I thought "this is ridiculous!" **Gaz** - You can get this thing now, because there's a lot of birdsong in our garden, you can record 30 seconds of it into an app and it will tell you exactly what bird it is!

Steve - Going back to fanzines, you'll read one fanzine from England or another from America or even from Poland, and they're all coming from different directions. I always found Polish stuff very industrial or proper working class. Italy would be really political. You'd think that because we're all into punk or whatever, that there'd be a general consensus. But it's really odd to discover how different the take is in different countries. I found that out when I was doing the tour last year in Belgium and we decided to do an encore of 'Ziggy Stardust'. We began doing it, but everybody was just stood still and I said 'right, stop this it isn't working, do "Owe Us a Living" quick!!'. Then, a couple of days later we were in Dijon and I was doing an interview with a mate of mine Jean-Christophe. He says: 'Steve, you often talk about David Bowie being a big influence on you, but to us he's just a pop star'. Then I realised of course that's the difference, because in England David Bowie was huge so there's different influences there. **Matt** - I know a guy in Sweden who loves Discharge and every record he owns and plays is a Discharge record. I said "there must be other stuff that you like" and he said "no".

Steve – Did you ever try to interview, say, Adam Ant or John Lydon? **Gaz** - We wouldn't have even have tried. Those people wouldn't have been our focus anyway. The Toy Dolls and Peter and the Test Tube Babies were probably the biggest bands we were interested in interviewing. As things went on, we got more and more into the DIY way of it. Interviewing bands with no manager or contracts, that's been the theme of it ever since really. We didn't want to be too samey, but we enjoy talking to like-minded people. There was a danger with the punk scene years ago, that it wasn't always too welcoming; it could be a bit insular. If you didn't know what was going on then you were on the outside. The DIY scene wasn't always very good at promoting itself or being more inclusive on occasions. **Steve** - The unspoken rules were very strict. **Gaz** - They were in a lot of ways, yeah. **Steve** - DIY can be 'don't involve yourself'. I know I've made that joke loads of times, but that's why. I remember Frank and Pete from In the City fanzine told me they'd interviewed Adam Ant and that he wasn't very nice about Crass. Well that didn't surprise me because by this time I was taking the piss out of him too. Apparently, they were allowed to ask three questions and that was it. At Rebellion, actually, you're only allowed to take three photographs and that's it. At a lot of gigs now, you have to get a special pass. I think it's so every photographer gets a chance from each magazine. But the problem is towards the middle of the set they are going to be the best photographs, because that's when the band are getting into it.

Jona - How do you actually start a fanzine Gaz? **Gaz** - The only way I can say you start a fanzine is to have enthusiasm for a certain genre of music, i.e. Punk, and you just want to get more involved. So if like me you can't play a musical instrument and you can't remember lyrics, then you can write about it instead.

Tony Suspect - DIY or DIE

I didn't know that I was looking for a local DIY scene, but when small punk gigs started happening I knew they were exactly what I wanted, and needed. These gigs were put on by people my age, they were welcoming and friendly and now I was part of something cool. Gaz is much more social than I am, and had been part of the initial discussions on setting up the STE Collective (which came after the South Hants Fanzine Collective who had initially put on local DIY gigs, putting in his £10 with the others. I don't know why I wasn't there, although Rich Levene surmises that as I'd stopped drinking by this point I didn't go drinking at The Joiners, which is probably correct.

So, although our new punk friends were open and accepting I still felt a little nervous and a bit of an outsider. I found it hard to mix, despite feeling like I was where I was supposed to be, and kind of hid behind Gaz's more outgoing nature. But I loved it, punk was becoming more than the music I listened to, it was fast becoming something I did. I had already been inspired and influenced by the Subhumans, but now I was beginning to see that there was a better way to approach the world with punk as my guide. My politics were changing as I became more aware. I was naturally left leaning, but then the sort of things the anarcho bands were singing about started to make more sense to me. I was finding that things really mattered and I could have a say in how much I contributed to the evils of the system.

Great new bands were right there, locally, formed by people I knew, and they weren't all the same, there was diversity and differences, but an underlying thread of co-operation, companionship and collaboration which unified us all. I still felt I wasn't cool enough or clever enough to have a real say, but I loved being there and being part of it, in some small way.

The second Issue of SD definitely shows more of a DIY influence creeping in, thanks to our new friends and the gigs we were now going to broadening our horizons. But although we interviewed Political Asylum and Last Rough Cause alongside GBH and Peter & The Test Tube Babies, reviewed local gigs and had adverts for DIY distros and labels, we were still reviewing major label releases by The Damned, The Alarm and The Clash and even devoted a page to the Sex Pistols! However, we were still finding our feet and we were having a lot of fun. I remember being sat at the table in the back room of his house while Gaz wrote a guide to being a Train Spotter, and laughing until our faces hurt, it may not seem so funny reading it back now, but at the time it was one of those silly things that seems like the funniest thing in the world. We also included our own punk rock crossword.

Again, this issue was printed by my dad on his work photocopier (I think Gaz got some copies of early issues copied at his work too. If these issues were mainly written and put together at Gaz's house, they were collated at mine.

I still felt a little nervous and shy at these early gigs, but the desire to be part of what was going on meant I just had to fight the awkward feelings because I knew this was what I wanted from punk. I mean, a few years before this, some huge bloke with a tall mohican and a Stranglers t-shirt was giving me hassle in HMV because the SLF I put on my faux leather jacket was done in tape. He gruffly said tape was naff and I should paint it on. His leather jacket did have a very cool painted Stranglers Raven on it. But I thought punk was working with what you had and making the best from what you could do, and I wasn't an artist, I didn't have easy access to paint, but my dad was an electrician so we had electrical tape in the house, and I used that. Anyway, our new friends were accepting, it didn't matter what you looked like, or what you had on your jacket, what was important was that we were there, creating something together. I was also eager to learn. I may have been a bit slow to get into the new bands in those days, but I was getting there. I was getting demo tapes, and buying more zines and starting to write to people all over the country.

This was still a time where my willingness to accept newer bands, unless they were local, was somewhat slower than Gaz's (It was Gaz who got into Minor Threat first and urged me to listen to them). I was getting there but I was still stubbornly dragging my feet at times. Up until this point my punk rock influences had been John Peel's show, the music press and Gaz, and our record collections were still almost identical. This started to change when this new scene got going, and I had my ears and mind opened to new sounds and new bands and a lot of them were coming to play in our town. We were hooked on the zine now, or at least I was, and issue three arrived, featuring lots of Gaz's drawings, including his cover drawing of Wattie. Whereas our first two issues featured collage front covers (mirroring Pete Zonked's current back cover creations for us), this issue's cover was just white, with Gaz's drawing in the middle and the bands featured underneath. In all honesty it's a bit of an uninspiring cover.

Speaking of the John Peel show, one of the new bands I heard him play one evening lead to our first face to face interview for SD. I would keep a notepad and a pen by the radio to note down any new bands he played that I liked the sound of. One night in 1985 he played a song called 'Wherever You May Run' from the first 7" by Portsmouth band Red Letter Day. As a long time fan of the UK Subs, their melodic punk struck a chord, so when Peel gave their address, I noted that down and wrote to them. They got back to me really quickly, within two days in fact, and this was the days when writing to someone meant actually writing a letter and posting it. Featuring them for the next issue of the zine seemed an obvious thing to do, and they suggested meeting up to do the interview. This was new territory for us, and I found it a bit daunting, but they suggested meeting in a pub halfway between Portsmouth and Southampton. It was only a couple of weeks of making contact with them, when we jumped into my rusty, less than trusty old Mini and headed over to Fareham, Gaz's old tape player in hand. Three of band were present, and they were friendly, and open and we had a good evening. This friendship with RLD lasted for a good while, and we would go and see them countless times over the coming moths and years.

As well as RLD we featured The Press Gang from Liverpool, after I'd bought one of their records from Craig Burton, Intensive Care and The Adicts. We were featuring more DIY releases and ads, including Rich Levene's The Plot Sickens distro, but there were still some major label releases covered, and another bloody page on the Sex Pistols! But, we were still learning, still growing and I, at least, was getting more used to being a zine writer, even if I still didn't really know how to achieve what I wanted the zine to be.

Gaz:
Issue #2 – This saw me getting more involved and I think I did the Test Tubes and Political Asylum interviews, with Tony doing GBH and Last Rough Cause. We were still tending to follow the bigger Punk bands that were still on the scene, but I'm pleased to report there were plenty of flyers printed up for DIY distros. It's left me wondering where a lot of those Punk enthusiasts are now?! Where is Louis who ran Cider & Chips distro out of Bristol? There was also this bloke called Gord, who lived in Frazerburgh in Scotland and did Punk & Oi tapes. He used to ask for your phone number so he

could give you a call. I actually remember him ringing me up and just asking me if 'I had booted in any dickheads round my way lately'. Rumour had it that he was quite a lot older than most people he was in contact with and was in contact with quite a few zines etc. All very odd and I'm glad he lived quite far away!

Issue #3 – Ah Yes! The cover of this was the silhouette of Wattie from The Exploited shouting into his microphone. More of my 'borrowed art is just inside the front cover with something nicked from the A Heads, Amebix and The Stranglers! This issue had interviews with The Adicts, Intensive Care, originally from Scotland, then their front man Iain moved to Sussex for work so it says in the interview! Iain went on to have a bit of success with Beerzone and then Control. The Press Gang from Liverpool also featured as did Red Letter Day from Portsmouth. I think this was our first face to face band interview too, which we did in a pub called the Delme Arms in Fareham, a town half way between Southampton and Pompey! Had to be a neutral venue for the football fans amongst us!

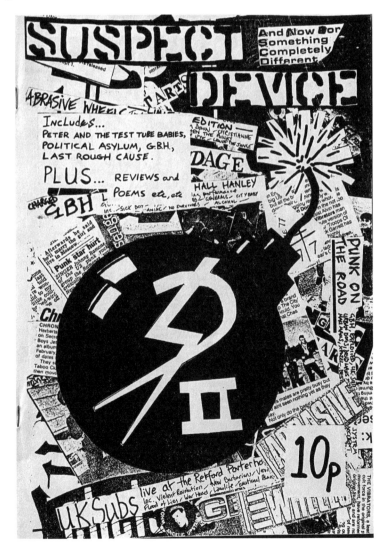

33

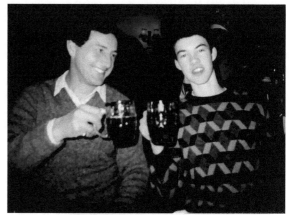

Gaz playing darts at Tony's house and drinking beer with Tony's dad

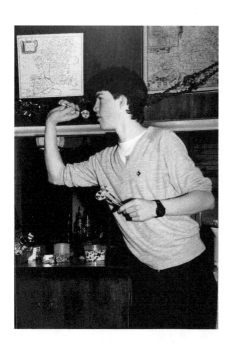

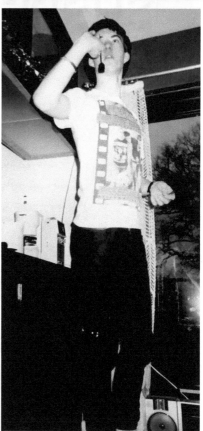

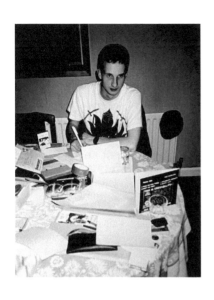

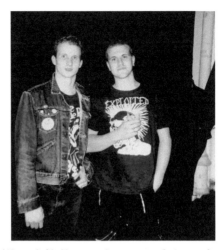

(Above left): Tony works on an early issue of SD at Gaz's house.
(Above right) Two Obvious Action drummers.

(Below left): Gaz and Tony out side Gaz's house. A finished issue in the envelope.
(Below right): Tony in Gaz's garden.

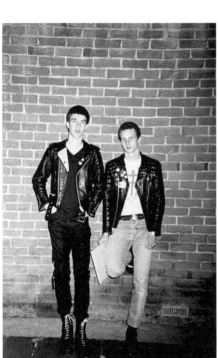

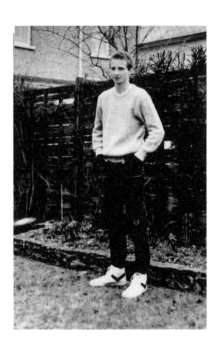

Birds Of A Feather, Flock Together Pt.1

Tony:
At this point it would seem a good idea to explain how the Southampton DIY punk scene came together. Gaz and me went over to speak to Rich Levene and Geraldine Lawrence about the beginnings of this local scene and the gig collectives that formed.

Rich:
By about '84 I was pretty close to a few people in Eastleigh, I'd become friends with Steve and Brendan, but didn't really know anyone in Southampton at all. I hadn't been to any DIY gigs in Southampton, just the big gigs at the Gaumont and stuff.
I started going to quite a lot of gigs in Bournemouth. I'd met Andy Anderson from Damage zine, which he did with Paul Chambers, he did an advert in Sounds and I wrote to him, and he started telling me about all these gigs in Bournemouth, which was people like Self Abuse, and things like that.
Because I went down on my own or just with another friend, as an excuse to talk to people I'd started doing the zine distro. I'd been writing to pretty much every ad that was in Sounds and then obviously once you started getting the zines, there were more addresses, so I was doing a Zine distro, and I met a few people down in Bournemouth. Probably about autumn 1984, I got a letter from Craig (Burton), he'd been to a gig in London, Subhumans or something like that, and he picked up a zine, and it had my address in there. So he wrote to me and said "I've seen your address, can you send me a catalogue?" which was basically just a handwritten list of what I actually had. So at that point he was just putting together the first Beercan, and he said "I'm doing this zine, will you be able to distro for me?" Then I went to see Conflict at Upstairs At Eric's in Bournemouth, and I was selling zines and he was there. So, we ended up getting a lift back from him. Then there was a Subhumans gig in Portsmouth, at the Hornpipe, I was selling zines, and me, Steve and Bren met Mike Fox and George at that.
I started writing to Craig pretty regularly and he told me that Suicide Pact were playing at the Joiners, between Christmas and New Year, and that was the first time I ever went to the Joiners, that was the first small gig I went to. Mike was there. I spoke to Paul (PJ) that night as well, and Simon (Suicide Pact/Nox Mortis), and I think Biff was there. Sid was there as well. Then in the early part of 1985, there was a couple of other Suicide Pact gigs. There was one at the Kingsland Hall, and one at the Labour Club.

So by that point I had got pretty close to Craig. I was chatting to him on the phone pretty regularly and he was telling me about gigs. He'd become friends with Mike as well around that sort of time, and we went up to see the Subhumans and Blyth Power at the 100 club, and Burt (Craig) drove to that.
Then pretty quickly, I met Bod, you and Rob Callen and Rut. And obviously Mike already knew some of the more kind of anarcho animal rights people, like he'd met Biff, and Sid and Muzzy, and then at the same time I'd met some of the Eastleigh people like tall Paul and Jamie from All The Glory. I'd seen both of them around before, but I've never actually met them. They'd become pretty close with the Suicide Pact people as well. So, it kind of came together quite quickly. Rut also knew Mark Barker.

All those people just came together really quickly. (There) was a gig at the West Indian Club, which was a gig Dave Carr put on, on Mayday. There was an anarchist picnic over on the common, and then there was a gig in the evening which was Pigs On Heat, and that was their last gig, and then pretty soon after that, the Thatchers (Mad Thatchers) started. Pigs On Heat were Morgan, Shane, also, Jim, who was in First Men In Space and Flick Spatula.

Then Mike was going, "we should put a gig on." Dave Carr had had done it, he had done things at the West Indian and he said, "that's really easy to do a gig at the West Indian Club." Mike was writing to Tez who'd just joined the Instigators, and they were going on tour, so they wanted to play in Southampton before they went off to to Europe. So we booked this gig, and we really had no idea. I think it was 3 weeks before the gig when someone said, "have you sorted a PA out?" And we were like "what's a PA?" We just, thought, get the band to come in and they've got their amps. And that's it.

The first one I got (Damage zine) was issue 2, which was the one that had Cult Maniax and A Heads and Subhumans in it. I was gutted because when the zine came there was a letter from Andy and he said "we've just put a gig on in Wareham 10 days ago" it was A Heads, Anthrax and Naked and all the local bands as well. So I started writing to him pretty regularly, and then he told me about that Cult Maniax, Screaming Dead, Self Abuse and Butcher were playing at Capones (in Bournemouth), and then me and a couple of other people from Eastleigh went down to that. I went pretty regularly to gigs in Bournemouth, pretty much every kind of out of town band that played down there, we would go and see.

But going back to how things kind of came together. Mike was kind of like, "I want to put a gig on" and then it's like, "let's put a gig collective together." So it was basically me, Mike, Craig, Craig's mate Neil, he was more kind of socialist, and I remember he would annoy us because he would always say "I'm part of the collective" and get in free, but not actually do anything. That's why when we started the STE, we were like, everyone, each gig will basically pay to get in, so that kind of if you weren't pulling your weight by doing anything for the gig, then you actually paid.

So, the Instigators didn't actually play because the line up had changed or something, and then they pulled out, so it just ended up being Suicide Pact, Atrox from Dorset, which was basically people that became Hate That Smile and Pro Patria Mori played as well. That was pretty busy actually. I remember we were so scared that nobody was going to come. I mean it actually, as it turned out, when the Instigators pulled out, it actually meant that we didn't really need that much money anyway, because there was three bands, (one) from Dorset, a band from Berkshire and a Southampton band, but it was pretty busy I remember.

Dave Carr was doing benefit gigs, and then when the Thatchers started, they were doing gigs at the West Indian Club as well.

So, we did a few gigs. The instigators did play, in the end (on 10th October 1985). We did Blyth Power, which was a really big gig, the first time they played in Southampton I think. That was a really good one.

The other thing that had happened, around that time was, obviously Craig with Beercan was the first zine, but then everyone else started doing their zines, like Mike did Another Krummy Zine, Rob did Bouquet Of Barbed Wire, I did The Plot Sickens, but only actually probably printed about 10 or 15 of them, because I had done it and it took so long to get it printed, that by the time I did it, I was like, actually, I don't even want to put it out now. So I just gave it to a few people.

Rob always had kind of quite broad taste anyway, he liked some of the Gothic stuff as well, like Skeletal Family and things like that and Spear Of Destiny. So Rob would kind of write about all sorts of things really.

Most of us were about the same age, left school sort of 82/83. that sort of time and, to me, it always seemed like it was people that were kind of quite isolated in their little geographical areas, and it was sort of a new scene, really, and the fact there was Suicide Pact who became Not Mortis, and The Thatchers and they were kind of our bands and we'd go and see them all the time and you'd know that there would be the same 30-40 people at the gigs. And (the bands) were more political, because at that stage, I would say probably none of us were really that political, not in the kind of way that we became later.
Dave Carr was really influential as well, because he was really supportive of the gigs we'd do and he'd be like "if you want someone to do the door so you can watch the bands..."

Some of those venues like the Labour club and The Cliff in Woolston, they were good little venues and it's a shame that they're not there anymore, even the West Indian Club.
The trouble with the West Indian Club was that you could never do a gig on a Friday or a Saturday night because obviously it was operating as a West Indian cultural club. So you could hire it any other night of the week, apart from Friday or Saturday. But as a venue, with the bar at the back, it was great. The Labour club was good because it was cheap, beer wise, but the dance floor became a skating ring as soon as someone dropped a drink.

Mike Fox offered his recollection separately:
We would all travel to London gigs together. From this friendship, the idea to put on overseas bands in Southampton grew. The South Hants Fanzine Collective put on a few gigs. Somehow, this developed into the Southampton Totton, Eastleigh Music Collective, or STE.
Rich, Steve & Bren had formed a band, CORPORATE GRAVE. I talked my way into the band. Rich left before we started gigging. CORPORATE GRAVE was given the first opportunity to play by Simon, Paul & Andy of NOX MORTIS, who were very important to the local DIY scene. I don't think it can be stressed enough that these friendships grew because of bands like THE MAD THATCHERS and SUICIDE PACT/NOX MORTIS. Not to forget the vibrant alternative scene that included I AM 7/FLIK SPATULA/ WHO'S IN THE KITCHEN/THE SACK and many more.

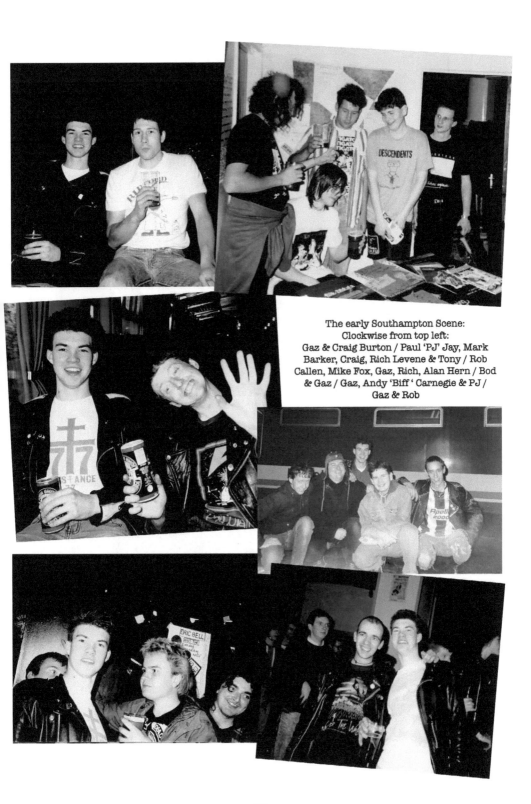

The early Southampton Scene:
Clockwise from top left:
Gaz & Craig Burton / Paul 'PJ' Jay, Mark
Barker, Craig, Rich Levene & Tony / Rob
Callen, Mike Fox, Gaz, Rich, Alan Hern / Bod
& Gaz / Gaz, Andy 'Biff ' Carnegie & PJ /
Gaz & Rob

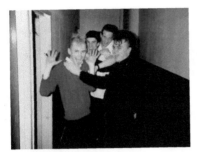

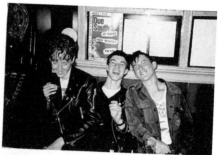

Rut, Gaz, Tony, Andy 'Biff' Carnige
West Indian Club

Rob Callen, Gaz, Mike Fox
The Joiners

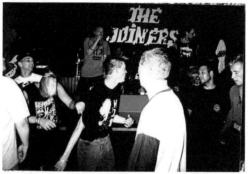

Sid, Rob Turl, Gaz, Rut, Craig Burton, Steve 'Punky' Littleton
Dancing to Older Than Dirt at The Joiners

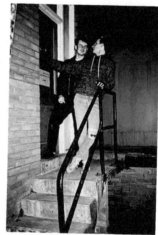

Crispin Erridge and Tony

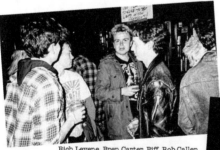

Rich Levene, Bren Carter, Biff, Rob Callen
Sir George Robey, London

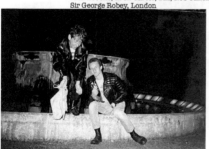

Above:: Luce, Gaz, Steve Burgess, Ady Howarth
West Indian Club

Left: Rob Callen and Tony
Southampton City Centre

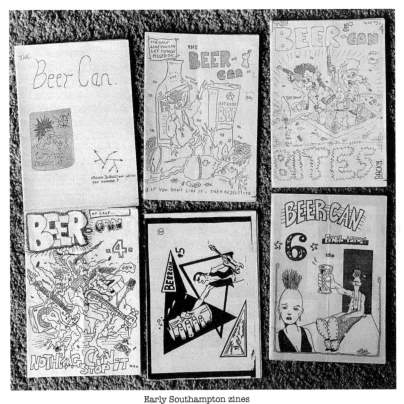

Early Southampton zines
Above: Beercan
Below: Another Krumy Zine, Bouquet Of Barbed Wire, Thrash Bash Newsletter

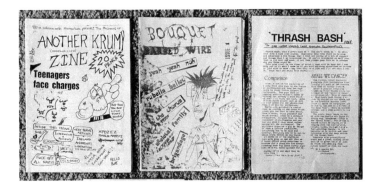

Tony Suspect - Into The Unknown

At some point, either late 1985 or early 1986, I received a letter from Peter & The Test Tube Babies thanking me for sending them a copy of the zine (SD#2) and offering us a guest list place for their gig in Southampton on February 24th 1986. It was at a short-lived venue called The Riverside. Before the big Itchen Toll bridge was built, the quickest way to get from Southampton city centre to the suburb of Woolston was by a chainlink ferry known, locally, as the Floating Bridge (there's a painting in the city's art gallery of the Floating Bridge done by Lowry). I think I remember going on the ferry, but it could just be that my dad had some cine film of me on there, and that's what I remember. Anyway, once the bridge was opened one of the old Floating Bridges was eventually turned into a venue, on the Woolston side of the river, and not far from The Cliff, the venue for a few early Southampton scene DIY punk gigs. This would have been the first time Gaz and me had been put on a guest list. I don't remember much about the gig, other than enjoying the Test Tubes, but I do remember, before they started, I was stood at the bar talking to Peter, he was working his way through what I guessed was their rider. He kept offering me shots, which I never accepted. Each time Peter offered me a glass of something or other, the conversation went something like "Here, have a drink." I would reply "No thanks." Peter would then look at me, almost as if I'd bought him the drink, say "Thanks" and down it. The same conversation happened several times.

Gaz:
They were drinking Jack Daniels that night, as I remember.

Peter seemed totally pissed, and I wondered how he was ever going to play a gig, but once he got on stage, he was great. During their set Peter introduced a song by saying "This one's for all those losers who try to get into gigs for free, it's called 'Guest List', it's for Tony and Gaz."
When they'd finished their set, we were made aware of a load of skinheads who had gathered outside. The Test Tubes were staying with our friend Rut that night, so we waited around for them to be ready, and when we eventually left the avenue the skinheads seemed content to be fighting amongst themselves, and didn't pay any attention to us.

Gaz:
Trapper went home after the gig, Rut says he had to go back to Brighton to sign on. Rut also said that the Test Tubes had a van or big car, and he got a ride with them to show them the way to his house.

Early in 1986 we were working on our 4th issue, an issue that showed our continued immersion of the DIY scene, especially locally, and had ads for zines, distros, labels and even a flyer showing dates for an Anti-Cimex/Napalm Death tour.
Now, criteria for featuring a band then was the same as it is now, if we hear a record or see a band live that we like then we want to feature them, there's no thought of being "cool", it was just bands that excited us. So although this issue features Oi Polloi, Attila The Stockbroker, Dead Men Don't and locals Act Of God, it also featured Condemned 84. They are a band we wouldn't touch with a bargepole these days, but then they had just had an album out on Roddy Moreno's Oi Records, and Gaz in particular rated the

record, so sent them some questions. Attila wasn't happy to be in the same zine as them, but we weren't clued up enough and assumed that as they were on Oi Records there wasn't anything dodgy about them.

I don't remember anything about Dead Men Don't, or how we came to hear about them, I assume they sent us a demo tape that we liked enough to want to feature them. But, one evening Gaz and me had gone to London for a gig at the Marquee, and as we were in London early, we went to a pub across Wardour Street from the venue, we may have been with others, I can't remember now, but we were stood in the pub talking, it was pretty packed, and someone suddenly said "Are you Tony who does Suspect Device zine?" (I hadn't yet been christened Tony Suspect, that came later from Mark Brennan and Lol Pryor at Link Records). It turned out it was a couple of members from Dead Men Don't. I have no idea how they knew it was me as, remember this was a time before social media, so contact was made by letter and you didn't often know what anyone looked like.

Also in this issue we had a contribution from Matty Blag, or Math from Complete Control as he was then, with a report on a gig he went to in support of the sacked Print Workers during the dispute with Rupert Murdoch's News International corporation. Matty would become a friend, and would sometimes ring up for a chat, and occasionally want to ask my dad questions about fixing his car. He also had a Mini, and knew that my dad had spent some time fixing mine.

The cover of SD#4 featured a drawing of the Slaughter & The Dogs snarling dog from the cover of the 'Do It Dog Style' LP drawn by, I guess, Gaz. We also went for orange front and back covers. My dad was still copying these after hours at his work, so he must have had a ream of coloured paper in the office.

Although this issue looked much more like the zine I wanted, I now feel a little uneasy about it because one band is featured, and that's a shame.

Later that year we had another issue done. The cover of SD#5 was back to black and white, it was a reproduction of an image from the back sleeve of Red Letter Day's 'Wherever You My Run' 7". Because we had developed a real friendship with them, and they had been doing quite a lot since their 7" came out, we arranged another visit to the pub in Farham for a catch up interview. This one really should have been edited as it goes on for 9 pages, which is a lot considering that both the UK Subs and The Neurotics interviews only covered two pages each. In hindsight we should have cut down the RLD interview and included more content, but it's easy to look back and criticise things, at the time we must have been happy. During the interview with RLD, a band who were a little older than us, Gaz asked them about their t-shirts and used the phrase "selling to kids like me", it's funny to read that now that we're in our late 50s, and still buying and wearing band t-shirts.

I think, by this time, I had been given a typewriter too, there's certainly no more obviously word processed type, and hadn't been for a couple of issues. I don't remember where I got the typewriter from, it was a smaller thing than Gaz had, but I used it a lot, and preferred the type to the word processor text.

Around this time I joined my first band. I'd seen Obvious Action at the West Indian Club with Instigators and really liked them, then when they played again at The Cliff I spoke to guitarist Colin after they'd played and he was saying that they may have to split up because their singer was leaving. For some reason I offered to be their new singer. I didn't want to be a singer, I didn't even know if I could be a singer, but I wanted to be in a band, and I didn't want Obvious Action to finish. In the days that followed I practised in my room, just singing along to records. I felt an idiot, which wasn't a good sign, if I felt an idiot at home on my own, how was I going to stand in front of people and sing. Then Colin called, not, as I was expecting to let me know where and when we'd be practising, but to say that their drummer was leaving now, so the band was over. "I have a drum kit" I said, which was true, although I didn't add that I didn't really know how to set it up, let alone play it, so Colin agreed to let me become the drummer. My usual nervousness had to take a backseat to my desire to be in a band, but I had to learn quickly how to play the drums, and basically learnt as we practised. Initially we were still looking for a singer, and Gaz even tried out, but in the end we decided to stay as a three piece, with guitarist Colin handling the vocals too. News of me joining Obvious Action was in SD#6, where we had a two page feature on the band. There was another interview here where we drove to a pub to interview Gosport band Free Beer, who'd played with Scream in Southampton, and Gaz interviewed Last Rites. There is a full page ad for Beercan's distro too. It also seems like we were starting to trade with other zines at this point.

Two other notable things about this issue are, first, the terrible cover that I did. I'm no artist, and it shows in the basic, black star with the name of the zine across it and the featured bands above.

The other, and more important thing was that Gaz didn't want to do the zine anymore. There was no falling out, we were still as close as ever, but I guess he had just had enough of doing the zine. I was disappointed and contemplated stopping the zine altogether. But as much as I didn't want to do a zine without him, I also didn't want to stop. I did think about changing the name, as Suspect Device was always Gaz and me, and I remember sat at the table in our kitchen with a list of new names in front of me, feeling totally dejected. But in the end I decided to carry on. As someone said at the time, "You've made a name for yourself now." That seems funny looking back now, as it's obvious we had a long way to go to make any sort of name for ourselves, but it was gratifying to have people think that the zine was worthy enough for me to carry on with.

It was January 1986 and we had put out 6 issues.

The next one didn't appear until June 1987. I think losing Gaz's enthusiasm and contributions played a part, but also being in Obvious Action was taking up my spare time. I was working in Winchester and band practises were in Salisbury, plus real life was also impacting on my time.

But, SD#7 is pretty good I think. Certainly the DIY scene was now a big part of my life, although the cover photo was of Joe Strummer, but the cover is still miles better than issue 6. I had interviewed The Sect as I'd sent off for and loved their 'A Free England' 7" and because this issue took me a long time to finish, I was also able to review their first album, 'The Voice Of Reason', which was the first LP that we were ever sent for review. I also interviewed Peter & The Test Tube Babies again, on the back of their 'Soberphobia' album. There was also Obvious Action news, and by this time I'd played my first three gigs and recorded a demo. I called this feature Action Times.

The first Obvious Action demo that I played on was recorded in Amesbury, Wiltshire at the home studio of Steve Collinson, the guy who'd engineered the Subhumans EPs 'Demolition War', 'Religious Wars' and some of the 'Time Flies...' 12" plus 'The Day The Country Died' LP, although those records were not recorded in his converted garage like our demo was (I think the Culture Shock demo may have been recorded in the garage though). I was definitely more excited than the others at having Steve record us as those Subhumans records were, and still are, big favourites of mine. I was probably too shy to ask all the questions I want to about the Subhumans, and I got a bit pissed off when one of my band mates asked "Were they smelly?" I guess I should have known then that our musical paths were going in different directions.

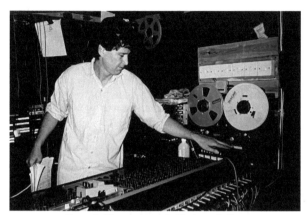
Steve Collinson records Obvious Action

After a long time between issue 6 and 7, SD#8 arrived in December in 1987 and it also saw Gaz back, but only as a "guest" reviewer. (and artist - the inside cover has his reworking of the UK Decay 'For My Country' 7" sleeve) I still like the cover, a moody shot of Mega City 4, but the intro sees me talking about new albums from Vibrators, 999 and Angelic Upstairs, and get excited about the reformation of Stiff Little Fingers. 999 were also interviewed, but we did feature more exciting bands like Instigators, Perfect Daze and Nox Mortis. Mega City 4 were featured after Gaz and me had seen them at the Marquee, supporting Chelsea, and I'd been blown away by them. I'd bought their demo and got in contact with Wiz, and we struck up a friendship. Action Times is featured again, and mentions our gig in London with UK Subs. I'd sent Charlie Harper a demo and he'd replied offering us a gig with them in Stoke Newington. Gaz and me hired a van, with him acting as our driver. We drove to Salisbury to pick up the other two and a few of their friends and headed to London. We got a bit lost, but saw a bus heading to Stoke Newington, so decided to follow it. Then the bus broke down, leaving us a bit stranded, I'm not sure how we finally found the venue, maybe someone had brought an A To Z book with them, we all seemed to have one back then.

Charlie Harper had said that we could use their drums and amps, and that we need only bring guitars and drum breakables. He was cool on the night, and after the Subs had done their sound check I went to the drum kit to get ready for our set. A big gruff Subs roadie stopped me and said I wasn't going to use the kit. Steve Roberts was back in the Subs at this point and came over to say that it was cool and I was welcome to use it. The roadie huffed a bit and said "ok, but don't move anything." Before stomping off. Steve Roberts just said "Move what you like, I know where I want stuff." I don't remember any interaction with the other Subs that night, but Charlie and Steve Roberts were both down to earth and very good to us. Gaz and me went to see the Subs in Portsmouth a few days after this and Steve Roberts was just as friendly, greeting us like old friends when we walked through the door of the venue.

We played an ok set in London, although it wasn't particularly well received, but then everyone was there for the Subs. It was, though, a bit shocking to see someone wearing a Screwdriver t-shirt holding a knife in the crowd.

The UK Subs were good and during the evening Gaz had indulged in a few beers, and as he was the designated driver, and I was the only one who hadn't been drinking, I had to drive the van home.

Action Times also mentioned that the band had had a name change, Obvious Action were now The Stand, named after the Alarm song. We recorded another demo, under the new name, and it featured an acoustic guitar. This was the beginning of the end for me with the band, in fact I left just a month after this issue of SD came out. The Alarm sound was the direction that the other two were wanting to go towards, and although Gaz and me had been to see The Alarm, and thought they were pretty good live, I was more interested in 7 Seconds, Dag Nasty and Instigators. I left the band soon after the demo was recorded, with my last gig being at the Salisbury Arts Centre, supporting Lords Of The New Church. Near the end of our set the snare drum stand collapsed, and the snare rolled off across the stage. And that was it, set over and my time with the band was too.

The Stand continued, eventually changing their name to The Magnificent, they recorded another demo, which Colin sent me. Colin had also opened a record shop in Salisbury, that Gaz and me visited a few times. We eventually lost contact, although I did run into him at a couple of bigger gigs in Southampton in the years that followed.

Gaz:

Issue #4 – A good issue really, but a bad one from the point of view that Attila The Stockbroker didn't like being in the same zine as Oi band Condemned 84. Rumour surrounded Condemned 84 politically, but my recall is firstly of my naivety and secondly that a lot of people liked them and were on the fence over the alleged politics of the members. I moved away from them after that and what they went on to do I didn't follow. I'm proud of my Oi Polloi interview though! Front man Deek did a great interview and still fronts the band to this day! Other bands were another Oi band from Oxford called 'Dead Men Don't and a local Southampton band called 'Act Of God'. Tony did both of them. Colour cover too!!!

Issue #5 – I've just read through this issue and it seems odd talking to Charlie Harper about ten years of Punk! We did a half decent interview with him, I think. Also featured again are Red Letter Day from Portsmouth and we met them once more in the Delme Arms on 23rd July 1986. This incidentally was the day Prince Andrew (Remember that twat?) married Sarah Fergusson! We also featured The Neurotics who were formerly the Newtown Neurotics and big favourites of Tony's and a fanzine called Concrete Jungle who helped us out. Where is writer Ian now? Hopefully still playing Punk! All in all an OK issue.

Issue #6 – Another half decent issue featuring Obvious Action from Salisbury, who Tony went on to play drums for and I tried to sing for! I'd have loved it if I could have made the grade, but they we're far too good for my limited talents. In fact, I have no memory for lyrics, no sense of rhythm and stuck to writing about Punk after that fail. Tony on the other hand has proved his worth to numerous bands and that really pisses me off! Why am I so shite at music? Other bands in this issue were Punky Herberts 'Vicious Rumours' who I interviewed and Last Rites from Scotland. A guy called Craig Ireland sorted that one for us, but the band didn't last to much longer after their feature in the zine. One of the members went on to sing for The Disturbed. Plenty of adverts for long gone fanzines and distros appeared too. Where are you all now? There was a great excitement to the pre-internet age and writing off to people for records and zines. Bandcamp just ain't the same! Recycled envelopes, soaped stamps and well concealed cash. Ha! What great times.

Issue #7 – For some reason, best known only to myself, I'd given up the fanzine and left Tony to go solo! I honestly can't remember why, but I suspect beer and the pub might have had a lot to do with it. That said – he carried on unfazed and without breaking stride to produce a quality issue. He managed to squeeze some decent answers out of Peter Test Tube for another PTTB interview and sorted other interviews with The Sect, Accident (formerly Major Accident) and a band from Northampton called Venus Fly Trap. Also, in the zine was 'Action Times' – Tony had joined Obvious Action from Salisbury on drums and I'd not been asked back as singer for reasons I've outlined earlier! Their loss, although you wouldn't have known it!

Issue #8 – Looks like this was my SD comeback issue with a few reviews and it turns out that my liking for the pub was probably a contributing factor in not doing anything for the previous issue! Apart from that Tony did a first class job with this issue and 999, Mega City Four, Perfect Daze, Red London, The Instigators, local band Nox Mortis and a band called Suspect Device were all well interviewed. Suspect Device the band were nothing to do with us though and came from Brighton, I think.

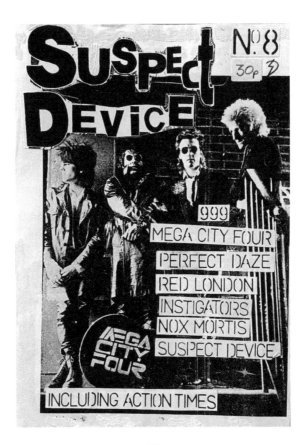

Tony Suspect - Back To The Known

SD#9 was a notable issue for several reasons. Most importantly Gaz was back, I guess he couldn't stay away. SD seems to have that affect on people, the long standing friends we have made through the years because of the zine are testament to that. Secondly, I got to do a phone interview with Ali McMordie of Stiff Little Fingers. Link Records had put me in contact with him on the back of their reformation and the live album Link Records released (I was later asked to write the sleeve notes for the CD version of that release).

This was also around the time that I was given my "punk name." Lol Pryor called, I think to set up the Ali McMordie interview, and mentioned that they called me Tony Suspect in their office.

I called the number that Link gave me, Ali answered and when I introduced myself, saying I did a zine called Suspect Device, he said "I recognise that name." He was very friendly and happy to talk.

This issue also sees the start of a long standing friendship with Mike Head, and he did some reviews for us.

Mike Head:

> "If my research is correct I wrote my first pieces for Suspect Device for issue 9 (a 999/Chelsea live review plus a Mega City 4 debut single & live review). I had been bitten by the fanzine bug after getting a copy of 20th Century Saints & To The Death zines, this opened up a new world to me. I started corresponding with Tony, sending well concealed cash for copies of Suspect Device (usually buying extra copies to sell to friends or at gigs). If I remember right Tony said I was welcome to write some reviews, we hit it off quickly recommending records to each other, lots of letters, later phone calls (pre Internet). The first time I met Tony was at a Ramones gig at Brixton, as years went on used to see him at other London gigs & on a few occasions in Southampton, met Gaz few times too both great people with morals, the enthusiasm they have for Punk still shines brightly, I consider myself very lucky to have contributed to this fine fanzine for so many years, looks like we are in this To The Death."

There's a feature on Corporate Grave and Gaz interviewed Foreign Legion and The Disturbed (Johnny, who answered the Disturbed questions, recently printed the Abrazos t-shirts). Sadly we also mentioned the sad death of Simon from Nox Mortis, which was a big blow to the local scene. Nox Mortis, following on from Suicide Pact, were such an important band, locally. Sadly they only did a demo and had three tracks on the Meantime Records compilation LP 'Shall We Dance?' alongside Joyce McKinney Experience, Decadence Within and Incest Brothers.

Other bands featured were Dutch band The Magnificent, The Abs, Joyce McKinney Experience and also 5 Star Rock n Roll Petrol, who had played a gig at The Cliff in Southampton that has become infamous, locally, for a short stand up set from a certain Gaz Suspect. That's all I will say about that.

There is a review of a Mega City 4 gig I went to in Salisbury, which was the first time I met someone else who would become, and still is, a very good friend, Crispin "Mumbles" Erridge.

Crispin:

> "In the late 1980s I was working for a shit pile of an insurance company. A few really good things came out of that Gods awful experience – one of which was that someone who I was working with, on discovering my musical proclivities said 'Oh, my boyfriend's into punk, you should meet him!"
>
> I am blessed with total recall of all incidents in my life so I am 100% positive that it was on the 28th April 1988 that I was waiting at Fifty-third and third standing on the street, Fifty-third and third I'm tryin' to turn... No I can't remember where it was.
>
> I have previously maligned Tony Suspect by claiming that he drew up in a red Ford Fiesta, he assures me that it was an Escort – a far superior car. Anyway, in I hopped and off we buggered to Salisbury, where Mega City 4 blew my mother-loving moobs off! It would appear that sometimes my memory and actual events are miles and miles and miles and miles and miles and miles apart!
>
> I came away from that clutching a copy of 'Running in Darkness/Miles Apart' which had been released the previous November and it got played to death. I had discovered that punk wasn't a thing of the past but a living vibrant thing if you knew where to look for it or were lucky enough to meet someone who knew where to look for it. For this reason and as it is probably the best capturing of their blistering raw energy on vinyl, this was a very special 7 incher for me and still is."

I remember that first meeting with Crispin, he was all about the Sex Pistols and Buzzcocks and didn't really know any new, more underground punk bands. The main reasons Gaz and me still do Suspect Device is because we love to let people know about the bands we like, so it was good to be able to take him to a small gig. We have all been in Crispin's shoes at some point in our lives, to some degree, and he had his eyes opened and he was eager for more. More importantly, that evening was the start of a long lasting friendship, and on the odd occasion that circumstances allow, we still go to gigs together.

Gaz:

Issue #9 – This is a fantastic issue of the zine I think, because of the great range of bands interviewed and the fact that I actually pulled my sorry arse out of the pub and did something positive! Bands featured in this issue were The Disturbed, The Magnificent from Holland and were on the cover, SLF, The Abs, the great Joyce McKinney Experience, Foreign Legion, Local band Corporate Grave and Brighton's Five Star Rock and Roll Petrol, who did a real sussed interview reading it back again. On the back cover of the zine is an advert for our first compilation tape that came out in early 1988 and we sold a fair few hundred of these I seem to remember, all for £1.25 including the postage. We were still in an age where the CD was yet to really arrive and Spotify would have been a work of pure Science Fiction! This issue really did capture what we were all about. A united Punk Rock!

Gaz Suspect - Press The Eject And Give Me The Tape (writing in 2004)

I suspect that for quite a few people reading this it will be something of a novelty for you to play a tape, or you will never have even bought one, depending on your age. But for most of us careering towards 40 years of age our musical upbringing was built around buying vinyl when we could afford it for, failing that, taping it. I remember waiting up to tape stuff from John Peel's show or even taping stuff from Top Of The Pops when the Top 40 was broadcast every Sunday evening on Radio 1. For those of you under twenty years of age I can only ask you to read and learn what us old bastards had to do to get our Punk fix prior to the digital age and the internet. Putting out music was never cheap back in the 1980's, only since the invention of CD burners etc has the price come down and the quality of reproduction got better for us DIY enthusiasts. Back then if you could not afford to get vinyl out then your fall back position was to get the best quality cassette tape out and make it look the best you could. So before Suspect Device Records ever came into being we ran a tape label, just like so many other fanzines and tape only labels at the time. What follows is the best write upon our tape label that I can put together as I've lost a lot of the artwork and info over the years and Tony does not venture into his loft that often to try and retrieve anything he might have.

Now That's What We Call Music (Released: Early 1988- Cat No SDT1)
This was the very first of our tapes and had the following line up: Red Letter Day, Red London, Nox Mortis (Local Southampton punks), In The Red (Our mate at footy's band! They sounded like The Jam), Mega City Four, 3 Blind Drunks, Last Rough Cause, Corporate Grave (Local Punx), Suspect Device (From Brighton- No relation!), Instigators, The Stand (Tony was in this lot - formerly known as Obvious Action and based in Salisbury) and Perfect Daze. I think this tape represented the punk scene quite well in the UK at this time. The scene was over for the early to mid 80's second wave of UK punk bands and pop punk as well as the American bands were beginning to provide the influences that are still with us to day even though things are beginning to go full circle again in my opinion. We did stick with tradition on the cover though and had the Leather, Bristles, Studs and Acne mob pictured! Where are they now? We sold hundreds of these believe it or not and I had to go and buy a new tape to tape recorder for the releases that followed. My copy is now very muffled but if anyone wants a copy I can still knock one out! Same goes for the rest although you're not guaranteed a cover or digital quality. The price will be as it was then - a quid and SAE. Oh! We also used to use the hard to come by D46 cassette tapes, which were actually designed for demo tapes I think. Can't guarantee I can supply them either.

Life On Earth (Released 1990 - Cat No SDT2)
With the mix of bands on this tape it carried on where the first tape left off, I think, in reflecting the punk scene in the UK and the influences that were around at the time. This tape featured The Abs, The Sect, The Magnificent, Five Star Rock n Roll Petrol, The Refugees, Foreign Legion, Guitar Gangsters, Rout Inc, Culture Shock, Identity, The Park, Red London and The Four Guns (Championed by none other than Mr Peter Test Tube!). I think we did a booklet with this but I can't find it for the life of me. It was also a benefit for Greenpeace and we gave them 25p for every tape sold which isn't bad as we only sold it for £1.25 (Mind you, you can burn a CD cheaper now). The cover was expertly hand drawn by me and had the customary typeface of my old

manual typewriter on the inlay. I know I keep on about it but you youngsters don't know what us old age punks (OPS) had to do back then. This was truly DIY, totally un-aided by Microsoft and all other manner of multi-nationals who produce PC's and software that we all now take for granted and moan about when all you have to do is hit Control, Atl and Delete. Tippex bottles must be in museums by now, surely? Once again we sold hundreds of these and all by post . Tony was only just beginning to try and flog stuff at gigs although we had sold records by hassling people end of a gig for a few years before that. In fact we once sold loads of the Intensive Care EP "Cowards" which is now quite collectible I believe.

A Far Cry From 76 (Released 1990 - Cat No SDT3)
The title of this tape had nothing to do with Punk beginning in 1976 to be honest but more to do with Southampton's FA Cup win in the same year, although it sold on the basis of the former. This compilation featured Flame On, Exit Condition, Exalt, Gunrunners, HDQ, Instigators, Sink, The Blaggers, The Price, Red Letter day, Suburban Filth, Hate that Smile,Blind Justice, Identity and The Sect. It came with an info sheet as I think most of our tapes did because we wanted the bands to get as much exposure as possible. Those were the days prior to email and you had to actually write to bands and visit your local post box. I would love to know how much we have spent on post over the years. Not sure how this sold but I don't remember it being as good as the first two. I've no idea what the cover looked like as I don't even have a tape of it. I'm hoping Tony will find one in his loft as my tape box in the loft failed to yield one. It sold for a quid and SAE as I found an old advert for it in issue twelve of Suspect Device.

Shouting Music (Released April 1991 - Cat No SDT4)
I think this tape got its name from Tony's niece as she felt all the bands we liked shouted a lot! Even though she's a lot older now I doubt she has changed her mind? Anyway we thought it was good and the line up was as follows: BBMFs, Rhythm Collision, Flame On, Older Than Dirt, Sleep, Herb Garden, Haywire, Couch Potatoes, The Abs, Goober Patrol and Walls For Effect. As usual it sold for a quid with SAE and had a shite cover drawn by me. I can't begin to remember how it sold but I don't think any of our tape releases sold more than the first two.

STE Benefit Tape (Released 1992 - Cat No SDT5)
This, as the title suggests, was a benefit tape. Nah, you don't say! The STE (Southampton, Totton and Eastleigh Collective) was and still is a collective of local punk's etc. who put bands on in Southampton. Despite my lack of involvement over the years I am pleased to say that I was at the inaugural meeting years ago and put a founding tenner in the hat for the first gig. This was also probably our best effort in many ways as we got a booklet properly photocopied or it may have even been printed. Anyway the line up for this tape was Exit Condition, Blaggers ITA, Shutdown, Strength Alone, Pseudo Hippies, Five Foot Nothing, Joeyfat, MTA, Reverse, Gan, Puzzlebox, Erase Today, CDS and Blind Justice. We sold this for £1.50 with 50p going to the STE and to the best of my knowledge it did sell quite well for a tape at this moment in time as the digital age was about to revolutionise DIY punk forever.

State Of The Nation (Released November 1993 - Cat No SDT6)
This was the last of our tapes as I think we had just or were just about to release the first vinyl on Suspect Device Records. I think we realised that the age of the compilation cassette tape was nearly over by this time and my note on the cover

would seem to back this up. However, no disrespect to the bands that appeared on this compilation as it was a good line up as the following proves: Wat Tyler, Thirst (Locals), Chicken Bone Choked (Locals), Distortion, MDM, 4 Past Midnight, Krapp, CDS, Wordbug, Another Fine Mess, Academy 23 and Indecision. I've no idea how this sold but I think it did have a booklet with it and the price was once again a quid with SAE. So there you have it, things have moved on and we were into the digital age here at Suspect Device just the same as almost everyone else. We still release vinyl on the record label as well as CD's but we have e-mail, a website, Microsoft, broadband and all the trappings that our beloved corporate gods demand we have in this day and age. However despite this the cassette tape and tape labels will be remembered as a statement of their time in the history of DIY punk and I'm glad we made the effort.

Tony:

I loved doing the compilations tapes, they were another step in our quest to "get involved" more. They were cheap and easy to do and were a good reflection of what was going on at the time in the DIY scene, the stuff we were listening to, and the bands we were now making contact with. Most tracks came from demos we bought from bands at gigs or from ones that we were sent to review. I don't ever remember a band saying they didn't want to be on a comp tape back then.

The cover of the first one was taken outside the West Indian Club after a gig there was cancelled (I think it was Brigandage, but I could be wrong, it has become apparent when writing this book that my memory is unreliable). I'm pretty sure it was the night that some people went off to to The Riverside in Woolston to see Tenpole Tudor, while others, including Gaz and me, went down to the Joiners to hang out.

Compilation tapes were an important part of the DIY scene, and at this time tapes in general were a cheaper way of hearing new music. Trading tapes was an important part of the country (and world) wide punk scene. Tapes would be criss-crossing the globe in envelopes which often had soaped stamps so they could be used again. You'd get a record, love it and want to share it with your friends. This was a time when you'd often buy records which would have an inner sleeve featuring the "warning" Home Taping Is Killing Music. Of course this wasn't true at all, in fact it was promoting music. If someone sent me an album on cassette and I liked it, I'd go out and buy the vinyl.

You could reuse tapes, over and over, they were an important part of this growing underground network of friends.

This was also the time of the personal tape player, which were more portable, meaning I could listen to tapes while riding my bike or sitting on the bus. For a while I would often buy new albums on cassette so I could take them with me; 'Germ Free Adolescents' by X-Ray Spex, "Machine Gun Etiquette' by The Damned, and albums by Killing Joke, Buzzcocks, The Police, Siouxsie & The Banshees etc were all bought on cassette and listened to endlessly on my brick sized tape player.

When Gaz and me first started going to record fairs, often the vinyl was expensive, but there were always loads of bootleg tapes available. I got cassettes of live sets from The Clash, Siouxsie & The Banshees, The Damned and the Sex Pistols final gig at Winterland in San Francisco.

We did try to resurrect the idea of doing a compilation a few years later, and compiled a couple of CDRs to give away with the zine, but somehow it was never the same. I don't play tapes these days, but there was something special about putting the SD comp tapes together and spreading the music.

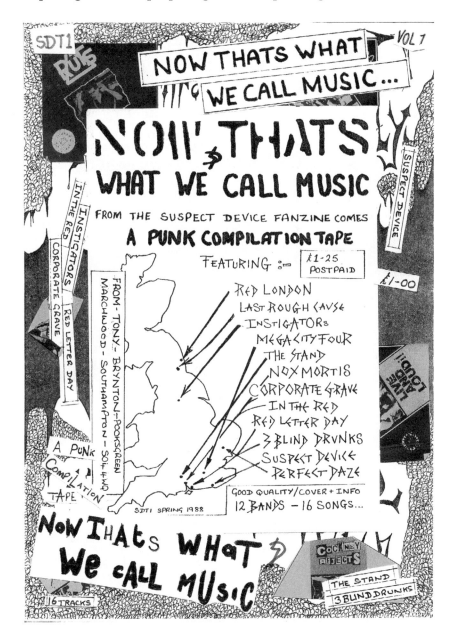

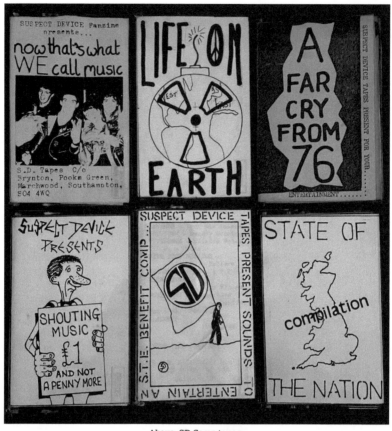

Above: SD Comp tapes.
Below: Info sheet for the first comp (left) / Booklet that came with the STE Benefit comp (Right)

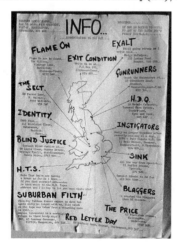
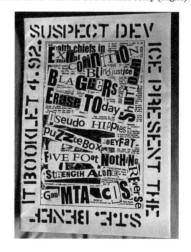

Birds Of A Feather, Flock Together Pt.2

Rich Levene:
So we were doing gigs and I suppose the gig that we were thinking, "maybe this isn't really for us", was that Scream gig when we got banned from the West Indian Club because of the trouble with that band Free Beer from Fareham, who ended up playing because, I think Nox Mortis were meant to play, and then Simon was ill, they had been contacted by Free Beer and put them on to us. They brought some idiots up with them and the toilets got smashed, so we got banned, and then they also nicked part of the PA, so the PA guy basically was chasing them down the down the motorway back to Fareham.

So we got banned from The West Indian Club and then we did a couple more gigs at the Labour Club. We did The Shrubs and also Rubella Ballet, and then that kind of fizzled out really. Then, for a while, it was left to local bands putting gigs on. Probably it was a good 18 months or so where there was no of out of town bands, certainly no DIY stuff. The Thatchers were still doing gigs and so were Nox Mortis.

(This was, time wise) probably through 87 and 88, and then probably that stage, things had moved a little bit from more of an anarcho (influence), and people were getting more into American hardcore. I remember there was a gig at the Cliff, I think it was Obvious Action and it was at the stage where everyone was wearing shorts and checked shirts and converse and stuff, and I remember someone from Obvious Action was going "Fucking hell, there's just loads of Americans here."

So hardcore became more of an influence on things, whereas before it was more English and Anarcho.

Also, as well, we were really influenced by the European stuff. Me, Mike and Bren and PJ had been to Holland in 87 and then we went again at Easter 88, which was the time Simon died. I remember we went to the Konkurrent in Amsterdam and we stayed with Hans from the Vernon Waters and we went with them down to a gig in the South of Holland and came back really inspired and Simon died, and I remember having a conversation with PJ going "We need to get things going again here, almost as a tribute to Simon." And then, I think there was a few people saying "Well, start another gig collective" and then I got a phone call from Kent Jolly, who was an American woman who was writing for Maximum RocknRoll, and said, "are you doing gigs in Southampton?" And I was kind of like, "yeah, we're just going to start again." "So, do you want to put Culture Shock on?" I remember phoning around a few people saying "I've been asked if we want to do Culture Shock. Should we start another gig collective?" We had a meeting at the Joiners and everybody was like, well let's start a kitty here and everyone pulled out a tenor at this meeting in the Joiners.

The gig was in June 88, so that would have been between probably April or May. 88. The other thing was we'd been banned from the the West Indian Club for two years. But we've been going there, there was a Thursday night indie night down there and we used to go there. I was kind of into that stuff, but some of the others weren't, but we'd go down there, it was something to do on a Thursday night. The bloke who was putting that on, a bloke called Ashley, who later did a runner with loads of money. He was doing these gigs and then I said to him "who's in charge of booking now?" And he said "oh, there's a new guy down there now." And I was like, perhaps he doesn't know that we were banned from here 2 years ago. So me and PJ went in and had a chat to him and like. He was like. Fine, you can do the gig. I just remember him saying, "But whatever happens, you can't have people smoking dope." I Remember Me and PJ going, you know, it's Culture Shock, there are some of their audience that's gonna be into it.

We were shitting ourselves. That, A, nobody was going to come, but also we get banned again for people smoking dope. The gig was really successful, there were like 200 people there, it was packed, but the irony is, we didn't have any problems at the gig. I think we just said to people, whatever you do, don't smoke (dope) in the in the venue, which people didn't, but the funny thing is, when we went to pay up afterwards, we went into the back room, which was kind of like the members area of club, and there was all these West Indian fellas in there playing dominoes. But it was like a sort of like a haze of smoke out there. It's like, so you're not worried about people smoking dope here, but you didn't want it out in the main venue. But, it was fine.

That was in June and then we hadn't booked anything else, and then Kent Jolly phoned me up again and said "I'm doing a tour for Christ On Parade. Do you wanna do them?" So we ended up doing them and that, again, that was successful.

That was sort of 88 into 89. And then we really started, after that we got on to the touring circuit. But the main problem with the West Indian Club was the fact that you couldn't do gigs on a Friday or Saturday and or obviously a touring band it could be any day of the week. But. if you wanted to bring like Joyce McKinney or an English band down, then you obviously wanted to do it on a Saturday night. Whilst we drank in the Joiners, we thought, maybe it's a bit small, obviously it was smaller than The West Indian Club, but actually, once we were in there and saw how good it was when it was packed, it was probably better to do it there.

We did the Joyce McKinney, Wat Tyler, Watch You Drown gig at the end of 89, that was really successful. We did a few more at the West Indian Club after that. I think in 89 we did Vernon Waters, Soul Side. Generic and Squandered Message, Victims Family and Bad Beach. Fire Party, Verbal Assault and that was through to the end of 89 and I think Joyce McKinney, which was the first one we did at the Joiners was maybe October 89 as well and then we did a few more. I think the last one we did (at the West Indian Club) was that Samiam one, we're ALL turned up, which was sort of end of 90, and I think the West Indian closed not long after that or basically they weren't doing gigs there anymore. But it was too big for most of the things that we wanted to do really.

I think the other thing was how people cooperated. There was various stages where we had a few gigs where we had a few financial disasters and stuff and people were like "Why don't you have a whip round then?" I really didn't want to ask people for money, just like donations or whatever. And then I remember you said "We'll do a tape for you."

Tony Suspect - Underground Rockers

There's a back page advert for our first comp tape on the back of SD#9. 'Now That's What WE Call Music'. Featuring local bands like Corporate Grave, Nox Mortis and In The Red as well as Instigators, Red London, Perfect Daze and others. Link Records were so impressed with it they asked me to compile an album for them, that became 'Underground Rockers'.

When it came to compelling 'Underground Rockers' I just asked The Sect, Red Letter Day, Instigators and Mega City 4, bands I was in contact with and liked at that time, if they wanted to contribute tracks. Gaz and me had seen Four Guns at the 100 Club, playing with Peter & The Test Tube Babies, so I guess I must have asked them off the back of that gig and buying their 7". Link Records wanted The Crack, Guitar Gangsters and The Magnificent included, so it wasn't totally all my choices.

I did travel up to South East London to meet up with Mark Brennan and Lol Pryor and go to a studio where The Sect were recording their two tracks. The tape they recorded on had previously been used for another Link release, I don't remember which one now, and they told me a story of using the crowd noise for one of their "live" albums (albums recorded in the studio, with crowd nose dubbed on afterwards) from 'Queen Live Killers'. Anyway, The Sect's songs sounded great as they recorded them live, it felt good to be there. I would have liked to have some local bands on there, I'm not sure why there aren't any, and despite that, and despite the bands I didn't choose, I was happy to be given the opportunity to get some of my favourite bands a bit of exposure. I did get £50 for compiling the album, and another £50 for writing the sleeve notes, but although that was nice, I wasn't really interested in the money, I just liked being involved in this project.

Stuart Armstrong writing in 2004:
"I'd just moved down to Dorset when, after two months I got a job in Eastleigh. Now, thinking that Bournemouth had Westbourne, Northbourne and Southbourne I didn't figure that Eastleigh could be too far away, having never been down here before. But, hey presto, I found myself travelling from Blindfold to Eastleigh every day for work, which was not a journey I enjoyed - starting off at 6:30 in the morning and not getting home until 9:30 at night. And with it being January I felt like I didn't see proper daylight.
My girlfriend, who dragged me 350 miles from home suddenly decided that she wasn't seeing enough of me and promptly ended the relationship. Now, bear in mind that she was what I came down here for and she and her family were all I knew in the area, so this came as a bit of a blow.
So, after only being at work for a month I found myself with nowhere to live, £30 in my pocket and the prospect of having to nick the company car to get me back to Morecambe.
Thankfully, the people I worked with were absolute gems and I suppose, saved me from doing something stupid. They spoke to their family and within a day I had a two bedroom flat, partly furnished and for very cheap rent in Eastleigh. I know this is long and drawn out, but there is a point to this story. Soon after moving in I decided to get away from things for a few days and went back to Morecambe to see my dear old mum. I visited some old haunts and a record store in Lancaster called Ear Ear and found an album called 'Underground

Rockers' which I paid £1.50 for. Mum didn't have a record player, so I had to wait to get back to Eastleigh to play it.

Back in my new flat I was listening to this new acquisition, and thinking that after all my years scouring second hand record shops for something punk that I hadn't heard before (which was becoming difficult as I've been into punk since the start, virtually), I had been missing out on some seriously good bands, and a brand new punk that was faster, more vibrant and FUN.

Whilst listening, I was reading the insert and came across a few fanzines being advertised and found an address for Suspect Device which was reasonably local, and as the title of the magazine was named after a song from my favourite band, I thought I would write to them to see if there was anything they could tell me about these new bands I was hearing, and if there were lots of others they could introduce me to.

I don't think I was really expecting a response. I'd written to people in the punk scene before and never heard anything, so when this packet arrived with a letter from Tony, and a couple of issues of SD I was most surprised and, I've got to say, over the moon. There were friendly people out there after all (I'd had some bad experiences in the local pubs that kind of destroyed my faith in Humanity).

I read these fanzines with renewed vigour, as if I'd never read anything related to punk before and found there were addresses of bands, how to contact them for demo tapes, reviews of new stuff, interviews and I was in my element. This was fantastic. So I replied and asked Tony if he wound't mind doing me a tape of some of the bands he was into and listening to that would give me an insight into this new found punk.

About three days later, this tape arrived of amazing music from Green Day, Jawbreaker, Jawbox, Instigators, Bad Religion, Fugazi, Life...But How To Live It? and many more. This blew me away, somebody I didn't know actually spent the time and effort in doing a tape for me. Now why would he do that? Because Tony is one of those guys who wants to spread the word and work of punk as I've found out in the years I've known him and also because he is a top bloke. This tape, like many others, were permanent additions of my car.

I kept sending blank tapes to Tony, and back they came filled with this awesome sounding music. Then Gaz got in touch and he started sending me tapes of old stuff I hadn't heard before, and that was it, I was an SD fanatic. Great music and great reading coming through the door, what more could a bloke ask for?

I wanted to meet both Tony and Gaz, because through letters they had become friends, and I had never met them, so when I got a phone call from Tony saying that this amazing band were playing the Joiners, I had to go.

The greeting I got was as if I was a long lost friend who they hadn't seen for years. We listened to a great live band, I bought a shed load of CDs and got drunk with Gaz, who, although we were strangers, spent most of the night getting to know us, as did Tony. I left that night feeling that I had met two of the soundest people on this planet.

I have since seen bands that have become strong rivals to all my old favourites, and I have met people that will never discriminate against who I am and the music I listen to. Tony and Gaz have become true friends, and even though I don't get to Southampton as much as I would like to, they still remain as friendly as the first time they wrote to me.

Since that first gig, they have inspired me to go to more and more gigs, listen to stuff that would never have crossed my path and brought me out of my ever-decreasing shell.

I'm sure you'll agree that Tony and Gaz are two of the nicest people you will meet in this underground scene.

I hope that I remain friends with these guys for a long, long time."

I had more freedom to choose bands for 'Underground Rockers 2' which came out in 1989. Manic Street Preachers had been in touch sending me their self released 'Suicide Alley' 7" and asked for an interview in the zine. I don't remember why we didn't feature them, because I did like that 7", but I did ask them if they wanted to appear on Underground Rockers 2, which they did, and gave us the two songs from that 7". I had been in touch with The Abs after getting their Turbosphinct 12", and they gave us two of the best songs they ever wrote. I had also struck up a friendship with Golly from HDQ by this point, so was really happy to have them on the record, and again they gave us versions of two of my favourite songs. Identity, The Price and Brighton's Suspect Device were also on there as were Senseless Things. They had sent me their debut 12", and I had got to know Mark Keds a bit, enough to chat at gigs and call him up from time to time. One day at work I took the opportunity to use my supervisor's desk phone when I had an empty office and called Mark to ask if they wanted to be on the album. Happily he was up for it and again their two songs are brilliant.

As an aside, when the Senseless Things came to Southampton to play at the University, the gig was taking place in the Student Union, and when we got there they were not allowing anyone in who didn't have a Southampton Uni ID card. I had one, having worked there for some time by then, but I didn't have it with me, but I only lived three miles away, so I drove home, got my card and rushed back. Some of the people denied entry had left, but there were a few people still milling round outside, so I went in, told Mark Keds what was going on, and he went out and made sure that the those outside could get in.

Back to the 'Underground Records 2' album. Once again I did the sleeve notes. Link had asked me to do a few of these sleeve notes by this time, always paying me, even though I'd have done it for free. I've never done any of this stuff for money, but if they were going to insist on giving me £50 to write a few words then I wasn't going to argue too hard. A section of the sleeve notes I wrote for Link's Peter & The Test Tube Babies 'Live And Loud' album appeared in a press released for a Test Tubes gig in Southampton many years later.

Crispin and me started a band after I left Obvious Action, called The Band From UNCLE. It didn't last long as only Crispin and me were into punk and immersed in the DIY scene, the others just thought it might be cool to be in a band. So with me on drums, Crispin on bass, my girlfriend at the time singing, another female singer and her boyfriend on guitar (I have forgotten either of their names but they worked with Crispin), we started practising. Crispin and me wanted to do something like The Joyce McKinney Experience, but as there were only the two of us in the band who knew JME, we could never get the sort of sound we both wanted. I remember writing a song about macho attitudes, and we did a cover of 'Wild Thing' because the guitarist knew it, but we must have had other songs as Link paid for us to record. We went back to Steve Collinson's studio, mainly because it was the only studio I knew at the time, and also because of his Subhumans connection. Link had suggested we appear on one of the 'Underground Rockers' albums, but thankfully saw sense when they heard what we'd done, and were honest enough to say that the band weren't quite ready. We certainly weren't, and we didn't ever get anywhere near playing a gig, and it all fell apart soon after. I didn't even keep a copy of that recording.

When Underground Rockers 2 came out, there was a gig at the George Robey in London, with some of the bands featured on the two Underground Rockers albums, plus others, spread over two days. Crispin and me went on both days, Craig Burton and Gaz went to at least one of the days with us too. It seems that the organisation on the first day wasn't good, but it did mean that we got to see Identity twice, who, according to my review, were great. We also enjoyed Red London and The Price, especially when Paul Fox from The Ruts joined them for a rendition of 'In A Rut'. But my favourite band of the day were The Sect. It seems that most of the crowd enjoyed The Crack, but I wasn't particularly impressed. We left before Splodgeenssabounds came on for some reason. The Sunday was the better attended day, and had more bands, including Suspect Device, Red Letter Day and The Abs, who's energetic set had Craig going a bit wild, so much so that he hurt his neck. We went outside into the bright sunshine, and as it was packed inside and getting hot we stayed outside and watched Culture Shock through the open door. Craig then had to take the week off work due to his neck problem.

Crispin remembers the weekend:

"In 1989, Tony – who was always very generous when it came to driving drunken (or planning to get drunken) punks to and from gigs – kindly did all the hard work which allowed me to attend what was in effect a launch do for Link records 'Underground Rockers' LP. Tony had come up with the line up at the request of co-founder Mark Brennan (formerly of The Business) who was one of Link's co-founders. A second LP was to follow but that, as they say, is another story.

From this line up: The Price, The Sect, Guitar Gangsters, Red Letter Day and The Instigators all featured on the LP and I went up with Tony and someone else for the Saturday. Through the scabs of my memory I do remember seeing Paul Fox climb up on stage and do a couple of songs with The Price, the highlight of course being a rendition of 'In a Rut'. The Instigators were as great as usual. The Price I always wanted to like but felt they lacked a bit in terms of guitar, Paul Fox fixed that all right! If Splodgenessabounds did play, we had left for reasons of time and good taste although I have a feeling that they may not have done.

I can be clearer about the Sunday as I compared memories with Craig Burton a couple of years ago as he was getting his Gigography up together. Burt along with Gaz came up on the Sunday with Tony again doing the drivey bit – what a guy! Various Cider fuelled Punks were lounging against the wall outside The Robey and one chirpy chappy chirruped 'have you got a pound?' in my direction. Feeling all brave I retorted "a pound, I thought it was supposed to be "have you got 10p?"' to which – and to my lasting admiration – the guy simply shrugged and replied 'inflation!'.

The line up did differ from the poster, for example I am sure that The Crack played somewhere over the weekend because I was very partial to 'Nag, nag, nag' and I'm sure I saw them do it there, it would make sense as they were on the album but we are talking 34 years ago, I was in my cups – to an extent – and I have never kept a diary or gigography so have to work from what's left of my memory. Be that as it may, my strongest memory of the event was this punk in a leather jacket wandering around the Robey, emptying everybody's dregs and leftovers into his pint glass. Suddenly I realised I was staring Charlie Harper straight in the eyes! Always a dude. There is a suggestion in the back of my mind that possibly either Culture Shock or The UK Subs changed day to headline instead of Splodge but I might well be wrong about that. The atmosphere certainly got a lot crustier when Culture Shock played and the atmosphere more, uhm, herbal! Culture Shock were great, My overriding memory of the weekend can be summed up in a word. Happy."

Underground Rockers was also the name of a column I had in a glossy magazine that Link were involved with called Beat Of The Street. I just wrote about all the new bands I liked. It was basically a round up of the sort of bands we were featuring in SD. My input only lasted for two or three issues, and I'm not even sure how many issues there actually were after I stopped writing for it.

My involvement with Link ended around this time too. I don't think the bands I was listening to were the sort that the magazine, or the label, were interested in.

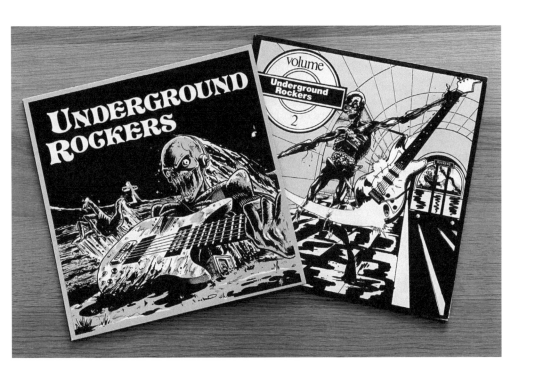

Tony Suspect - Network Of Friends

SD#10 featured HDQ, Government Issue, Culture Shock, Refugees, Exalt, Released Emotions Records and Last Rough Cause.

My favourite Government Issue song is 'Hall Of Fame', and the 'Boycott Stabb' 12" is a masterpiece, but I love their later stuff too, and their 'You' album was a real favourite at the time, and still is, so I was delighted to get a response from Tom Lyle returning some interview questions. Having them in the zine alongside HDQ and Culture Shock was great, three bands who's records I was playing a lot at that time. Dick Lucas sent his answers to our questions back on a cassette tape, which was a first, and very cool of him. We'd become friends with Vince who ran Released Emotions Records initially through his zine, 20th Century Saints, and his label would release records by The Sect, Red Letter Day, Anhrefen, Last Rough Cause, UK Subs, Crucial Youth, Lurkers, Flame On, The Price, Chelsea, Vibrators, Maniacs and Oi Polloi.

It was Wiz of Mega City 4 who'd originally recommended HDQ to me, and I'd bought 'You Suck' on the strength of that. I was a fan instantly, they were one of those bands that I knew I wanted to have in the zine from the first listen. A friendship developed with singer Golly and, to a lesser extent Dickie Hammond. HDQ have remained firm favourites ever since, and although contact with Golly has been sporadic, I still regard him as a friend.

Golly:

> There were lots of fanzines back then and all of them very important to the DIY punk/hardcore scene as we obviously didn't have the benefits of social media back then so they were one of the main sources of how we discovered bands and what was happening within the scene. Every single fanzine played its part and was as important as the other but Suspect Device was always one of my favourites. I think it is testament to how good it is even back then that it is still going strong today.

Gaz interviewed both Exalt and Refugees.

There were also reviews of Hate That Smile, Lemonheads, Fugazi and The Vernon Walters amongst many others. Mike Head was also back doing more reviews.

The cover is a reproduction of HDQ's 'You Suck' album cover that worked pretty well as a zine cover.

HDQ became a huge favourite of mine, they were excellent at the West Indian Club when they played with Verbal Assault, and their second album, 'Sinking', remains one of my favourite albums. They came back to play in Winchester and afterwards they stayed at my flat. We stayed up late into the night chatting, and I remember Dickie Hammond being so full of life and friendly, dominating the conversation. What struck me was their politeness, I guess when you toured as much as they did, being nice people was a necessity as you often relied on the generosity of others for a place to stay. Anyway, I was happy to offer them a place to stay, showers and, in Dickie's case, a radiator to dry his socks on. In the morning they all went to the little shop right near the flat, and made themselves a cooked breakfast. After more chatting they left to head to the ferry to Europe (I think that's right). As I waved them off I remember thinking that I'd have a kitchen to clean up, but when I went back into the flat, they had done the washing up and left everything clean and tidy. I was already a fan, but the few hours they stayed with me just enhanced my admiration for them.

It seems there was about a year between issues 10 and 11, but a hell of a lot had changed in the meantime, the biggest being that I'd left home, and was now living in a flat on Millbrook Estate, not far from where I was born.

Although the initial copies of SD#11 were printed by my dad, I had also got a new job, and after the first 20 or so A4 copies, photocopied by my dad as usual, we switched to getting the zine printed, rather than copied, at my new work, and due to the cost, most copies of this issue were printed A5 size. Looking at the reviews, we were still going to a lot of gigs, and getting a few more records in to review. I like the layout, and the bands featured were all particular favourites from this period, Instigators, Identity, Senseless Things, The Sect, Sofa Head and locals Corporate Grave.

I was a fan of the Instigators before Andy Turner joined, but after meeting him, briefly, at their West Indian Club gig in 1985 I had stuck up something of a friendship with him. We corresponded quite a bit, as I'm sure he did with a lot of other people at that time. He kept me up to date with Instigators news, and recommended bands and records too. He was good at promoting the scene, and his enthusiasm was infectious.

I asked Andy if he remembered when he first became aware of SD, and the impact of the DIY scene:

"I used to buy every zine i found at gigs and we traded loads too and sold them through both distros and on tour if we were in it. Probably met you guys first time at the West Indian Centre in Southampton in 1985. Was one of the first with Instigators after the line-up change. We had a tour booked and had been rehearsing solid for the 7 days we had until it kicked off.

There's a line I can trace that goes right back to when I was 14 and got into punk and all down it DIY defined who I was and who I am now. To do what you loved and what you wanted to do you pretty much had to Do It Yourself and picked up a multitude of "job Skills". I did a zine, I did a record label, I printed shirts, I made badges, I booked shows, I wrote songs and some. What I do now is only because of what I did between then and now."

I saw the Instigators a fair bit, with various lines ups, and Andy always took the time to have a chat. It has to be said that Andy did a lot to inspire me, not just with his music, but the encouragement, and the bands he introduced me to over the years. I still listen to the Instigators on regular basis, and their music and the memories of those times never fails to put a smile on my face.

I think, by this time, I was feeling much more comfortable in the local scene, I didn't feel so much an outsider. I have to say that those feelings of alienation had nothing to do with anyone else, our friends had always been supportive and inclusive, it was just what was going on in my head, not feeling cool or knowledgeable enough, and feeling like an imposter with the zine. But now I was starting to put those thoughts to the back of my mind, although even now I often feel awkward and alone in a crowd of friends.

Crispin sums up how welcoming the local scene was to new faces:

"As I have already related, good fortune led me to meet one of the loveliest people I have ever known, Mr Tony Suspect. Over the years, he has been a far better friend to me than I have probably deserved as through my own idiocy, fate and Kermit or is that Kismet, I have never been a particularly pro-active member of the scene. My bad and I can only say that people like Tony, Rich

Levene, Gaz 'air guitar' Suspect, Rob Callan, Paul Jay and too many more for me to here mention, have my undying respect for their work over the years. After meeting Tony, it wasn't long before I was attending gigs at The West Indian Club as it was then – best venue ever – and although I don't remember (to my ever-lasting shame) which was my first gig there, I soon became a regular. I knew all about punk of course because I'd listened to a few records, had a leather jacket – in which I had spelled 'Sex Pistols' on the back done in safety pins, DR Martin's boots and had been to a couple of gigs. I was therefore somewhat confused to see this bloke there in jeans and a matching denim jacket! Well, he can't be a punk I thought but stone me, when the music kicked off, he was down the front like a cider fuelled rocket. Also there was this guy in a t-shirt which I didn't recognise stood slightly back from the main mess, rocking to and fro approximately in time to the music and apologising if he bumped into people!

I had gone to the gig with my warbly voice, slight acne and carefully gelled hair expecting spikey tops, violence, and mayhem, not people helping each other up when they fell over whilst dancing down the front. Everybody was so bloody nice I nearly asked for my money back!

So my education began. The more I spent time with Tony, attended gigs and spoke to people, the bigger fool I felt – I knew nothing but that, as they say, is the first step on the path to enlightenment. Mainly in Southampton but also occasionally in places like Winchester, I attended many gigs – usually thanks to THE Rock Star, Tony Suspect (remember he was in bands and did a zine – WOW!) and was bowled over by how nice nearly all the regulars were. I expanded my mindset and eventually at least learnt what being a punk was really about and still is.

It isn't about major record labels, leather jackets and famous bands (although many of those first bands I still love), it was about this community of nice, welcoming kindred spirits who had a thirst for some blistering guitar driven noise with words that meant something. About helping if you could because why the fuck wouldn't you. About community and a sense of belonging and in fairly short order, I was convinced that I belonged. A lot of the bands not only produced great music but were there to chat to before during and after their sets. They didn't live on Mount Olympus, they were ordinary folk who had time for you.

For REAL punk to exist you had to get off your arse and do something and even I contributed just a tiny bit because at the end of the day, the lesson is, you've got to do it yourself."

We interviewed Sofa Head after seeing them live and having their album sent for review. I've never asked for review copies of anything, and I'm always grateful for anything that people feel they want to send us. I felt very privileged getting stuff from Meantime, because I would have bought their releases anyway. Unfortunately I was out when the Sofa Head LP arrived, so the postie folded the LP sized cardboard package to get it through the letter box. Amazingly it didn't snap, but it did look like a half pipe, so I flattened it out by placing it under a pile of heavy books for a few days. The first track on each side still jumped, so I bought myself another copy. Gaz took the copy I was sent, and as far as I know he still has it. I still play that first Sofa Head album, it's one of my favourite records.

I like the look of SD#11, the cover was of Andy Turner singing with the Instigators. The Instigators were an important band, not just for me, but for the UK scene in general. Andy was good at encouraging people and promoting what was going on in the UK at that time. He also helped spread the word about SD.

Steve Lee (Vision On zine) remembers his introduction to SD came through Andy:
"I can't remember specifically but I'm guessing it was through hanging around the Full Circle office in Huddersfield – which seemed like a drop-in centre for the area's punks who were more than likely signing on, usually skint and always on the blag for a cup of coffee – which distro'd Suspect Device. I'd probably seen reviews in other zines as well, specifically the big American ones MRR and Flipside which were something resembling punk and hardcore bibles back then. I remember poring over every issue, reading every review and advert of those two, especially MRR. It wasn't easy to pick up underground, independent releases back in the late 1980s and equally difficult to get onto decent, underground publications. Sending off the ubiquitous SAE with a few coins to God knows where for a zine was a leap of faith, but it soon became apparent that SD was an enthusiastic, entertaining, reliable, politically sound, knowledgeable zine which you could genuinely trust."

The layouts for SD#11 looked good, we were still using typewriters and putting each issue together meant getting out the scissors and several Pritt Sticks, but we had a better idea of how we wanted a zine to look.
Mike Head was again involved, doing some reviews, but it seems Gaz and me were still not adding our names to our reviews. I can tell which are which as I recognise our individual typewriter fonts.

SD#12 features two of my favourite interviews, we spoke to both Sleep and Target Of Demand on the same night at The Joiners. My memory tells me that we got there early and interviewed Sleep in The Joiners itself, they were, as they always were, good company and easy to talk to. Then we went out to Target Of Demand's van and spoke to them there. Again they were easy to talk to and we had fun. Both bands then went and played fantastic sets, as did the other band on the night, Joyce McKinney Experience. I think most regulars at STE gigs over the years remember this one very fondly.
My dad may not have been printing the zine, it was another A5 zine printed at my work, but I was now obviously using his Amstrad home computer, instead of the trusty old typewriter. I'd have to go to my parents to use their computer when I wanted to type up the zine, Gaz would write his interviews and reviews out on paper and I would type them up. I would also make use of their CD player as I still didn't have one and we were starting to get one or two CDs sent in for review.
We were finally crediting ourselves with the reviews we were doing, so that was some progress, other reviews were from Crispin and Rut, and HDQ's Golly did a write up of one of their European tours.

Golly:
"As for touring in the mid to late 80s and early 90s, the UK had some great venues but could also be a bit of a slog for us as not everyone appreciated our melodic punk sound that was heavily influenced by the American punk scene of the time and bands like Dag Nasty and the Descendents but Europe was

totally different. They really seemed to get what we were doing and we toured throughout Europe a lot. I think it was about 6 European tours we done and most of them were long tours lasting over 4 weeks at a time. We played Germany a lot and also France, Netherlands, Austria, Switzerland, Belgium and Hungary which was a very eye opening experience. We always seemed to play to larger crowds in Europe and if you speak to any band who played over there they will all tell you how much the gig organisers looked after the bands. There was always a meal waiting for you and of course an endless supply of beer haha. The punk hardcore scene especially in Germany was booming at that time. I remember travelling thousands of miles in the back of a transit van with mattresses on top on the equipment so we had somewhere to sit. It was basically a death trap if we ever crashed. Great times and great memories and I met some lifetime friends in the process of doing what we loved to do to people who loved it too."

One of our mates at football was a photographer, and worked in a camera shop developing photos. I'd had the roll of film I'd taken at the Target Of Demand gig developed, and had selected a suitable photo of Rainer (Target Of Demand singer), took the negative in to my mate's shop and he blew it up to A5 size, and we used it for the cover. I thought it worked well, it was just a shame that the printing was a bit dark.

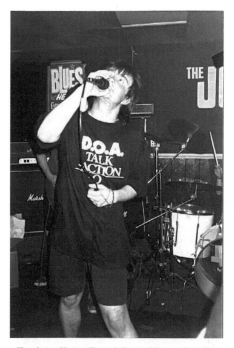

The photo of Rainer Knispel (Target Of Demand) at The Joiners, Southampton, which was used for the cover of SD#12

When we got to SD#13 our network of friends was widening, and we had by this time made contact with Aston of Boss Tuneage, and Mike Head was doing more reviews for us. The interviews show how much we were now being fully inspired by the local scene. Not only were there interviews with Rich Levene about the STE, Older Than Dirt and Haywire (still based in Dorset at this point, but regularly at gigs in Southampton), but also US bands we'd loved when seeing them in Southampton at STE gigs. Verbal Assault had played with HDQ and had blown me away. I didn't interview them on the night, but got an address and sent off some questions, getting a reply very quickly (and remember this was a time of actually hand writing letters and posting them overseas). We also featured ALL, they weren't supposed to play Southampton, but turned up unexpectedly at the Samiam, Ultraman, Older Than Dirt gig at the West Indian Club. But as they were there they and ended up playing, and went on first, which was cool, but did mean Older Than Dirt didn't get to play. Goober Patrol were also featured, if they hadn't played in Southampton at that point, they soon would. They had a split 7", with Vehicle Derek on Boss Tuneage out, and we took some copies to sell at STE gigs.

The ALL interview was done one the night at the West Indian Club by Crispin, Shaun Hemsley and Paul Chambers. I didn't go along as I wanted to see Samiam who were headlining the gig. I hadn't heard them before but wanted to check them out.

Crispin remembers:
"Time plays funny tricks on that which I am pleased to call my memory and so, it is thanks to some helpful nudges from an invaluable source that I shall now record how, accompanied by Shaun Hemsley and Paul Chambers (at that time of Hate That Smile), clutching Tony Suspect's tape recorder and without an effing clue as to what I was doing or what to ask, ended up interviewing ALL for Suspect Device.

It was on the 2nd of October 1990 that saw me arrive at The West Indian Club for, what I have established thanks to sources that must remain anonymous (thanks Tony!) must have been STE gig number 19! The fact that I was there at all casts some serious question marks over me as a person I now realise. It was my brother's 13th birthday and our Dad had died less than 8 months before and here I was gallivanting. Oh well, he was probably eating jelly, eating bits of cheese and pineapple on sticks or shooting up. Whatever you did for your birthday when you were 13 in 1990.

Anyhoo, despite or because of my personal failings, the 2nd of October 1990 saw me down at, what was called, The Tinder Box which I hadn't remembered till I caught sight of the flyer (thanks Tony) and which, to me, will always be remembered happily and simply as The West Indian Club. To see Berkeley California's Samiam and I note a band from St. Louis, Missouri – Ultraman. I was also very much there to see our very own Older Than Dirt who were leading the way in Southampton as our very own Hardcore outfit as my education into the new sound continued.

I am not afraid these days to admit to things that don't cast me in a particularly good light, which is probably just as well all things considered and so continuing the trend, I have an admission to make. At the time, I held contemporary American Punk music in some disdain! On the whole and despite the mix tapes that Tony had cooked up for me, there weren't many bands from across the pond that did it for me. Those that did do it for me: The Dead Kennedy's, Black Flag and The Descendents were all long defunct by

1990 but I remember that Soulside had blown me away the previous year and a gig was a chance to catch up with some familiar faces and have a bit of a boogie once the beer had kicked in, if I felt so inclined.

We'll take it that the scene has been far more than necessarily set and get to the nub and grist of the whole brouhaha. As the night got underway, it became apparent that Older Than Dirt were not going to be playing, shenanigans had taken place which I only found out about decades later and it soon became apparent that ALL, despite not being on the bill, were going to open proceedings. I was hobnobbing with Tony and Paul and Shaun from Hate That Smile when this became apparent and even I knew that ALL were the remains of The Descendants and even contained a former member of Black Flag in the form of Bill Stephenson (okay, he wasn't in them for long but then apart from Ginn, who was?).

I think that they were touring Allroy Saves but I couldn't honestly tell you what they played as I wasn't a fan and only heard a few tracks and possessed none of their vinyl but I knew the excitement was palpable. They played their set to an enthusiastic reception then made way to Ultraman who I dimly remember as being quite good but like so many other bands of the time, I doubt that I got terribly excited. Samiam I mainly missed as I was otherwise engaged.

As I hadn't heard about Older Than Dirt missing out on playing, I couldn't understand why the intrepid Tony Suspect, who was clutching a tape recorder, wasn't carpe dieming and taking the chance to interview ALL. They were famousish and surely anyone stealing a sneaky interview with them would ensure that the next edition of SD would sell millions, garner a Pulitzer and probably be the next Jools Holland or whatever. Thing is Tony had heard about OTD losing a gig and he wanted to see Samiam. Never mind! I was here and I'd had some Dutch courage so I squeaked something about doing it myself had obtained possession of said tape recorder and was busy blagging my way backstage to the band's room to have my name cast in stone.

To my shame, I have to admit to being a little piqued when Paul and Shaun said that they would come too! This was going to be MY big exclusive – as I've said before I was (and probably still am) a bit of a prick – but thank every deity, God, false God and Cthulhu that they did because they actually knew what they were talking about. Thanks to their presence, the interview didn't grind to a halt after I'd asked the obligatory What do you think about England and How's about the weather then? They knew the Band and the music and elicited insightful answers to questions related to the band buying a house together so that they could fish and about songs that explored the subject. They literally saved me from making a gigantic plonker of myself, well that and the fact that Bill Stephenson and other band members were so nice. Responding kindly to a question I think I pitched about Black Flag.

So, small thanks to me, SD ended up with an interesting interview well worth printing, I met some very nice chaps and overcame some silly prejudices against American bands, Paul got the Pulitzer Prize for Journalism 1990 and Shaun went on to present Hootenanny (although I could be making some of this up!)."

The Older Than Dirt interview is in two parts, the first chat was at The Joiners when they played with Sink and Can't Decide, that was cut short for reasons I have long since forgotten, so I finished it with Mike and Paul before the Samiam / Ultraman gig at the West Indian Club. As they ended up not playing that night, they were, understandably not particularly happy, but agreed to finish the interview. We did it in a room behind the stage and I was surprised to find that there was a boxing ring there. We sat on the floor in front of the ring to do the interview.

I did the interview with Rich at his house in Eastleigh. Periodically I'd visit and Rich would introduce me to new bands, a lot of whom would become real favourites. I felt awkward doing face to face interviews, but Rich made it easy.

We featured a Samiam interview, conducted via mail after making contact at the West Indian Club gig, in SD#14. Other interviews were with bands who'd played in Southampton; The Abs, Herb Garden, Juice and BBMFs, along with Dumb, Wanton Thought and Jawbox, who's debut EP Rich had introduced me to on one of my visits, and it had really excited me. SD#14 also has another Euro tour report too, this time from The Sect.

Shaun Hemsley interviewed The Void, and also did quite a few reviews. By this time I was in Fusion with Shaun, Paul Chambers and Iain Ratcliffe (Iain had also done some reviews in this issue). There is mention here that Fusion had played our first gig, supporting Quicksand at The Joiners. As a band, Fusion was split between Dorset and Hampshire, so two practises took place, alternately, in both locations. Iain and me would drive to Wareham, and then the next one would see Paul and Shaun come to Southampton. One practise in Wareham was so cold, and the heaters were up in the rafters, and heat rises, so we had to stand on chairs and reach up to try and get some warmth in our hands.

This was the first band I'd been in that had a more Hardcore sound, so I spent ages listening to the drums in Government Issue records before we got together for our first practise. I felt intimidated at my lack of drumming skills, and the other's obvious musical talent, but I did enjoy being in the band.

Before one of our gigs, I'd bumped into Iain during the day and we arranged to both wear Captain Scarlet t-shirts for the gig. We were so cool!

Mike Head was still involved, and we were in contact with people who contributed from Greece, the US and Germany, and the thanks list in this issue mentions a certain David from Cambridge.

David Stuart:

"I recall reading this fanzine that I had heard about and just totally feeling in line with the writing, the attitude and the friendship/unity that it gave off as the pages turned, I did an interview to start with for my 3rd zine, still got that interview somewhere! I don't recall how I started contributing, you must have asked me to do something... reviews? I just remember being so enthused about fanzine stuff again.

I had seen the name and knew SD was a fanzine, but I think I only picked up from issue 11 (1990?) or something. I had been putting my own fanzines out since 1986 and had just had the disappointment putting together a split zine with someone, who then disappeared after receiving my half of the project! There was a superb in-depth and beautifully(?) laid out interview with the late Mick Magee (RIP) of UK hardcore band Mayhem that never saw the light of day. I was gutted, but once that project was a no go, I started on another zine of my own and along with an interview with Resistance 77 (who had just come back with a brand new 7") and local guitar pop heroes Color Factory, I also interviewed the SD guys to make a change from bands being asked questions! I had read the fanzine, connected to it and wanted to promote another publication that was well deserved of some exposure."

There was a lot going on in our lives in the autumn of 1991, Gaz had started a relationship, while mine had fallen apart. Around the same time as this Fusion weren't able to practise, play live or record a demo as Iain had gone to the US and hadn't come back. But the local scene was thriving and we had a lot to pack into SD#15. Majority Of One had played in both Southampton and Winchester, and after being impressed at The Joiners, Iain and me had interviewed them in my car before their Winchester gig. My memory tells me that the same week as Majority Of One had played in Southampton, GO! had also played. Shaun and Paul were now doing their own zine with their friend Jim. Before the GO! gig I joined them when they interviewed Mike Bullshit in the alley beside the Joiners. When that was done I spoke to Mike for SD, but instead of going over the same questions, knowing that Shaun and Paul's zine would be out at roughly the same time, we mainly spoke about our shared interest in Native American culture and history. I had written some lyrics for Fusion on the subject, and GO! had 'Victim Of Civilisation', so it was good to hear what he had to say on the subject. I thought GO! were tremendous that night, I loved their super short, fast songs and abundant energy.

We also included an interview with straight edge band Headway, local gig promoters Urbcore, Wards Of Warning Records, Rhythm Collision, Blitzkrieg and M.T.A. Plus there's a short piece on Shutdown, who had sent us their demo. This was the start of a longstanding friendship with Neil Cox. David Stuart had a two page feature and also did some reviews. The cover is uninspiring, but the issue is packed and pretty good I think. Oh, and there's a Fusion interview done by Shaun and Paul's mate, Jim Daydream too.

Gaz:

Issue #10 – I have to say that this is another decent issue and one where again - it looks like I pulled my backside out of the pub! We interviewed HDQ, Last Rough Cause, Culture Shock, Exalt, Government Issue, Refugees and Released Emotions Records. The legend that is Dick Lucas did a great interview for Culture Shock and we featured Roddy Moreno's SHARP – Skinheads Against Racial Prejudice and what they wanted to achieve, which was basically to get the right wing twats out of the Skinhead movement. By this time, we were also beginning to pick up other contributors, most notably Mike Head, who is still doing his bit to this day and a guy called Cal from Plymouth, both did reviews for us. I gave special thanks to Marcus from Foreign Legion in this issue too – he was always a great help to us and an enthusiast of all things Punk, sadly he passed away this year in June (2023). Gone mate, but not forgotten and the same for Dickie Hammond and Lainey of HDQ who we've lost since then. On the back cover of this issue was another compilation tape from us too! Life on Earth, which also had a booklet and was another £1.25 including the postage bargain! We even managed to get 25p from each tape off to Greenpeace! Think we shifted a fair few hundred of these too!

Issue #11 – This issue saw us reduce the zine in size from A4 to A5 – not sure why? I guess it was on the grounds of cost! It also looks like we heralded in the 1990's with this issue, which featured Sofa Head, The Sect, Identity, Senseless Things and local Punk favourites Corporate Grave. Not much I want to pass comment on here apart from it was another solid issue and our most expensive to date! Yup! We were into the era of proper printing as our circumstances had changed with access to work copiers. This one set the Punks back 30p! A massive rise from the previous issues 20p cover price. By now we were looking to bank offshore along with the Politicians and uber rich. We had ambitions to own football clubs, write the zine from our penthouses in Monaco and generally flaunt our wealth like those bunch of cunts from Made in Chelsea. Sadly, we were dealt a savage blow by reality and continued to make a loss! Oh well, Punk Rock never made any money for you and me did it dear reader!

Issue #12 – While trying to justify the massive price rise for a copy of the zine we decided to keep the quality high too! The excellent Target of Demand from Austria, Sleep from Brighton, Leatherface, Flame On! and Blind Justice from Wales were all interviewed. Yet another compilation tape was also launched – A Far Cry From '76 and featured Exit Condition, The Blaggers, The Instigators and many more. Again, we managed to flog a fair few of these for a quid with suitable SAE. 'Play it to yer Granny' I wrote at the bottom of the advert in the zine! As I sit here typing this I am a Grandad!

Issue #13 – Still charging 30p and sticking to A5 we had to justify it all, so we brought you – ALL, who I think were formerly The Decendents, local punk outfits Older Than Dirt & Haywire, Goober Patrol, the excellent Verbal Assault and The STE Collective, who I can claim to be a founding member of (little else though!) and we put on gigs in Southampton for a fair few years. Most of the credit must go to Rich Levene and Rob Callen for being the real movers and shakers though.

Issue #14 – Another packed issue and another price rise! 40p brought you Juice, Samiam, Herb Garden, the totally good fun BBMF's, Dumb, Jawbox, The Abs, Wanton Thought, The Void and more! Struggling to read the small print that came with an A5 zine, but its another solid issue with plenty of variety.

Issue #15 – Ha! Yet another price rise! 50p for flip sake – mind you I think you were getting your money's worth?! It's a great shame we didn't do the zine A4 anymore, because it would have looked great and I may have been able to read it! Packed out with interviews though and our mission to mix up the Punk genres and divisions went on as we interviewed Majority of one, Headway, Fusion, Urbcore, M.T.A. Words of Warning record label and Rhythm Collision. One thing I have noticed and not mentioned so far is that at some point we must have mothballed our old manual typewriters and entered the computer age. That's Tony's department as like musical talent, I also had no talent for computer operation although I've improved through necessity over the years!

(Right) The STE flyer for some
early gigs.

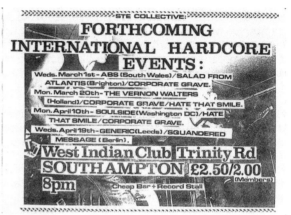

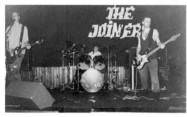

(Above) SMOG UK, The Joiners
(Below) NO SUBSTANCE, The King Alf

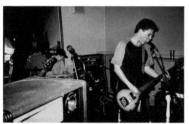

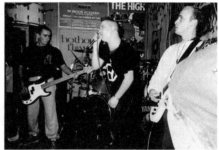

(Above) OLDER THAN DIRT, London

(Below) Some early demos and live tapes

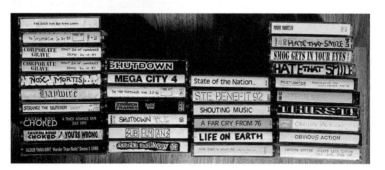

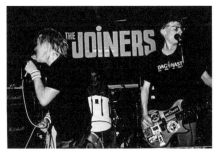

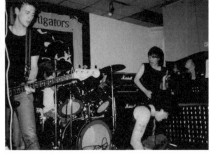

(Above left): SLEEP, The Joiners
(Below): HDQ, The West Indian Club

(Above): INSTIGATORS, West Indian Club
(Below): THE SECT, Hype Club, London

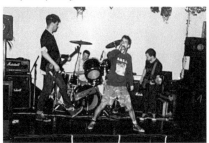

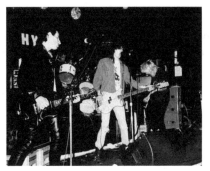

(Left): MEGA CITY FOUR, West Indian Club
(Below) THE TONE, The Railway Inn, Winchester

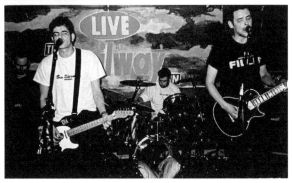

Tony Suspect - The Pleasure And The Pain

It would seem that as 1991 ended things were starting to look up for me. We put out the first of our infrequent mini-issues. Vince from Released Emotions Records had given us a load of sampler flexis for his label, featuring The Price, Red Letter Day, Red London and The Lurkers. We also had some stuff that didn't quite make it into SD#15, but we didn't feel would still be particularly relevant by the time we got to number 16. So we decided to do an Xmas issue, calling it issue SD#15 1/2, giving away the flexi as a little Xmas gift. Stu from Older Than Dirt did an Xmas version of the OTD stage diving character, and we used some Xmas wrapping paper as the background.
Mike Head and David Stuart did reviews, as did Ian Arnold, Chris and Lloyd Pearson The latter three had contributed to the previous couple of issues, but I don't really remember Lloyd and Chris and I lost contact with Ian Arnold many years ago (sorry guys). The other person to do some reviewing, for the first time for us, was Paul Fox.

Paul Fox:
"I first heard about Suspect Device from David Stuart (DS), I was tape trading with him on a regular basis and he was fuelling my obsession with, typically, American hardcore punk, he was, and still is, quite an authority on the subject and I liked his dry wit and American influenced slang and attitude, I can't quite remember how we got onto the subject of SD, he may have sent me a copy of one of the early issues, I distinctly recall reading one of Tony's anecdotes which was deeply personal and referred to a relationship breakdown and the lyrics to an HDQ song (incredible melodic punk band from Sunderland featuring the late great Dickie Hammond, also of Leatherface, on guitar), this instantly struck a chord with me and I immediately reached out to Tony, feeling a degree of empathy and sympathy, I'm not sure why I did that, but as Tony's a good sort, he responded straight away and we too became regular corresponders through letter writing, progressing onto tape trading, and good friends, having never met and there being some pretty hefty distance between us."

There are short features on Turkish band Moribund Youth and also the Obscene Females. David had his Cambridge page, and he did a quiz/word search page, and we included a recipe for my mum's mince pies.
This mini issue also includes my first ever column, inspired by David's writing. I pour my heart out a bit, it seems the months of feeling like a failure after the relationship break up had made way for a new feeling of hope. I remember listening to HDQ's 'Soul Finder' album over and over during those lonely months and all of a sudden, the hope I was feeling seemed to have a soundtrack, and I printed some words from the song 'Things Seem A Whole Lot Better Now' from that album in this issue...

You put a smile on my face / You don't turn away / You wiped the tears from my eyes / You sweetened that bitter taste / So thanks to you, things seem a whole lot better now //

What I didn't know at that point was that the relationship I had been in wasn't a good one, it was a situation I found myself in while I was concentrating on bands and zines and records and gigs, and it really wasn't right for me and I wasn't happy. I needed it to end, but I still felt like a failure. I think I was beginning to realise that it was the best thing that could have happened, and that the new friendship I'd found would blossom and has endured to this day.

Once again punk rock, and the friends that punk had brought with it had got me though a shitty time, 1980s were fading into the distance, the zine was becoming what I'd always wanted, and I could finally see some future.

I remember being disappointed with with cover of issue 16, even though I did it, and it seemed funny at the time. I think Stuart Pearce had recently had a top ten records published in a newspaper or magazine, and it was all punk, so we put a picture of him on the cover over a background picture of a Shutdown t-shirt.

Interviews featured new and older friends. Shutdown became real favourites of not just ours, but the Southampton scene as a whole, and I was in pretty regular contact with their singer Neil.

Neil Cox:

"Can't remember the first time I read SD. It would have probably been 88/89/90 as I was getting more involved in the punk scene in the UK, sending off for fanzines to be delivered to very sleepy Gloucestershire and generally soaking up a world beyond the Peel Sessions I'd been hearing of The Stupids, HDQ et al.

I do, however, remember meeting Tony and Gaz for the first time. At an STE gig at the Joiners. Well, obviously! I remember an instant bond beyond the music, with them both being big football fans and from there on in a friendship began.

Tony and I corresponded pretty regularly and it was great to find a kindred spirit who not only loved punk and football but also a bit of the old mod revival so close to my heart. And with Gaz, our musical tastes were a bit further apart but we had our darts and no one will ever take that away!!!

I played in a band that went down to the STE/Joiners a few times and it was always great. Suspect Device were always massive champions of what we did and I will never forget that. Some brilliant memories from Tall Man playing and first hearing 'Play a song for Totton/Tottenham/Rotten (delete as appropriate)' to a few very memorable Shutdown gigs, none more so than a tribute to Steve Burgess, band mate of Tony's and STE founding member (I think). STE was the essence of the Southampton punk and SD was the heartbeat.

I was asked to do a few columns in SD which ranged from my excessive drinking, the real meaning of emo, football and even a stupid (but still makes me chuckle) feature of an imaginary record label and bands.

As life goes one we all find our paths and we all have other things that take priority in our lives. Tony and I hadn't corresponded for a good few year and then I found myself in another band that played the STE anniversary gig and it was brilliant to catch up. I occasionally saw Gaz at Rebellion over the years, I could pick out that chunky bracelet amidst a sea of black leather jackets a mile off.

Then a few more years pass by and you kind of lose touch but just about keep in contact with all the wonderful things that social media gives us (maybe). By my estimation it's a friendship of 35 years +. Not bad going, but not a patch on Gaz and Tony's which has always been the crux of SD and made it so lovely. Two friends who discovered punk and decided to channel their energy into something positive. Sometimes I miss an issue coming out but I do try and keep up with it, and it's like an old friend popping through my letterbox. I still get the same excitement as I did many moons ago. Is enduring a patronising description? I hope not.

We're all still here, still appalled by modern football, still kicking around the punk rock scene. And most of all, SD is Tone and Gaz and always will be.

Great people, great read and great times ahead I have no doubt.

The real deal. Thanks chaps. X"

Boss Tuneage Records were included in SD#16, we had been in contact with Aston for some time, and I had even contributed a little to his zine IG, but his label was taking off. Also, Exit Condition were featured after drummer Richard had made contact and had sent me tapes, both of bands he thought I'd like, and the first Exit Condition demo. Gaz was in contact with Blind Justice, and they had sent us a tour report. The Instigators were featured again as they had reformed, and Andy Turner was a mate. Iain Ratcliffe now living in the USA may have meant that Fusion had ended, but he was still contributing to the zine, and for this issue he had interviewed JFA. There was also pieces on Subbuteo and Comics.

Older Than Dirt had released their flexi, which we loved, and there are two reviews of it here, and the back page is an ad for it. Also, it looks like we got the page count wrong and there is a flap on the back where a blank page had to be cut off.

I've talked about how the local scene was inspirational and one of the main reasons we persevered with the zine in the early days, and the STE in particular were responsible for giving Southampton a thriving and close knit DIY punk scene, and by the end of 1992 they had a bit of a cashflow problem, so SD#17 was a benefit for them. We also did another compilation tape, complied by Gaz, as a benefit.

We started the zine as a way of getting more involved, and now that we were part of a great scene, we wanted to do what we could to help and give a bit back. I doubt we were able to give them much, but we tried our best.

The cover featured photos of us with lots of locals, with text running round the pictures in a Crass style. Gaz did quite a lot for this issue, not just reviews and interviews, but even a column too. David Stuart was back, and there was a short interview he'd originally done for a Cambridge area zine that didn't end up coming out. Aston (Boss Tuneage) did some reviews, Shaun interviewed Comb from Seattle and we also featured CDS, Nux Vomica, Subversives, Gan, Reverse and Erase Today, plus a bit on the STE. Gaz and me also did some reviews where we sat at his house, played some records and reviewed them together.

There is a call to Stuart Armstrong to contribute too.

According to my intro for SD#18, we made a "tidy sum" for the STE, which was good. It's another packed issue which has lots of interviews, including Wat Tyler and one with the editor of a FC St Pauli fanzine done by Paul Pomonis who would send me lots of Greek records, and would go on to write for When Saturday Comes. There was also a tour report, contributions from several people, columns and a review section typed and laid out by David Stuart. The cover photo is of Face To Face, who's first 7" I loved, but who's answers left a lot to be desired.

We also advertised SD t-shirts, and I remember my sister, niece, Sarah and me going out into the road outside my parent's house to take photos of us wearing the shirts. I'd bought an old skateboard, so we played around on that while the photos were taken.

By this time I was in a new band called Thirst! It was started by Steve Burgess, me and Shaun, who'd been in Fusion with me, and Shane who'd been in Mad Thatchers. Shane and Shaun left before we'd done more than a few practices and were replaced by our friends Rob Callen (bass) and Jon Fry (vocals). Musically the influences came from bands like Embrace and Marginal Man, although I did get us to cover 'Walk Together Rock Together'. Steve and Rob were the main writers of the music, but I ended up writing a lot of lyrics, and I have fond memories of recording our demo. At the time I was watching a lot of Italian football, and the day we recorded, the Milan derby was on TV, so Steve suggested calling it 'Milan Derby" and we used a sample from the televised game at the end of the tape.

David's contributions had expanded, he always had a lot of content to submit, and we were more than happy with that, so we decided that our next issue would be a split issue with his Cambridge zine.

SD#19 turned out to be a huge issue, over 70 pages, and some of the Cambridge half had really small text, so was a whole lot to read. Amongst all the bands featured, including Older Than Dirt who had a new line up, was a question and answer thing instigated by David with him, Gaz and me. Looking back now it's a bit unnecessary, especially with the amount of content we already had (4 Past Midnight, Sugar, Zimmer Frames, Down By Law, Screeching Weasel, Devil Dogs, Posh Boy Records, The Queers, MDM, Chicken Bone Choked, Dole Drums Distro plus columns, reviews etc). This issue came out in September 1993.

The next issue, SD#20, came out in March 1994, and a lot had happened. First of all it marked ten years since we decided to start the zine, and the cover features a repeating list of all the bands we'd featured up until that point. Any celebration of our decade of bashing typewriters was overshadowed by the death of our good friend, and my bandmate at the time, Steve Burgess. Just after Christmas 1993 Steve had a sudden heart attack that shook us all. If anything good did come out of such a shocking and upsetting time it was the way the local scene grouped together offering support and comfort. A poetry zine had been put together to celebrate Steve's life, finishing a project that Steve and Rob Callen had started. In this issue Rob writes a heartfelt column about the poetry zine and finding out that Steve had died. There was a piece by Shaun too, a letter to Steve as he prepared to emigrate to Australia.

I still remember the last time I saw Steve, he'd actually come to watch me play football, as he was going to join my team. He picked a good game as I scored four goals, and after each one I could hear him shout "Schillaci", mimicking he commentators of the Italia 1990 World Cup where a Toto Schillci, a relatively unknown, scruffy player scored goal after goal to get Italy to the semi-final.

The last time I spoke to Steve was when he called me to apologise for pulling THIRST! out of a gig at the last minute after feeling unwell. He'd had chest pains and had gone to the hospital, but had been sent home. He said he was feeling better and we talked about what we wanted from the band, Steve wanted us to record a 7". That conversation was just before Xmas.

In between Christmas and New Year, I was round my parents house doing some zine work when Rob Callen called me to tell me that Steve had died. The shock of what he was telling me left me numb, and it took a while to really sink in. I remember just sitting in a chair staring into space trying to take in what Rob had told me.

As usual David wrote a lot for this issue, and we had a lot of other contributors, including Rich Levene who did some reviews and Neil Cox who wrote a column about

Oi! His band, Shutdown were also interviewed alongside K.R.A.P.P. (featuring Dave Morris and Pete Northam, who are both now living in Southampton, and James Domestic), KBO! Wordbug, Short & Curlies, Distortion, S.A.N.D. No Fun At All and an interview with The Ruts, done by someone called Chris Jones, but sent to us by Aston. There is a lot of text, but although the layouts are quite simple, I think they work pretty well.

The other notable inclusion in this issue is a column written by my dad.

Dad also has another column in SD#21, this one about football. It's another packed issue, although looking at it now it seems to have a weird vibe, I can't put my finger on why though. David contributed his usual amount of good stuff, and Gaz's enthusiasm is plain to see in his contributions.

It was interesting to see that our irregular Great Forgotten Album feature was originally Crispin's idea. I hadn't remembered this fact, and I would never have said that we started it this early on.

Quite a varied issue when it comes to interviews; Campus Tramps, PMT, Rhythm Collision, Naked Aggression, Terminus, Bedlam Hour, 100,000 Bodybags, One Bloody Fanzine (from Serbia), The Harries, Piss Drunks and Scratch Bongowax who were interviewed by Stuart Armstrong.

I hadn't really thought about Bedlam Hour for a quite some time, but out of the blue, recently, they posted a video of them at The Joiners, it featured a little intro from Rich Levene, and some footage of Thirst! playing live that I'd never seen before, and it sounded good, faster than I remember us being.

Mike Head was back contributing, and it seems we hadn't been in touch for about three years but had recently bumped into each other again at a gig in London.

Mike Head:

"Looking back I think I had some health issues, that combined with me being a bit jaded with music. Mega City 4 / Senseless Things had changed direction there wasn't much going on that I liked. Then things like Skimmer got my attention, Green Day putting Dookie out opened up doors for other bands, it became easy to get a Screeching Weasel album, I became as hooked on hunting down new music as I had been before & some of my all time favourite records came out soon after (Rancid , Jawbreaker etc). Seeing you at that Down By Law gig and you saying I should write something for SD possibly sparked me in to action a bit, buying even more records so I could review them etc."

Gaz:

Issue #15.5 – This was our first Xmas special I think? We featured Turkish hardcore band Moribund Youth and Cambridge fanzine, which was written by long time Suspect Device supporter Dave Stuart. We also launched our final compilation tape 'Shouting Music' which I think got its title from Tony's Niece, because she thought it was a lot of shouting! Anyway - the tape had eleven bands and twenty songs from the BBMF's, The Abs, Sleep, Haywire and more. I think the age of the CD was upon us as this was Christmas 1991 and we'd already abandoned manual typewriters, so why not analogue tapes!

Issue #16 – We put footballer Stuart Pearce on the cover as we'd heard he was into Punk! I think Tony even sent a copy to Nottingham Forest his then team, so he could have a read. Needless to say, he never replied! That said, was he into DIY Punk? Over the years and having listened to him give a talk at the Rebellion festival I don't think he went to many DIY gigs or boasted Crass and UK Subs records in his collection. I'd like to be proven wrong! Anyways in this issue were JFA, Instigators, Exit Condition, Boss Tuneage Records and Shutdown who's front man Neil Cox has always avoided me on the Ockey. I've called him out on numerous occasions over the last thirty odd years and it's always been a 'no show' from him! Someone told me that he's moved to Australia!? Not sure if that's true or just fake news, but it's a long way to go to avoid a showdown!

Issue #17 - We went for a Crass style cover with this one and packed it out with CDS, Gan, Reverse, Comb, Erase Today, Nux Vomica, Subversives, Puzzlebox and Cambridge zine. We kept the price of this issue a secret following a succession of oil company style price rises and duly foisted it upon a few hundred true to the cause punters in November 1991. We also did an STE benefit tape! The STE being our local gig collective and many of the bands on the tape also featured in the zine. It hit the streets for £1.50 including post and quite how many we sold remains as much a mystery as the price of this issue!

Issue #18 – Think we'd given up with advertising the price of the zine on the cover after being accused of turning rebellion into money. Our adoring public were on the verge of a punk coup, so we threw up a smokescreen to deflect their attentions. As the smoke cleared, we hit them with Another Fine Mess, Obscene Females, Pseudo Hippies, Threshold Shift, Victims Family, The Krayons, Wat Tyler, Joeyfat, Glue, Face to Face, FC St Pauli and Chicken-Bone Choked. We were so confident that this new tactic would work, we didn't even bother them with a compilation tape!

Issue #19 – A split issue with the mighty Cambridge fanzine! Why did Dave Stuart call it Cambridge? For no other reason than the fact that he lived there! Anyway, we spotted an opportunity to expand our empire and Dave was up for it. We skilfully hid our reputation for not putting the price on the cover anymore and he went for it hook, line and sinker! We gave the Punks a packed issue though as our half hit em' with Down By Law, Screeching Weasel, Zimmerframes, MDM, Sugar, 4 Past Midnight and local hardcore barnstormers Older Than Dirt. The Cambridge half came back at us in equal measure with The Queers, Devil Dogs and Posh Boy Records. This issue hit the DIY gigs of Britain almost 30 years ago to the day as I type this! 05/09/1993.

Issue #20 – This was our tenth anniversary issue! I think its true to say that we were well into some sort of chaotic stride now and we'd built up a fine base of contributors too! This sound issue featured KBO! Krapp, S.A.N.D., The Ruts, Wordbug, Distortion, No Fun At All, Short & Curlies and Shutdown – That's right! The band fronted by the darts match avoider Neil Cox everyone! I'm not afraid to name names and his Lawyers don't scare me! The saddest thing is though – he's actually a nice bloke! The situation between us kind of reminds me of the Heavyweight Boxing world at this moment in time. The big reputations avoiding each other in their prime as no one wants a defeat on their record and we'll only meet on the Ockey when we've blown our fortunes and need to fill the pension fund up!

Tony Suspect - Another Cheap Product for the Consumer's Head

Suspect Device number 21 coincided with us starting SD Records. It had been something we'd been talking about after seeing how well our tapes had been received, and so initially we discussed doing a compilation album. One evening we were sat around in Gaz's house talking about how we were going to afford it, and Sarah was encouraging us to just go for it.

This was just before Steve died, and at his funeral Steve's wife Chrissy spoke to me and said we should keep the band going. I don't think any of us had considered doing THIRST! without Steve, but when Chrissy said this we decided to carry on, and asked Phil Beavers from Chicken Bone Choked to join on bass, with Rob moving to guitar.

Rob and me both wrote some lyrics about Steve, and with Phil in the band we got the music together pretty quickly for two songs. I still think the words I came up with are among the best lyrics I've ever written. I was driving home in the pouring rain and realised that it seemed to have been raining non-stop from the day I got the news about Steve, and then the words just came.

So we decided the first SD Records release would be a 7"EP by THIRST!, with any profits going to Steve's wife and daughters. We backed up the two songs we'd written about Steve, with a couple from the demo that Steve had played on, he had wanted THIRST! to put a 7" out so even though he wasn't with us any more we could have him on the record. We also included a poem Shaun had written about Steve, which he read out over acoustic guitar played by Rob.

Sean Forbes was a huge help in helping us get it this record cut and pressed. He'd written a piece on how to put a record out, that we'd printed in the zine, but he went above and beyond and offered to show us the ropes and came with us to Porkys in London's Shaftesbury Avenue to get the record cut, and then over to Mayking in Battersea to deliver the lacquers and arrange the pressing.

Sean:
"The year is 1994 and Tony who was part of the Suspect Device fanzine gets in touch by letter. It's the 90's everything is done by letter. They want to make a 7" for former guitarist of Thirst! and friend Steve Burgess who passed away. I know fuck all about 99% of things in life but the one thing I do know about is how to make a record. In the 90's it's still a mystery to many and as Rugger Bugger Discs had already released a heap load of average and over appreciated records, they asked if I could help. Being the hostess with the leastest I go the full hog and take them first to Porky's in Shaftesbury Avenue in the West End. The place is where 90% of people cut their records. George from Porky's is a legend and having him etch Porky prime cut on your run out groove is like a seal of excellence. George always pretended he was into the music - click his figures, nodded, squealed and then turned the volume up. You came away feeling great, even though really you had no idea what he did. Basically he just made your record sound louder.

George handed you the lacquers, after a cash transaction and from there you take them onto Mayking Records who manufacture your records. Tony, Gaz and Sarah who came up seem bewildered with the process but excited as well. It was lovely being around people excited and as they say "You always remember your first time". Mayking was in some mini industrial estate in Battersea and seemed posh to me, but I was living in a Co-Op house in Gipsy

Hill that was pretty run down. You took the lacquers direct as it saved money on biking them over. I was happy to help as the Suspect Device were doing such a great thing by releasing the 7". However, if truth be told I wasn't screaming at the rooftops that Thirst! were gonna change your life.
In Mayking the Suspecters emptied their wallets and paid for 1000 7"s without sleeves and we all sat back and waited for test pressings. The rest is history and now nearly 40 years later the 7" is for sale for 87p on Discogs. Well fuck that - it doesn't matter. The sentiment was more important."

Sean is right, George was always enthusiastic about what you'd brought in, or at least made you think he was, and he'd press this button on the huge consul in front of him, that made the songs sound huge, blaring out of the massive pig shaped speakers built into the wall. Whatever you took there sounded brilliant once he had pressed that magic button, and it was pretty cool watching the lacquers being cut on the machine in the room.
If you check your old punk records you'll find a lot of them have "A Porky Prime Cut" scratched into the run out, so it was exciting to have that on our records too.
I don't think Gaz and me ever lost that excited feeling of going to Porkys. Going into this posh looking building in the heart of London's West End seemed surreal, people like us didn't go into posh buildings like that. Once in you'd go down to the basement to this magical place, where some great records had benefitted from George's magic button treatment; the UK pressings of those classic Dead Kennedys singles and LPs were cut there, as was (side A of) Crass' 'The Feeding Of The 5000', Buzzcocks albums 'Another Music In A Different Kitchen' (A Side) and 'A Different Kind Of Tension' among so many more great records, so it seemed amazing that our little records were getting cut there too.
It was a fun day, and I think we got carried away with it all and went for a pressing of 1000. We never got anywhere near selling that many, but we we able to donate a bit of money, not much but I think it got Steve's daughters some Christmas presents or something like that.
I didn't mind that we got way too many of that first 7" pressed, we did it for all the right reasons, and the process was exciting to be part of. Part of the problem, apart from releasing a record by an unknown band, was that neither Gaz or me are great at publicity or self promotion, and THIRST! never played outside of Southampton. We work hard on what we do, and enjoy it, but when it comes to promoting ourselves and what we do, we are, and always have been, a bit lacking. But, it was another example of how if you embrace the DIY ethic, you can do whatever you want, and there will always be people willing to help you and pass on knowledge they have.
Later that year, 1994, Gaz had the idea of doing another mini Xmas issue, it was a rush but we finished it on December 9th. We gave away another gift, we put a bubblegum, a kids temporary tattoo and a balloon in a paper bag and gave it away with the mini issue.
The issue is actually pretty good, we called it issue SD#21 3/4, David was press ganged into contributing his usual high quality stuff, there's an interview with MTA from Brighton, Mike Head and Lloyd Chambers did a tour report of their week following Jawbreaker round the UK and they helped us with the Jawbreaker interview at the Joiners gig. The back page is a reprint of an Animal Aid flyer about having a cruelty free Christmas. The cover was, once again, Xmas wrapping paper. There were always gigs around Xmas, and we'd always have a stall, so the Xmas issues were generally meant for these gigs, although we did, obviously, sell them via mail too.

Before we got another issue out we were busy on other things. After seeing J Church several times by this point, and because of their friendship with Sean Forbes, we asked if we could release a split 7" featuring J Church and War Tyler. Of course, both bands were happy to donate songs, so we went through the process again.

When we got the records back from the pressing plant, we had the job of folding the wrap around sleeves. The J Church side was pretty much all black, and the ink made my fingers black, so I had to keep constantly washing my hands to stop me getting black fingerprints everywhere. I'd done a couple of hundred of these sleeves in one day, and that night I woke up with a really itchy face and head. I went to the bathroom and looked in the mirror and didn't recognise the reflection. My face had swollen up, and my head had lumps all over it. I'd had a reaction to the black ink. Thankfully it hadn't affected my throat, so I could breath, but I couldn't really eat or drink very well because my lips had swollen up. I had to get medical help and was prescribed some drugs which made me feel a bit woozy. I made sure I wore gloves to do the rest of the sleeve folding. However, since that day I haven't been able to comfortably wear most black t-shirts as they aggravate my skin, and some print still makes me feel itchy and the smell gives me a headache and makes me sneeze.

This record caused us a bit of a problem with MCPS, the music copyright people in the UK. John Peel played one of the J Church tracks, and as they had copyrighted their songs the BBC tried to pay up, but MCPS didn't know anything about the record and apparently you have to register any release with them. They even turned up at my flat to get a copy of the record. Luckily I was out, so they sent me forms to complete with the information on all the songs and who wrote them (I also had to do this, retrospectively for the THIRST! record). After submitting the forms they then wanted a copy of the record as they thought 'Smells Like Dog Poo' was a Nirvana cover. It isn't.

We haven't registered a record with them since.

After all that excitement we put out SD#22, the cover was a reworking of the original 'Feeding Of The 5000' cover with the Crass symbol on the flag replaced by the SD logo. It was either done by Gaz or he got someone to do it for us. We liked it so much we also used it on a t-shirt. I wish I still had that shirt.

The issue has a couple of short interviews that Mike Head did, with Broccoli and China Drum, a couple of face to face interviews done at the Joiners, early in 1995, first with Skimmer in January 1995 and then Smog UK in February. Those early interviews show how long it took us to get this issue out. I also interviewed Swedish band Taste Like Soil, after they sent us their demo. It looks like I liked it, but I can't remember what they sounded like now, but my review compares them to Nux Vomica, Cowboy Killers and Beastie Boys' early hardcore stuff, and their interview mentions that they were political with lyrics condemning war, the police and racists. Plenty of contributors providing reviews, columns and interviews, alongside David's usual packed pages. The layout is a little messy in places, but there is quite a bit to read.

At Easter 1995 Gaz, Sarah and me went to San Francisco for a week. I didn't get to meet up with Iain, despite speaking to him on the phone, but we did have a good time. We did the sights, went to Alcatraz, rode the trams, went to the waterfront, City Lights Bookshop etc. On one of our days there it day rained heavily, so we went to Epicenter Zone, the Maximum RocknRoll run record shop, and spent a lot of the day there. At one point while I was flicking through a rack of LPs I heard a voice behind me say "Hello Tony." Both Gaz and Sarah were in front of me, and I knew Iain wasn't about so who else in California knew who I was? I turned round and it was Lance Hahn with a big smile on his face. We had a little chat, I caught him up on the progress of the split 7" and then he went off to do a bit of volunteering at Blacklist distro, which was run out of the same space. With the weather being bad Epicenter was a good place to hang out, there was a pool table, comfy sofas, a zine library and of course we bought some records. When the rain stopped, we went off to do more touristy stuff, and made sure we rode the J Church line on the Subway. We also made a trip over to Oakland to Gilman Street, but it was closed.

SD#23 featured a report of our trip to California, as well as travel diaries from Rob Callen and Mike Head who both had also been to SF. The cover shot was of Rancid, which is odd as they are not in the zine, other than David's review of one of their early releases. It seems strange that we had them on the cover, even if they are stood in front of a sign for Gilman Street. There is, however, a good mix of bands featured (Jumpin' Land Mines, 4 Past Midnight, Jay Langford, Public Toys, Travis Cut, Contempt, Toast and Spithead) as well as a chat with Pete who does Land Of Treason distro. Shaun sent another contribution over from Australia and Rich, Mike Head and Crispin did some more reviews alongside David's customary packed pages.
We had also opened a PO Box, manly, I think, as Sarah and me were in the process of moving house, and also because we were getting more and more stuff through to review.
There was also mention of another adventure that Sarah and me had, this time Crispin was our companion, rather than Gaz. J Church and Broccoli had played at the Joiners and then had gigs in London and Harlow to follow, so we decided to go to both. Lance from J Church and Sean Forbes, who was travelling with them, had arranged guest list places for us at the Venue in New Cross. In those days parking in London was much easier, so we were able to park on the main road right outside the venue. Broccoli weren't actually playing that night, but Travis Cut were, and so were The Muffs and Snuff. The best thing about this gig was the friends that were there. I have fond memories of hanging out with Mike Head, Mac and Chris from Travis Cut and Sean. Mike Head had arranged for us to stay with a friend of his in Bromley that night, and the next day we went to Shake Some Action Records in Croydon where both Broccoli and J Church were playing sets in the shop. After that, we went off to Harlow for a gig at The Square and more fun and frolics, including Crispin trying to slide down a fire escape railing and ripping his shorts. They had been three enjoyable gigs, but our adventure wasn't over yet. After staying over at Mac's house in Harlow we were up early and went off to Cambridge to spend the day with David.

We had planned to do another mini issue to go with our third release on SD Records, which was the Shutdown / Smog UK split 7". However, David had some stuff that didn't make it into the last issue, so, in October of 1995 SD#24 ended up as a slightly rushed full issue. Shutdown and Smog UK were interviewed, from what I remember Smog UK came to our flat to do their interview, but Shutdown's was done via mail. David had chats with Swingin' Utters and Riverdales, Gaz did Retch Records and Chopper were featured too.

Gaz:

Issue #21 – This is a very decent issue with 100.000 Bodybags, Scratch Bongowax, Naked Aggression, One Blood Fanzine, Rhythm Collision, Campus Tramps, The Harries, The Piss Drunks, Bedlam Hours, Terminus and Norwich's finest PMT. They are an all female Punk outfit who still turn out occasionally! This period in our history also represented our first venture into the world of running a record label! We released a benefit record for the family of our mate Steve Burgess, who died very suddenly in his early 20's and this release was his band Thirst. Tony played the drums and it seemed a fitting tribute to Steve that we should kick off the label with Thirst.

Issue #22 – Another plagiarised Crass themed cover for this issue! Well, why not?! They are kind of responsible for this whole DIY Punk thing let's be honest. Inside were interviews with Skimmer, Taste Like Soil, Leadbelly, China Drum, Broccoli and local favourites Smog (UK). I actually thought Smog were fantastic live, had a sound that was best live and were one of the few bands who probably were difficult to capture properly in the studio. Meanwhile Suspect Device Records was marching on with the release of a Wat Tyler/J. Church split EP. This was probably our best seller as I think we went to a repress and sold well over 1000 copies. The legend that is Sean Forbes really helped us out early on too.

Issue #23 – We were well into 1995 now and for some reason we put a picture of Rancid on the cover! Probably due to the fact that a sign for Gilman Street was over their heads and we'd been on a trip to San Francisco and the Bay Area visiting this famous Punk venue. It was only a visit too as there were no gigs that week and we'd walked to a dusty industrial estate to find it – another prime example of why we struggled to run a bath between us! What we didn't struggle with was zine content. Jumpin' Land Mines, Land of Treason, 4 Past Midnight, Jay Lansford, Public Toys, Travis Cut, Contempt, Spithead and Toast were all interviewed.

Issue #24 – Shutdown and Smog (UK) got featured again because we'd released a split EP of both bands. Notably Shutdown front man was still avoiding me on the Ockey! Don't think I'm labouring the point - do you?! The Swingin' Utters, Retch Records and Chopper also featured too.

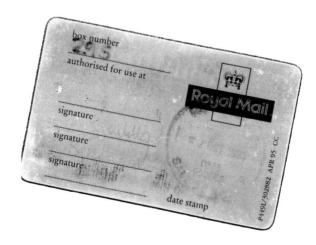

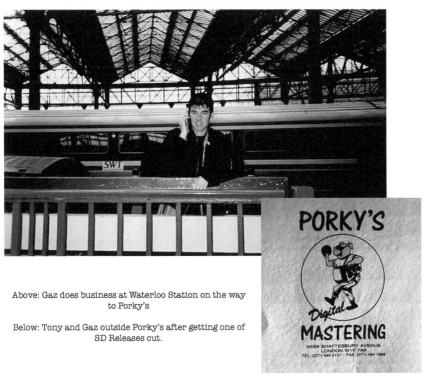

Above: Gaz does business at Waterloo Station on the way to Porky's

Below: Tony and Gaz outside Porky's after getting one of SD Releases cut.

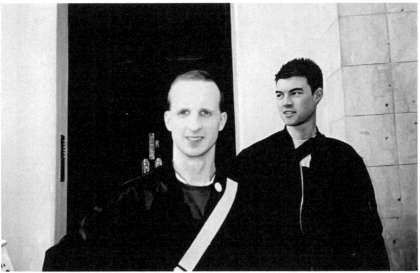

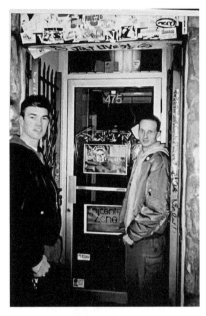
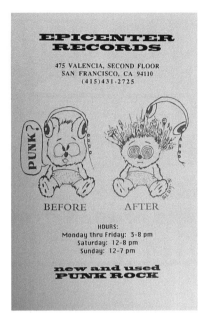

San Francisco 1995
Above: Gaz and Tony outside Epicenter Zone (Photo Sarah Whatley) / Shop Advert
Below: Tony on the J Church line

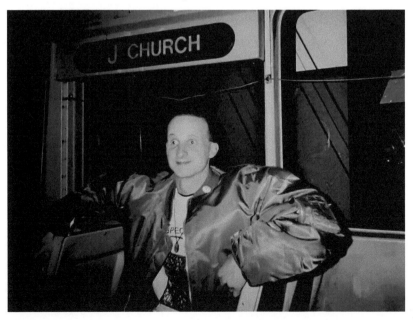

Tony Suspect - Friends Of Mine

SD#25, which came out in early 1996, had a cover that I really liked, but Gaz didn't. It was a picture I'd taken of Broccoli at one of the gigs we'd seen on our mini-tour mentioned earlier, that I just put on a white background. I'd been inspired by an issue of Armed With Anger, and it seems Gaz wasn't too impressed with my attempt at being "arty". But that aside, I like this issue, David had done a great interview with Mike McGann of Channel 3, a band both Gaz and me also loved, as well as his usual packed pages of reviews and comment. Broccoli were interviewed, as were Burnside, Down By Law and One Inch Punch, who were from Australia and were interviewed by Shaun, who also did some reviews. Sean Forbes wrote a column and gave us a report of Wat Tyler's US tour. Plus, someone called Stan had been writing to us, he was setting up a label and it turned out he was the original drummer of Anti-Pasti, playing on their 'Four Sore Points' 7"EP and the 'Don't Let The Bastards Ground You Down' the split live EP they shared with The Exploited. We took the opportunity to send him some questions, which he was happy to answer. Rich Levene, Mike Head and Stuart Armstrong also did some reviews. Over 60 pages made for a pretty good read I think.

Our next issue came out in July 1996, and SD#26 is a huge issue, it was back to A4 size and is probably the biggest we've ever done. I think there are a few reasons for this, one is that we were getting a lot of stuff through too review, a crazy amount in fact, up to 20 CDs a week were arriving at our PO Box, because the US bands on the bigger labels like Revelation, Fat Wreck, Epitaph etc were being well promoted over here, and as well as all these CDs turning up, their tours would include a handful of UK dates with "interviews" being requested in return for guest list places. Also, an influx of young people locally meant motivational levels were given a boost as this injection of energy into the local scene meant we were getting inspired once again by what was going on around us.

This issue makes mention of two gigs I remember well at the Powehaus in London, the Youth Brigade / Bouncing Souls gig where Sarah, Gaz and me met up with Mike Head and other friends, plus the Samiam, Texas Is The Reason, Shutdown gig, where we met up with David, as well as Pete Osman (Land Of Treason distro) and of course Neil Cox. It was at this gig that Sarah, me and Pete interviewed TITR on their tour bus. We spoke to drummer Chris and bassist Scott, who were nice guys and happy to talk. One thing I also remember when I think about this interview was that, at the end, Pete said that he'd interviewed a lot of American bands who said that when they get back home they are splitting up, so he wanted to know if TITR would do the same? They told us that they weren't and that they had another tour to do. Of course they promptly got back and split up! I did see them again, many years after this when they reformed for a tour and Si Briggs asked me to if I wanted to go along to to see them at the Electric Ballroom with him. I wasn't all that fussed about TITR by then, but I was always up for going to a gig with Si so I went along, and I have to admit that they were pretty good, but it wouldn't really have mattered if they were rubbish, I got to spend the day with Si.

There are a lot of bands featured in this issue, with Farside, Bus Station Loonies, Funbug, Peter & The Test Tube Babies, Goober Patrol, The Shreds, Casum, Capability Green (who featured Andy Turner of Instigators fame), Maniac Miracles, Four Letter Word and Dave Smalley.

Contributions had also increased with columns by Mike Head, Wolfie (Perfect Daze), Sean Forbes, Stuart Armstrong, Crispin Mumbles, Nail McGuirk, Neil Cox, Jim Hart and first columns from Jamie Goddard (Minute Manifesto/Whole In The Head) and Paul Fox.

Paul Fox:
"After becoming friends through tape trading and letter writing, Tony asked me if I'd like to contribute a column to SD, I jumped at the chance, knowing that SD was a big deal in the underground UK punk scene and were at this time, throwing out packed issues with diverse bands and written opinions and stories from some other like minded souls from the underground DIY punk scene, I rubbed shoulders with a couple of other individuals I knew, namely DS, and an old friend from the north east town I grew up in, Middlesbrough, which was Si Briggs, a dear old friend who I initially met at skateboarding sessions on a wooden vert ramp at a roller skating rink, we later also became good friends and still are, even if we don't correspond as regularly, he's still a dear pal and is held in the highest of regard. I eventually met Tony (at the Paint It Black / Pilger gig in Hull) and then again in Leeds, at a Strike Anywhere show around 2006, ironically a month before I emigrated to Australia, it was lovely to meet him after many years and felt like I'd known him even longer, I remember when my daughter was born in 1995, Tony very kindly telephoned me congratulating me, which I'll always remember as being a most kind and touching gesture. I also met David Stuart in Bradford at one of the many all day weekend punk gigs some years before."

This issue also featured an Ipswich scene report from Wolfie and a Skimmer tour report from Dave of Crackle records, Mandy from MDM did the Maniac Miracles interview, and Keef did the Goober Patrol one.
Gaz, me and David each did a whole lot of this issue.
We also gave away a free CD with this issue, it was a Dr Strange Records promo. They sent over a box of these CDs, from California, and they got held in customs. I seem to remember Gaz having to do some negotiating to get them as they wanted quite a bit of money in duty. They didn't seem to believe that we were getting them for free and were going to give them away, so no one was making any money.
Inside the back cover is an advert for our 4th release on SD Records, this time a Travis Cut / Spithead split 7". Two completely different sounding bands, but both who'd played great gigs in Southampton. We went to Porkys as usual for the cutting, but we weren't using Mayking anymore to get them pressed up, we were using a place in Wimbledon. When the records were ready Gaz and me had a plan for the day. We were going to drive to the pressing plant, sleeve some of them up then drive over to the distributors to save on postage costs (I think we were going to use Cargo, but my memory is hazy here). Then, as Saints were playing Wimbledon at Selhurst Park that night, we planned to go to Shake Some Action records in Croydon and then go to the game. As it was a Monday, we'd both taken the day off work but it meant that neither of us had a car available and going on the train wasn't practical when we'd have several boxes of records to collect and get across London, so we had to hire a car. The only car we could afford was a little Fiat Cinquecento. I think an electric shaver had more power then this car, but it got us to the pressing plant ok, which was in an Industrial Estate. We collected the boxes of records and took them out to this little car, but when we opened the boot we found that we had forgotten to bring the sleeves. We

sat in this silly little car, and swore, loudly. Not at each other, but at our stupidity. Then it started raining. We did go to Shake Some Action Records and then to the game, but the rain didn't let up, and Saint lost 3-1. It was a TV game and because my parents didn't have the channels that showed football, my grandad, who was living at my parents' house by then, went to one of my aunt's house to watch the match. During the game he had a heart attack, and although he was taken to hospital, he never recovered and never left the hospital. It wasn't one of the best days I've ever had.

Gaz: Do you know I'd completely forgotten about this day and yet another triumph for the Suspect Device DIY Punks!
When Tony jogged my memory about this my strongest recollection of the day was the shite game at Selhurst Park and the pouring rain! The only way I can add to this is to warn you all off putting out your own records and the total loss you'll make in doing it – that's if you want the financials?! DIY Punk at the SD level has never paid and will never pay! What you get from it though is the sense that one day you'll look back and think – 'well we helped a couple of decent bands and made some mates' and that for me trumps the fact that we'll never break even let alone make a couple of quid towards the next release! We were a couple of 'Wilfs' that day and continue to be until this day! What I find the oddest thing about all of this is that we know we're rubbish at it and still carry on! Mind you we're lucky to be telling this tale having been driven to football matches by Tony's Grandad on numerous occasions.
I was once trusted to go to Porkys on my own and get an SD Records release mastered and cut. The actual release escapes me, but I'd arrived early in London and went to a pub for a couple and when I arrived at the studio, I'd forgotten what the plan was! Using my inebriated initiative, I managed to get the bands on the wrong side of the record and tracks in the wrong order. When the error was pointed out to me, I had to go back and get it done again! With no SD funds left I had to personally pay up for the lot. Another loss making adventure in DIY Punk land kids and probably the dearest beer I've ever bought.

Our next issue didn't come out until January 1997, not sure what happened, my intro is a little cryptic, but does mention my disillusionment with the UK punk scene. I don't remember what that was about, although I do say that I was still dedicated to SD and DIY punk.
SD#27 is another packed issue, although it's back to A5 again. The cover drawing was done by Pete Osman (Land Of Treason), it's Ignite's singer and guitarist and is taken from the sleeve of their split 7" with Good Riddance. I had interviewed Casey Jones from Ignite in London for this issue, another chat set up by the promo team in the UK, and meant I had a midweek trip to London on a freezing November night with Rich Levene and Jamie Goddard to see Ignite at the George Robey. As it turned out I sat and chatted with Casey on the very same bus I'd been in with Sarah and Pete Osman, to talk to Texas Is The Reason. Casey was friendly and good fun, and after we'd finished the interview, he kept coming up to talk to me in the venue throughout the evening. I thought Ignite were great that night.
I remember getting back to Totton station about 2.30 am and the frost on the pavements crunching under my feet as I walked the mile or so home. It was freezing, and I was really cold by the time I got into into bed. It was only about three hours

before the alarm went off and I had to get up and go to work on my little Vespa Scooter. It was still dark, and freezing cold.

Mike Head interviewed J Church, with his friend Nick Evans, in San Francisco, Gaz spoke to Intention while I also did a phone interview with Turtlehead and an unplanned and unprepared, off the cuff interview with Travis Cut, conducted in my car outside the Joiners.

David contributed interviews with Descendents and Weston. There was a tour report from Broccoli and Chopper's tour of Japan by Sean Forbes, and a brief feature on Stoke band Destination Venus.

The deluge of CDs and records arriving for review was continuing, so the issue has loads of reviews all throughout the zine. Looking at the reviews now, there are a lot of CDs that I have recently given to Gaz to sell (the ones he doesn't want to keep), with the money going back into the SD pot for printing and SD Records releases.

By this time I was in a new band, Portiswood. I think Cov John and PJ had already come up with the name when we started it, I certainly don't remember any discussions and lists of names being written. From what I remember the first practise was just (Cov) John Baines, PJ (Paul Jay) and me. Rut joined soon after and we quickly got a set together and played a few gigs, We recorded a demo at The Joiners one Saturday afternoon. I remember I had a football match, and didn't want to just not play, so I arranged with the team manager to just play the first half, then I dashed down to the Joiners, still in my kit, to record the demo. Rut decided to leave after a while and Mike Fox joined. I had known Mike for around ten years by this point, but this was the first band we'd been in together, and it quickly became apparent that our tastes were very similar, and the band took on more of a hardcore sound. Mike wrote a song called 'Death Comes Screaming' and it kind of set a template for bands him and me would go on to do together over the next ten years or so. Practises were usually really good, but often gigs would see me behind three people who'd had a bit too much alcohol and I felt we never really did ourselves justice live. We did a second demo with Mike singing, that we called 'Too Punk For Lennons', as we had played a gig at a Southampton venue called Lennons and we were told we wouldn't be invited back because we were "too punk" (the venue has now closed, and had various names since it was Lenons, most recently called Suburbia, and has in recent years hosted gigs by Anti-System, Culture Shock, Liberty and, towards the end of 2023, Pegboy and Peter & The Test Tube Babies). One or two of the songs from this demo went on to be included on a couple of CD compilations.

Gaz reviewed our first demo, with Rut singing, in this issue. It was called 'The Relegation Battle Continues', and one of the songs was asking what we'd be doing when we're 40 years old. Seems funny thinking about that now, with all the members of the band in their 50s and 60s, and still going to gigs. As it happened, on my 40th birthday I was practising with Pilger.

Before this issue, a rather important event happened, one that still means a lot to me now. I went to see the Descendents in London (that's not it) and met up with David (still not it). We went to a pub near the venue, where he had arranged to meet up with a friend he had been in contact with who lived up in Middlesbrough. It was in this pub that I was introduced to Si Briggs and his wife Paula. Not long after that, Si wrote for a copy of SD#27, and when I sent him the issue I asked him if he'd like to write something of the zine, and his column in SD#28 perfectly summed up Si's humour, and reading it now left me with a huge smile on my face; he wrote a column about how he couldn't think of anything to write about so wouldn't be writing a column.

Si and me have remained good friends ever since and recently Si and Paula let us stay with them as we broke up our drive to Scotland with a visit to the North East. They looked after us very well, as they have done countless times in the past.

What Si got to read in SD#28, our second issue of 1997, were interviews with Rhythm Collision, Ben Weasel, Assert, The Devices, Airbomb, Dogobah, Machine Gun Etiquette, Antibodies, Armed With Anger distro and Chicken Sex Death.

The Chicken Sex Death interview was done by Keef, one of Gaz's mates who contributed quite a lot to SD in the 1990s. CSD were from Boston and the questions were answered by their singer, Marv Gadgie. This was a long time before I knew Marv. I had no recollection of this, and I didn't remember the band name, so I re-read the interview and when I saw that the questions were answered by Marv, I sent him message. I don't think he believed me initially, so I sent a photo of the interview.

His reply was:

"My word what a blast from the past. I remember being in touch with Keef a lot and then he sort of disappeared. We had his band on at the IQ and he often turned up with touring bands. Wonder what happened to him. It's a bit mad him doing an interview as we weren't really band, we were just a few mates messing about as we had nowt better to do. To have an interview is ridiculous, probably figured it would be a good way to promote the growing IQ scene which at the time was just taking off."

I had been talking to Marv, via Messenger, about when he first became aware of SD, and so mentioned to him that this issue came out in June 1997. He said:

"This is hilarious! I didn't even know that this had been published and as it is in Suspect Device 28, it was at least five issues before I even saw an issue of your fine zine. To say Chicken Sex Death deserved an interview is ridiculous. We were a bunch of daft lads who, between us had two guitars, a knackered bass, a mic that barely worked and a tape recorder. A few of us had what could best be described as a "rudimentary grasp" of how to actually play the guitar. One of us was good at shouting. Ahem. Our "band" consisted of us messing about in our flat while on the dole or in the summer holidays and we made up a sort of pretend band just 'cos we had the name Chicken Sex Death and it was too good a name to not use. Well, we thought it was, as we were idiots. I had been in touch, through writing letters and swapping tapes and the likes, with a fella called Keef from Barnsley. He had a pop punk band called Leadbelly who we put on with Worm at the IQ and he turned up a few times when the latest Paul Raggity tour rolled in to town with bands like The Manges, Stinking Polecats, The Apers and Peawees. Keef started a short lived label called Irritation Records and his first release was the Stinking Polecats album followed by a Raggity Anne/Worm split 7". He gave me the last twenty copies a year or so later to give out free with the zine. I gave 'em away at an IQ gig to anyone who wanted one and as a result every bugger and their dog in Boston loves the Worm songs "Prozac Queen" and "Another Love Song." Any Worm gig that anyone from Boston is at will see them made to stay on stage until they have played "Another Love Song" ever since. They must bloody love that I imagine. Sorry Worm. My bad. Anyway ... Chicken Sex Death were barely a band, so having an interview in an esteemed publication like Suspect Device, is utterly ludicrous! I'm aghast! At the time I was writing to folk all over the place, trading tapes, zines and sending fliers and what have you so probably mentioned to Keith our our Chicken Sex Death antics. He was pretty keen at writing stuff and sending it to zines so when he offered to do an interview – must be what? 1997? – I figure I must have viewed it as more like a scene report sort of thing to get the word out for Boston and the IQ. I had done such things in Knucklehead and Why zines so more publicity for the Boston scene, that is the proper bands who could write songs and play them, is an opportunity not to be sniffed at right? Assuming I must have mentioned our lampoonery in a letter to Keef at some point, I can't imagine that I thought he would have taken it seriously and thought we were a "proper band". Thinking back, I recognise the band logo as I just wrote it left handed to give the appearance of a four year old writing it. That sums it all up better than any description really doesn't it? I was never sent a copy by Keef of the finished zine, and must've forgotten all about it until you sent me it yesterday! I was on a train to Stamford travelling to a Punk all day BBQ/gig carry on and seeing that made me laugh and recoil in horror as well as amazement. I finally get to see an interview I did, but can't remember, twenty five(?) six(?) or seven(?) years after it was published. Lawks-a-lordy. I stand by some of the shit I spouted too! Some of it though ... well the folly of youth, eh? Keef disappeared from my radar not long after and I never heard from him again, just a Stinking Polecats CD, a Worm/Raggity Anne 7" split, a few bits in Gadgie that he did – an Australian scene report in issue 3 and an interview with him about the label in Gadgie 4 – and now this long lost artefact ... the Chicken Sex Death story is told in more detail in Gadgie #49 which will be out very, very soon ... how timely of this to turn up eh?"

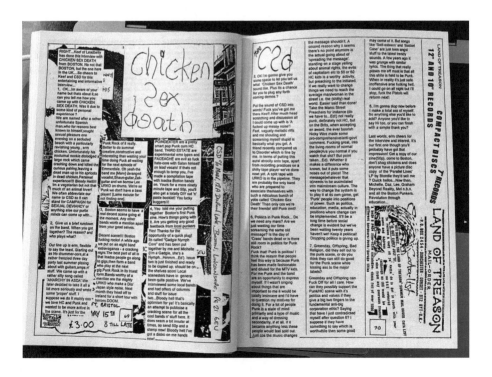

The whole thing is a bit odd as the name Chicken Sex Death is not on the cover with the other featured bands. So it was a big surprise to re-read this interview and find that they were from Boston and Marv was the one that answered the questions. I didn't know Keef who asked the questions, he was a contact Gaz had, but Marv is now a good mate and a regular contributor to SD.

Marv:
"Digging in the Gadgie Towers archive I have discovered the first issue of your esteemed periodical to come my way, was issue 33 from 1999. I had been living in Boston for about three years at that point and was pretty involved in the Indian Queen punk scene with Urko and co. Gadgie fanzine was on about issue 8 or 9 by then so I'm guessing we traded issues maybe? Maybe I taped some coins in to a bit of card and sent 'em your way in good faith, as we did back then, after reading a review or seeing a flier? I had come across the SD distro/label before though as one of my first DIY Punk experiences was an STE all dayer at The Joiners in Southampton during the summer of 1996. I met quite a few folk there who, unbeknown to me at the time, I would come to know pretty well and be mates with to this very day. This gig was a pretty important moment for me as it opened my eyes to the wonderful world not just of Punk Rock but of DIY Punk Rock. I bought a couple of records from your stall (I think) of bands who had played like Shutdown and Ex Cathedra so it is very possible that this was the first time I met you Tony but at the time we obviously had no idea who each was. Can't imagine why I wouldn't have picked up a zine if there were any on offer but I took home the STE programme and poured over every word of it on the train, fascinated by this amazing new, and seemingly secret, world ...
A side note: I have written about this gig in Gadgie in much more detail and, also, as part of a film column in Lights Go Out where I managed to tell the tale of meeting Martin Einon and sharing a love of Doug McClure films with talking about a gig and The Land That Time Forgot! I have added them should you wish to read them/use them/completely ignore them!"

There's also my report of Sarah and me going to see Nerf Herder in Boston (Massachusetts) in a blizzard. We'd gone to Boston over the easter break, and both had our birthdays there. On my birthday it was sunny and warm enough that I remember wishing I'd worn shorts. Sarah's birthday is the next day, and we woke to rain. While doing the touristy things Sarah wanted to do over in Cambridge, the rain turned to sleet and then as she liked Nerf Herder, and they were playing at the Middle East we decided to go and see them. As we got to the venue the sleet had turned to snow. We enjoyed the gig and emerged into a blizzard. Thankfully we managed to get what turned out to be the last train back over the river to Boston before all but the central underground routes were closed. As we emerged from one of these underground stations into the full force of the blizzard, to see a snow plough coming towards us, sideways. It veered off to one side which was lucky as I'm not sure we'd have been able to get out of its way. The hotel wasn't far away but we had to make the short walk inching along the wall of a building as that offered some small shelter from the high winds. The next day we woke to find two foot of snow had fallen and the city was pretty much shut. We did find somewhere to have breakfast, but with the snow up to and above our knees and my only shoes were flimsy Converse All Stars, and Sarah only had trainers, our feet were getting cold and wet. We thought we'd spend sometime going to a cinema that was showing a Star Wars film for some reason (it was one of the original trilogy), but like most things that was closed. We did find a shopping mall that had a book shop open, so we spent some time there. It was quite nice to have the city to ourselves, despite our cold feet, and at least the few underground lines that were running you could use for free.

Of course, when the weather allowed, we did more touristy stuff, which included the site of the Boston Massacre, the Boston Tea Party, Paul Revere's house and Newbury Comics.

Gaz:

Issue #25 – I actually don't own a copy of this issue so I'd better refer you to what Tony has written.

Issue #26 – Don't wanna be seen to be blowing the SD trumpet in public, but on this occasion, I feel I have too! This issue returned to A4 and had a massive 82 pages! From front to back cover this issue had loads in it. I did an interview with Peter Test Tube over the phone and remember having a microphone off an old mono cassette recorder taped to the receiver! High tech eh! Dave Smalley, Texas Is The Reason, Farside, Casum, Funbug, Capability Green, Bus Station Loonies, The Shreds, Maniac Miracles, Goober Patrol and Four Letter Word all interviewed. Loads of different contributors too and this is what we wanted the zine to be by this time in its evolution. A proper collective effort with all of our contributors bringing their spin on all things Punk!

Issue #27 - Out at the start of 1997 and returning to the A5 format. J. Church, Ignite, Travis Cut, Destination Venus, Intention, Descendents, Weston and Turtlehead all featured. Really good looking hand drawn style cover too. Bit of relief in Tony's editorial that he'd found the energy to get this one out!

Issue #28 – Six months after SD27 came out we produced this 74 page offering and again, looking back, it's not half bad! Rhythm Collision, Ben Weasel, Assert, Armed With Anger, The Devices, Airbomb, Dagobah, Machine Gun Etiquette and Antibodies were all interviewed. It also coincided with us putting out a Down By Law 7". We ambitiously got 1000 pressed and as I write this bit on that record, I've just sold the last copy I have for sale on eBay! 26 years to sell a thousand records must be some sort of record!

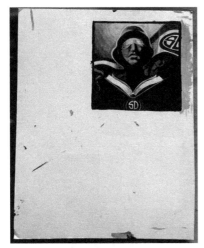
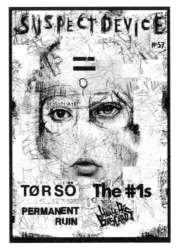

Dan Roberson's original painting of the image used on the compilation CDR given away
with SD#37 (above left), the cover he did for SD#57 (above right)
The logo Dan designed that we put on.a t-shirt (below)

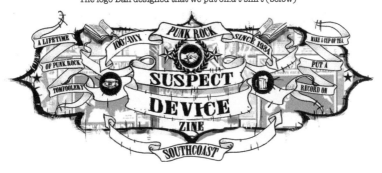

Below: Pete Osman's original artwork (left) that was used for the cover of SD#27

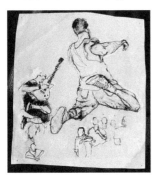
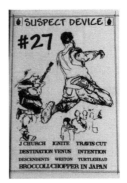

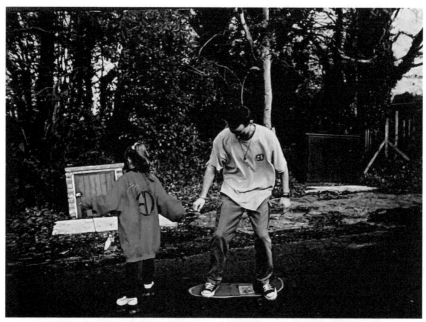

Merchandise, it keeps us alive. SD shirts modelled by Sam Tear, Jane Capers and Tony (photos Sarah Whatley)

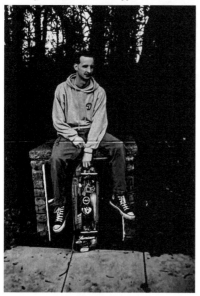

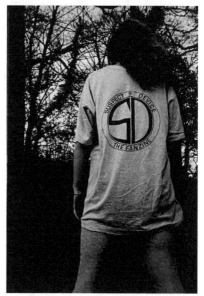

Tony Suspect - A Simple Gesture

J Church were back in the UK in the autumn of 1997, and were touring with Wat Tyler. I'm not sure who came up with the idea, but it was decided that we release another split 7" featuring the two bands for them to take on tour with them. Sean and Lance were up for it so we set the wheels in motion. The pressing plant offered us some left over colour sleeves from a record that hadn't sold as well as expected, so this record came in the sleeve for the 'We Love You' 7" by Menswear. We got a load of stickers and wrote the names of the bands, the track listing and info by hand and stuck them on each sleeve. Each one was individual and as well as Gaz and me, we got some others involved, including Sarah and my young niece (Sam) and nephew (Josh).

I asked Sean about the split EPs they did for us:
"Wat Tyler and J Church were both absolute slags when it came to releasing records. Both bands had no or little standards, so it only seemed a matter of time before we joined together in harmony. The only band at this stage who could rival us for split 7" releases was the mighty Agathocles. After being involved with Suspect Device Records Number 1 - it only seemed natural to be part of number 2. The sleeve on the Wat Tyler side was typical of our humour - IE not really that funny. The songs were a mix of all sorts. Played For and Got is pure indie pop with Julie from Dan on vocals and a hook stolen from the Commodores. It was recorded for a release by our fake Indie Pop band Eggplant but hey - why release something once when you can release it twice under different names. Smells Like Dog Poo is pure Smithy comedy Gold. Purile and childish and nearly 30 years later - still kind of makes me laugh. It was recorded at London's most fruit loopy studio Redchurch Studios with a Hippie - Fred, man. The final song is a cover of If the Kids are United but with kids singing it. Darren and Duncan were an absolute joy to be around. They came and did it at a gig once, at the Dublin Castle and ran everyone and the place wild.
On the Flip J Church destroy a Wat Tyler indie pop song At The End Of The M1. Lance is a master songwriter but his voacls were always somewhat dodgy and this is proof. The other track If I'm Lonely is a J Church gem - a two minute golden nugget. If you have a spare 1.73 pounds sterling - then this magical split 7" can still be yours. Who ever said that all 90's vinyl is worth a fortune has been proven wrong.
As if by magic a few years later in 1997 Wat Tyler and J Church were back together for another split 7" for the bands September / October 1997 UK Tour. This time we all upped the game and you got no proper artwork, and even worse songs. The barrel was being scrapped and we must have forced Suspect Device to release it. The Wat Tyler side contains two shocking covers of the Stranglers Go Buddy Go and Lynyrd Skynyrd's Freebird which were both recorded with Frankie Stubbs as part of a session for a soundtrack for a horror film for a geezer from Thirsk. It was a horror recording session and sounded pretty bad and we scrapped nearly everything. Well in true Wat Tyler style, we scrapped it and then gave it away to compilations over the years. I fucking hate both the Stranglers and Lynyrd Skynyrd but the Stranglers were Smithy and Tuck's favourite band. it also ended up on a Stranglers tribute album which in all honesty should have been a one sided 7".

The J Church side features Alone When She Dies which is a slow chugger which sounds like the hook has a bit of Slade to it whilst Crop Circles has everything you could want from a J Church song. That typical Lance Hahn guitar work and a solid rhythm section. Looking on Discogs it seems that someone has paid over 30 quid for this 7". There are some truly mad men in this world."

The write up on discos says:
"WAT TYLER / J CHURCH tour 7" - From J-church.com: Released to promote the two bands' September / October 1997 UK tour. The covers are all individually hand-designed. To be exact, the sleeves originally belonged to a 7" called We Love You by Menswear, a crap British indie band who had lots of hype and precious few record sales, hence all the available covers. Each was adapted with handwritten stickers on the front for the band names and on the back for the track list and record label address, all in various bright colours. DIY or what?"

We must have asked Sean and Lance about using the Menswear sleeve, and when I asked Sean if he remembered he said:
"I think you probably did mention it, but we probably didn't care. It was the first ever cover of a cover."

There are less bands interviewed in SD#29, but one of them was our friends Shutdown who we thought were about to play their final gig. Shutdown were a special band for me, they, like Travis Cut, had became an honorary Southampton band, and each time they played at The Joiners they were fun, and their songs were brilliant. I can still vividly remember actually feeling them as well as hearing them at The Joiners. I was stood at the back behind the SD stall and their songs pounded in my chest as well as assaulting my ears. The cover of this issue was a shot of Neil taken at what we thought was going to be their last gig. Sarah and me had driven up to Cambridge to see them, and Crispin came along for the ride. David was our host and I seem to remember Goober Patrol also played. The interview was conducted in my car, but I'm not sure if it was at this gig or an earlier one in Southampton.
Blew were also interviewed, by our Japanese friends Tomomi and Yuko, who thankfully translated it for us too. Tomomi and Yuko had spent time in the UK and did Love Love Love fanzine. Lithium Joe were also featured, and although there were a fewer interviews than last time there were still 60 pages.
Gaz was busy with SD Records, so didn't have any interviews in issue 29. But when when it came to SD#30 I was the one who didn't do any interviews, it was down to Gaz, Keef and Ashley Coleman. My life was about to the change, but I'm not sure that had anything to do with me not doing any interviews. There is another travel report from San Francisco (was there anyone who didn't go to SF in the 1990s?), and a piece from Chris Evens (Travis Cut) about their trip to Washington DC to record their second album, which SD released. It's a story that includes them recording at Inner Ear with Don Zientara and Dave Smalley, going to Dischord house, mad drummers and blowing up Brian Baker's amp (both Brian Baker and Dave Smalley appeared on the album). During the recording of the album Chris called me from Inner Ear, and then when I called back Dave Smalley answered the phone. It was a surreal time. By the time this issue appeared, Gaz was reporting that we had sold 500 copies of the album and he only had two left.
This issue also contained the first contribution from Pete Zonked!

Pete:

    Come the mid-Nineties, having put down permanent roots in Brighton, I'd regularly make the journey West on the A27 to Southampton for S.T.E. gigs at The Joiners, which were always a good time amongst friends. And it was at The Joiners I first properly encountered Tony and Gary of Suspect Device 'zine. Gary in his leather jacket, bondage pants 'n clutching a beer, was the more outgoing. Tony, his more reserved partner-in-crime, sported a hoody, Converse 'n strictly no-alcohol. They made me feel very welcome on their turf, and I liked the pairs dynamic.

    There were a lot of paper 'zines in circulation, some excellent ones too, but Suspect Device had stood out for me. The guys behind it had deeper Punk roots, were my age, had stuck it out when Punk wasn't hip and hadn't walked away. There was plenty in their 'zine I connected with. So it was excellent to meet the people behind it, and a slow-steady friendship was made with the two of them. It was cool learning we'd been at some of the same gigs in the later-Eighties at The Richmond in Brighton, as well as bonding over our mutual love of bands like The Subhumans, Cult Maniax, D.O.A., Instigators, 7SECONDS, U.K. Subs, Dead Kennedys... and of course The Test-Tubes! One of these days we will all make that pilgrimage to Peacehaven, meet up the flats up Roderick Avenue, and hope Seaford or Saltdean don't turn up for a ruck. (Note to self; purchase some red laces).

A huge change in my life happened between issues 30 and 31, but not one that was unexpected. In April 1998 our daughter, Becca, was born. This meant that there was about 6 months between issues, and I also decided to leave Portiswood. There was no fall out, I just felt that I couldn't commit to regular practises now we had a baby in the house and my focus would be on family rather than the band. Cov John wrote a bit in his column about me phoning him to say I was leaving, and him comparing it to a relationship break up. It was funny, and a little sad, but I knew I was doing the right thing. I played a final gig with them at the STE Festival and that was it. I don't feel too bad about it, though, as Haywire drummer Saul joined, and I think they were a better band with him in it.

There were other reasons this SD#31 was delayed. I had a panic where a disk containing all my reviews was corrupted and it took ages to recover the data. Then there were holidays, a World Cup, gigs and Gaz doing SD Records stuff. But, the issue is pretty good I think. David interviewed Tim Armstrong, Keef did The Destructos and Babies 3 and I did Minute Manifesto and Annalise. Annalise also gave us some free CDs which we gave out with initial copies of this issue.

There are a lot of columnists, which is good, including Sean Forbes, Jamie Festo, Mike Head, Steve Lee, Em Watson, Andy Thompson, Si Briggs, Pete Zonked! and some people I don't remember (Claudia from Germany for instance).

I had been in contact with Steve Lee for quite a while, and loved his Vision On zine. Steve even printed some SD stickers for us, so it was good to have him writing a column in this issue. Although contributing to SD isn't something that Steve remembers well, as he said recently:

    "Can't remember if I've ever written anything for SD, to be honest. If I have, it certainly wasn't a regular thing."

Steve wrote quite a few columns for us, including some under a pseudonym. But, when talking about the network of friends and the DIY scene at this time and zines in general Steve said:

"The only way you could find out about new music – any non-mainstream music really – was through friends, through tape trading and through fanzines. You learnt which opinions you could trust and often went blind into buying albums, something that was quite a big outlay at the time. During the late 1980s and early 1990s there was a real network of zines, labels and distros that seemed to keep the scene going . . . actually, along with gig promoters and, of course, the bands – they WERE the scene.

I don't think the scene was terribly insular by choice, I just think it was quite small. Everyone you spoke to, no matter where in the country, always seemed to have mutual friends and acquaintances. Communication was via phone calls and letters, people meeting up at gigs, talking to bands, stopping at each other's houses, trading tapes and zines . . . the same names always cropped up when you were talking about who you knew, what you read and which bands you listened to.

During the early 20th Century there seemed to suddenly be more money around for advertising and promotion and there were more and more releases coming out. While this was obviously a good thing for almost everyone involved I started to get totally jaded by the amount of mediocre music that was getting pushed and swamped by stuff to review for my zine, a lot of it totally uninspiring. Likewise, gigs started to become bigger and, again, while this was usually beneficial for bands you started having to turn up early and queue to ensure you got into some gigs, loads of bell ends started to show up, venues like Leeds Duchess started having bouncers on the door . . . it just seemed like that feeling of everyone being in the same boat was ebbing away and, in some cases, the 'us and them' divide between bands and audiences started to become a factor."

The cover photo is of Becca in her cot wearing a T-shirt that David and his girlfriend at the time had made up which had the SD logo on the front with The Next Generation underneath it.

Andy Thompson also started contributing to SD. It was good to have him on board, not least because he had been instrumental in opening British ears to punk from around the world, with his Xcentric Noise label releasing cassettes and records.

Andy:

"When in Rome : Be Yourself. :-)

My memory is a bit sketchy, but I've been a fan of Suspect Devine for many years and still. In a way it kind of got me back into Punk. When I went to Blackpool, as so called mature student .. Ha .. to do photography, I wasn't doing, buying or seeing much Punk stuff anymore, so after leaving Blackpool and heading to London reading Zines like Suspect Device and in the great tradition of Maximum Rock n Roll, their excellent column writers (also a big up here to Real Overdose and Zonked) they got me enthused again about new stuff. I still always loved the old stuff, but they covered so many bands I'd never heard of, for me it it was like the 3rd wave (after 77/78. and then Early 80s DIY) and through Suspect Device and people like Pete Zonked Craven, who I had even been in contact with back in the old Xcentric Noise days, and David

Stuart (who would send me some great compilation cassettes) I got into Jawbreaker, Rancid, Riverdales, NOFX then onto Lag Wagon and a lot of that scene, and learned there was a good scene and cool new bands in the UK too. I suppose I've always been a bit jealous of the Southampton and Brighton scenes, they always seemed to have and still have an active and enthusiastic scenes, but at least I could get my taste of it back then. (I know I should have gone down there more)

I even wrote a few columns for Suspect Device, it's always been so well laid and and a cool read, so was great to be asked but what the hell would I babble on about, I wasn't involved in the Punk scene anymore, more a fan on the outside, rather than like my early 80s days. So I wrote about getting into Punk originally and then the early Hull punk scene, but it was your bit ! what you wanted to say ! all their columns were so varied. I distinctly remember writing one while caught in the bad earthquake in Taiwan in 1999 and its aftermath, found some crazy internet cafe, felt like some kinda reporter . . haha . . I suppose I knew my writing was done, for a while at least, when I went into broken relationship and silly stuff like that, and didn't feel I had a lot to say, especially about Punk, but feelings are feelings and emotions are emotions, and i'm a big believer nowadays of people really opening up, but I guess it wasn't so much the norm back then talking about about that kind of personal inner feelings n shit. Maybe I guess I felt like a bit of a dick and didn't feel my writings were then worthy of a Punk Zine (especially this one) and thought I best back out for a bit, but the last few years I've really got back into Suspect Device again, still a great effort and dedication all round from Tony and the team at SD HQ. Nowadays technology has changed massively of course but you still can't beat holding the printed matter in your hand and I'm still learning about new bands around the world and the great thing you can do these days is go straight online and watch or listen to them. Keep on.. AndyT/Shesk "

Gaz:
Issue #29 – I refer you to Tony! Another gap in my collection.

Issue #30 – Well into 1998 now. 68 packed pages and interviews with my mate Welshy, who was fronting External Menace, another mate of mine Clara, who was playing bass in the newly formed Zero Tolerance, Stinking Polecats, Sad Society, Age of Chaos and Travis Cut also contributed to another good outing for the zine.

Issue #31 – I think that the thing that stands out for me with this October 1998 issue, is that Tony was about six months into Fatherhood (Baby Becca on the cover!) and my late wife Helen was expecting our daughter Hazel. That said we marched on and this issue was again packed with Annalise, Minute Manifesto, The Destructos, Babies 3 and Tim Armstrong all giving a good account of themselves. We also released our first vinyl LP on Suspect Device Records in the form of the Seventh Inning Stretch album from Travis Cut. We got about 500 pressed and sold the lot! I think quite a few went abroad too!

SUSPECT DEVICE 31

ANNALISE MINUTE MANIFESTO
THE DESTRUCTOS BABIES 3
TIM ARMSTRONG

Tony Suspect - Past Tense, Future Perfect

Something that would turn out to have a big affect on me happened towards the end of 1998. Mike Head, sent me a tape of an album he thought I would like. I don't remember now who that was, but he filled the space on the tape with another new album he'd just got, it was Kid Dynamite's debut, and it blew me away.

I reviewed the Kid Dynamite album in SD#32, as I had got myself a copy of the CD. This issue appeared in April 1999, so quite a gap after the last one. But we had a new baby in the house (The "finished" date on the inside cover is just a day before Becca's first birthday), and Gaz's daughter had arrived in March 1999, so we both had a lot going on domestically. It seems that when we did our 20 year book I stated that I wasn't happy with the clean layouts I did, or the cover, but looking at it now I think the layout is ok, and although the cover is a little dark, I quite like it. I do remember being amazed that Gaz was able to do the Airbomb interview with all he had going on at home. The Tone were also interviewed, and Ben also did a report of their European tour. I have fond memories of interviewing J Robbins before Burning Airlines played in London. The interview was set up by Scott Stewart, then working at Southern Records, and I remember meeting up with Scott in London and, in one of those surreal moments that seem to happen when you do a punk fanzine, ended up sat in a cafe talking to Scott and the band. This wasn't where the interview happened, this was just a social chat while they ate. I then found myself helping them load their gear into the venue, before sitting down with J Robbins in a deserted bar to do the interview. He was cool too, very friendly and happy to have a lengthy chat.

Before all that though, I was in central London, making my way to a tube station when a young kid (he must have been 11 or 12 I guess) stepped into the road and was hit by a motorcyclist. It was horrible, the guy on the bike went flying as he hit the boy. It was central London so he wasn't going too fast, but the kid was screaming and was quickly surrounded by passers by. The biker was walking around, looking in shock. There were a lot of people around both the biker and the kid, and it didn't seem worth me getting involved too, so I walked on feeling a little shaken.

David didn't do as much for this issue as he was working on a book that him and me did, called From Inside As Well. We had both been inspired by the books of Dan O'Mahoney and, in the spirit of DIY punk rock we decided to publish it ourselves. I got it properly printed and bound by the Print Unit at work, rather than the copy room who did the zines. We called it From Inside As Well because one day when I was writing some pieces for it I happened to be listening to The Vapors, and in 'Turning Japanese' there's the line "I want the doctor to take your picture, so I can look at you from inside as well", and as the book would feature thoughts, feelings and stories I thought it would be a good title. I phoned David to see what he thought, and he was also listening to The Vapors. It seemed to seal the deal. There is an advert for the book on the back cover.

I don't remember how many we had printed, but I do remember taking a couple of boxes of them over to David when he was living in London. They all sold out though, in fact I didn't keep a copy of my own. Gaz had a copy, but I don't think he's ever read it, which is understandable, it's not really his sort of thing, although I do mention a train in one of my pieces.

I think the good sales were mainly due to David's half of the book, that's where the good writing was, I was just along for the ride and didn't feel my stuff had much merit. David had sorted out an ISBN number which meant that there is a copy in the British Library.

Some time later we decided we wanted to re-print it, but when I went back to the Print room to ask about getting another batch printed, they had lost (or thrown out) the disk, and by then I didn't have a copy, and neither did David.

I now have a copy, it was the one my dad had, which we only found when sorting out his stuff after he died.

In SD#32, Cov John wrote about the first Portiswood gig without me, and it just so happened that it was at that gig that I spoke to Mike Fox and Phil Hedges (Phil also had a column in this issue) about starting a new band. It had only been about a year since I decided to leave Portiswood but, during 1999 one of my favourite bands, 7 Seconds released their 'Good To Go' album, a back to basics album full of the sort of short, fast hardcore songs that made me fall in love with them in the first place. This album, along with the Kid Dynamite album, had me itching to play in a band again. But I wanted it to be a back to basics fast punk band. By the time our next issue came out the three of us, plus Dan Roberson, had started Chokeword.

By November 1999 Chokeword were up and running, and my column in SD#33, which came out that month, mentions an incident I witnessed that lead me to write the words to the Chokeword song 'Break The Cycle'. The big news this issue is that Andy Morris had leant us some money to buy new stock for the distro, and because of that nice gesture we asked him to take over the running of the distro, which he did. We had also just put out the Annalise/The Tone split 7", our 9th release on SD Records. Featured in the zine are my chat with Kevin Murphy of Farside, Gaz's Bug Central interview, which has a great layout, David's talk to Stephen Egerton from ALL/Descendents and for some reason he laid out my Shonben interview too. I don't remember why he did that, it's not as though he hadn't contributed enough of his own stuff, as well as, by this point, starting to write for Fracture.

Our next Xmas issue, SD#33 1/3, which had front and back covers done by my niece and nephew. Gaz did a Rotunda interview and we printed our distro list, which was growing thanks to the work Andy was doing for us.

It was the end of 1999 and I explained why I was back in a band:

"I had hung up my drumsticks, I was tired of being in a band, I hated practising, I hated playing gigs and I wanted to concentrate on zine stuff and being a dad. Then Kid Dynamite came along and gave me a huge kick in the pants... Then I got the 7 Seconds album. They were back on top form and Kevin's voice and lyrics were as inspirational as ever. I listened to it one morning and wrote three songs. I haven't been as inspired by two records for years."

It was May 2000 when our next issue (SD#34) appeared, and a lot had happened for my new band, Chokeword. We'd written a bunch of short, fast hardcore songs, recorded them, played a gig and then decided to release a 7". The gig was at a venue called Volts in Southampton with Belgium straight edgers One X More, who had a 7" out on Dutch Label Commitment Records.

One X More were great live and so it was obvious we were keen to have them in the zine, and thankfully they were happy to answer our questions. Andy Morris interviewed Bouncing Souls, there was also a chat with Imbalance, and I interviewed Golly and Dickie of HDQ. They were no longer a band at this time, but 'You Suck' had just been re-released on CD and after running into Dickie at a gig in London and talking about featuring HDQ in the zine again, I got back in touch with Golly and the interview was done.

David didn't do much in this issue, just a piece where he explained why he didn't have time for this issue. Partly due to a deadline we'd given ourselves as we wanted this issue out for the STE two day festival.

Chokeword were probably not ready to release a 7", but we were happy with the songs, Gaz liked them and we had the money to do it. We called the EP 'D.I.Y' as that was something that was important to us. Dan did the sleeve with Nath Haywire and we gave away a Chokeword sticker that Steve Lee (Vision On zine) had printed for us. We had a stamp made up with a circle A (to signify which side was which), Dan joined us at Gaz's house to hand stamp each record and fold the sleeves one evening while Gaz and me looked after our very young daughters. It was never going to be our biggest seller, but it was a good document of where the band was at that point, and a good record of a particular moment in my life. We had comparisons with Minor Threat and Negative Approach in reviews, which was good enough for us.

SD#34 had a column written by Welly detailing the problems his band, Four Letter Word were having after being sued over their name by an unknown boy band in the US. He, and the band, were fighting it and so we decided to do another mini issue to raise awareness and a little bit of money to help with their costs. By a stroke of luck, with issue 34 just having come out we were able to call this one SD#34LW.

It featured an interview with Welly as an update on the case, plus a few columns about the fight. It felt like we were standing up to the corporate world, but in reality our little zine, although it sold out, didn't raise too much money for them, it was just something we felt we had to do.

It's like anything else we do with the zine, we realise we can't do much but if we can do a little bit to help spread the word about a band or a zine or a cause then we will.

October 2000 saw us put out one of my favourite issues of the zine, SD#35 featured an interview with Dan O'Mahony. I can't remember how I got in contact with him, but I loved and had been inspired by his books and had been a fan of No For An Answer, 411 and Speak 714 and the 7" he was about to release with a band called John Henry Holiday remains my favourite thing he's done. Anyway, once I had made contact, Dan proved to be friendly, patient and very open and was happy to conduct the interview over a series of emails. I have fond memories of writing out questions and sending emails to Dan while at work.

Elsewhere in this issue, Gaz catches up again with Red Letter Day, 14 years after we first spoke to them. Gaz was impressed by Ade's continued enthusiasm for the band, and so arranged to speak to them again. Gaz also interviewed Instant Agony. Our friends Yuko and Tomomi spoke to Cradle To Grave over in Japan and we also had a Four Letter Word interview. Lots of columns included pieces by Mike Head, Pete Zonked, Chris Cut, Mike Fox, Si Briggs, Paul Fox, Tanya, Welly, Wes, Steve Lee and Andy Morris.

David's pages featured a moving tribute to his brother who had recently died, and reading it again now I can feel the pain he was in at the time.

In December of 2000 we did another mini issue, SD#35 1/2, although it didn't turn to to be so "mini". We tried to inject some fun with a feature where all our contributors answered questions about their year and their favourite Xmas song. There were also interviews with The Movielife, Sunfactor, Swellbellys and the usual columns and reviews. I think we gave away an SD badge with this issue.

It was five months before we did another issue, but we hadn't been idle, we had put out a Four Letter Word CDEP. There was some issue with the CD covers, although neither of us can remember what the problem was, but they had to be reprinted. As well as that we were working on a new issue, and SD#36 featured locals Parade Of Enemies and One Kick Wonder, Reason To Believe zine, Runnin' Riot and Turtlehead, plus a feature off Crass' Dial House situation where they were in danger of being evicted. Gee Voucher answered a question via email and pointed us to details on their website, which is where the rest of the details in the article came from.

I was still getting issues printed at work, and they were always done quickly, and it was cheap, but any image was always a little dark.

David's section is basically a few pages of reviews, done in a conversational style. I wrote about getting chicken pox at the age of 34 and how excruciating it was, but Stuart Armstrong trumped me with a tale of discovering and having an operation on a tear in his bowel.

In my intro I talk about the deaths of Jaz Toomer and Joey Ramone, plus there's mention of Chokeword's trip to Middlesbrough to stay with Si Briggs and play a gig in Stockton, with Imbalance.

I was still playing a lot of football, but in April 2001 I had to stop. Up until that point, although punk rock was my main focus, I enjoyed playing for the team I'd been at since I was 19. I did have offers to play for other clubs, some playing a better standard, but my team didn't have any macho attitudes, and that was perfect for me. I was never going to earn any money playing so I may as well carry on just enjoying a run around on a Saturday afternoon. However, that season a couple of younger lads had joined the team, they were stereotypical football lads, with accompanying racist views. Quite soon after they joined, one of them saw a badge on my bag, it was a home made Dead Kennedys Nazi Punks Fuck Off badge, although it didn't show the name of the song, or band, it just had the crossed out swastika, and one of these idiots came up and said "are you BNP?" He seemed confused when I said it was an anti-Nazi badge. Then, a couple of months later, the other one came up to me as we prepared to start a match, he pointed at one of the opposition players, who happened to be black, laughed and made a racist comment. He looked surprised when I told him to fuck off. It ruined the atmosphere of the team for me, and I had decided to leave the team at the end of the season. I was 35 then, and so qualified for veterans football. My cousin had asked me if I'd like to join his veterans team, so I had decided that I was going to do that for the following season. Then, just before Easter of 2001, right near the end of the season, my knee exploded, during a game, when I went to shoot at the same time a defender was going to clear the ball. I remember thinking that I was going to score, then the next thing I knew I'd collapsed and my knee felt like it was on fire. I should have gone to hospital, but we had a holiday booked for the Easter break, so I didn't want to jeopardise that. When we got home from holiday, after a week of my knee painfully giving way, frequently, I got a call from a mate asking if I wanted to play at Southampton's then ground, The Dell. The stadium was due to be demolished, and the club had lined up a few events to say goodbye to the old ground, one was a five aside tournament for fans. I didn't tell my mate about my knee, I just agreed to play. So I strapped my knee up as tightly as I could, and went out there. I lasted two minutes before I collapsed in agony. Again I should have gone to the hospital, but Chokeword had a gig that night, so I went and played that instead, in agony. It was my right knee, so the bass drum may have been missing from a lot of the songs that night.

I had one more go at playing football again, some months later, in a friendly game, but collapsed again and this time did go to hospital, which eventually lead to an operation. But I have never been able to play football since that day, and even now, my knee still periodically gives out.

Our next issue, SD#37, came out in November 2001, and a lot had happened since the last issue. In our own little world, we had decided to put together a compilation CDR to give away with this issue. We wanted to do something in the same vein as our old comp tapes, so this featured a good variety of bands (Imbalance, Jumpin' Land Mines, Portiswood, Four Letter Word, DC-9, Rhythm Collision, Smog UK, Knallkopf, Red Letter Day, Annalise, Parade Of Enemies, Zero Tolerance, Wat Tyler, Brambilla, External Menace, Chokeword, Humans The Size Of Microphones, The Good Time Charlies, John Henry Holiday and MiDlifeCrisis) and the cover was done by Dan Roberson, it was in the style of the old Anarchist Spanish civil war posters, and it's an image I still love to this day, it's my phone background, and I still have the original painting he did. The issue started off A4 size, then we went to A5 for some reason. I guess we needed to print some more and A5 as cheaper? Lots of contributors this time, including Dan O'Mahony who I'd kept in contact with since the last issue, he let us have three pieces that were going to be in his next book.

The zine featured DC-9, Disposable Heroes, HHH, Open Season gig collective, Bus Station Loonies and Good Riddance.

We had been offered the chance to interview Good Riddance by their label's UK publicist at their gig at the Wedgwood Rooms in Portsmouth. So we agreed and were told it was all arranged. Gaz, me and Andy Morris got to the venue early, to do to the interview, but security wouldn't let us in. By the time the doors finally opened Gaz had gone off to the bar next door, and when Andy and me said we were there to do the interview we were told that the band wouldn't do interviews once the doors were opened. We explained that it was all arranged, but we weren't allowed into the venue earlier, and so singer Russ Rankin came down to talk to us. We went to the bar Gaz was already in and Russ looked really pissed off, not with us, he was happy to talk and wasn't trying to put us off, he explained that he was just tired. We talked about their new drummer, who was Dave Wagenschuts from Kid Dynamite, I had never met him, but in the coming years he would become a friend and Si Briggs and me would end up staying at his house in Philadelphia.

Dave Wagenschutz

"The UK? So... that's most of them spots over there 'cept the Republic of Ireland, yeh?! My 1st trip in a music related capacity was the August Bank Holiday Weekend 2001. The fabled Reading & Leeds Festivals! Good Riddance played the 'Concrete Jungle Stage' with Snuff!!! According to the flyer, there were other cool bands but I love Snuff and was blown away that we got to play with them. We hung with a local (my wife's cousin, Richard), the catering was good (lol) and I saw concert goers sit down in areas where other attendees had previously relieved themselves. Our quick-trip over was smack in the middle of a North American tour that eventually ended in Portland, Oregon on September 9th, 2001. A crazy few days followed (as you can imagine) and when I finally arrived back in Philly (flight cancelled, found a few trains) I flew out for my 1st Euro tour EVER). While I don't specifically recall the UK gigs on that tour, I do recall Chuck & I getting a 'knob' at the local barber. This may sound silly but the shows felt the same but everything else was different but in a "I was always fascinated with England" good way. The money, the food, the Football!! I had played soccer as a kid and felt like I was in the motherland."

Chokeword were also finished. It was a shame, but real life intervened and practises became difficult; children, jobs and Phil joining Parade Of Enemies all contributed to us not being able to get together as much, it was no one's fault, it was just a culmination of these things that made it all frustrating. It was a shame as it had been fun, and I still like the songs we wrote. Mike Fox and me decided one night, when a practise had been cancelled at the last minute, that we wanted to do another band and call it Pilger as we'd both been reading his books and watching his documentaries. Initially Mike was going to go back to singing and I was going to play guitar. I wasn't a great guitarist, but I had been practising, and had even played guitar on a version of 'Young 'til I De' that went on the CDR given away with SD#37 (also present were Cov John - Bass, Mike Fox - Vocals and Andy Morris - Drums, we called ourselves MiDlifeCrisis, Si Briggs even did some backing vocals). As we were discussing the new band, Kevin Borrett got in touch as he'd moved to Southampton and asked if I knew anyone who needed a bass player. We hastily arranged a practise, and somewhere along the line I was back behind the drum kit and Mike was the guitarist. Phil Hedges then offered to do vocals. I had written a few simple riffs, which Kev, Mike and Phil knocked into shape and the first one we worked on, which Phil would call 'God Free Hardcore' ended up being played at every gig we did.

The big world event that happened in September of that year was the plane attacks on New York and Washington DC. This gets mentioned in some columns in this issue, and we printed some emails that Lance Hahn sent out with some thoughts, and facts, about the whole thing.
I remember being at work when the news broke. We didn't have a TV in the office, but the radio was put on and we heard the report of the second plane hitting the tower. I was emailing Andy Morris while this was going on, and we speculated that it wouldn't be impossible for George Bush's government to somehow be involved. News sites on the internet were not loading as too many people tired to find out what was going on, but I was posting on a Southampton FC fans forum, and one of the posters worked in TV and was sat in a news room, so he was giving updates as they came through on a football forum.

Just a month later we put out another Xmas mini issue, SD#37.5. It seems, from my intro that there wasn't much enthusiasm for it, from me anyway, but I'd done another interview with Christopher Jones of Verbal Assault, and it hadn't arrived back in time to go into SD#37. Not sure why I was feeling so down, as everything seemed to be going well, personally. I know that I'd had a bit of a crisis of confidence earlier that year. Again I don't remember what brought this on, but I'd started to give away a lot of my punk rock t-shirts, and I do remember wondering if it was time to stop wearing shirts with band names on (I can't remember my reasoning). Then, at some point in 2001 I'd gone along to see Endstand at The Hobbit in Southampton, I knew the name, but hadn't actually heard them at that point. I stood to the side, doing a distro, as always, as they played a set that was so positive, so energetic and so great that my enthusiasm was given a real boost. I remember Janne speaking between songs, I can't remember exactly what he said, but it really resonated, and I realised that although I didn't know this man, and he was from Finland, what he was saying was universal, that there was a connection between us forged in punk rock. The venue was small and the connection was there, not just with me, of course, but with everyone in the room. They ended their set with a cover of Negative Approach's 'Can't Tell No One', it was fast, it was fun and I think everyone was singing along. A moment where we were in the present, but sharing a celebration of our history. It was an uplifting end to an inspirational gig.

I spoke to Janne at the gig and he was so friendly. I bought their 'Fire Inside' 10" and also a t-shirt and left feeling so much more positive. I'd wanted to feature them in SD#37, but it didn't happen, so I was really happy that we could feature them in SD#38, which came out in May 2002. That was my only interview for this issue, but Si Briggs spoke to Solea, Dead Inside and Speedwell while Clara Zero interviewed Rabies Babies and Deadline for us. The cover was taken from Endstand's 'Fire Inside' 10".

A few years later, Si and me took a trip to the 1in12 Club in Bradford to see Endstand. Again Janne was friendly and happy to chat, in fact we laughed that we'd spent a lot of the time talking about our kids, rather than records or bands. On that same tour Pilger got to play with them when they came back to Southampton. Some time after that, Si and me had gone to London to see Lifetime, and while they were playing I felt a tap on my shoulder and turned round to see a familiar looking man smiling at me. It was Joel, bass player for Endstand. He was in London for a tattoo exhibition and happened to see that Lifetime were playing and found himself standing next to me. It was cool to see him, and even nicer that he recognised me. Endstand remain an important band for me, and I often think about that first gig, in fact every time I go to The Hobbit I think back to that night.

Janne:

It was September 1998 when we toured Europe with our Swedish friends Outlast. My friend Leo Harrison from Leeds helped us out getting six gigs in England (Brighton, London, Manchester, Bradford, Liverpool and Southend). On that trip we made a lot of friends who we kept meeting on our future trips for the next few years. Plenty of great memories from that first tour there! My notes say that the first time over there (in Southampton) was 2001. Thought it was earlier, but guess not. I remember the place, I remember you and your zine. We had a warm welcome there with you and your friends, that's what I remember the best. We played so much, especially during those years that all the gigs get mixed in my head. I remember the places and people better than how the actual gig was. But Southampton is a great example of a place that I would never have visited without touring. We got to so many places with the band, met so many amazing people by touring - I just can't put it in words how much that all affected my life. It was a great university for life, really! I had gotten some copies of the zine before I got to know you, so it was an honour to meet you and to see that you actually liked what we did. It felt good! And all the nice words you wrote and said really meant a lot, I really appreciated your feedback big time, so thank you once again for that all!

It's amazing to see that you still keep going with the same passion you had years back. You don't see that kind of dedication too much around. As a grown up person it takes a lot more than as a teenager, so you really must love this all a lot, haha! I do too, but somehow it just feels very hard to find time for anything else but buying some records and listening to them - scene-wise I mean. I do go to some shows, but not that much of that either. Punk still means the world to me and it has shaped me who I am today, but being too active in the scene anymore feels too much. Glad to see there's people like you, and a younger generation keeping things alive - huge respect for that."

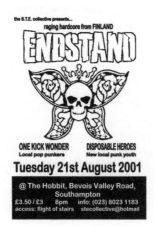

We gave away another CDR with this issue, it was another international compilation featuring Endstand, Pilger, Speedwell, Solea, Net Weight, The Horror , 24H Hell, Stegel, Cross Tide, One Last Thing , Chamberlain, Mallorkaos, Les Dipsomanes and Dead Inside.
Andy Morris did the intro in this issue as it seems SD had received some criticism which he objected to. Gaz and me didn't see the criticism, and if we had it probably wouldn't have concerned us too much, but Andy wasn't happy.

SD#39 is an important issue for me. It features the first interactions with two bands who remain favourites to this day and who Si and me had a few adventures with. Funny enough, a few days before I pulled this issue out of the box I was talking to Lloyd Chambers about the time he introduced me to Thomas Barnett at the Joiners in Southampton so I could do the interview that's in this issue. We just sat on the pavement outside the venue and had a really cool chat.
I'm pretty sure it was Si Brigs who sent me a tape of Strike Anywhere's 'Change Is A Sound' album, and from what I remember they didn't hit me straight away, I mean I liked it, but there was no indication of the effect they would have on me. It took a few plays, but it wasn't long before I "got it" and I bought the album. Then I went to their Joiners gig, spoke to Thomas and watched them deliver an explosive, energetic, politically charged gig and I viewed them in a whole new light. Just like the Endstand gig from the year before they really moved me, and I listened to the album exclusively for days and days after the gig. I wrote in SD#39 how, again like with Endstand, I was

struck by this band from thousands of miles away who came to our little town, be so engaging, open and friendly and make a connection through their music and politics. In the years to come I would see them countless times, usually with Si, we'd travel to their gigs, we'd have adventures and we'd sing along to their songs. I remember one night at the Camden Underworld we were carried away with the music, and at the same time we both punched the air to one of their rousing choruses, then looked at each other and laughed. We were men in our 40s and we were at a punk rock gig punching the air to one of our favourite bands. And it felt perfect. Si and me live 300 miles apart, but were brought together by punk rock and have been friends for years. Our musical tastes differ wildly a lot of the time, but there are bands we both love and the good times we've had seeing them have reinforced the bond we have.

My column in this issue was about the excitement I felt watching Strike Anywhere and talking to Thomas, it was certainly one of those special gigs that has a lasting affect on me.

Another of those special bands for us are Paint It Black, and they are in this issue too. I can't remember how I got contact details for Dan Yemin, but it was probably through Jade Tree records. I was eager to interview him because Kid Dynamite had meant so much to me, and when I first contacted Dan he initially seemed positive about doing an email interview, then after sending questions about his life in punk rock, Kid Dynamite and Lifetime, I didn't hear anything back, for a long time. To say I was disappointed was an understatement, in fact I felt let down, and was prepared to add Dan to the list of bands and people who'd never bothered to reply, and forget all about it. However, Dan did eventually get back to me and explained that he'd had a stroke and nearly died. I felt so bad about doubting him. Thankfully, Dan had recovered and told me about a new band he'd put together that also featured Dave Wagenschutz from Kid Dynamite, which certainly had me interested. He shared a couple of demo tracks and a short video of Paint It Black playing live. I was instantly hooked. The original questions I sent were forgotten about, and I sent more concentrating on Paint It Black. Again, Si and me would have many adventures going to see Paint It Black, both in the UK and the US.

Also featured in this issue were Friends Of Ed, Active Slaughter, Mike Thorne and Arwen Curry of Maximum RocknRoll and Gaz's round up of the Holidays In The Sun festival. There is also an interview with the anarchist punks from the J.A.R Collective in Chiapas, Mexico, done by three Zapatista solidarity workers from Bristol linked to Bristol anarcho ska-punks Disruptive Element. J.A.R. stands for Juventud Anit-Autoritaria Revolucionaria, which translates as Revolutionary Anti-Authoriatarian Youth, and was created in 1992 at a meeting of various collectives and punks after a demo against the celebration of 500 Years of the "discovery" of America. As well as wider political aims, they wanted to reclaim punk in Mexico from drugs, violence etc and create more of a community. It was good to see that there was also an interview with the J.A.R. Collective in Raising Hell 24 recently.

Clara Zero did the Active Slaughter interview, and we also printed her reply to Andy as it was her piece in Terroriser magazine that prompted him to write the intro in the last issue. She makes some good points, and as neither Gaz or me had read the original article it was hard to comment either way, so we just left the two pieces as they were with no comment from either of us. We've always been more interested in co-operation than division.

We rounded 2002 off with another mini issue, SD#39.9. It was an issue that I put together while recovering from an operation on my knee, and it was slow going because although I was off work, sitting at a PC was painful, and I could only do it in short blocks of time. So although this is a mini issue, it took a while to put together. I'm guessing that I was back at work in time to get it printed.

This mini issue was also a benefit for Reason To Believe zine, with both Gaz and me saying how we wanted to help in some small way with their cashflow problem because, as much as we liked Fracture, Reason To Believe best represented what we were all about, and we wanted to help them keep it as a free zine. Pilger also played a couple of benefit gigs for Reason To Believe too.

Clara interviewed Dutch band Antidote, and I spoke to Boxed In, one of my favourite bands at that time. Pilger played quite a few gigs with them, including two in one day, when both bands, along with Swedish band DS13, played at the Free Butt in Brighton in the afternoon and headed back down the coast to play at the King Alfred in Southampton in the evening. A photo I took of Boxed In at the Free Butt gig was on the cover of the mini issue.

This is the issue that has my infamous review of the first Intent CD. They were a new band to me and had released the CD themselves, and it had a barcode on the back, which I moaned about in the review, saying it wasn't very punk rock. It wasn't long though before I'd call Intent my friends, and we became pretty close. They never let me forget this review though.

David would start to write less and less for us as he started writing more for, and getting involved with Fracture. I never contributed to Fracture at all, but I would take a bundle of each issue to give out at local gigs. They'd arrive in a big mail sack each month or so. It was a shame that David and me/SD grew apart, but these things happen. We never fell out, but it was a shame as the friendship was strong at one point, but we had our own things going on and we both let things drift. We're now back in fairly irregular contact, which is a good thing.

David:
"We started hooking up in London for shows, first meeting with Tony was in line at a Down By Law gig at the old Powerhaus venue in Islington, buying a cheap football and having a kickaround over Finsbury Park before gig at the new Powerhaus (old Robey) or I'd go and stay at Tony's in Southampton and go to those classic STE weekenders. Tony came to my first gig promotion in Cambridge with Goober Patrol, Shutdown & The Shreds I recall. We hung out quite a bit and those memories are cherished. Somewhere down the line I got involved with a bigger fanzine called Fracture that had appeared as a "national punk and hardcore magazine"... I drifted away from a lot of things at this point and as much as I supported fanzines within that magazine, I lost touch with a few folks and stopped writing for other zines. I kinda sold out in a totally non-profit fashion!"

Pilger were playing quite a lot at this point, getting to places like Portsmouth, Leeds, Bradford and Stoke and as well as Boxed In, we played quite a few gigs with The Mingers and Jets Vs Sharks, so it made sense to feature both of these bands in SD#40. I was particularly eager to feature Jets Vs Sharks as they were very popular locally, and we great people too. Paul Fox progressed form writing columns and doing reviews to interviewing The Last Chance, Si contributed an interview with Cold Blue Sky and Clara interviewed Sick On The Bus. We have always wanted to reflect all aspects of the DIY punk scene, but I remember feeling a little disappointed with Sick On The Bus as I felt their answers had them coming across like stereotypical drunk punks. Gaz really like them though and I was happy to have them in the zine, I just wish they'd done a better interview.

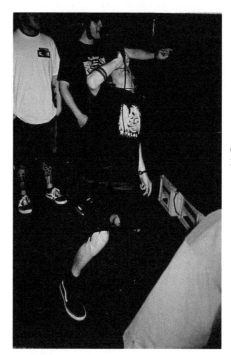

Boxed In
The Free Butt, Brighton
Image used for SD 39.9

Gaz:
Issue #32 – This issue I think featured Burning Airlines, The Tone and others! I can't elaborate as I actually don't own a copy! I'm actually not that bothered by the issues I don't have as I take the view we must have achieved and provided someone with a good read.

Issue #33 – It's November 1999 now! I'm a Dad and despite a lot happening on the home front we interviewed Farside, Shonben, Bug Central and Stephen Egerton, who played firstly in The Descendents and then All. We also had a split EP out on SD records by The Tone and Annalise. It was £2.50 including the post! As I type this, the second class postage alone is that much! Don't you just love inflation and privatisation?!

Issue #33 1/3 – Probably our two quickest back to back issues to date! #33 and this Xmas issue. I managed to interview the excellent Rotunda from Birmingham and the rest was filled out with reviews, views and great forgotten albums. I think we also gave away a free gift with this issue, but can I remember what it was? Nope!

Issue #34 – I'm not actually sure what my contribution for this issue was? I can't even see an introduction – not that I've ever wrote that much for any of my intros! You can now see that even as this issue took us into the new Millenium my old mate Tony was still Mr Motivator. One X More, Imbalance, HDQ and Bouncing Souls all featured as did a small advert for our latest vinyl release on the third page. You can see why we never picked careers as salesmen can't you?! Although Chokeword were a little known local band and had Tony on Drums, we could have bigged them up a bit better! Ha! Anyway, as the poor advertising deserved, I still have half a box left if anyone would like a copy!?! I think our old mate Andy Morris had something to do with releasing and funding this too.

Issue #35 – I think I made a bit of a comeback in this October 2000 issue as I've done an intro and interviewed Instant Agony! Also featured were Dan O'Mahony who fronted 'No For An Answer' amongst many other US Bands with Four Letter Word, Cradle To Grave and our old mates Red Letter Day completing this issues line up. The back cover gives the Chokeword DIY EP another plug, but again it has little fanfare! We really are masters of the hard sell.

Issue #35 1/2 – Another year nearly over and another Christmas issue! The Movielife, Sunfactor and Swellbellys all interviewed. Besides Tony and myself I've counted another dozen contributors to this issue. Pretty good even if I do say so!

Issue #36 – Not sure if it's a figment of my imagination, but we put a cover price on this issue. The princely sum of a quid would make a copy yours. For that money you got Parade Of Enemies, Turtlehead, One Kick Wonder, Reason To Believe Fanzine, Runnin' Riot and a feature on the Punk institution of Dial House, home to members of Crass. We featured Dial House because at that time (May 2001) the members of Crass still resident we're under threat of eviction. Luckily, they secured the Cottage and I can happily report that as I type this, Penny and Gee are still resident to this day. The back cover of this issue featured a full page advert for the latest release on SD Records. Four letter Word got unusual treatment of us actually giving a release some push! Not sure how many of this CDEP we actually got pressed, but if your interested I still have a couple of copies left.

Issue #37 – It's November 2001 and this issue saw us giving away a free compilation CD, which Tony sorted and our mate Dan Roberson did the artwork inspired by a Spanish Civil War poster. Think he will be doing the cover for this book too. Time and technology had by now moved on significantly and the CD now usurped the humble cassette tape. DC-9, Disposable Heroes, HHH, Good Riddance, Open season and the joyous Bus Station Loonies made for a very decent line up in this issue, which we printed in A5 and A4 I've just discovered! Not bad for £2 and SAE looking back.

Issue #37.5 – By now a Christmas issue was becoming the norm. On the cover we asked if anyone remembered a band called Verbal Assault, who by this time had split up, but we had an interview with their former singer Chris Jones who was reviving their recordings. For the record I think Verbal Assault played one of my favourite gigs in Southampton back in the late 1980's. This issue was a Pay No More Than – 50p!

Issue #38 – Endstand, Solea, Deadline, Rabies Babies, Speedwell and Dead Inside made for a packed May 2002 issue and our old mate Andy Morris was now well involved and contributing, so much so, he even wrote an intro for this issue. Great days.

Issue #39 – Onwards to October 2002 and this busy issue had interviews with Friends Of Ed, Paint It Black, Strike Anywhere, Active Slaughter and Maximum Rock 'N' Roll. Great variety of bands, contributors and again we were only stinging you all for a quid!

Issue #39.9 – Christmas 2002 mini-issue! Boxed In and Antidote interviewed and most of the quid you were asked to pay was a benefit for Reason To Believe, who were a free fanzine and we wanted to help them keep it that way.

Issues #40 - #45 – I'm really hoping Tony has written about these issues as they are a missing from my collection!

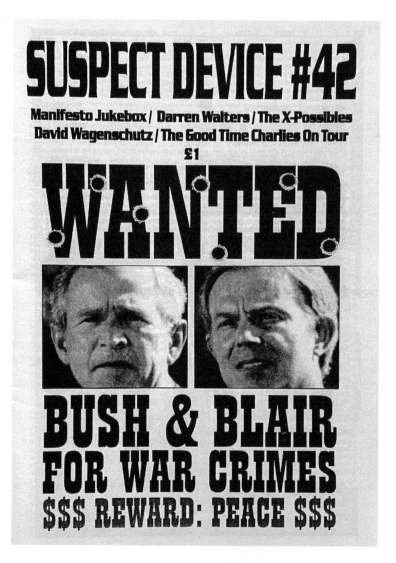

Tony Suspect - Blatant Localism

For SD#41 we decided to focus on the local scene. Not just Southampton, but Portsmouth too as well as reflecting on Basingstoke, Winchester and Bournemouth. Ged Babey let us use his interview with original Southampton punks State Jacket, we spoke to Southampton gig collective OOMF, Portsmouth's When All Else Fails and Chillerton, Ian Canty's Part Time Punk zine and Mike Fox, who was, at the time, in Pilger with me and was also doing a zine called I'm Only Doing This Zine To Get Free CDs. Both Gaz and me were really pleased with this, and it felt good to shine a light on what the locals were doing, as there were a lot of dedicated, creative people around at that point.

I planned to have a cover full of gig flyers form the local area, but then realised that the only ones I had were Pilger flyers, but I used them anyway, as a lot of them featured other local bands and were for gigs put on locally.

The title of Mike's zine came from a silly conversation we had, that he ran with. I really liked the zine, as it was funny and featured Pilger a lot, although one cover had a very tabloid like quote attributed to me. Pilger had pulled into a service station on one of our trips north, and a couple of Great Tits had landed on a bush in front of the car, and, being quite a fan of our feathered friends I said something like "Oh, look at those Great Tits." Mike put those words on the cover of his next issue, and with no context the innocence was lost, it would have made the editor of The Sun proud!

Jets Vs Sharks seemed to be at the hub of the good things going on in Portsmouth, with the gigs often at The Horseshoe, being fun and inclusive. The Portsmouth bands also played regularly in Southampton and became good friends. By this time Pilger's bass player, Kev, was living in Portsmouth, and the two cities were part of one vibrant south coast scene, so much so that Mike Fox got soutHCoast tattooed on his leg.

One notable, non-local inclusion in this issue is my review of Paint It Black's debut album 'CVA'. Needless to say I quite liked it!

Away from our cosy little scene on the South Coast, bigger things were going on in the world. The attack on the World Trade Centre in New York inevitably lead to the US and the UK attacking Iraq, a country not involved in the attacks, so our cover for SD#42, was a reprint of a Wanted poster that had Blair and Bush's faces on the front, calling for their arrest for murder. There was a little bit of a mess up on my part in that I forgot to include the Manifesto Jukebox interview that Joe Watson did, so I had to print up some pages and insert them in after it was printed.

As I was in contact with Darren Walters of Jade Tree Records, and because of his love of British football, Dave Wagenschutz got in touch as he was also into British football. Dave was working at Jade Tree at that point, and because he had been in Kid Dynamite, Lifetime, Good Riddance and now Paint It Black I was keen to interview him. Si also interviewed Darren. Ged Babey, again was generous enough to give us another interview, this one with The X-Possibles and Andy Morris did a Good Time Charlies tour report. It was the last thing Andy did for us for a long while, and we lost contact for a couple of years. It was a shame because Andy was (and still is) a good friend, however he had things going on in his life which, obviously he needed to deal with.

After my rant about their barcode, I became good friends with the guys in Intent, they were now very involved with the local scene and Pilger formed a bit of a bond with them.

Paul Samain
"The 4 of us formed Intent in 2001 through friends of friends, but Matt was already buying the fanzine long before we got to meet Tony and the SCHC crew. Stew had already been the front man for 'Older than Dirt' which was part of the punk scene in the late 90's and Neil had already started following Pilger. After a year of rehearsing and jamming we were invited to the play our first show at Manifest in Winchester. We then decided to record our first few tracks which was to become the 'Everyday' EP which was reviewed by Tony and Suspect Device, and was our first big introduction to SCHC and the fanzine as a band."

Stew Watt
"We had all attended STE, OOMPH and other DIY gigs before Intent formed. Initially we were not sure how to get involved or if we would be considered for gigs but it only took a couple of convos with people and we were included.
We always tried to contribute to the scene, putting on gigs ourselves, attending as many as we could, also running a decent PA that people could access I think really helped.
We were all about playing for the joy of it. I don't think anyone would consider we were musically particularly innovative but always brought energy and fun to shows."

Matt Coleman:
"We only did it for the fun, we never took ourselves seriously, practices were the most amazing times of being silly and messing about. We would be the 4 man pit for many bands and always had a blast. We would always play early as possible as I would often get anxious and throw up before gigs so we would get it over with and all have a blast."

Neil Clelland:
"That was all really driven by Mat, really - I think the rest of us were pretty clueless about it to start with! He would talk about going to some smaller gigs and I remember him showing us a copy of the Pilger - Silence CD with it's folded paper sleeve. Certainly at the time, I did not get it. But, Intent only ever started as a bit of fun - certainly for Paul and I. For Mat though, it was much more his passion, he was the driving force behind much of what we did in the early days: we got our first gig, at The Railway, through a friend of his; and after we recorded the Everyday record, it was him who sent it out to loads of places to get reviews. Obviously he sent it to Suspect Device and that is the review I remember him reading back to us. Then it was fairly organic....the four of us became fast friends and just started turning up to gigs, you get to know people and they were kind enough to give Intent some opportunities: in those first couple of months the fellas from Oomf included us in their 2002 Xmas Party; we were asked to play an Anti-War Benefit at The Horseshoe and Pilger asked us along to play the Totton Youth Club. That was a really nice time and opened my eyes to the local DIY scene. Just a great group of people

having fun and helping each other out, it was an easy thing to get involved with.

I think we were accepted fairly quickly. I always felt we were a little different though. In that, we were quite late to the scene, so we seemed like an anomaly. We were older than the younger group of bands, so we had different responsibilities and a slightly different outlook.....and we were a closer age range with the more mature bands, but we hadn't been there from the start, so we were missing the history."

Gaz's sister was working at a Youth Club in Totton, and she invited us to come and play for the kids there. Pilger played there a few times, often with Intent, but we did have other bands along too, including No Substance and one formed by some of the youth club kids. Initially the kids were into it, they'd put soft mats down so they could throw themselves about without getting hurt and they loved it. The Halloween gig was particularly memorable, Intent dressed up, and I decided it would be a good idea to play the Pilger set wearing a white hockey mask with my hood pulled up. It was very hot. Becca came along and, dressed as a witch did a bit of dancing on the stage too.

Stew Watt:
"The Totton youth centre gigs really cemented our sense of belonging to a pretty positive scene, I think we played there 3 times, did loads of give away goodies and stuff. It was great fun and a nice way to give back to the broader community."

Paul Samain
"Intent was always about friends first, we met weekly for rehearsals but it was about being together rather than having to jam. There were occasions we would set up but just sit around and chat all night. Our unique value was to be positive and not swearing in our songs, however in Punk it is very easy to get into the anti theme. We chose to sing about friends, family and even the scene itself. When it came to gigs we would promote 'Posi Pits' and trying to be inclusive so everyone could join in with no one getting hurt. This came about more after we played a gig at Totton Youth Club. The club supported kids from a deprived area of Southampton, and there was a definite gap between the kids in age and size. The kids didn't mix much and stayed in their groups, but Intent & Pilger taught the kids to have a laugh in the pit and before we knew it the bigger kids had the little kids on their backs and having friendly piggy back fights in the pit. There was also an occasion the bigger kids lifted the sofa full of the little kids, and started to crowd surf them. Of all the gigs we played, the Totton Youth Club gig is the one we always talk about, it was also the basis of the bands anthem 'Posi Pit'. Neil and I were left in the rehearsal room whilst the other 2 went to get some food, and by the time they got back we had written the bass and drums, and pretty much sorted out the lyrics. When we came to officially recording it, Neil threw in "Totton Youth Club Crew" in the last chorus as a salute to the club and how much they influenced us and the song."

Neil Clelland:

"Intent played the TYC three times - including a great time in October 2004, when we all turned up and played in full Halloween outfits. These gigs were quite different, as there was quite a mix of reactions. For a start, the kids were mainly early to mid teens and some were younger than that. The bands set up on a low-riser stage area and we had crash mats laid on the floor in front, with sofas going down the side wall. I remember one time Phil from Pilger really got the kids going, they got whipped up with circle pits, they started throwing themselves off the sofas and Phil managed to find himself at the bottom of a massive bundle on the floor. Hilarious."

The last time we played there, I think the kids' musical tastes were changing and they didn't seem to be so into it, and as much as we loved playing there, it was time to stop. It was their space, and we were just their guests.

Matt Coleman:

"First (Totton Youth Club gig) was great, really really great to see the kids with all this energy. Second one was a bit quieter and I tried to do some audience participation/rap thing that seemed a great idea before but in reality failed terribly. I hope a few of those kids started bands.
(Posi Pit Crew) was the first song we all wrote together so we decided to sing a line each on rotation. We wanted a song about the good parts of the community, silly dancing, 'crowd surfing on 2 mates' etc. Lovely that Tony would come play drums with us sometimes and Paul could take the mic and run around."

Neil Clelland:

"I think that is probably the fastest that we ever wrote a song! I think they were riffs that I had brought to practice and Paul and I were just joking around and messing about with it and trying to make it as stripped back and simple as possible. As we were being so silly with it, Stew got bored or annoyed (or both) and went off to get food for us all.....as he left Mat, Paul and I then resolved to try and write all of the lyrics before he got back. And we did. It was very much a song about us. The first verse about the antics we'd get up to at gigs (mainly Pilger gigs, if we're being totally honest) and I think the second verse was some ramblings about Stew and his very serious approach to lyrics and some reference to Paul and I being the rhythm section. It was ridiculous, it's still ridiculous, but it was a lot of fun to do and it was always a lot of fun to play, as Paul and Stew would switch to let Paul sing it."

When Neil was about to get married, instead of a stag night, his bandmates had put on a gig called Neilfest, at the King Alfred Pub in Southampton, a venue that was then home of DIY gigs, hosting bands like Career Suicide, Tear It Up, Annihilation Time, Endstand, Tragedy, Fucked Up etc. Anyway, the money Neil made from the gig all went to the youth Club, and they were able to put it towards updating their kitchen area.

Neil Clelland:

"Neil Fest came about as a convergence of a couple of different ideas about my stag do. It presented the opportunity to get together and have a bit of a celebratory gig - by this point, Intent had kind of run its course. Mat had moved away to Brighton and whilst we had toyed with the idea of bringing in Dave, as a replacement it really didn't feel right. Mat and Dave are contrasting guitar players, so when we had tried it out, the songs had a very different energy. And besides, Intent was really Mat's band from the start, he was the common link that had originally brought us all together, so it felt wrong to continue without him. Neil Fest became the first excuse to get back and play together again. I also wanted to try and do something positive with my stag do, so we decided to donate the door money from Neil Fest to the TYC. I had loved playing there and really admired the work they were doing to help these kids and give them a space to just be. So I think we got them a couple of hundred pounds to buy some kitchen equipment or something. I was grateful to the bands and everyone involved that worked to allow us to do that. The gig itself was a blast, we had Circus Act, No Substance, Pilger, Intent and Jets vs Sharks all play. Unfortunately Kev was busy, but that did mean I got to play bass for the Pilger set - after learning the songs for the Paint It Black tour. Also the Intent guys also surprised me with a band karaoke at some point and made me sing a couple of my favourite songs, I think it must've been Discharge, Misfits, Slayer and Rudimentary Peni. It was a special night for me and I felt very loved."

Stew Watt:
"Neilfest and SD 20th Year gigs were really special, we were so lucky to have such a great group of friends in so many bands that we could put shows together and just have fun with each other.
I remember singing Meantime with Trend Abuse at Neilfest which is possibly my fave track ever and Intent learning and playing a passable version of the track Suspect Device at the SD gig."

Paul Samain:
"Intent did play quite a few gigs looking back, the very first gig in Winchester started off quite funny. The band after us were a young Ska band, the trumpeter had left his trumpet on the train which seemed daft. The only gigs that really stood out was Neil Fest and the Totton Youth Club shows (I think we played 2 in the end). I set up Neil Fest for Neil's stag do, we asked his favourite SCHC bands to play with us and we even invited some guest appearances in the Intent set."

Neil Clelland:
"Well, I always tried to have fun whilst we were actually playing! I never really took it too seriously, so I didn't feel any pressure to have to play well or put on a show. For me, the fun was just in getting the opportunity to actually play. It probably meant we were often a bit of a mess though! In terms of a favourite gig, that is a tricky question....there are a lot of gigs I enjoyed being a part of: the Punks Picnic in the Park, the gigs at the TYC and definitely having the chance to get together again after a couple of years for Mat's 30th birthday in Brighton were all a lot of fun. But if I had to say what I thought my favourite Intent gig was, from a purely band performance perspective, that would have to be this random gig we played at The Bang Bar in Basingstoke. It's a venue I'd never been to before and never went to after and I think it's closed now. It was a great place for gigs though, the drums were set up in the front window

by the door and the floor space was limited as you ran straight into the bar. I think we always benefited from small places which required less people to like us. Everything just really came together and everyone was really into it which was great. I have a recollection that we only came up with the setlist after we arrived, which was unusual for us. I think even Mat enjoyed playing that one, so it must have been good!"

It seems that SD#43 was a real rushed affair. I think I wanted it to be a bigger 20th Anniversary issue, but we decided to do a book to mark that, so because we had interviews with Intent and No Substance, along with Gaz's chat with Assert and Clara's Discharge interview we decided to to a regular issue. In my rush I messed up the page count and so had to quickly add more stuff in, then there was a problem with the printing, and that had to be done again. It was all a hassle and a bit of a mess, but we got it done.

We did manage to get one more issue done in our 20th year, and it featured one of my favourite bands, 7 Seconds. I didn't think it would ever happen, but 7 Seconds came to play in the UK, and had a gig at The Free Butt in Brighton. Gaz and me went down with Neil and Matt from Intent. Pete Zonked was there, of course, and lots of other friends. It was a small venue and 7 Seconds were superb. I felt like a little kid, so excited to hear those songs live, punching the air and singing along to songs that I'd loved for years. I then sent Kevin Seconds some questions once their tour was over, after he'd gave me his email address that night, and I was thrilled to be able to have them in the zine. Another band that Gaz and me have loved for years are The Partisans, and they also released new music that year. So not only did we get to see 7 Seconds, we also got to see The Partisans. Gaz and me drove up to Croydon to see them. They were another band that I never thought I'd ever get to see, and it was great to be able to do that with Gaz. It wasn't the classic line up, no Louise or Shark, but they were fantastic. I'd been in contact with singer Spike for a little while before ewes them, and he had answered some questions, so it was cool to have both The Partisans and 7 Seconds in the same issue. Si interviewed The Loved Ones from Philadelphia, a band that featured Spider from the second Kid Dynamite line up and Dave Hause from the first Paint It Black line up. We also had an interview with Si's son's band An American Obsession.

There were so many reviews, because we were getting so many bundles of CDs each week to review. Sarah and me would be making the trip to our PO Box every other day and coming back with an armful of packages.

Nath Haywire wrote a piece about Wickham Animal Testing Laboratories, and Gaz wrote a piece on DIY breweries. I filled a couple of extra pages with a piece about Coca-Cola, inspired by going to see Mark Thomas, and also seeing his documentary on their practises; Workers killed for joining a union in South America, villages in India deprived of water as the nearby coke factory had diverted it all. Sadly, Abrazos have a track on our album (released in 2022) called 'Coke Costs Life'. Nothing changes for the many while big money is being made by a few. The message remains the same, don't buy Coca-Cola.

It seems Pilger were getting quite prolific, we'd just had an EP released by Peter Bower Records, and SD had released our split 7" with the Isle Of Wight's Biff Tannen.

We'd also played a gig in one of the parks in the middle of Southampton, which was cool. Not only did Sarah and Becca come along, but my mum and dad and sister too. Si and Dan Briggs also made the trip down from Middlesbrough.

SD Records were busy as we were also about to release the Intent album 'Double Positive' on CD. Intent had also played at the gig in the park, and their singer Stew wrote his first column for us in SD#44.

In the column I wrote I tried to make the case for the best Clash album being 'Give 'em Enough Rope', something I stand by today. That album holds a special memory for me. When it came out in 1978 I was eager to get as many punk records as I could, but money was scarce, and I had to save up my pocket money, which wasn't very much. I didn't yet have a paper round, so it took while to save up enough for an album, and there were always lots of singles I wanted. However I really wanted this record after seeing someone with it while at Lymington market with my family. It was a Sunday and I wasn't well, a chest infection meant I was struggling and so was lagging behind the others, and while they looked at the usual stalls, I happened to see a spiky haired older youth wearing a Dennis The Menace jumper, sat on some steps looking at this colourful record sleeve. I noticed The Clash written across the top, which stopped me in my tracks. The next day I was too ill for school, and had been left in the front room under a blanket in front of the TV. At some point a music show came on, and remember this was a time when there wasn't much daytime TV other than educational programs, but for some reason there was a music show on, and they interviewed The Clash about their new album. They showed the red, yellow and blue cover of 'Give 'em Enough Rope', that I recognised as the one the Lymington punk was holding. The band also talked about how they refused to go on Top Of The Pops and mime, but were on this show as they could play live; they then played three songs live in the studio. It was fantastic. It took some time to save up for that album, but although I was so determined to get it, it would have been well into 1979 before I actually owned a copy. I've loved it ever since. I realise their debut is the one that's full of punk rock energy with the rough edges evident, and I know I'm usually put off by slicker production of their second one, but the opening three songs are fantastic, and if I choose to listen to a Clash album, this is the one that I'll put on. It was 'Tommy Gun' that really made me want to play drums.

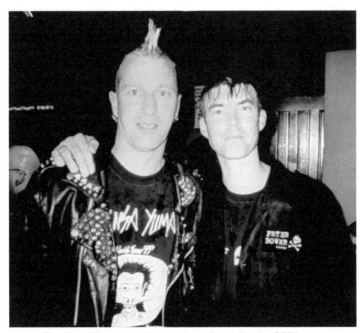

Spud and Gaz at the Birmingham Punx Picnic, 2005
(Photo by John (Welshy) Welsh)

You're Only Looking for Vinyl

Graham Sleightholme - Distros

Somewhere along the line in the mid 90's I was young, very enthusiastic about punk and had already ticked off the other tasks in the scene. I had written a zine and I had by some sort of miracle started promoting gigs. Putting on gigs on my own always felt a bit awkward, but I was in a city where bands didn't come and my enthusiasm won out. I was completely blagging it and thankfully ended up in a gig collective. So fast forward a bit and a local who was running a label and distro (they always went hand in hand) was fed up with it. Myself and a friend decided to take it on and a deal was struck. Releases by Spite, Restarts and Haywire were out and we had plenty of stock to trade with. I had to learn a whole new way of thinking about how the punk scene operated. Writing to distros was always a thing I did but how did stocking their releases work? How did you get that new release on Prank, Profane Existence, Slap-a-ham, Skuld etc? Turns out you did the same as a regular customer but with added involvement. Trading releases meant you needed to start working out what people wanted and what would sell in your local area. You did not want to start losing money, although it was somewhat inevitable. So lots of letters to European and US labels start flying back and forth. Bigger labels and distros in the UK like Looney Tunes, Flat Earth, La Vida Es Un Mus and Enslaved came to the fore.Getting to know these people was par for the course, they were in the same boat.

So I was set. Once I had sorted trades and made new mailout lists to be photocopied at the printers I was taking endless parcels to the - soon to be 1st name terms - post office worker.

I now needed to get into "doing a stall" which was the only aspect a lot of people at gigs ever saw of what you did. It was a great place to be as you were putting names and faces together as you travelled to places like Southampton, Bradford, Leeds, Bath, Sheffield, Bristol, London etc. It soon became the default that you would be hanging out with these people. You would be a magnet for the record nerds, and there were a lot. Sometimes a certain person would walk in and you'd know they were going to buy something. Pre-internet you would be expected to know everything you were selling and be able to describe it. I occasionally got laughed at by regulars for talking them out of buying something as I knew they wouldn't like it. A lot of people knew the cool stuff but a lot of the smaller bands would get passed over. Gordon Solie Motherfuckers and Young Wasteners weren't on everyone's lips straight away. So I became a salesman, it wasn't hard as I was overly enthusiastic. The distro also meant driving to gigs, and driving meant you were everyone's mate for lifts to out of town venues. I ended up with a solid crew of degenerates, who were up for gigs and carrying boxes of records across the land. The fun of gigs was also that if I went to somewhere like Southampton i would be doing a stall next to Tony and Gaz inevitably. Other towns had their regular stalls and people behind them. A lot of it was talking shop but at the same time we all knew we could leave our stalls in their hands and that upon return they might hand you £20 for records you had sold. The community of support between us was brilliant. It wasn't competitive, we might even be selling the same stuff.

There were downsides to doing a stall, you had to be there early, people at gigs don't want to give up their tables for you. Getting their early also meant getting out last after the bands had finished. People were also great at buying something and asking you to hold onto it til after the gig, last orders, chatting to their mates and going home having forgot they`d bought something. You were expected to wait. There was also the problem of being stuck behind a stall for loads of poor bands you just couldn't avoid, conversely you might be in the other room next to the gig and see hardly any of the bands you wanted to see. Swings and roundabouts I guess. Eventually you would know the venues based on stall potential. Getting a table in The Junction, Bristol meant being in early and grabbing the long tables as the round ones were shit. The 1in12 was a law unto itself though with the cafe snooker tables being covered and a stall-fest taking over. I loved those weekenders for that. It was our place and all the DIY distros gathered together. As a record buyer it was the best.

Most shops didn't carry DIY Punk releases, maybe one switched on shop per city (Replay, Bristol) would do sale or return. Labels and the bands we dealt with didn`t want to be in HMV or Our Price. It just wasn't the point. A lot of this was down to the Anarcho ideals of the 80`s which carried on strongly in the UK / Europe and from the pricing point of Not for Profit which was still a very much debated topic. Dischord records being torch bearers for a similar, but different approach to say the Crass ethic. It was a debate which raged in the DIY arena. We were fighting against commercialisation via the likes of all the pop punk stuff which always felt pretty vacuous barring the odd exception. The distro was what made your punk gig different along with the Hunt Sab stalls, the local zine on sale and the touring bands whose records were only available at the gig or via the likes of me who took 10 off them when they stayed at your house. Distros were a very uncool part of punk. There was very little in the way of ego from any of the people I encountered. The love of music and the ideals were the main thrust. During the week we would be stuffing EPs into envelopes with loads of flyers, it wasn't glamorous. There was the inevitable zine nights where you would pore over MRR / Fracture / Reason to Believe / Engine / How We Rock etc for the reviews / adverts section to work out what to get in. I can still remember the address` of distros / zines from 30 years ago! Alternatively we might be topping up the boxes for the next gig.

There were other upsides to this as well. Punk Post! I cannot state how great this was as a network of pure trust. Touring bands especially, but also distros would lug parcels up and down the UK and even to Europe at no charge to avoid the postal charges. This never ceased to blow me away. You were giving boxes of records to strangers or mates and not thinking twice about whether they would get delivered. I've not encountered this sort of thing in other parts of life. It went hand in hand with the anarcho beliefs of the 80`s, as did occasionally giving lifts to people from gig to gig, or letting people you'd never met stay at your house.

After about 8 or 9 years I decided to get out. I'd just had kids and I knew I wouldn't be able to commit as much time as I needed to it. I was lucky and sold all my stock at cost price in one go. After almost a decade I made enough profit to buy a new jacket, an Ipod and an Infest EP. My hourly rate was shocking, but I guess that wasn't the point.

Its very easy for the role of the distro in the punk scene to be forgotten, the internet killed it to an extent. Online ordering direct from a label became quicker and easier than waiting for me to get 10 copies via punk post. But a distro made a punk gig more interesting, it took effort to do our own thing. The distro meant small DIY labels could exist, we provided the network for it to get out there. We would lug bizarre zines around as well. I even carried the Banksy small books on my distro before he became famous. We gave opportunity. Bands and labels who made it, and some that didn`t, have whole books dedicated to their fleeting existence. Thankfully zines are starting to get some recognition as important parts of the punk eco-system. I'm not sure a book on a distro will ever happen but those of us who did it have plenty of hilarious tales of disaster and fun times. If you're over 40 and still own records, there's a chance you bought one from a gig. There's a chance it was me. There's no value in that. It just was that way.

On a final note. Some people are still at it doing this punk distro malarkey. It's not a stall at a gig but it's done for you, for the love of it. Paco/ LVEUM, Jules / Missing the Point, Urinal Vinyl, Superfi Records. They have rooms full of records waiting for you. They're run by people in bands / labels / promoters. You should support them over larger corporations.

Tony:
I'm not sure when we properly started the SD distro. Very early on we had copies of the Political Asylum 'Winter' 7"EP to sell, and we would do some limited trades for early issues of the zine, but neither Gaz or me were very good at walking round asking people if they wanted to buy a zine or record. Having a stall at gigs was a perfect way for us, we could layout what we had and people could come to us if they wanted anything. We took quite a few copies of the first Boss Tuneage release, the Goober Patrol/Vehicle Derek 7"EP, and I think our early distro stalls were just SD zines and the couple of records we'd bought to help out friends' labels or bands. We would also have the next few releases from Boss Tuneage, the Wanton Though 7", Damage 12", Goober Patrol LP and Life...But How To Live it LP, and many more in the years that followed. Once we had made contact with Sean Forbes, we would have the Rugger Bugger releases too.
Having local gigs put on by our friends helped too, we could get there early and set up our stall, getting a good spot so we could watch the bands as well as sell stuff. Initially, at the Joiners, that was against the back wall, facing the stage, which was then at right angles to the left of where it is now. Often we'd be sharing our space with Dave Carr and Dan Roberson who brought along their October Books stock, records as well as books, and occasionally t-shirts. Of course we'd always make space for bands to put their stuff out if they wanted to. Then, when the Joiners stopped using the bar in the back room we'd use that. It wasn't such a good view of the bands, but it did give everyone more space.
When Pilger started playing up and down the country, I'd take the SD distro with me. That was a time when we were not only trading for SD and Pilger stuff, but I was also buying in CDs from Revelation Records, as well as UK labels. Revelation would send CDs through in air mail envelopes without jewel cases, as it was cheaper for us to pay the air mail postage costs and buy blank jewel cases over here. Si Briggs would send in his requests and take the "northern branch" of the distro to gigs he went to, or just to sell amongst his mates up in the North East.

Some of my favourite memories of gigs is doing a distro, sat alongside friends or people who became friends after sharing a distro table. I used to enjoy sharing distro space with October Books, it was nice to sit and chat with Dave, Dan and Nath. I'd often end up buying stuff from them and Dave Carr would order in records for the shop and he'd sometimes say that he'd ordered in a particular record that he thought I may like. I would always make the trip to the shop to get that record, he wasn't often wrong in thinking I'd like it.

Hot Water Music came to play at a Health Club in Southampton, it was an odd venue, and one that the STE were never able to use again, but that evening I set up the SD distro at a low table which was placed in front of a sofa. Not only that but they sold tea. What better way to watch a couple of bands than sitting on a sofa next to my good friend Dan Roberson, both of us drinking tea and selling records to people?

Rich Levene:
"I remember that gig. Afterwards, the bloke who who ran the club said. "It's not really my thing. Didn't like the music and I don't really want to do anymore gigs, but I have to say, your crowd you punks are far more polite than most of my regulars are." First of all, he was sort of on the defensive, but then he's going "Everybody said please and thank you when they ordered drinks.""

Obviously the best place for a distro table is in the venue where you can watch the bands, but another of my favourite memories was setting up the distro at a table in the front bar at The Joiners at the STE 25th Anniversary gig. There were a few distros set up and I spent a lot off the day sat next to Graham Sleightholme, and chatting to Pete Zonked! and Ralf, Steve and Baz of Violent Arrest and lots of other people who stopped by, often just for a chat. It made the day more of an event, more than just music and I remember the time spent sitting at the distro stall with more fondness than I do the bands. It's not that I didn't enjoy the bands, because I did, it's just that sharing space and time with the other distros and those buying stuff is what the DIY scene is about; friendship, co-operation and fun.

When I was in Pilger, and we were playing a lot of gigs, we had built up quite a good distro, but in the years after the band finished the distro had dwindled somewhat. But I wanted to build it up again. Postage costs were growing and as I had a contact at Grave Mistake records, I was going to buy US releases in bulk to sell at a fair price over here. My mum and dad offered to help with some money initially, and I set up a web shop. I would regularly get stuff sent over from Grave Mistake and Revelation, and I'd also take stuff from La Vida Es Un Mus, Static Shock, Boss Tuneage as well as zines, including Maximum RocknRoll, and stuff I'd trade for zines. I'd always pay up front and usually took up to ten copies of whatever it was.

The on-line shop has gone now, and I don't do a stall these days, but Gaz sells anything we have on eBay, and it does feel weird going to gigs on my own and not going to stand behind a table. I found that easier, like there was some protection. People generally wanted to talk about the records I was selling, without that I find it a bit more difficult. I have to say it is nice to not have to carry in heavy boxes of records, and deal with money, and worry about people putting glasses or bottles of beer down on top of zines and records, but I do miss it some times.

As with most things Gaz and me do, I'm sure we lost quite a bit of money over the years, but that was never our motivation, we just liked being able to have records and zines available at gigs, and make them as cheap and accessible as possible.

Gaz has started selling stuff on eBay. Initially it was copies of Suspect Device and the CDs from my own collection that I wanted to get rid of, and that he didn't want. It was mainly old promos I had been sent for review over the years, but also many other CDs that I now have digitally on my hard drive, and so never play the actual disc. He has also sold SD records releases and some distro items. All the money he makes goes back into SD funds for zine printing and, these days, Abrazos releases.

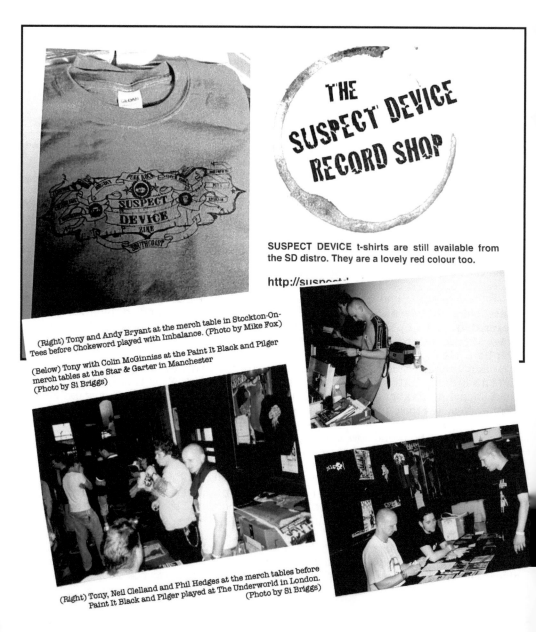

THE SUSPECT DEVICE RECORD SHOP

SUSPECT DEVICE t-shirts are still available from the SD distro. They are a lovely red colour too.

http://suspect

(Right) Tony and Andy Bryant at the merch table in Stockton-On-Tees before Chokeword played with Imbalance. (Photo by Mike Fox)

(Below) Tony with Colin McGinniss at the Paint It Black and Pilger merch tables at the Star & Garter in Manchester (Photo by Si Briggs)

(Right) Tony, Neil Clelland and Phil Hedges at the merch tables before Paint It Black and Pilger played at The Underworld in London. (Photo by Si Briggs)

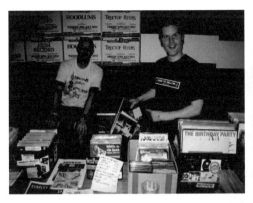

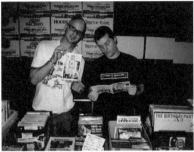

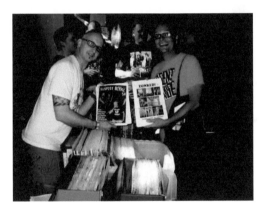

Distro stalls at the STE 25th Anniversary gig. (Above) Graham Sleightholme and Tony ready to serve. (Left): Pete Zonked! and Tony with the latest issues of Zonked! and SD.

Doing a distro isn't always glamorous.
Below left: Rich Corbridge (Armed With Anger), Janne (Endstand) and Graham Sleightholme at The IQ, Boston
Below right: Tony and Andy Morris (The Railway Inn, Winchester)

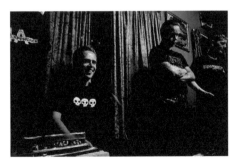

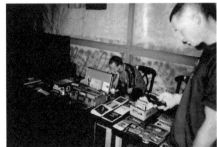

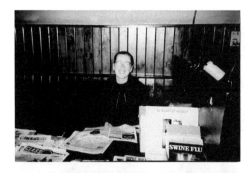

Sarah with the SD distro stall.

The Joiners, Southampton

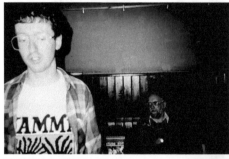

Dave Carr with the October Books stall
with Rob Callen in the foreground.

The Joiners, Southampton

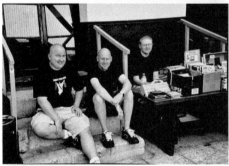

Dan Briggs behind the SD stall
with Mike Fox and Si Briggs.

The Hobbit, Southampton

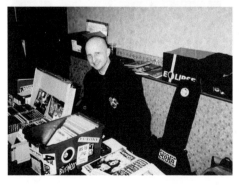

Tony at the SD stall.

The King Alfred, Southampton

Tony Suspect - Twenty Years On

Our next venture was to put out a book called Twenty Years Of Suspect Device fanzine. Stew from Intent helped us put the book together, it had a run through of all our issues up until that point, along with sections on the distro, the tape label and the record label, plus contributions from some of the people who'd helped us along the way.

When the book was printed, we had a gig at the King Alf, where everyone who came got a copy of the book. It was a night of good friends and good fun. During Jets Vs Sharks' set I was stood on a chair, behind the SD stall, and Matt White indicated that he wanted to speak to me, so I bent down and then before I knew it he grabbed me and slung me over his shoulder before I was passed around above people's heads and deposited in the middle of the band as they played. I then didn't know what to do, so just meekly shuffled off back to the safety of the SD stall. You couldn't have called it a crowd surfing, it was more Crowd Kidnap.

Gaz was also picked up and handed around above the crowd's heads, but he took to it with much more enthusiasm than me, and even attempted a back summersault just like the young kids were doing at the time.

It was a fun night that, I think, celebrated the closeness and fun of the local scene as much as 20 years of SD.

Paul Samain

"Before (Intent) decided to have a break we were invited to play the 20th Anniversary Suspect Device gig, which was an absolute pleasure to support Tony and SCHC. I seem to recall Neil playing in Circus Act for a while and on one I played for 2 different bands and Neil ended up playing in 3. The fact you could play in multiple projects was also a reflection on how tight the SCHC was, no one cared who you played for everyone just wanted to get involved where they could."

Daz of Cat n Cakey records also put on a gig for us in Whitchurch, and I'm embarrassed to say that I don't remember who played that.

There's an account of the Twenty Years gig in SD#45, along with interviews with Self Abuse, Circus Act, The Mercury League, Gameface's Jeff Caudill, OneWay System and None More Black. Again there are tons of reviews, and mention of an Amnesty International benefit gig that Stew from Intent was organising, a gig that Pilger played. Unfortunately the printing is very dark, which is a shame as there were some good photos from Self Abuse's first gig back in 20 years.

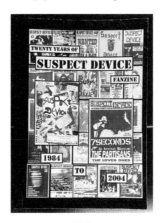

Again, there was a lot going on in the second half of 2005, and we tried to cover a lot of it in SD#46. There is mention of the London bombs, and of "terrorism" in general, there are interviews with Abandon Ship, Dirty love, The Black Veins, The Varukers, The Fire Still Burns and Fighting Shit. But, apart from the stupid amount of reviews, a lot of the zine is taken up with two adventures that Si Briggs and me had. The first was the short tour Pilger did with Paint It Black around the UK.

After getting in touch with Dan Yemin, then Darren Walters of Jade Tree Records and Dave Wagenschutz, Pilger were offered the support slot for the UK dates on Paint It Black's 2005 European tour. Of course we jumped at the chance, so on the 20th June we rounded up the Pilger crew, which included Neil Clelland who had learnt our set in case Kev couldn't make it as his partner had just had a baby; most bands take spare equipment, we also took a spare bassist. Also along for the ride were Stew Watt, the designated driver, and Si Briggs, merch guy, roadie and reserve driver. We hired a van and headed off to Norwich, stopping in Basingstoke to pick up Neil and change a tyre which had already got a nail in it. Not the best start when we had a long drive to Norwich ahead of us.

Not only were we going to get to hang out with Paint It Black and Darren Walters in Norwich, but our friends Jets Vs Sharks were playing that first night too. It was a week that also took in gigs in Hull, Manchester, Bristol and London. We had a lot of fun, spent time with friends new and old and we got to watch Paint It Black be fantastic every night.

What follows are excerpts from the write up that appeared in SD#49, to give an idea of the way the tour went:

Si: The journey to Norwich went smoothly, lots of excited good natured banter about what the next 5 days would hold for us and in no time at all we were there. We arrived early and so a few of us had a wander along to the footer ground, a fave pastime of Tony Suspect I have come to discover, and had a look around.

Mike: We were the first to arrive at The Ferry Boat and I can say that this was the best location for a gig. The venue is in an old boat house that backs onto a canal. Sweet, this was picturesque and a scouting party made it to a not so super market for provisions, okay I got 12 cans of cider for stupid money.

Si: The Jets guys were there when we got back, with the legend that is Benny Boy as their driver We chatted a while and enjoyed the fine weather and after a while another van showed up and all of a sudden we were amongst the Paint It Black peops, and I am not afraid to admit I was pretty fucking nervous! Wasn't sure what to do in such a situation and so I played it nonchalant, when in doubt, appear aloof and ignorant I always think. Eventually I walked over to Tony who then introduced me and Dan Yemin said "Hi I'm Dan" and gave me a very firm handshake, not sure what my response was but I'm pretty sure it involved drooling and gibberish. Met the rest of the guys, and I think I managed to actually make sense to at least one of them, and we started taking stuff in and setting up, and this is where I discovered being a Pilger roadie was a bit of a doddle, they've got nowt, which pleased me no end. Had a look round the venue, The Ferryboat, and found the merch area, only to discover the PIB merch guy was Darren Walters, oh fuck, the odds of me stringing a sentence together was looking pretty slim. However, it turns out that Darren Walters is a really nice guy and chatted to me and from somewhere deep within I found the power of speech, WOOHOO! It soon became very obvious that he was also a much better merch guy than me, which was good 'cause he was crazy busy for the entire 5 days. So yeah it became obvious straight away that none of the American guys were in any way arrogant or egotistical, but what they all were was pretty fucking amusing, some more than others, but before the gig started I knew it was going to be a good tour, I was happy.

The gig in Norwich, at The Ferry Boat (which was a pub across the river from Norwich City's stadium), was a strange one, there was a big cage round the stage, which wasn't great for Phil who liked to go into the crowd while we played, and it was something none of us were used to. We didn't like it much, and I think it's fair to say that we didn't play our best gig that night. But Paint It Black didn't let the cage put them off, they were great, and it was exciting to see them play those songs live, the intensity was quite something. After the gig PiB went off to wherever they were staying, while we stayed the night in the venue. The room stunk, and during the night Mike thought there were rats in the room, luckily he realised it was Neil's foot before he battered it. It was also supposed to be haunted, but we never did see the Grey Lady; she was either put off by the stick in the room, the noisy punk rock of the evening before, or perhaps ghosts just don't exist.

Si: The gig was amazing, though not as well attended as I had thought it would be. Saw most of the bands, Black Veins were really good, and their demo I bought is one of the most aesthetically beautiful things I ever saw! Jets vs Sharks were amazing, as always, even with the stand in drummer, I love those guys. I know the Pilger guys were pretty nervous but they were excellent, again as always, and then Paint It Black were on, I wasn't sure how Dr Dan would fair as a front man, what with being a guitarist in all his other bands, but I need not have worried, they were awesome, well actually better than that! And when Dan took of his shirt, it was kind of like some strange human TARDIS thing, man he's BUFF!!!! So yes, a truly amazing first gig. Chatted to lots of cool folk and even sold a bit of merch! And then we had the delight of sleeping in the Ferryboat Pool Room. Not the nicest or comfiest of places but it was very nice of them to let us stay so I'm not complaining. We were all a bit disappointed when the "Grey Lady" ghost didn't show up at midnight, though we weren't that hopeful anyway.

In the morning we realised that we were locked into the venue and couldn't get out. We had to wait until the staff arrived to let us out. Once released, about 10am, we went off into Norwich centre to get something to eat and do a bit of record shopping, meeting up with some of the PiB guys in the city, before getting back on the road to Hull. On the drive we went over the Humber bridge, which thrilled me.
The Hull gig was in a big venue, but it was a really good night. We got to the venue quite early, so before the gig we went off to a local park to kick a football around, and then when PiB arrived most of our group went off with them to eat. As our friend Paul Fox had turned up, Si and me sat in the van with him and had a lovely chat.

Paul Fox:
"I first met Tony (in person) when his band, Pilger, toured the UK with Philadelphia band Paint It Black, they played one date in Hull, which was about an hours drive from where I lived, I immediately went into mother hen mode and baked loads of goodies for the tour warriors to consume and thought it

would be comforting what with them being so far from home, apparently, as Tony reminds me, we sat on the bus chatting before the gig while everyone else was getting food."

Si Briggs:
"Paul is a skate bro' from way back, and a top chap indeed. He had made us some grub, banana cake and flap jacks, how cool is that? And beautiful it was too. The gig was much better attended and was another absolute stormer! I missed the first band, through chatting to people, though they sounded good, indie rock kind of stuff. Next up was Black Tax and they were excellent stuff, real fast thrashy, but a bit stoppy starty too, and they seemed to go down real well. Then the mighty Pilger, and as good as they were in Norwich they were a whole lot better in Hull, excellent stuff, and got a great response from the crowd which is always good."

We had fun playing, and seemed to go down pretty well, then Send More Paramedics played and were a bit of a force to be reckoned with. They were lovely people, but musically not my sort of thing, so I took the opportunity to join Darren Walters at the merch tables and cooled down. I was unprepared for how good PiB were. I thought they were amazing in Norwich, but the energy they put into their set in Hull was phenomenal, it's been a long time since I was blown away by a band like that. Neil was even moved to jump up and sing with them, Stew dived into the pit too. It was one of those special nights, and one where I was kicking myself for leaving my camera in the van.

Mike: Hull was good, lots of really nice kids turned out. Black Tax from London were pretty good, I missed some bands, well a man has got to eat. Paint It Black were on fire tonight, really kick arse good, everyone agreed and Neil and Stew took southern style tomfoolery to the pit. Afterwards we indulged in a lot of back slapping, everyone had such a good night.
Si: Said our farewells to friends and then headed to Sheffield for the night to stay with Dave, a friend and band mate of Stew and Neil Intent/1UTBS. Had a bit of a to-do with the van and an underground parking place but not too bad.
Mike: I will not mention parking in the underground car park, other than to say Si Briggs could fit extra sardines in any can, a genius in parking terms!

After a better night's sleep, we had a wonder round Sheffield, met up with Dave again briefly during his break from work, and got back on the road. I quite enjoyed the drive through the Peak District, it was a little slow, but it was nice. As we entered Derbyshire I hoped we'd go through New Mils (I know it's near Manchester, but I have no idea where it is really), the home of Blitz, but we didn't. Once again we found the venue quite quickly, Paint It Black's van was already there, but they'd been there a while and had gone off to see the sights.

Mike: Once we had offloaded our gear to the safety of the venue a trek into Manchester was called for. Needless to say, people wanted to look at record shops. I needed a piss, so I lost everyone, found a toilet and lightened the load. The toilet was kitted out with fresh, nicely packaged spare needles, for the desperate drug taker. Cool. Better to stop the spread of AIDS and shit, me thinks. If you're gonna stick a needle in your arm, better it's a clean un! I found a punk exhibition. Fuck me, punk in a museum, now that is sad, but it was a fuckin' top quality display, loads of Seditionaries clothes, lyrics hand written on scraps of paper from various Sex Pistols, loads of video footage of all your old favourites, a cracking documentary on the 2 Pistols gigs in Manchester and a bunch of old fanzines from 76/77, a bloody good time.

Tony: We wandered off into Manchester and gradually got split up. Kev and me bumped into Darren Walters and Andy Nelson, Darren was just back from doing the stadium tour of Old Trafford. After a brief chat we met up with Si and walked back to the centre of town where we met Neil and lost Kev. Somehow we then lost Neil, so Si and me went for a little walk, found a couple of record shops and my need for the toilet eventually led us to a shopping centre, and then a vegetarian food outlet, it was cool there, as in not baking hot like it was outside, so we sat and ate and were eventually joined by Stew, Phil and Neil. They ate and we enjoyed the coolness. After a brief visit to a health food shop we went in search of Mike who'd phoned to say he was near by. He'd found a gallery with an exhibition of early punk rock and recommended it. Unfortunately it was closing by the time we got there, if only he'd phoned earlier!

Si: I'd been to Manchester a few times and knew of a few good record shops and skate shops so we weren't wandering totally blind, bumped into some of the PIB guys who were having a good time. Mike found a Punk Rock exhibition thing but by the time he let us know about it, it was too late to go in. Tony was not best pleased at all! Mike said it was really good, Tony gave him one of his looks, funny.

Before the Manchester gig, at the Star & Garter, we were in the car park talking to Andy Nelson, Kev threw a football out of our van, he threw it straight up in the air and it came down vertically straight into Andy's hands. Andy wasn't one of the American's on this tour who likes football and said in a deadpan voice "Shit! Football's just fall out of the sky in this country!" A little later, Dave and Darren came back from visiting places in Manchester associated with The Smiths, and Dave was threatened with arrest for filming Strangeways Prison. Darren thought this was very funny.
Si and me we doing the Pilger merch stall next to PiB's, being manned by guitarist Colin McGuiness. Colin was moaning that he hated doing the merch stall, and told us how he'd done it with Kid Dynamite, but quit early in the tour. Si and me offered to do the Kid Dynamite stall for him as we were there with the Pilger stuff. But he said he wanted to fave fun "fucking with the kids!"
And he did, but did it with such a cheeky smile that no one seemed to get offended, even when a typical conversation went something like:
Kid: "Can I have a medium t-shirt?"
Colin: "No, fuck you!"
Then there would be a huge smile and a cheeky laugh and the kid would happily leave with his t-shirt.
When it quietened down a little Colin started reading through a copy of SD, but it wasn't long before he exploded again, after reading the article calling for a boycott of Coca Cola, saying "Oh man, what's wrong with coke? They just want to make a delicious drink that gets you addicted and makes you fat!"
He then noticed my "boycott Nestle" t-shirt and he was off again, "Nestle? They make chocolate, right?" I love chocolate!" He spent the week commenting on my t-shirts and slapping me on the shoulder with a good natured laugh.

Kev wanted to get a picture of Pilger with The Star & Garter in the background, so we went outside took a couple of pictures, then Dan Yemin appeared and insisted on joining us in the photos.

The gig was good, Fight Back and Down & Outs also played. We played well, and I enjoyed it, but not too many people were that interested in us. At one point Colin ran in front of the stage taunting me with a can of coke.

Si: My good mate Neil Swan showed up and his bro' Ian and we had a good chat as always, great, fun guys, and Neil was putting us up for the night. Another fantastic gig, The Down and Outs were excellent, Oi! Oi! Oi! Pilger put on another really great show as did PIB, this time with a bit of a strop from Dave the drummer, throwing a broken cymbal down which caught Dan the singer on the hand as he tried to stop it going into the crowd I think, which resulted in him having a cut hand, nothing bad though, and its' all Rock n' Roll right? Colin the PIB guitarist turned out to be a really funny, as well as a fantastic guitarist. The drive back to Neil's house was fun, his bro' Ian kept us amused with drunken anecdotes like "Don't stop the van here, they'll steal your feet!" and other pearls of wisdom. We had to be quiet at his house due to his young daughter Isobel which I think we about managed to do? Neil Intent went to the bathroom but returned rather sheepishly saying he'd walked in to find Neil the house owner stood there naked having a shave, we laughed rather, but quietly. We'd been provided with plenty of bedding so a comfy night was had.

Mike: I kipped in the van for safety of the equipment; boy does the sun rise early in summer!

Si: A decent journey, with Stew once again doing all the driving. I may have had a little nap and listened to my MP3 player and the time flew by. The venue took a bit of finding, but we got there, mainly thanks to Phil Pilger. A very odd venue, small and a funny shape and the Pilger guys weren't expecting much.

The gig had been moved from The Croft to The Junction because the soundman at The Croft was working at the Glastonbury festival. We'd played at The Junction before, a couple of times, neither of which had gone too well, especially as at one of them we'd managed to wreck a guitar amp belonging to What Happens Next?.

Once parked up, everyone headed off in to Bristol, apart from Mike, Neil and me, we took the first shift with the van, ready to ward off Traffic Wardens. When the others got back, Mike and me nipped down to a supermarket for some supplies. When we returned PiB turned up and started the load in. I saw Colin outside and I had on a No Sweat t-shirt which depicted Mickey Mouse and Donald Duck working in a sweatshop, with Misery written Disney style underneath. I knew he'd look to see what shirt I had on and he did, right away. This time he said "Disney? I hate Disney" and gave me one of those heavy handed "friendly" slaps on the back before adding "I'll be drinking a coke and eating chocolate, but I'll be pissing on Mickey Mouse!"

After interviewing Dan Yeman (with help from Si, Stew and Neil), the gig got under way, and it was good to see some friendly faces turn up, including Punky Steve and Graham Sleightholme. I missed one of the bands as Pilger were asked to do an interview, so we headed out into the garden to do that.

Despite our reservations of the venue, we played really well and I thoroughly enjoyed it. It was the first gig of the tour where I felt really relaxed. We got a good reaction, we were fast, Phil was on form and we had some fun on stage too. I don't know if it was because we didn't have monitors and just set up like we do at practise, but the sound on stage for me was the best yet and although it was hot and sweaty it was just an awesome feeling. Paint It Black were once again wonderful, almost from the start Dan was buried under a pile of bodies as people went crazy. The energy was brilliant. Mike was in the pit from start to finish, punching the air and singing along, and when one idiot started to swing his fists about, Mike tickled him, it seemed to work as he stopped and moved away from Mike, ending his macho silliness. It was a brilliant bit of non-violent positive action I thought.

Si: The gig turned out to be a total stormer, as they often do when you're not expecting much. The two support bands were pretty poor I thought, one of them professing to not having a name? But Pilger played an absolute rip roarer of a set and I sold a good bit of merch too! Also met an ex-Boro guy, cool! And then once again PIB blew the place apart, without doubt one of the best live bands I've ever seen. Fantastic stuff!
We had decided to drive back to Southampton that night and we had a most amusing episode watching Mike trying to help unload the van whilst half asleep, Tony was a bit tired and grumpy and Kev and I were giggling like naughty school boys.

There was a bit of hanging around and chatting after the gig, and then we were off back to Southampton, we did a drive round dropping Stew and Phil off before heading to my house, where the rest of us were spending the night. Becca had allocated everyone their beds, and we all went straight to bed. Mike was a little worse for wear after an evening of cider (well we had been in Bristol) and I was so tired I was getting very grumpy, calling everyone fuckwits!
It was nice to be able to walk Becca to school the next morning after being away for a few days, and once everyone was up and had showers, we ate toast, drank tea (or coffee in Mike's case) and sat around until mid-day when we loaded the van set off to collect the rest of the Pilger crew and got on the road to London.
Thanks to Neil's expert navigation and Stew's driving we pretty much went straight to the venue, parked up and unloaded our gear, then while Stew an Neil went of to park the van, Mike, Si, Phil and me headed off to All Ages Records. They managed to park the van in the road the record shop was in and joined us in the shop. After a few purchases we wandered back and met Dave, Dan and Colin outside the venue. I hadn't been so careful about my t-shirt choice today, and hadn't even thought about it as I'd put on a When Saturday Comes shirt. Still Colin looked at it and said "What you boycotting today? Soccer? Oh that's ok!"
I'm not sure where the PiB boys went, but Mike and Neil went for a drink, Stew and Phil went for food so Si and me went for a walk after stopping to get a tea.

Si: We walked up to All Ages Records and got a few things. A couple of the guys decided to have a sit in the pub but not fancying that Tony and I had a walk along Camden High Street after getting a cuppa. It started raining so we sheltered under the bridge, had a bite to eat and drank our very weak tea, bloody Southerners, and turned down several offers of "skunk". Skunk, in the rain, is that some kind of sick joke? We were well impressed with the free grub the venue put on and we sat with Colin and ate and chatted. Though when I got back downstairs I found Tony a tad non-plussed at the time I'd taken while he was stuck doing merch, for us and PIB, got one of his looks, ouch!

I missed out on food at the venue as I was minding the stalls. Seemed there was some nice stuff laid out for us, including chips, but I didn't get any.

Some friends turned up to this gig, including Mike Head, who I hadn't seen for some years. It was good to see him.

The first two bands kind of passed me by, no reflection on them, I was once again manning the merch. But soon it was time to set up and play. We had a good time, Phil stayed on the stage for once, but he couldn't resist jumping down in the crowd a little, and with Paul, Mat, Neil and Stew there the Intent Posi-Pit crew was in full effect. Near the end of our set I noticed Dave and Colin stood near me at the side of the stage. Dave then moved one of my cymbal stands out of reach, and as we went into the last song, that stand disappeared, then Dave started to remove more of my kit until I was left with a bass drum, snare and high-hat and played the final drum roll with a t-shirt over my head. I hadn't noticed that Colin was stood behind me, it was his t-shirt, and he was still wearing it. Dave said later that it our last song had been longer I'd have been left with just a snare.

Si: I decided to do a bit of photography tonight, it being the last one and all. Pilger were really great I thought, Phil stayed up on the stage a lot more than usual and I realised what a really great front man he is. Toward the end of the set Dave Wagenshutz decided it would be fun to slowly start removing Tony's drum kit as he played, and he was right, most amusing it was! Poor Tony, he finished with half a kit and his head stuck inside Colin's T-shirt, but still they rocked! And then Paint It Black hit the stage once more, and with the help of a very enthusiastic crowd they once again totally blew me away, what a fucking band! I took up a position side stage, right next to the band and used up a load of film and just totally loving being there, we all got thanked by PIB and I realised this had truly been one of the greatest times of my life.

Paint It Black were, once again, brilliant and at the end of their set, during 'Memorial Day' I felt compelled to run on stage and sing the last bit with them, Stew joined me. I punched the air and lost myself in the music, it felt like a great way to end a wonderful week. I did contemplate a stage dive at the end, but then thought better of it.

As we had at all the gigs on this tour, as soon as PiB had finished Si and me ran to the merch stall and tried to help Dave who was getting swamped with kids wanting shirts, but we were also struggling to keep up with people wanting Pilger stuff. It got hectic, but it was cool that people wanted our stuff, and also it meant that we missed the loading of the van, which was a bit of a bonus.

With most of the gear loaded we headed to the back stage area for the traditional tour photos. Both bands and crew huddled together with Colin dressed only in his underpants which he'd pulled up to make a very fetching (I think that's the word) thong. Kafren from Household Name Records kindly offered to take the pictures with various people's cameras. Then we said our goodbyes, and it was sad to think that one of the best weeks I've ever had was at an end. Kev went off to sort out the money with Dave W, and the rest of us let PiB have their showers and went out to the van. I finally got some chips. Then we drove home via Basingstoke to drop Neil off. After taking Stew, Mike and Phil home, Kev and Si came back to my house and we drank tea and talked about the week. It was nice to be home, but the adrenaline was still running and I just wanted to talk to everyone about it.

The next morning we got up early and took the van back to the hire place and dropped Kev at the station while Si and me went home via the SD PO Box. Not long after we'd arrived home Sarah was leaving to take Becca to dancing, and as she was passing the station on the way Si went with them. Then, for the first time in over a week I was on my own, and it was quiet. I found myself just walking around the house with a huge grin on my face while playing "Paradise" over and over.

Dave Wagenschutz
"Where to start! That PIB tour was weird due to the fact the we played all different kinds/sizes of venues. It felt like we were "at home" in the smaller DIY spaces and yet played some larger (semi-empty) spaces. Looking back it felt like we were punching above our weight class. I was way too wrapped up in the business end of things. Put undue pressure on myself and the band to "be profesh" and not lose money. Kinda soiled the tour as a whole (looking back). I did have fun, my wife was along for the tour. Playing with you guys was great. Hanging with friends and playing music, there's nothing better. Didn't the Ferry Boat close shortly after we played Norwich??! I remember hopping the train to Liverpool. We played Manchester that day but I wanted to visit Anfield and the find the yellow submarine on the waterfront. I ended up with a sunburn (no one told me the statue had moved) and found coins equal to my entire train fare in between the seats!! The show at Underworld was awesome, love that venue!"

(Yes, the Ferry Boat in Norwich did close not too long after we played there - Tony)

Si's last paragraph in the zine was:
I never thought at the age of 41 I would get the chance to do this, I'm a lucky guy and I want to thank everyone involved from the bottom of my heart; Tony, Mike, Phil and Kev Pilger for letting me tag along, Neil and Stew for being great, fun guys, and Stew for doing all the driving; and the PIB guys, Dan, Colin Andy and Dave, and Darren Walters for being a very cool merch guy, and their driver T-Bone. The train ride home back to Boro was spent with a big smile on my face thinking about the last five days.

Stew Watt gave his thoughts on the tour:
"I remember lots of driving and singing. I remember Neil walking in on our host who was stark bollock naked in the bathroom in Manchester. I remember sleeping on the floor in the pub in Norwich. I remember the Billy Idol look alike with the "this isn't punk" hand written sign for PIB in Manchester. I remember playing football (me very badly) in a park in Hull. I also remember eating a really nice curry with Dan Y from PIB. I remember watching someone kicking off in a nightclub doorway when I was outside the underworld in London in the van after the show and it getting quite nasty. I remember the amazing banter in the van for the week."

The interview I'd done in Bristol with Dan Yemin was the second part to one I'd done before the tour started, via email after he sent me an advance copy of their new album, 'Paradise'. SD#46 also featured an interview with The Black Veins who we'd played with in Norwich, Si interviewed The Fire Still Burns, Mike did Abandon Ship, while Gaz did The Varukers and Dirty Love. There was also a chat with Fighting Shit from Iceland too. Gaz also did a report form the Wasted Festival and Mike wrote a good pice on self harming, and there was more about the vivisection going on in Wickham, and a brief bit on Blair and Bush's murderous obsession with Al-Qaeda. Finishing up what is one of my favourite issues was a write up of the trip Si and me took to the US to see reunion gigs by Lifetime and Kid Dynamite.

We flew into New York and went straight to the Knitting Factory to see None More Black play with Smoke Or Fire and Planes Mistaken For Stars (we'd missed Glass & Ashes). We were knackered, but NMB were great. We met up with Dave Wagenschutz (then playing drums in None More Black), and he took us back to his house in Philadelphia.

Despite being knackered I don't think either of us slept that well, and we spent the morning visiting a huge Health Food store then going back to Dave's to watch an English football match on TV. We did think we were going to Hellfest in New Jersey where Lifetime and PiB would be playing, but that had been cancelled. As that was meant to be Lifetime's reunion, a gig had been arranged in Philly's Starlight Ballroom where Lifetime would now be playing with Smoke Or Fire and 108, but not PiB, unfortunately. After getting to the venue, Si and me were treated to a meal at a totally vegan Chinese restaurant by Tim Owen and Darren Walters of Jade Tree records. Back at the venue, it was also cool to meet up with Andy Nelson and Dan Yemin again before joining Dave W back at the merch table. Dave was a bit pissed off that the security of the gig was being done by a gang who, apparently had no problems with stabbing or shooting people they didn't like. They were all huge guys wearing shirts with FSU New Jersey on them. Dave's point was that having them as the security validated their existence. Andy Nelson had put the gig on, but I'm not sure what the reasoning was for having them there. Needless to say Si and me stayed well away from them.

We were with Dave as he did the Lifetime stall, and he was getting swamped by kids wanting their shirts, it was unbelievable. They sold so many that I didn't get one. Si did, but then he is the bigger Lifetime fan out of the two of us, so it was fair. Smoke Or Fire were really good, but I wasn't all that fussed with 108. Lifetime were brilliant though, and it was good to see Dan Yemin playing guitar.

The next day, after a morning of looking round Philadelphia's South Street, our driver turned up to take us to a None More Black gig in Baltimore, it was Jason Shevchuk. Dave introduced us and Jason said "Hi, I'm Jason." Like we didn't know who the singer of Kid Dynamite was! We got into the van with Dave, Jason, Paul (NMB bass player) and a couple of their friends and headed off to the Ottobar. We played silly word games on the way, with the American's having trouble with our accents. I think they had more problems with the way Si spoke, and when he said "The Ruts" they couldn't understand at all and I had to translate. With people from New York in the van it felt like every conversation was an argument, even though it wasn't and they were all being very friendly, it was quite an odd feeling and I found it a little unnerving.

The line up was the same as it had been in New York, but this time we did get to see Glass & Ashes. Smoke Or Fire were great again, and None More Black were fantastic. There seemed to be a bit of tension onstage, which made their set even more intense. Dave would later say he thought that may be his last gig with NMB. When we finally got back to Dave's house it was pretty late, and as we got to his front door someone walked up the road with a dog and said hello. It was Jared Shavelson who would go on to replace Dave in both None More Black and Paint It Black.

We had a quieter morning the next day, which was good as that afternoon we were off to CBGBs to see Kid Dynamite. Dave's wife was coming to this gig, along with a couple of their friends, which made for a packed van. Si and me had to travel in the "loft" which got uncomfortable after a couple of hours. It was still a thrill to see the Statue Of Liberty as we drove past, and when we pulled up at a crossing in the Lower East Side, Roger Federer crossed in front of the van with his wife (the US Open was on at the time).

When we got to CBGBs the queue was right round the block, some of them had been there all night. It was hot, and Jason Shevchuk had been out and distributed some water. It did feel a bit weird arriving and walking past them all into the venue carrying some Kid Dynamite equipment.

It seemed unreal to be stood in CBGBs, and as they got ready to set up, Si and me took the opportunity to stand on the stage. I took a moment to think about all the bands who'd played on that stage over the years, and wondered how the hell I had ended up there? Next thing we knew we were watching Kid Dynamite soundcheck.

After all that, we had a little walk around the area surrounding CBGBs, just Si and me. Then when we got back we were able to walk past the queue again as we had our green CBGBs wrist bands.

We wouldn't be heading back to Philly with the others after the gig, so we had our bags with us, and were stashed with the Kid Dynamite gear. While waiting for the gig to start, we found ourselves sat in the CBGBs "dressing room" talking to Vinnie Value, the Kill Your Idols Drummer who was playing with Grey Area that night.

A couple of other bands opened up proceedings, Take My Chances and Voice In The Wire both sounded pretty good, then Grey Area, who had been persuaded to get back together for the gig, went on and were superb, so much better than their recorded stuff. They even did a cover of 'Young til I Die' with Ernie telling a story of him seeing 7 Seconds at CBGBs when he was 14.

Excitement was building, and it was soon time for Kid Dynamite. The crowd were packed in, but Si and me had a good spot at the side of the stage. Jason said "Thank you for being here, we're Kid Dynamite from Philadelphia, let's have some fun." They started the intro to 'Living Daylights' and the room exploded in a mass of bodies. They were stunningly good. Kid Dynamite meant a lot to me, and I'd listened to their songs hundreds of times, but I never thought I'd get to see them, let alone at CBGBs. I couldn't believe I was in that venue watching Kid Dynamite with one of my best friends. Fantastic.

After the gig, we said our goodbyes as we were staying in New York over night ready for our flight home the next day. We spilled out on to the pavement to see Tim Owen and Darren Walters outside, and they had a Lifetime t-shirt from me, what great guys. It was later and we weren't entirely sure how far away our hotel was, so we then got a yellow cab. It was dark, we were tired but amped up about the day we'd just had, so I didn't take much notice of our surroundings

The next morning I opened the curtains and there, right outside the window was the Chrysler Building. We walked miles that day, seeing the sights and buying records before getting a cab back to the airport.

Going through passport control, I got stopped by security as I'd set the metal detector off. A right shitty security guy shouted at me and took me to a room where another, slightly more friendly guy, put on rubber gloves before searching me. I was worried about what was going to happen, as I didn't like the look of those gloves, and there was a tense moment when I said I thought it was the 'poppers on my shorts" that set off the alarm. I didn't know that poppers meant something else in the US. Apparently I should have said "snaps"! I finally got out of the room unmolested to find Si laughing at me.

When we wrote about his trip in the zine, Si's last comment was "All this happened just out of punk rock and friendship. Unbelievable." And he was dead right.

I asked Dave Wagenschutz if he remembered us coming out for the Kid Dynamite gig:

"Heck yeh! That was so much fun. To finally play CBs (RIP ☹) and to have you fellas there. I can't believe you both flew over!!"

After all that, and the fact that Gaz was in the middle of moving house and working permanent night shifts, we still managed to put out another mini Xmas issue. SD#46.6 came with a free Intent CD called 'Make Your Own Luck', featuring what would turn out to be their final recordings. The zine features Intent's drummer, Paul's account of Neil fest, the gig mentioned earlier that they arranged as Neil's stag do. Intent played, along with Jets Vs Sharks, No Substance and Pilger. Kev was unable to make it, but Neil stood in on bass, after all he'd learnt our set for the PiB tour. He wore a ginger wig while playing too. It was a really fun night and Neil had good time. It was initially meant to be a free gig, but in the end they decided to charge a small entry fee and then donate the proceeds to the Youth Club in Totton, where Intent had played a few times with Pilger. They were able to hand over £300, which was great and just showed what a valuable part of the Southampton DIY scene Intent were. They loved the scene and they love being able to do a little bit to help the Youth Club, they even wrote a song about playing there, called 'Post Pit Crew', and at Neilfest I played drums on it so Paul could jump around at the front. I have very fond memories of watching Intent play. Neil would end up joining Pilger and we'd play together in both Screwed Up Flyer and The Shorts.

Along with all the fun stuff I'd done in 2005, Pilger had recorded an album. Chris from Peter Bower Records had seen us pay in Boston, and offered to put a 7" out, which turned out to be the 'These Times' 7", then he asked us to do an album. We recorded half of it earlier in the year, then we had the Paint It Black tour, and after that, Phil went off to the US, leaving Kev, Mike and me to sort the music for some more songs, which we did, then all went on family holidays. When all that was done, Phil came back just as I went off to the US with Si. Eventually we got back to the studio to finish the album. We sent it off to Chris and heard nothing. For quite awhile we were left wondering if he hadn't liked it, as he wasn't returning emails. We then had a gig in Bradford and Chris was there, it turned out that his email wasn't working and when he'd called me I was out. Thankfully he liked it and was going to put it out on vinyl and CD.
There were a couple of interviews in the Xmas issue too, Flamingo 50, from Liverpool, who I'd loved when Pilger played with them in Southampton, and old favourites of Gaz and mine, Violators.

We were back with SD#47 in June 2006, the Pilger album had come out on vinyl, and again it seems we'd had some good times to report. As the Subhumans were back playing again, we decided to ask Dick for an interview, of course he said yes, because he's good like that. Gaz and me have always loved both The Partisans and Subhumans, right from their earliest records, so it was good to be able to interview the Subhumans and print Gaz's review of the Partisans gig, a gig we both loved, so much so that I added a little bit of my own after Gaz's piece on the gig.
The zine cover is a reworking of the 'Demolition War' sleeve, the first Subhumans EP.

Si interviewed Smoke Or Fire and Latterman and also mentioned a trip him and his family had to our house when Middlesbrough were due to play Portsmouth. We went to the game and, because Dave Wagenschutz and his brother, James, were also staying with us we took them too. They were quite intimidated by the atmosphere in Fratton Park, despite it not being all that hostile. We got stuck trying to get out of Portsmouth and were late back, but we all went out for a meal afterwards. The following day we took the Americans to see a match at St Mary's, against Millwall. It was a far calmer atmosphere, despite a little tomfoolery from some Millwall fans in the ground. After the game the Briggs's went home and we took Dave and James to Stonehenge. The next day I drove James and Dave to London where they were spending a day sightseeing before flying back to the US. When he got home Dave messaged me to say that he had left Paint It Black, saying he didn't tell me while they were staying with us as he didn't want to ruin the trip.

Dave Wagenschutz:
"I'll always remember our trip to St Mary's (wonderful), Fratton Park (yikes) and Stonehenge (Spinal Tap!). Thanks for hosting us. I barely made my connecting flight in Toronto! Last time I saw Si (in person) was December 2018, My brother James & I were over for a bunch of matches and we hooked up in Manchester. A trip to the National Football Museum and a bite to eat. He's a bit of a traveler and I recall hanging with him in NYC a few times. You've been doing SD since '84?? That's crazy. I am proud to call you friend and am amazed by your dedication to the zine and the scene. Thanks for having me along on this ride!"

I also interviewed Casey Jones after getting back in contact with him via MySpace. We'd got on well when I interviewed him at the Ignite gig some years before, but after sending him a copy of the zine the interview was in I didn't hear from him again. However, I found him on MySpace and reached out, he remembered me and since that point we have been in contact ever since. He was kind enough to answer some questions about his punk rock life, taking in Justice League, No For An Answer, Ignite, The Killing Flame etc. Casey was also always very kind about Pilger, and has remained interested in my bands ever since. I'm glad we got back in touch as he's a valued friend.

Casey:
"I first met Tony at an interview when we played a show in England in the mid-90's. I don't know exactly when or where the show was or even remember doing the interview (sorry, brother) but I'm sure they both happened because the Suspect Device 20th anniversary issue write up on Issue #27 recaps both! It also states that he interviewed me on the same bus that he interviewed TITR in. I remember crossing paths with Texas on those tours and getting to play with them a few times...one of my favorite bands from that era. I'm sure the bus stank horribly both times you visited but I hope you've made a full recovery by now.
Here's what I do know though – Tony has become a dear friend as we started corresponding a decade or so later and have ever since. He has been a steady voice through some pretty tough times, and I am forever grateful. Not surprisingly, I have met most of my close friends through hardcore. For me, that's the best thing about this music that binds us all. The friendships. The

music gets us in the same room and then this scene of ours does the rest. I've always liked that pretty much every band is accessible. A friend and I also did a zine in 1984, also on a friend's parents' photocopier. We didn't have the tenacity that SD has and only got one issue to print, but we thought of the bands we wanted to interview and then just went up and asked them if they wanted to be in the zine at shows or through the mail. No one turned us down, including another 15 or so bands I interviewed in the year or two following for (the never released) Issue #2. I would guess that very few other genres are as tight knit and accessible."

The other interviews in this issue are Gaz's one with Drongos For Europe and Neil's with Propagandhi. There'a discussion piece on the old Southampton scene, instigated by our friend Ralf with input from Mike Fox, Paul Vary, Craig Burton, Rich Levene and me. Ralf did the intro about how it was important for the continuity of a DIY scene that the older generation are still involved and a history is not forgotten. Ralf being from the Netherlands and moving to Brighton was looking in from the outside and had been impressed with the amount of older people still active in Southampton. His introduction to this piece is really good. Even all these years later I'm still friends with these fine people and still see Rich and Craig regularly at gigs.

Ralf's intro:
"What better place to start on an introduction to an article on the 80s punk scene of a small south England town, than in a flat in Sarajevo? I'm in Bosnia at the moment and as I always do before I visit a new country, I've tried to unearth information about anything DIY punk over here. Sadly, I've failed to really find anything. What I've come across though are a number of articles and interviews, in which all seem to agree that whatever was happening before, however small, came to an abrupt standstill when the war happened. The punks left the country and did not return. With all links with the past severed, it being up to new generations to start from scratch, their predictions for an active DIY punk scene over here anytime soon, seem to be pretty pessimistic.
Now even though Southampton and war torn Sarajevo are two entirely different worlds, there's still a point to be made here. The conclusions these ex-Yugoslavian punks reached, namely the importance of the continuous involvement of older generations and knowledge about our own punk past, to ensure the survival of a healthy DIY community, are valid everywhere. Be it Sarajevo or little old Southampton. Educating ourselves to gain an understanding of the history of our own communities and culture, will help us keep moving forward, taking inspiration from past successes and learning from past mistakes. The great thing about punk is of course that that's actually a whole lot more fun, than I'm making it sound right now.
The way I see it, one of the main strengths of the Southampton scene is the ongoing involvement of many of the "older punks". Their being active, in quite a few cases since the early 80s, has helped to ensure that basic punk knowledge and ideas were not lost, where as this sadly has not been the case in many other parts of the world. It's my belief that the S.T.E. and OOMF gig collectives, Suspect Device and Passivity Is Compliance zines and bands like Older Than Dirt and Pilger have helped sustain links between the 80s, 90s and the current decennium. Whether they realize it or not, they've helped pass on

the D.I.Y. ideology and ways to do things to a number of new generations; inspiring many in the process.

By now it should be pretty clear I'm an enthusiast for the Southampton punk community. Ever since I moved from the Netherlands to Brighton, I've been inspired by the people of this small south England town. It's because of this I also take a special interest in its history, trying to understand how it became the great place it is today. Where knowledge about all things "D.I.Y." is all over the Southampton punk community, it being a living breathing example of what can be done in a small town when punks put their mind to it, knowledge about the actual scene of yesteryear, appears a lot less commonplace.

I somehow must have pointed this out to Rich, because when he came over to visit me in my new hometown of Amsterdam he, ever the missionary when it comes to great punk, brought with him a tape with four 80s Southampton area bands. Nox Mortis, Suicide Pact, Mad Thatchers and Corporate Grave. As that tape kick started a process which eventually lead to the article in Suspect Device you're about to read, I guess I don't need to mention I was blown away? I played little else for weeks, these four bands sounding as fresh and amazing today, as they must have done back then. After enquiring about them a bit more, it became clear these great and inspiring songs have probably never been heard by most of the current Southampton scene though. Especially with some of their band members, like Mike and PJ, still so involved, that's really something I feel can and needs to be corrected soon. I hope the following article will lead to the post-80s generations enquiring more about these fantastic local bands that came before them, thereby gaining an understanding of how their scene turned into what it is today. I also hope the 'older punks' step up to the plate and make sure to get these songs out to them. There's a reason Rich's tape is now with me in Sarajevo, playing on the stereo. I hope it'll be playing on many stereos in Southampton soon as well, for the exact same one: the fact these bands are amazing, inspiring and parts of our communal past that should not be forgotten."

What followed that intro were questions about the early Southampton DIY scene answered by Rich Levene, Craig Burton, Mike Fox and me. Most of what was said was covered by Rich earlier in this story. But some excerpts are below:

What sort of memories do you have from the early Southampton DIY punk scene?

Rich: Very fond memories mostly, although tinged with sadness when I think about friends like Steve, Simon & Tracy who didn't make it through until today. This was definitely one of the greatest times of my life. I also began travelling to gigs further afield in London and beyond around this time. I was in my late teens and the ideas and attitudes that punk rock had nurtured in me, were definitely cemented by exposure to the local bands and scene of that time. The local scene coalesced around that Suicide Pact gig at the Joiners and further ones in early 1985 at the Labour Club and Kingsland Hall, plus around the same time there were Act Of God gigs at the Queens pub in the City Centre and a May Day gig at the West Indian club which featured Pigs On Heat (who would evolve into The Mad Thatchers). Groups of people met at these gigs, as us Eastleigh punks (me, Steve, Bren) met all the Totton punks (Gaz, Rob

Callen, Rut and a sober, quiet Tony!); Mike Fox, the aforementioned Burt; Mark from Netley, plus of course the people in the bands.

Particular memories? Going with Nox Mortis / The Mad Thatchers / All The Glory to a gig on Shanklin Pier on the Isle Of Wight and all the chaos and shenanigans that followed. Nox Mortis playing a Xmas gig at the Labour Club in drag. Corporate Grave's impromptu first gig where they played a cover of The Stupids' 'So Much Fun', which went down so well, they played it again as they didn't have any other songs! Countless drunken laughs and scrapes... Above all, it's the wonderful people I met at this time.

Many of these friendships have endured 20+ years and for that I am truly grateful.

Craig: In the early days because gigs were so few and far between everybody turned up for every one and that's when friendships were forged that have lasted ever since, and the music became the soundtrack to my life.

How involved were you in that scene?

Craig: It didn't take too long before I thought I want to get to get more involved with this and I'm not sure whether a fanzine in Southampton had been produced before but I thought I can't play music so a magazine is something I could tackle. The early Beercans were a bit sloppy and lacked any professionalism but I enjoyed doing them and once again I met loads of people through the zine and even had a bash at putting a few gigs on with some of the bands I met through it to varying success.

Favourite bands from that era?

Rich: Early on the big two bands in Southampton were Suicide Pact (end of 1985 when Tracy left they became Nox Mortis) and The Mad Thatchers. I probably saw both these bands at least 30 times each and they made a huge impact on me both musically and politically. Nox Mortis in particular were important in that they taught me that it was possible to live a life based on solid ideals but also to have a sense of humour and come across as warm, friendly people. PJ was later a cohort of mine in the S.T.E. and I still count him as one of my best friends. Suicide Pact / Nox Mortis were tuneful, mid-paced anarcho punk, while the Thatchers combined political lyrics with a potent mix of Crass and 77 punk, plus some spacier effects. Of the bands that didn't record, Act Of God only really played a couple of times but were good fun. Eastleigh's All The Glory had some good tunes and later when my best friend Steve was in them I used to watch them practice and loved some of their songs. Later came Corporate Grave. Now I was the person who formed and named (from a Zounds lyric!) the band but I never had the patience to learn my bass and by the time they began gigging in 1987 I had left. Corporate Grave were the first self-consciously hardcore band in Southampton, with big influences from Minor Threat, Dag Nasty and The Stupids and it always gave me a buzz to see my mates Steve, Mike and Bren thrashing away. Later still came the wonderful Older Than Dirt in 1990 but I guess we're talking about the '80s here.

Mike: Suicide Pact, The Mad Thatchers and Nox Mortis. They were my favourite local bands, though there were a smattering of others that didn't have quite the same impact on me. All The Glory, Act Of God and UXDiver. I also have to say I liked Ad Nauseum from Pompey, only saw 'em twice.

At the end was a piece by Paul Vary, who'd been in Older Than Dirt, and has written a few things for us over the years. His piece is below:

Southampton DIY Scene by Pablo
My first DIY gig in Southampton was Culture Shock at the West Indian club in 1988 which by chance also happened to be the first ever STE gig! A group of us were going to get the train down from Winchester but after an early start in the South Western pub my mates couldn't be arsed, so after calling them a bunch of boring bastards etc I went on my own. I don't remember that much about the gig apart from between songs the singer Dick asked everyone to "make friends with the person standing next to them, as that's what it's all about" or words to that affect.
There was a great scene in Southampton in the late eighties and early nineties. There were loads of great bands a lot of whom I suppose you'd call indie punk. The names I remember are; Whose in the Kitchen, Flik Spatula, the Green Egg, First Men in Space, Malvinas Brothers, Pogrom, Corporate Grave and two bands I was in, Time to Kill and Older than Dirt.
There were some great 'illegal' gigs at that time as well. Two memorable open air ones were at Farley Mount in Winchester where I saw Corporate Grave for the first time and Lepe Beach on Southampton Water where my band Time to Kill played. I'll never forget that gig as it was on my 21 birthday!
Another totally DIY gig was at Shawford Village hall (between Winchester and Eastleigh) with Time to Kill (we changed our name to Psychic Slam for the gig) and the Mad Thatchers. We rented the hall, hired a PA, bought loads of booze and did our own bar and put up 100s of posters, which included train times! The turn out was incredible, about 150 people, which was especially amazing seeing as it was our first gig. Two of Mega City Four even came down for it. (Me, name drop?) I remember playing the intro to one of our songs when a very pissed Mike Fox got on stage and started shouting in my ear about train times back to Soton which made me fuck up the riff!
Back then Southampton had one of the best punk/hardcore scenes in the UK and loads of bands that played there said it was the best date of the tour! I saw so many amazing gigs that it's hard to pick out favourites though the two NOFX gigs at the Joiners were special (even if they were arseholes about the money), Leatherface was a great gig and from a personal point of view some of the early Older than Dirt gigs were excellent due to all the great people that came to see us, more than the racket we made! Happy days!
Now, I think people have got too lazy/comfortable and think advertising a gig means putting it on one or two websites so you get the same group of friends turning up rather than putting up posters all over town and putting an ad in the local paper etc. Still, at least a fair few of us from those days are still involved in the scene even if it's only a case of going to the gigs!

Paul now lives in Mallorca, but we're still friends and he is still active, his band Bomba X recently released an album which SD helped release.

My column in SD#47 recounts the time Sarah accidentally dropped a cup of boiling water in my lap while we were out in town, and the pain, blisters and pus that followed.
Again, so many reviews took up several pages at the end of the zine, but the look of it all kind of set the template for all the issues to come.

Gaz:
Issue #46 – Ah! It's September 2005 and Paint It Black, Abandon Ship, Dirty Love, The Black Veins, The Varukers, The Fire Still Burns and Fighting Shit have graced the pages. In other news, Tony and Si Briggs had made it to the legendary CBGB's in New York where they witnessed Kid Dynamite blow the place apart. Sadly the place is no more, but what a place to say you've been to for a gig as it's etched in Punk legend.

Issue #46.6 – Another year and another Christmas (2005). The Violators were asked some great questions by Tony - Flamingo 50 and local band Intent provided great support.

Issue #47 – For one reason or another this June 2006 issue is probably one of my favourite issues and probably our biggest seller to date. It also signalled a much needed return to A4 as we were getting fairly good at this Fanzine lark even if I do say so myself. We put the famous Subhumans skull on the cover as they were in it and an impressive array of bands were packed in around them. Propagandhi, Smoke Or Fire, Drongos For Europe, Latterman and Casey Jones for the record. We went mad and printed about 400, the printers made a slight error with one of the pages and we got another 400 for free with error corrected. That was more than we were ever likely to sell, so I took the misprints to Rebellion or whatever it was called back then and gave hundreds away for free! The Punks gathered in Blackpool lapped them up and I was really proud to see so many enjoying a pint and reading SD.

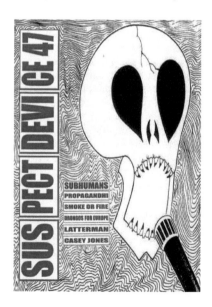

Pilger on the UK tour with Paint It Black

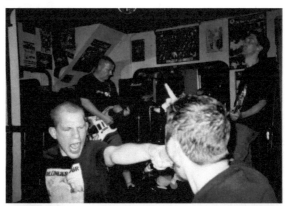

(Right & Below) Pilger at The
Junction, Bristol
Neil Clelland joining in.
(Photos by Si Briggs)

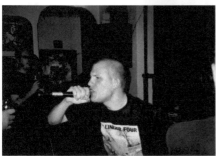

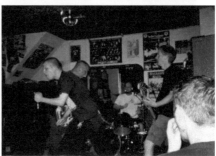

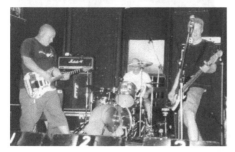

(Right) Pilger at The Star & Garter, Manchester.
(Photo by Si Briggs)

(Left) Pilger at The Underworld, London.
(Photo by Si Briggs)

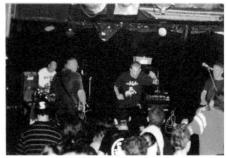

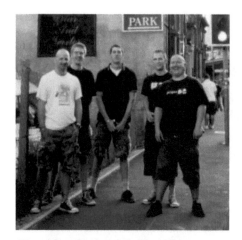

(Above) Dan Yemin briefly joins Pilger,
Star & Garter, Manchester.
(Photo Si Briggs)

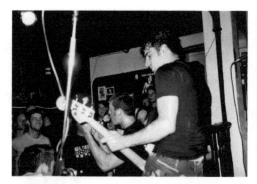

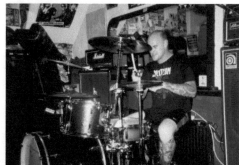

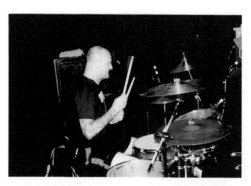

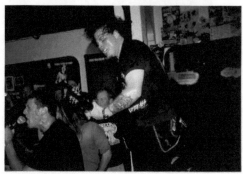

(Above) Paint It Black at The Junction in Bristol.

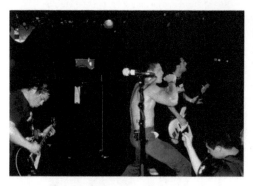

(Above) Paint It Black, Underworld, London
(Right) Paint It Black, Pilger and crew after the
last gig of the tour at the Underworld (photo by
Kafren (Household Name Records)).

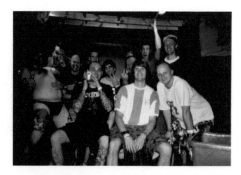

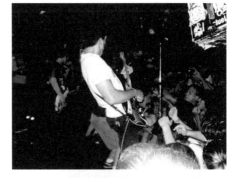
Kid Dynamite at CBGBs

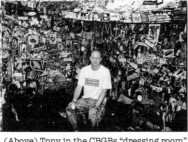
Si Briggs, the morning after

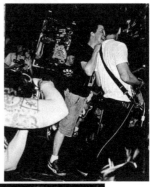

(Above) Tony in the CBGBs "dressing room"
(Photo by Si Briggs)
(Below) The infamous toilets

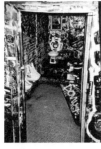

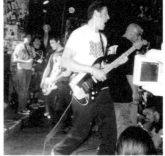

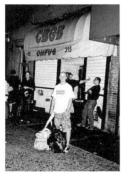

(Left) But after the gig...
Tony outside CBGBs
(Photo by Si Briggs)

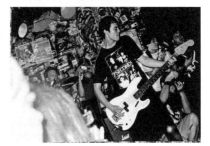

Tony Suspect - Begging For A Silver Lining

After all that positivity, by early 2007 things were not going so well. Pilger's album had come out on CD, which also included all the tracks from the two EPs we had put out. The CD sleeve opened out to have all the lyrics, but there were no credits or band info included, so we made our own, we took the info sheet that came with the LP, made it CD size and inserted them in each CD we had. However, in SD#48 Mike mentions that the band was no more. As it tuned out, our last gig was as a five piece, with Neil Clelland on second guitar, supporting the Exploited at a nightclub in Southampton, an odd venue for us, not really the DIY gig we would normally play and for the life of me I cannot remember why we ended up playing it. I don't think we knew at the time that it would be our last gig, but that's how it happened.

I wasn't happy when Phil, and then Kev decided to leave Pilger, but with hindsight it was probably for the best. Pilger had been fun, we had written some good songs, released a couple 7"EPs, and two albums (I'm counting 'Silence' as an album), had tracks on several compilations, and played some great gigs up and down the country, with some great bands. But all things come to an end and I think it was probably the right time to call it a day.

When Phil decided to leave we initially considered carrying on as Pilger with Mike singing, and Neil playing guitar, Phil's vocals and delivery style were unique and it would have sounded very different with Mike singing those songs, so Mike, Kev, Neil and me, with Paul from Intent, carried on practising with the idea of writing a completely new set under a different name. We initially called ourselves The Blast Shadows, which was a lyric from the Strike Anywhere song 'Sedition', the first track on their 'Dead FM" album that had just come out, but when Kev also decided to leave quite soon after Phil, Paul moved to bass and we became Screwed Up Flyer. Mike turned up to practise one day and in his guitar case was a gig flyer that one of his children had screwed up, it seemed a better name than The Blast Shadows.

The initial line up of Screwed Up Flyer was Mike Fox, vocals, Neil Clelland, guitar, Paul Samain, bass and me, drums (We were eventually joined by a second guitarist, Simon Lewis, who had been in Business Of Death and is now a BBC Wildlife cameraman). We did a few gigs, including playing with Paint It Black in Newport South Wales, Deny Everything in Richmond, TV Smith in Southampton and at Ralffest in Brighton with Seein' Red, Geriatric Unit, Whole In The Head, Constant State Of Terror and Fix Me. We recorded two demos and also had a track on the 'Good Times' 7" compilation that Town Clock Records put out. When the band eventually fizzled out, I did think, for a while that it would be the end of me playing in bands.

My column in SD#48 saw me feeling pretty down about going to gigs (or more precisely some of the people who were going to gigs then) despite recalling how much I enjoyed Strike Anywhere when I went to see them in Leeds and London with Si. Gaz, though, had the worst time of all at this point as his wife had died suddenly, which explains why he didn't do much for this issue. The front cover is a cool picture of The Varukers he took though.

Despite all that negativity, there is some good stuff in this issue. We talked to Jallu about Phoenix Foundation and Kieltolaki, Affirmative Action Jackson (the band that featured Andy and Josh from Paint It Black), The Steal, Hank Jones plus Portsmouth band You Me & The Atom Bomb and ex Sleep bass player Danny Leigh, now an author and film critic. Plus, after our Southampton scene feature in the last issue, we did one

on the early Dorset DIY Scene with pieces by Andy Nazer (Self Abuse, Zimmer Frames, C-30s) and Paul Chambers (Atrox, Hate That Smile, Damaged zine). Although Gaz and me never made it down to too many of the DIY gigs put on in Bournemouth and surrounding areas, a lot of those that would be instrumental in the local Southampton DIY scene getting started did travel down there and friendships were made that have endured to this day. We will reprint both pieces in the following pages.
Of course SD#48 also had hundreds of reviews.

Gaz:
Issue #48 – This was another great issue and the picture of Rat from the Varukers on the cover was one of my finest photographic moments. It was taken from behind the band at Rebellion and a decent member of the stage crew let me backstage to take it. Sadly, this was my only real contribution to this issue as in between the last issue and this one I'd lost my wife Helen very suddenly to a Brain Haemorrhage and was in the midst of adapting to life as a single parent. Although this was a time of great loss it was also when I found out who my friends were. All I'll say is that I didn't realise I had so many, and outside of close family, the Punk community gave me fantastic support for which I'll be forever grateful. This February 2007 issue had The Pheonix Foundation, Kieltolaki, You Me & The Atom Bomb, Affirmative Action Jackson, The Steal, Hank Jones and a guy called Danny Leigh who used to play in a great band from Brighton called Sleep.

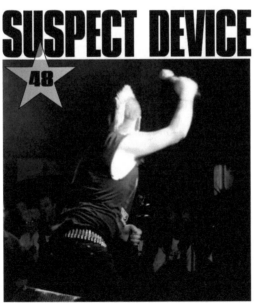

SUSPECT DEVICE
48

The Phoenix Foundation / Kieltolaki
You Me & The Atom Bomb
Affirmative Action Jackson
The Steal / Hank Jones
Danny Leigh
The Early Dorset DIY Punk Scene

State Of Mind - The Dorset DIY Scene (from SD#48, 2007)

Early Dorset Punk Scene by Paul Chambers

I'm not going to go through all the stuff I wasn't around to witness myself. Hopefully there will be others who can do this. I will be mainly discussing the Weymouth and Bournemouth scene circa '82-'85.

It has to be said that both towns are known for being seaside places where pensioners come to die, Bournemouth especially. Both towns were (and still are) very conservative and the fact that a scene existed there at all is a miracle.

The epicentre (!) of the Weymouth scene was the local 2nd hand record shop. Handsome Dicks was off the beaten track in a residential area and stocked loads of old punk stuff, all of the pay no more releases and old comics. There was however a Weymouth Anarchy Centre that I never visited. How long this ran for and what form it took I don't know, however, I do know it wasn't someone's bedroom! My 1st gig was at the Rock Hotel in late '81 I was fourteen, the line up was The Mob and Dirt with Weymouth band Dead Popstars, who were named after the 1st Altered Images 7". The Dead Popstars were the main local band that released the "Hopeless In Hotels" tape. It came in a bag with an 'I'm a Dickhead' badge, a toy soldier, an Opal Fruit and a lyric sheet. My favourite track of theirs was "Manufactured Stars"; they also had a good track called "Stinky" that was later covered by Weymouth band, Admass. The Popstars were a pretty basic punk band with a slight Anarcho feel and good live. In '83 they left for London to find fame and fortune. After this gig I must have missed a few classics in Weymouth, with the Mob, Null & Void, Red Factory and many with the Dead Popstars, Manic, Admass etc. Communication was virtually zero, with only the Sounds gig guide to tell me what was going on. I was born in Weymouth but lived in Wareham, slap bang in between Weymouth and Bournemouth. I didn't know anyone else who had any idea that these bands existed.

All of the big bands that played Dorset ended up playing at the dreadful Poole Arts Centre. It has the worst acoustics known to man. This was because the floor was hollow and pivots over with the seats bolted underneath. I saw the Ramones there in '87 and it took me over a minute of each song to realise what they were playing. My second gig was at this very establishment – what should have been Blitz and Channel 3 became the Defects, the Meteors and The AntiNowhere League in June '82. This gig was the main reason I became disinterested in, shall we say the 'Burning Britain' punk stuff. In hindsight, this was unfair but I could only go from my own experience. The Meteors set was just a big fight with bare chested young men strutting their stuff and the atmosphere throughout was dismal. This was the only '82 type gig to happen in the area.

The third gig was Stiff Little Fingers, again at the Arts Centre in around September '82. This is where I first met members of Self Abuse after the gig. This gig again had little in the way of atmosphere and seemed redundant, there were people spitting at SLF for most of their set!

The Mob at St John's Ambulance Hall in, I think, November '82 was in my opinion pivotal in the local scene. There was a huge crowd and a real buzz going round. The Dead Popstars tape was being sold and a zine that I can't remember the name of now. The support that night was, I think, The Peaceheads and The Dead Popstars. The main talking point at this gig was the upcoming Dead Kennedys date in Southampton. I had to outbid a friend of mine for a ticket being sold – final price £7!! Worth every penny as it turned out, for MDC alone!

1983 was the most prolific time for punk in Dorset. The 1st major gig was what should have been Flux and Chaos UK became The Subhumans and Cult Maniax. This was an awe some gig and very eventful. Support bands Manic and Admass both from Weymouth were excellent, all of the Dorchester and Weymouth bands seemed to be Anarcho, it was hard to believe at the time. I remember taking a piss during the gig and this guy in a black cape with skull broaches stood next to me, looked down and said 'Alright mate' in an outrageous Devon accent. Huge he was, tall as well!! It was Big Al, singer of the Cult Maniax!! The Maniax stopped their set due to a bunch of Weymouth skinheads attacking people indiscriminately. The Maniax jumped off the stage, gave the skinheads a kicking and carried on playing as if nothing had happened. An interview with the Maniax later that year questioned the band on what happened that night. The answer was 'Nobody fucks with the Maniax'. Quite! Andy Anderson my later cohort on Damaged zine got his head kicked in by his brother John while Andy was doing backing vocals for the Subhumans. Bruce had lost his voice that night, so Andy had stepped in. During "Zyklon B Movie" it was, pulled him right off the stage he did, fucking mad. I can't recall what they fell out about but they were always arguing. Somebody stole a skeleton from one of the back rooms and a police dog van turned up for the remainder of the gig. Suffice to say this was the last punk gig held at this venue. Devon zine Never Surrender (issue 3) was sold at this gig, I don't have it anymore but it was a great issue and had an advert for the classic "Raw War" International Punk Tape on Xcentric Noise. Never Surrender editor was a guy called Higgs who was also a roadie for the Maniax.

The 1st Dorchester gig I saw was Butcher, from Bournemouth Shock To The System and Screaming Disorder, both from Dorchester in April at the Boy's Brigade Hall. Screaming Disorder had Paul Simmons on guitar who later joined STTS/Atrox. Shock To The System were my favourite local band from that gig onwards. They sounded Anarcho played Subhumans covers and were all around my age and after talking to them it turned out that they were doing a fanzine as well. This gig another last for a venue due to a nutter from Poole smashing the toilets. This was the catalyst for the STTS track "Banned Again". This was also the 1st of many gigs that I recorded of the local scene. The Boy's Brigade was later used as a practice place for Atrox. Chainsaw zine was sold at this gig. It came with a free Butcher and Riot Squad flexi disc. Around this time Damaged zine was really taking shape. John Anderson and I had been planning for over a year while at school. We were inspired after getting Rising Free zine free with the Insane's "El Salvador" 7" in '82. I sent off for several zines and demos advertised in Rising Free including IQ32 #1 and the Anthrax demo. Unfortunately John's parents had decided to move to Germany and as John was under sixteen had to go with them. This left John's older brother Andy, who was nineteen to look after the house. He also took over John's place as Damaged coeditor. While at school in May '83 a girl in my class was going out with a member of a certain Bournemouth band. One day in class she was passing around one of those yellow things you get in kinder Eggs and was getting people to open it to see what the 'liquid' was inside. I'll leave the contents to your imagination.

She also had copies of a Bournemouth punk zine. Hydrophobia was the 1st and only Bournemouth zine from this era. The last page had a map of how to get to the Subhumans gig that was happening on 11.6.83. It also had interviews with Bournemouth bands that we had never heard of – The Demented, Mad Are Sane and the Parasites, as well as Butcher and Self Abuse. Another classmate having nearly joined Self Abuse as singer got me a copy of their recently released "Teenage" demo.

The Self Abuse demo was amazing and still is excellent and well worth getting hold of. I played it recently and the lesser known tracks like "Derelict" and "You're So Cold" still stand out as unknown classics as they were dropped from their live set early on. During this period I was spending all of my spare school time typing up Damaged #1. Me and two other punks had taken typing & office practice as options and we were the only three boys in the class. I was stopped from doing Home Economics as well, as apparently that would be "too many girls' subjects!"

The day before the Subhumans gig was the infamous Weymouth Beach Party on Friday 10.6.83. There were other Beach Parties before this but this was the 1st I attended and I think it was the last. The line up was Omega Tribe, Cult Maniax, Manic, STTS and The Peaceheads. Omega tribe were openers and were truly excellent, much better than on record. The Peaceheads were next who played covers by The Mob, Null & Void, The Stooges etc. The last band were STTS who were, as usual, excellent. Unfortunately their set was stopped short by the Police after some complete idiot was dancing in the middle of the road and was caught in between a lorry and a bus!! Damaged interviewed The Cult Maniax at this gig.

The day after was the release date of the Subhumans "Evolution" EP and their 1st Bournemouth gig. They opened with "Evolution" and played "Joe Public" for the 1st time. I recorded this gig and it was released officially and sold via Sounds classifieds. The Subhumans were supported by Bournemouth bands Self Abuse and The Parasites. This was the 1st time Andy and I saw Self Abuse and we were blown away by how good they were. The Parasites who organised the gig played 1st and played very fast punk, covering "I Don't Give A Fuck" by the Partisans and ending their set with ANWL's "Woman" with Mark of Hydrophobia zine on vocals. Loads of people met for the 1st time at this gig and saw the turning point in Bournemouth taking over from Weymouth as the place to play.

26.6.83 was the date of the 1st gig at the excellent Capone's nightclub in Bournemouth. Access to the club was via a lift to the top floor. The club was large and plush with round tables with tablecloths! Now here my memory lets me down a bit as I believe there were several gigs at this venue in a very short space of time with the same bands on the bill. The 1st though was amazing – Butcher, Self Abuse, Confession Of Sin, Shock To The System and Admass. Butcher were the biggest band in Bournemouth at the time and already had their "On The Ground" 7" out for quite awhile. At this gig though, the crowd seemed bored of them and they didn't really seem a part of what was going on. After these Capone's dates they seemed to disappear for a while. The support bands got a far better response. The STTS set that night was used on their "Last Breathe (sic) For Humanity" demo. Confession Of Sin were from Parkstone in between Poole and Bournemouth. They played Stooges/ Velvets stuff and released an excellent demo that came in a cardboard sleeve. Their singer Tony was a great front man and came across as being very professional and probably the best in the scene for spectacle. Later COS gigs saw the band cover "Loose" by the Stooges which was just awe inspiring, a bit like that Hendrix gig that was never recorded where everyone cried. My favourite band of that evening was Admass. I had been in touch with Admass bass/vocalist Andy Rendall for a few months after phoning him up after buying the "Raw War" comp tape. Their track on "Raw War" was their most infamous – "The Garry Bushell Song". It was taken from their only demo that was recorded in a bedroom in '82. Andy was the only other person I knew at the time who had the Meat Puppets "In A Car" EP and a taste for US Hardcore and Rudimentary Peni. They only played two songs that night – "Garry Bushel" and "Mayor Of Weymouth Part 2". Nobody had really heard Admass in Bournemouth and they blew the place apart. Their sound was heavy, noisy and fast with Andy screaming in a Nick Blinko/Chris Kirkwood fashion.

The 1st Capones gig was also the release date of Damaged #1. My Dad had a mate who worked in an estate agents and he had agreed to let me use their photocopier. All was well until he found me copying a hundred copies of each page and he went totally feral and chucked me out. Obviously my Dad hadn't told him the whole story!! We couldn't find anywhere to get the zine printed so my Dad, thinking I was becoming a budding Richard Branson bought me an old photo copier for £50 that only printed one sided. It served its purpose though and I spent many hours printing up 50 copies all of which sold that night at Capone's. Andy printed other copies as he had got a job that gave him access to a photocopier, total printed was 175.

Damaged #1's cover was lifted from the Pistols "Something Else" 7". I fought long and hard not to have a picture of Sid Vicious on the cover but Andy was bigger than me so that was that. Although Andy and I had common ground musically – Subhumans, Cult Maniax etc we didn't agree on many things. I was into Anarcho and US Hardcore and he was into some Goth and Oi stuff as well and this gave Damaged quite a wide appeal and a fair bit of controversy. The cover quote was 'For Punks, Skins & Other Wise People!' and had interviews with Anthrax, AHeads, Riot/Clone, The System, Destructors, Uproar, Red Alert and Patrol.

Shortly after this Mentally Unstable #1 came out. Coedited by Alex Vann of STTS and STTS friend and 'Manager' Andy Thorne. As well as interviews with AntSystem, Disrupters, Attack and Instant Agony there were several local bands included: Admass, STTS, Genetic Malfunction, Manic and The Disciples Of The Elder. This was the 1st zine to include bands from Dorchester and Weymouth.

By this time Andy Anderson was upping the anti when it came to doing interviews. We were already good friends with Self Abuse and were spending most Saturdays dossing around Bournemouth in record shops and cafes. Bournemouth had 2 central record shops – Subway and Uptown both stocked punk stuff and were excellent. Both are closed now but the two 2nd hand shops: Snupeas and Bustop still remain today. Andy had arranged for us to interview the Subhumans and the AHeads in Warminster and we spent the weekend there to watch both bands practice and hang out. It was a great experience and everyone was very warm and friendly, I got to read Dick's lyric book too! Our second jaunt was the 100 Club to interview Charlie Harper just before his 40th Birthday. He was a great bloke and spent over a couple of hours talking to us. Our 3rd outing however was a real eye opener! A weekend in Bristol was arranged to stay with Disorder at their squat. We were to interview them and any other bands around at the time. On arrival we were greeted by a friend from Weymouth. I can't mention names but our friend was holding a glue bag and was totally out of it. He died soon after this but I am unsure of the cause. When we got in the squat we were told that the music was upstairs (Disorder practicing) and the drugs were downstairs! I was only 15 and had never been around drugs before and was frankly a bit scared. The squat had, for the umpteenth time been burgled a few days prior and the feeling of impending doom was in the air. That Saturday was the printing day of 'Be Glad Be Bad' #3, by far my favourite fanzine to this day. It was coedited by Disorder but mainly written by Tim who did Children Of The Revolution Records who also lived in Disorder's squat. We went down the printers got the pages, went back to the squat, stapled them all up and then went out to sell them. Disorder selling zines was a real insight, they just stopped anyone in the street, including pensioners, really fucking mad. This was not as mad as trying to interview the Amebix though. We arrived at their squat to find two of them in a room lying on a mattress. We knew things were amiss after the first question: 'What have you been up to recently?' Answer: much giggling. 'Do you like being in Bristol'? Answer: much more giggling. Obviously totally out of it, we left bemused. Of all the bands I've ever met, Disorder were the only one who I thought really lived what they preached. They were totally independent and very sorted despite their intake of whatever they were into. That weekend was fucking mental. On the way back we went through Warminster and we saw Mel Bell of the AHeads in a chip shop. Seconds later our coach broke down so we ran back to the chip chop, met Mel and went to have a coffee at fellow AHead Jock's flat. Then it was back to the coach that was just about to leave and back home in time for tea. I'm not making any of this up!

Damaged #2 came out in July '83 with a cover drawing by Mark of the Mad Are Sane. The cover headline was: 'Cheaper & Better Than Sounds!' Bands interviewed were the Subhumans, AHeads, Mob, Omega Tribe, Peter & The Test Tube Babies, Resistance '77 and Attak. By this time I had found a printer in Wareham hidden in a small industrial estate that printed the local parish news. I agreed to do day release to keep the costs down. During this time Hydrophobia #2 was also printed there. This was the last issue and included Admass, STTS, Mad Are Sane, Idiom Tribe, Confession Of Sin and Amebix (the latter had been done by post, which would appear to be the best way to interview them!).

26.8.83 was the date of the notorious Wareham gig. I managed to cajole the local vicar into renting me the Parish Hall, which was situated on the picturesque Wareham Quay. I had acquired a huge list of telephone numbers of bands and started making calls. 1st choice was the Subhumans but they already had a gig that day, Flux Of Pink Indians were a bit too expensive and Conflict seemed a bit dodgy through no fault of their own but the local skins were guaranteed to make an appearance. As I had previously made contact with Anthrax through Damaged I called them and they said they would bring their PA and the Naked along too. A call to Mel of the AHeads arranged the last main band for the night. The task of choosing local bands was a bit of a nightmare as everybody wanted to play. I was adamant to make it an all Anarcho affair so this trimmed things down a bit. The local band line up became STTS, Admass, Mad Are Sane (their 1st Gig) Manic and Genetic Malfunction (their 1st and only gig?). My Dad had offered to do the door for me (still believing me to be a budding Branson) and everything was sorted. A tip off on the day enlightened us to a plan by the Weymouth Skins to come to the gig to fuck things up, so my Dad unknown to me told the police. This turned out to be unnecessary as the skins had hired a van and on the way flipped it causing a fair few injuries, problem solved.

The gig was due to start at 6pm, by 2pm there were over 50 punks already enjoying themselves on the sunny Wareham Quay much to the annoyance of many a local. This event was already becoming a huge culture shock to what was usually a very quite, small country tourist town. By 4pm there were over a hundred punks in attendance and the bands had all turned up. With 8 bands to play in 5 hours, things were hectic. I just told them all that there was no agenda and to sort out who was playing when for themselves. During the gig there were accusations of punks stealing from shops and a few local casuals came in to throw glasses around. A police presence was inevitable and over 20 had turned up to try to stop the gig but with over 150 punks acting peacefully they just decided to stand around and watch. By this time the vicar had sussed that he'd been conned after a neighbour of the Parish Hall had called to complain about the noise. It turned out that the neighbour was a 'Big In The City' solicitor on holiday and was going to get me sued by the Performing Rights Society.

I was also nearly arrested for putting rubbish in a litter bin! The Police finally stopped the gig at 11pm during the AHeads set. Jock of the AHeads shouted 'Fuck The Pigs' but fortunately everybody left the hall without further incident. However, two Bournemouth punks had been arrested for cannabis possession and the area was cleared systematically. This gig is still talked about by locals to this day and gave me notoriety for the next ten years I lived there.

Mentally Unstable #2 had by this time had come out. Bands interviewed were Screaming Dead, Blitzkrieg, Protest and Cult Maniax but also local bands, Self Abuse and Butcher.

In July '83 STTS had lost their bass player 'Wimp' and had played 2 Capone's gigs without a bass. The 2nd one on 24.9.83 had Andy Nazer of Self Abuse standing in to play STTS's longest track "Last Flight Of The Phoenix". At the end of this gig Andy Anderson, in his usual flamboyant manner was shouting that he knew someone who could play bass for STTS and was pointing at me. I was terrified, I could only play "I Hear You Laughing" by the Mob and "Warhead" by the Subs, both badly! STTS guitarist Paul sat me down, showed me how to play "Total Blackout" I played it back ok and I was in! I couldn't believe it; I had joined my favourite local band!

Another Bournemouth gig in September in a small suburb was probably the smallest turn out. Usually all gigs had around 100-200 in attendance. This gig had only around 50 and the bands were Manic (their last gig) Admass (their last gig before changing name to Madmass), Fallout (ex Six Minute War) whose bass player had a picture of Jimmy Saville stuck to his forehead and the Amebix. Manic had played a few gigs in Weymouth and Yeovil and had been banned from many venues. They sounded like the Mob and could have been a really excellent band had they practiced more but alas split up shortly after.

21.10.83 was the date of my 1st gig playing for STTS. I had been to Dorchester to meet the band properly a couple of week's prior and we had no time to sort out a practice. Paul had written down which frets to play for each song. I had to practice to live tapes on my own.

After joining STTS I had far less time to do Damaged and also stopped doing Harmonious Dischord Tapes. HDT started as a live and demo tape label in early '83. I had advertised in Sounds and put fliers in record shops. I sold tapes of the last Pistols gig and other rarities, Banshees and Slaughter & The Dogs demos and loads of Anarcho Tapes including Conflict, Subhumans, Rudimentary Peni, Mob etc. As I said previously I had been recording all of the local gigs and sold/traded those as well. Apart from these a few proper tapes were released:

HDT #1 – Admass 3 Dates In '83
HDT #2 – Subhumans Live B'th 11.6.83
HDT #3 – Shock To The System Live & Demo
HDT #4 – Omega Tribe Live Weymouth Beach 10.6.83 HDT #5 – Anthrax Live & Demo
HDT #6 – Sod The Quality Hear The Content Compilation

Damaged #3 was released in September '83 and was to be my last issue. Andy and I were already at odds as to which bands were ok to have in the zine. I was far more pretentious and just wanted mainly Anarcho bands and the inclusion of the Macc Lads was a bridge too far; 'We're The Lads From Macc And We Want Some Crack!'. This was before Crack was a drug you understand, I was not happy. The Macc Lads cover of 'Hey, Hey We're The Monkeys' proved worse: 'Hey, Hey We're The Macc Lads And We're Not Fucking Queer, We Like Chips & Gravy...'Damaged #3 included The Screaming Dead, UK Subs, the Apostles, Lost Cherrees, Cult Maniax, Naked, Instigators, Icon AD and local bands Self Abuse, Manic, Mad Are Sane and Admass.

Late '83 was a quite time and there were no local gigs. A lot of us however did travel to the 100 Club for the Subhumans Xmas Party. Also on that night were the AHeads, Naked, Organised Chaos and the Instigators.

Early '84 saw the release of Mentally Unstable #3 now coedited by Charlie Mason, who had also become vocalist for Atrox, the renamed STTS. This was the last issue. I don't have a copy anymore but anyone read it couldn't forget Charlie's tirade against Simon Edwards Riot City records. Somehow the idea had gone around that Riot City had connections with EMI who at the time were helping to finance the arms race. All of this turned out to be unfounded of course and much embarrassment ensued. A piece of scene history for sure.

Andy Anderson had now become the 'Manager' of Self Abuse and had begun finding gigs further afield. He had come up with the brilliant idea to hire coaches to take the band and local punks to little places like Bridport, Illminster, Westbury etc. These gigs were mainly supporting the Subhumans and/or the Cult Maniax and every one was awesome. This also gave a lot of people the chance to go to gigs where they normally couldn't, as the bus would do stops along the way through Bournemouth, Poole, Wareham, Dorchester and Weymouth.

In Jan/Feb '84 STTS had their 1st gig under the new name of Atrox. I had to phone Mel of the AHeads to get us on the bill to support Self Abuse, Confession Of Sin, A-Heads, Breakout and Idiom Tribe (the latter being a cover band from Bournemouth) getting gigs for ourselves was getting harder as there were more bands around.

In spring '84 there was a large squat established in Cotlands Road near the train station. It used to be a Barclays bank and became home to members of the Mad Are Sane amongst others. Two Miners Strike benefits were organised there. The 1st on 5.5.84 started in the afternoon and on the bill were Atrox, Mad Are Sane, Disgusting Pukey Scarves, Toxic Shock and Helius. The Mad Are Sane now had Tony of the now defunct Confession Of Sin on vocals. The Bournemouth Echo newspaper came down to take pictures. They came down early, so as Atrox were the 1st band we got our photo in the paper. The 2nd benefit was in June/July and was a Bournemouth classic. There was some guy absolutely out of it sat in the corner with a glue bag. The next thing I know he's on stage playing bass for Eat Shit who were a thrash band that used to lie about from being from America. Other bands that night were the Mad Are Sane, Dirt, Virus and Polemic. There was a big crowd for this one and a lot of LSD going round. During Polemic who played last, there were loads of us linking arms and dancing in a circle. There was a real feeling of scene unity at this one. (Remember kids, unity is fascism!)

June '84 saw what was to be, the last Stonehenge Festival. A lot of locals had returned with fantastic tales and bands doing Hawkwind covers wasn't far away. There was a definite shift towards festivals and drug taking and a more pretentious, 'We're more Anarcho than you are' mentality.

In late '84 a new venue had been found in Bournemouth. The Pembroke Arms (now The Goat & TriCycle) had a bar and a small stage upstairs. Downstairs was The Pembroke Shades a dire hole that was used as a 'last chance motel' for scoring drugs. I went to see Wretched there 3 times and they never turned up! Atrox 1st gig there was supporting Self Abuse and a local skinhead band called the Victims. The Victims had no drummer for the night so their singer approached Atrox drummer Alex and said 'Oi mate, would you mind drumming for us?'. Alex replied: 'No thanks' and the Victims singer said: 'You fucking well are mate!!' Seeing Alex with his very long hair and a rather frightened expression playing along to 4Skins covers will always be an enduring memory. Atrox 1st demo "Hit The Oxide" was now out and before long Alex had received hate mail from a certain Bournemouth band. Two sheets of paper arrived, one saying 'Hit The Oxide – Really?!' and the other proclaimed us as 'Atrox Children'. I thought this was great. We were kids! The scene had an average age of 17 and was for the kids! The Bournemouth band in question were sad and old, life was good.

The last gig at the Continental was a classic Cult Maniax night. The venue owner had decided early on that he wasn't going to pay the band so Big Al told the crowd to tear out the seats, which they duly did. This night was the last time I saw Vernon The Carrot do his 'thing'. Vernon was an ex Marine who had become a roadie for the Maniax. He would get on stage and get the crowd to sing carrot wine to the tune of 'Here We Go, Here We Go'. He would then get his dick out, piss into a pint glass and drink it. Happy days!

The next Pembroke gig was another classic. Disorder, Atrox and new Weymouth band Haywire. Haywire had the recently returned John Anderson on bass and they played, as they do to this day, punk in the Chaos UK/Crusty vein. Disorder were awesome that night and the highlight was bass player Taff getting electrocuted. When he came to, his 1st words in a very quite voice were: 'Cider, need cider'.

By late '84 early '85 things were slowing up. A few more dates at the Pembroke saw the likes of Lunatic Fringe, Mass Of Black etc being supported by new Bournemouth bands General Belgrano and Bad Noise who were influenced by Crass LP "Yes Sir I Will". Atrox had played with both bands at two gigs in Bridport one of these being an Anderson organised coach trip. Charlie and Alex of Atrox organised two gigs at Upstairs At Erics, the renamed Capone's. The 1st was Conflict, Icons Of Filth and Eat Shit. The 2nd was the Lost Cherees and Butcher.

Gigs in Bournemouth had ceased and Atrox organised 2 gigs in Dorchester and played 2 more in Southampton organised by Rich Levene who later formed the STE Collective. Self Abuse had become Pale Shade Of Black a goth band who played with us at the last Atrox Southampton gig on 19.9.85. I remember all of us being really shocked as Self Abuse had been improving with every gig and this was a totally different band. The last band I saw from the scene in '85 was the revamped Mad Are Sane who now had local musos Graham on bass and Shamus on guitar. They were excellent and could have gone far but after a handful of gigs they were finished too. Punk gigs and the scene were over in Dorset by late '85 and bands such as Here & Now, Blyth Power, and Inner City Unit were the alternative. I have to say that I was into all that too but then New Model Army came along. They were worse than the Meteors.

Late '85 saw the release of the hideously named Xcentric Noise compilation LP "Party Pooping Punk Provocations". Atrox and Self Abuse had 2 tracks each alongside UK Hardcore heroes the Stupids. It was a great moment but both bands were over, we weren't meant to be kids anymore.

Andy Nazer (from SD48)

I remember my first gig proper being the Undertones at Bournemouth Winter Gardens [sadly now demolished], in 1980 on the "Hypnotized" tour with the Moondogs supporting. The Undertones were brilliant and totally inspiring. I went with Dave Brown from Self Abuse who I also went to school with and the seeds were starting to be sown about getting a band together.

After an abortive attempt with some other school friends [I was kicked out for not having bass lessons!], eventually Dave realised the band just wasn't happening and after a chat on the way home on the bus from school we decided to get something else together with him on guitar and myself on bass. Luckily he showed me how to tune my bass and we haphazardly went from there! Around this time, Dave and another schoolfriend and punk fan, Rich Waterton had been to see the local punk band Intestines [along with The Mob, Null and Void and the Revue who were on the same bill] at Poole Arts Centre and this was the first time we were aware of a local punk band in existence...[although as time went on we'd get to hear of other short lived bands such as Aggravation, Annexe, UBoats, Illegitimate] and Dave promptly bought their double "Borborygmus" tape from the legendary Armadillo Record shop in Westbourne. This was our first taste of local DIY punk rockall the covers were hand made Xerox affairs and recorded onto old David Cassidy cassettes bought from a bargain bin!

In January 1982, we met Roger and Steve via Dave's guitar lessons at Studio 95 and started rehearsing in earnest [we never did find out who Earnest was, poor sod!]. By this time we'd heard of a couple of other local punk bands- Butcher [formed from the ashes of Intestines and having just released their debut single 'On the Ground'] and Confession of Sin.

Realising that they were playing together at the Brewers Arms in Poole, we trooped over to catch my first local punk gig. It was certainly a bit different from the big gigs I'd seen up to then[Stranglers/SLF/Undertones at Poole Arts Centre], the bands playing at the end of a small function room without a stage. Buoyed by a couple of pints of lager and blackcurrant, it was a cracking gig, friendly and it made you think "shit! We can do this too!" Also on the bill were Shock to the System from Dorchester, [Alex Vann, the drummer also did the 'Mentally Unstable' fanzine] and I remember being really impressed with them as well.

Come October 1982, Steve booked our first gig at the Sloop Hotel [a biker pub in Poole] under the pretence that we were a rock band they wouldn't have let us play if he'd said we were a punk band! Roping in another punk band called Barbed Wire from New Milton via our Studio 95 connection, we were shocked that upon arrival at the gig, there was four punks sat in a corner there to see the gig![notable for the fact that they were from another B'mth punk band who were just getting started 'The Demented' [who within a few months would become The Mad Are Sane]. Our set was pretty ramshackle but good fun [I've still got the tape of it somewhere...] and we realised we needed to get better and tighter especially as Barbed Wire were pretty good...and luckily the biker who threatened to put Steve's bass drum over his head as we were leaving didn't carry out his wish!

In early 1983, the whole local scene really started to come alive; Self Abuse recorded and released our "Teenage" demo, more bands were appearing, Idiom Tribe [from Sway/New Milton], The Parasites [Bournemouth], and we met Andy Anderson who did the excellent 'Damaged' fanzine and who started to help manage us, getting us gigs further a field and organising things like coach trips to gigs. in Ilfracombe, Ilminster, Bridport, Trowbridge and Westbury. Every coachtrip was packed! Andy was a really good guy and helped us a lot, as did Dave Parsons our ever present roadie [and still is to this day!]. There was also Hydrophobia' fanzine run by a guy called Mark [Golding?] which ran for a couple of issues and there was also a local magazine called 'Coaster' that would have local punk features in its pages as well as other interesting articles on local arts.

As for keeping ourselves 'entertained', on a Saturday we'd generally hang about town, frequenting Uptown Records at the Triangle, flicking through the new punk vinyl releases and playing the pinball tables and space invader machines that were in the bargain basement. Then it was off to '31's cafe next door for a cup of tea and a teacake followed by a stroll down to Bournemouth Gardens or Horseshoe Common to see who was about.

Saturday nights would find us in the Branksome Arms at the Triangle [Ken the doorman obviously never did read my date of birth on my provisional driving license correctly!] or at the Pinecliff in Southbourne.

During the evenings in the rest of the week that hot summer, we'd hang about with the Mad Are Sane and others at Roger's folk's house [where we'd rehearse sometimes] or drinking cider over the road on Redhill Common armed with a ghettoblaster loaded with various punk cassettes.

Sundays we're spent on the end of Boscombe pier playing more space invader games in the Amusement arcade [soon to be demolished] and occasionally throwing French bangers off the end of the pier in paper cups.[or each other-don't try this at home folks!]

Local DIY gigs were great, we had Subhumans/Self Abuse/Parasites at St Andrews hall in Boscombe in April and Cult Maniax/Self Abuse/Last Orders/Parasites at the same hall in June, no trouble or fighting at all £1.50, bring yer own booze!

Then there was Amebix/Mad Are Sane/Idiom Tribe/Admass [who later became Madmass does anybody have any tapes of this great band?!] later that summer at Shrubsall Hall in Boscombe.

We played the Regent Centre in Christchurch with Shock to the System and Idiom Tribe, then Cult Maniax also played with us at the same venue [some front seats got ripped out after encouragement from Big Al the Maniax' singer, suffice to say we didn't play there again, luckily Rogers dad came down and bailed us out].

After then, the gigs came thick and fast, put on by either Butcher or ourselves we had Cult Maniax, Screaming Dead and AHeads all at different times at the great Capones venue [Rooftop Hotel on the top floor of a multi story car park]. Upstairs at Erics [below Capones] hosted gigs by Conflict/Lost Cherrees and New Model Army amongst others.

In October of 1983 the Mad Are Sane released their 'Reality' demo on Inept Products [Rob Banks from Butchers' label] this has got to be one of the best recordings of a band from this area and era Mortarhate released the track 'Animal Crimes' on the "Who, Where, Why, What, When" compilation.

Another important event from this time involved some of the Mad Are Sane and other like minded individuals who squatted the soon to be pulled down houses in Northcote Road. They formed the Bournemouth Housing Action Movement [BHAM] in response to the lack of decent affordable accommodation. To be fair, a lot of the bedsits rented by unscrupulous landlords were little more than glorified slums anyway.

From there, they moved to the Holdenhurst Road Squat complex, which Mad Are Sane was a huge old disused garage surrounded by flats and houses [now home to the massive Abbey Life building].

There was a couple of benefit gigs held there and bands that I remember playing [from what I remember through a haze of pot smoke and tasting Rut's homebrew!] were The Mad Are Sane, Atrox, Idiom Tribe, Self Abuse,

Madmass, Virus, Toxic Shock, Polemic, Disgusting Pukey Scarves, The Thing, General Belgrano [or Code of Hate?] and The Conspiracy. It seemed that quite a few punk/anarcho/freethinking types were moving to Bournemouth from sleepier towns.

2CR radio even seemed interested in the events going on in the town, some of the squatters got interviewed [got the tape somewhere!], and also various members of Butcher, Idiom Tribe and Self Abuse were all dragged into the studio to be interviewed by local DJ Toby Rose!

As things dragged on into the dreaded 1984, the Continental Cinema [again, now demolished] in Winton [Bournemouth] hosted gigs put on by a chap called Greg [who would go onto front Bournemouth premier glam/sleaze band Poze!] Once again, Subhumans and Cult Maniax, on two different nights [both with Self Abuse/Madmass supporting] and cracking nights they were too, the Subhumans one being particularly memorable, with a queue right up the street before the doors opened and due to the fact that the Continental sometimes showed soft porn movies, the more 'righton' brigade tried to rip some seats out. Dick from the Subs chastising them 'you want to lose another venue do you?' [To whit, we did...]

The Self Abuse EP "[I Didn't Wanna Be A] Soldier" was eventually released that summer [after about a year or waiting for it to be released] and was flying out of the local Our Price records, was played by John Peel and got to number 2 in the Melody Maker charts [?!]

To be honest, after that summer, things started to decline, I guess as things do... Self Abuse played their final gig on December 29th 1984, no great falling out or arguments. The Mad Are Sane had disintegrated then reformed as a completely different band. Butcher continued for a good couple more years. Pale Shade Of Black formed from the ashes of Self Abuse [although in my honest opinion it wasn't a good move] and played their first gig in Southampton.

There were still other bands formed and gigging around that time, Bad Noise and Victims spring to mind, but personally I think the punk/anarcho scene was on the wane and people had moved on or away.

Personally I slogged on with bands here and there [what else was I gonna do?!], stayed in Pale Shade Of Black for a couple of years until I could take the more goth tinged affair no more! [No disrespect to either Dave or Steve, musical differences!] then I was in Inside Out for a while [a reggaeish punkish thing] before joining the Zimmer Frames in 1990 on vocals and guitar. A breath of fresh air!, back to kicking up a racket and a laugh.

And, when we played a few gigs put on by the STE at the Joiners in Southampton a couple of years later, it sorta felt like what it did playing in a punk band in the first place, with friendly people and a healthy scene!

Strange tho', the year is now 2007, I'm still in Bournemouth. Self Abuse have been back together for 2 years, we've been gigging and writing new material, there is new punk/alternative bands springing up, Demonic Upchucks [who've been together since leaving school and have been going for 8 years!], Spitroast, Diablos, Extinguishers, Boneyard Creepers, Death Valley Riders, Sludgefeast, Thunderdump and probably more! Oh yeah, and Virus from Gillingham are back together, there is rumours of the Intestines doing something...and Haywire never went away or for that matter did Suspect Device! Just one thing, as you've probably noticed, the powers that be in Bournemouth seem

hell bent on knocking down venues [they've not long demolished the Winter Gardens with its excellent acoustics] and older places of interest and erecting flats and other monstrosities in their place [anybody seen the Imax building?]. Culture? Bournemouth?!
But we're still here who woulda thought it eh?!

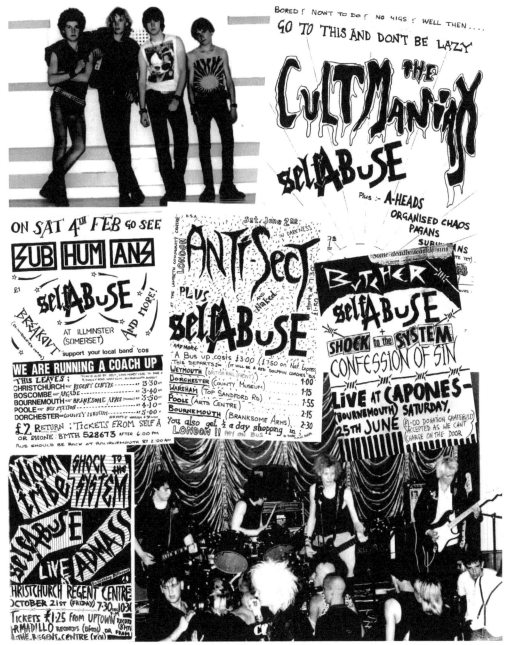

(Self Abuse flyers and photos supplied by Andy Nazer)

Tony Suspect - Summerpunks

Si Briggs and me had another adventure, that we both mentioned in SD#49, which came out towards the end of 2007. We'd decided to nip over to Amsterdam to see Strike Anywhere. We didn't bother booking accommodation, just flights. So, after a short flight from Southampton airport, we got to passport control, and it was Si this time who was held up by security. They made him take his belt off, and I can still see him shuffling away holding his shorts up as he went.

We got the train from the airport to Amsterdam's central station and the first thing we needed was something to eat, so we stopped at a kiosk and got some chips (not wanting either mayo or ketchup on my chips nearly caused an international crisis, or so it felt). After finishing our chips we went looking for a Tattoo Museum I'd heard about. We wandered up an down this street by a canal, past lots of women enquiring if we wanted to visit their establishments. We politely declined each request and carried on walking. Not finding this museum, we made our way back down the street, and there were now two guys stood with one of the girls outside one of these buildings. They called out "Come on in guys, you know you want to.' We thanked the gentlemen for their kind offer, but insisted that we really didn't want to go in, and we scuttled off, abandoning our search. We never did find the museum (did it even exist?).

Soon after that, we met up with Lloyd Chambers and Thomas from Strike Anywhere and headed off to the venue with them. We hung around a bit, and then went off to get some food with Thomas. That night Strike Anywhere were great, as you'd expect, and after the gig the band invited us to their backstage room and told us to help ourselves to their food. Punk rock takes you to some unexpected places, and there we were sat in the dressing room of a venue in Amsterdam with Strike Anywhere, eating their food and chatting like they were old friends. After the gig, we were outside on the pavement talking to Lloyd and Thomas. Perry Farrell had been playing in an upstairs room of the same venue, and he was stood near us, surrounded by young, blond, giggly girls. I pointed out to Thomas that in contrast to Mr Farrell he was just surrounded by three old, bald, British guys. Thomas seemed ok with that. When all the band arrived, we found ourselves following the local support band round the streets of Amsterdam. As we walked down the street that had women behind big windows, all red lights and curtains, I had a conversation with Thomas about whether the women were empowered as they were unionised, or if it was still exploitative? We didn't ever come up with an answer, neither could we decide how we felt about it.

As the evening went on we found ourselves in a bar where everyone, except Si and me, were getting more and more drunk. Thomas was funny, and the alcohol seemed to make him ask more and more questions, grilling us on European political history. We struggled a bit with some of his questions, both going through schools where history was very UK centric, but it didn't seem to matter and the questions kept coming. Si and me went from laughing with the band to laughing at them. At various points people drifted off and when we left the bar, at about 3am, there were only Si, me, Lloyd, Strike Anywhere's guitarist Mark, drummer Eric, bass player Garth and merch guy Josh left. We ended up back at their hotel. It was pretty small, but when they found out we had no accommodation booked they insisted we crash on the floor in their room. One of the band even made up a little bed for us to prove there was room. As tired as we were, and as tempting as the offer was, we had an early morning flight and thought that if we stayed, we'd over sleep and miss it, so we thanked them and left, the two of us were the last men standing as we trudged through the rain back to the train station, getting more chips on the way. There was a bit of a wait for a train, but we got to the airport very early in the morning, so had time for a bit of a snooze on the uncomfortable airport chairs before boarding our flight.

SD#49 also mentioned the deaths of the Ruts' Paul Fox and Killing Joke's Raven plus, closer to home, J Church's Lance Hahn. The first two deaths were sad as those two people had been in bands who created some of my favourite songs, but we knew Lance, with J Church being featured in the zine several times, and, of course, we'd released two split EPs with J Church and Wat Tyler.

In the zine Sean Forbes wrote a short, but moving top ten facts about Lance:

1. Lance was like a brother to me. Admittedly we looked pretty different (except when he piled on the pounds) but we were the same in mind, musical tastes and political views. He was 40 - same age as me and we grew up on other sides of the world but we lived the same life. We didn't have to talk - our friendship was rock solid and that never changed. Not having you around is gonna tear me apart.

2. First time we were in touch was when he sent a letter to All The Madmen Records with some Cringer recordings in it. He wanted us to release it. Not a fucking chance pal - they were rubbish. In fact they never really improved apart from the European tour with Citizen Fish when Kamala broke her hand play flirting with Dick and they had Trotsky on drums.

3. The last time I saw Lance was in Japan. We had a game going on with who could go to Japan the most times. I was winning 9 - 8. He sent a cocky email saying J Church had a tour booked and that would make us 9 times each - however two weeks later Hard Skin got the nod and we were gonna be there at the same time. Taking me into a 10-9 Lead. We played a couple gigs together (Oi and pop punk uniting for two nights only) and got to shop hard and eat even harder. Some geezer wanted to show us around Japanese temples but me and boy wonder slipped out the historical lesson and went to Shinjuku record shopping. He found Crass 'Reality Asylum' the Japanese pressing on Rough Trade and I got a Japanese copy of the 2nd and totally shit Abrasive Wheels album.

4. Lance was fucking useless at replying to emails, sending records to people who he'd promised things, saying no to food and singing in tune.

5. He has got to be one of the unluckiest people I know - Heart problems, Kidney problems, Housing getting burnt down and Gardner J Church's bass player getting deported from Japan twice.

6. If you want to do something in his honour - buy 'Arbor Vitae' on Honey Bear - the best album J Church ever recorded and a pop punk classic. I'm not sure I'll be able to listen to it again in the same way I can no longer listen to Lush.

7. It's almost Christmas 2004 and we are hanging out after a gruelling five week euro crust tour for J Church. We are watching Queen on DVD from Live Aid and eating Veggie Chinese. Neither of us are Queen fans but the performance blows us away and we watch it two more times. It's a nothing moment - but we were both so content just eating, watching a 'classic' band and talking shit.

8. Someone has to complete and publish his long term project which was a book on Anarcho Punk (don't call it Peace Punk!!) called 'Let The Tribe Increase'. Please don't let all his work go to waste.

9. With tears running down my face, I'm sad that he's not here, sad that I'll never get to eat with him at the Gipsy Rose Cafe, sad that he wouldn't get to hear and see the proposed Hard Skin benefit single of 'My Friend in a Coma'. I know you'd have laughed. We laughed long and hard with Tim Yo when we suggested to him releasing an album of his most wanted rare singles on an album 'Killed by Cancer'. I miss you now and I'll miss you forever.
10. At least I won't have to buy a new J Church 7" every other week to complete my collection.

I added to that with some memories of my interactions with Lance, both in relation to J Church and our last few emails before he died.

I don't remember how many times I saw J Church, or met Lance, but each time he was nothing less than very friendly and seemed genuinely pleased to see me.

When the house he was living in with his girlfriend burnt down, and he was selling records to help raise some money, I contacted him to see if he needed any of the first split 7" sent over to try and sell to help get some money back; we didn't want anything from him in return, and I'm not sure if the ten copies I sent actually made any difference, but I felt I wanted to do something to at least try and help.

I followed Lance's health problems via the regular email updates he sent out; occasionally I'd send him a reply, always getting one in return. The last update he sent out with news of his faltering health really disturbed me and I replied straight away; this time I didn't get a reply, a week or so later I got that text from Si with the news that Lance was dead. Death is a funny thing, and the feelings that come from hearing that someone you know has died is strange. I didn't know John Peel at all, but his death seemed to hit pretty hard, which I remember was a little confusing. I did know Lance, but hadn't seen him for a few years and so couldn't ever call him a close friend, but I do feel very sad when I think that he's not still around playing with J Church and writing his histories of UK anarcho bands in Maximum RocknRoll, probably more than I would have expected. I guess good people leave their mark on you and you remember them with great fondness; Lance certainly was a good person.

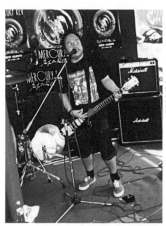

Lance Hahn - J Church playing Shake Some Action Records, Croydon

I was on a train on the way home from visiting Si and his family, when Si sent me that text letting me know Lance had died. Coincidently, on the train trip to the see Si a few days earlier I'd read about the death of Paul Fox.

Gaz's life was still in turmoil, and he was planning to move to Norfolk, but in his intro he mentioned the Postal workers strike, saying

"Please support the Postal workers who take shit hours and shit pay to get it to you then get fucked over by a 'Labour' government more interested in supporting all the bent and corrupt bastards walking this planet!"

It was good to feature Whole In The Head in this issue, as well as Social Parasites and German band Deny Everything. Si had brought down the Deny Everything EP as he thought I'd like it. To start with I thought "They just sound like Kid Dynamite." Then realised, of course, that I love Kid Dynamite and Deny Everything were really, really good. I saw them a few times, and Screwed Up Flyer played with them in Kingston on the first dated of their tour. Their drummer had bought a batch of cheap drumsticks before they left Germany, and by the end of the set at that first gig he'd broken them all, so I gave him a set of mine. I went to see them a few times on that tour, in Brighton, Southampton and Reading and he was still using my sticks.

Si came with me to see Deny Everything at The Engine Rooms in Brighton, and of course we met up with Pete Zonked. I always enjoy gigs in Brighton because Pete is a good friend and it was always good to catch up with him. It was nice to have Si there as well.

The gig was great, and we had a good time, and I guess that high of being at a brilliant gig with good friends stays with you for a while, so the following day while thinking about a conversation the three of us had at the gig, it stuck me that there was a real connection there between three people from different parts of the country, brought together by punk rock and friendship. Our 50th full issue in our 25th year of SD seemed like a good moment to celebrate one of the things that Gaz and me have always valued, co-operation and collaboration. Suspect Device maybe our zine, but we have always included contributions from others, and Pete had been writing stuff for us for quite some time at this point, and we also loved Zonked! so I had the idea of doing a split issue.

Pete had the idea of dividing the cover for SD#50, with some barbed wire running at an angle to separate our stuff from what was in Zonked!#11. Career Suicide spanned both covers as it was an interview both Pete and me collaborated on.
It took me ages to work out how to do it, but I got there eventually, and I have to admit it was a good idea and is still one of my favourite front covers.

Pete remembered:
"It was his suggestion that to mark Suspect Device's 25th year/50th issue we put out a split 'zine, which was great fun – including an interview by the two of us with Career Suicide. I'd forgotten about that until we went to see Career Suicide recently. Tony was chatting to their singer. I asked how he knew him; "because WE interviewed him"!!! Oh right! I'm guessing that split-issue must have been a great success for them because I was persuaded to do it all over again for their 58th issue (and my rather lowly 13th, haha). Only now do I realise that possibly this was their masterplan all along (he kids himself)

because I transferred my creative energy's increasingly to their 'zine. Or maybe they've just been too polite to serve me a P45. Sorry fellas, maybe we can discuss it during my mid-year review."

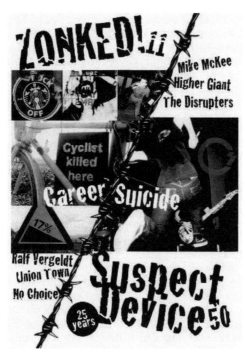

I'm not sure who came up with the idea of doing a joint interview with Career Suicide, but as well as each zine having three interviews of our own we got together to sort out some questions for Career Suicide. They had recently played in the UK, taking in both Southampton and Brighton, and were phenomenal. I guess, like us, Pete had already been a fan, but their new album, 'Attempted Suicide' had taken us all by surprise with it's speed and power.

Pete interviewed No Choice, Union Town and our friend Ralf Vergeldt, and as well as Mike McKee we featured another Philly band, Higher Giant, who's drummer was our friend Dave Wagenschutz. Gaz also interviewed The Disrupters. Pete and his friend Ian wrote pieces about visits to Palestine and Israel, while Si mentions another little adventure we had, going to stay with Gaz in his new Norfolk home and going to see Strike Anywhere in Norwich.

We kept our reviews to a minimum, we were now using the website for a lot of them, so most reviews in the issue are Pete's.

One of the things that surprises me about this issue is that we interview Mike McKee (Kill The Man Who Questions, Amateur Party, Armalite), someone Si and me met on another trip to Philadelphia. It's not surprising that we interviewed Mike, he's an interesting, friendly man, the odd thing is that neither Si or me mention our trip to Philly (I seem to remember we did a write up on the website, which is sadly long gone, but it's odd that there is no mention in the zine).

Needless to say it was another of our silly ideas that we actually went ahead and made happen. Paint It Black had planned a couple of release gigs for their new album, 'New Lexicon' and we decided we wanted to go. Dan Yemin offered to put us up, so we made plans and went. It was cold when we got there, and I don't just mean the usual frosty US immigration "welcome", it was like -5 at midday on the day we arrived. We got the train from the airport into Philadelphia and I remember walking out of the station into a cold but sunny day. We made our way to the location we were to meet up with, Dave Wagenschutz, at the Health Food Store he was then working in. He took us to a cafe while we tried to make contact with Dan. At some point Andy Nelson arrived and sat with us for a bit. It does still make me smile thinking of Dave calling Dan and saying "The Brits have arrived, I have them."

We eventually ended up back at Dan's house, and before long we were off to a gig. Several gigs had been arranged around the two that PiB were playing to mark the release of their new album. On that first night we went to Disgracelands, which was actually a house where the downstairs had been gutted, this was where bands played. But it was still a house so it was packed. The Unloveables and Static Radio NJ both played (there were at least one more band, but I forget their name) and it was great. What was odd, at least for us UK punkers used to a more collaborative scene where bands shared equipment, was that every band had their own equipment, so after each band played they dismantled their drum kit and amps and squeezed them through the crowd, or in the case of the drum kit carried it above the heads of the crowd. Then then next band reversed the operation with their own gear. It was quite an experience, and the bands were really good. We ended the evening out on the pavement talking to the guys from Static Radio NJ.

The next morning Dan drove us to a PiB practise, on the way we listened to Hard Skin in his car, with Dan occasionally asking about some of the very British language and references. PiB were so good, even when they were just practising in the basement of Josh's parent's house. Of course the guys in Paint It Black are certainly not egotistical enough to assume they were anyone's heroes, they were our friends and we were just hanging out with them, but I still felt very privileged being there watching them prepare for these gigs. It was quite an experience.

After that we did a bit of record shopping in Philly before going back to Dan's, where we listened to more records.

That evening PiB played at the First Unitarian Church, the other bands playing that night were The Marked Men, Mike McKee's Amateur Party, Wold/Inferno Friendship Society and Dustheads. Before the gig got underway, Dave W stopped by to see us, although he wasn't able to stay for the gig.

After all that excitement, we went to another venue, which was more of a bar, to see a Hard Skin inspired "Oi" band called Combat 215 who featured Mike McKee and Andy Nelson, playing covers of UK punk and Oi songs. They were a lot of fun. After them were Pissed Jeans, but unfortunately, by this time I was so tired and the fact that there was smoking allowed in the venue, something we'd got used to not having in the UK, I was feeling really grumpy and out of sorts, so I didn't really enjoy their set. I'm sure they were great, I was just feeling wiped out.

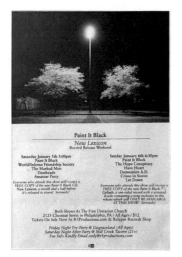

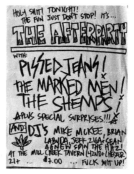

(Left) Poster for the Paint It Black 'New Lexicon' album release weekend.

(Below) Flyer for the After Party on the Saturday. I don't think The Marked Men played, and I don't remember The Shemps, although I was pretty wiped by the time we got to this venue.

The following day's gig, back at the First Unitarian Church, was more of a "hardcore" affair, with Damnation AD, Have Heart, The Hope Conspiracy, Crime In Stereo and Let Down also playing. But before that we had breakfast in a cafe with lots of people who were at the gig the night before, both bands and people who'd travelled. After that Dan took us to a big building that seemed to have some DIY printing operation going on (My memory is hazy here) to pick up some record sleeves which we took to Andy Nelson's place where Si and me helped him and Dan hand number the sleeves, which were for a 7" they were giving away at that evening's gig (people at the gig the night before had been given a copy of 'New Lexicon' on CD).

After watching PiB from out front the night before, we watched this set from the side of the stage, although at one point I found myself stood behind Andy's bass amp. Once again Paint It Black showed how you play punk rock, it was another amazing set of speed, power and intensity.

We were up early on our last day, Dan had to work so we left his house when he did, walking into Philly for a day of seeing the sights. The Rocky Steps weren't too far from where Dan was then living so we went there first. Then on to the Liberty Bell and the LOVE sculpture. We may have arrived in Philadelphia to find sub zero temperatures, but this last day was sunny and warm, and we'd been lugging heavy bags around with us, so we walked to Dave W's house as he had offered to look after our bags for the day. We went back out into the streets of Philly and, after a long, but fun day, we met up with Dave again, and he took us to a 50's style diner which sold vegan burgers. Once fed, he drove us back to the airport. It was another packed, tiring, but very cool weekend, and once again our Philadelphia friends looked after us very well, and gave us so many more fantastic memories.

I am still in contact with Andy Nelson, Dan Yemin and Dave Wagenschutz, and to a lesser extent, Darren Walters. So I spoke to Andy, via Skype, to get his memories on the times we've had together, and also about his thoughts on friendship and punk rock.

T: There's a big part of the SD story that involves Paint It Black and to a certain extent Jade Tree. There was the PiB tour with Pilger, and then Si and me coming out to Philly...

Andy: Yeah. And also to ours, it's very mutual. I know the line up of the band has shifted a little over the years, but I know me and Dan feel that way, and Wagenschutz as well.

A thing that has been constant, another thing I've been fixated on, as far as continuing to make punk do punk stuff at a rapidly advancing age. I am kind of really thinking about, more specifically hardcore, because I'm in that world too, that's gotten more mainstream over the last five years, probably, on some level that's great, but I do think it's interesting how much of that seems to be completely devoid of any of the things that made me interested in punk to begin with. Y'know, anti-establishment, anti-mainstream, anti-corporate, all these things, those sort of ideologies seem to be entirely absent from young people doing it now. Which is upsetting to me on several levels, but mainly because I think, what punk is, is community, a network of friendships, relationships, and you need that in order to survive. For me it's less a matter of aesthetic, or any particular ideology, it's more about survival. And you can't do this for 40 years without friendships and relationships, and we couldn't be a band for 20 years without those things. So I feel like a lot of those people who are doing it now are approaching it as if they were pop stars.

So if there's anything that makes this what it is, it's the friendships and camaraderie, because your friends have your back forever. So if Tony Whatley emails me, I'm jumping on Skype, no questions asked. Y'know. If my friends need something I'm there, I'm an intensely loyal person. So, corporations may give a hardcore band money in 2023, but in 2024 they're not going to give a fuck about them, they're going to be on to what happens next.

T: Friendships are so important to us, I don't think we'd have got past two or three issues if we hadn't had that network locally. And we've still got that. (Alan) the bass player of Abrazos has moved to Scotland, but he's such a good friend that there was no question of getting someone else, we just work round it. We haven't played a gig for over a year, but we have released an album and we have an EP due out soon.

Andy: I think that's great. I am incredibly opposed to careerism in punk music. Paint It Black, as a band, have never done anything that we didn't feel was worth everyone's time, not ours, but people in the world. I mean we didn't put out bullshit records, or play shows we thought were wack, so sometimes that means we don't do that much. If you take it seriously and put care into what you do, maybe you don't put out an issue of a zine for a year, or maybe you only put out a record, but you don't play any shows. But I think it's really important to make that contribution, and I think it stands in direct contrast to now, where everyone is just a content creator, like, churn out as much fucking bullshit as possible, there's no staying power, no one's going to remember what any of that stuff is in a week, let alone ten years. But to me, Suspect Device was a crucial and important thing, both as a zine, but also you as a person, and you as a friend, for like fostering a really important connection, that swung both across the pond to England, and back to the US.

T: I just wondered if you had any memories or stories of stuff we've been involved with, when Paint It Black came over to the UK, or Si and me came over to Philly? Or your experiences of DIY, because you've seen it over in the US and you've seen it over here. You've played a small hall in Guilford, and also bigger venues like the Underworld, so you've seen it from all angles.

Andy: Yeah. Paint It Black are one of the few bands from America who've played a small hall in Guildford, and then the Reading and Leeds festivals. You're going to have to help me with the time line a little bit. We met you guys the first time we came to England, right? That was the Wagenschutz, Colin tour? 2004, 2005?

T: Yeah, Paradise had just come out.

Andy: 2005. Yeah.

T: Because I had been in contact with Dan, I think Darren (Walters, Jade Tree) had put me in contact with him, and then Dave contacted me, about football, not punk rock, funny enough. Dave asked Pilger to be on that tour, and I think that was when relationships were cemented.

Andy: Yeah. I just remember meeting you guys, and knowing about Pilger, probably through Dave, or Dan, and thinking it was Rad. I was really young when we met, I was like like 23, but I had been doing shows for a long time, in Philly, I'd booked British bands, like Voorhees. But I remember being blown away, there was like a zine you've heard of from another country, that is like the longest running UK punk fanzine, and I was like "The guy from that zine knows who we are? That's crazy." Y'know. Because I've always been into British stuff, not just punk, but everything, so it seemed crazy at the time that we could possibly be on someone's radar, like yours, it was both like really exciting to me but also validating, like "Ok, yeah, we're cool, if this guy knows who we are we must be kinda cool." Over the years I'm hard pressed to think of a punk hero that we haven't met or played shows with and you eventually just learn that they are just regular people. That is not just why punk is cool, but I kind of genuinely think that in order for you to make punk stuff that is good, that will connect with people and that stands the test of time, you have to be a regular ass person. You can't be like a rich person, or someone that's just having a dalliance with subculture, you have to be a devoted regular guy with some sort of ethic.

But at the time I remember getting to England and being so psyched and thinking "I can't believe we're in England, and we're going to play shows." I think the first show was, I could be wrong, but I think the first show was in Nottingham?

T: It was in Norwich. A strange venue with a cage round the stage.

Andy: Yeah, Norwich. That's the Alan Partridge place, right? I remember getting out of the van and it feeling so British. And then you guys rolling up, and then playing the show with the cage. It was like a harbinger of things to come where you play all sorts of strange places. Was the the same run where we played in Hull?

T: Yes. Hull was the next night.

Andy: I was talking about that show last night. I was at a party and my friend, who is in Touche Amore, was there and he had just gotten back from six weeks in Europe, and he was like the one thing that Touche hasn't done is a British tour. They've done the usual Europe thing where you pop in for a couple of days, but never done a British tour. And he said "I bet you have though?" And I said yes, we've done a few, and we'd like to do more. And I said that maybe the craziest show, in terms of how good it was and where it was, was in this place called Hull, and he was like "I've never heard of Hull."

You have so many experiences when touring, and I have forgotten 95% of the stuff we've done, but I have in my house some tour posters of British tours, the one we did with Ceremony and Paint It Black, and the one Paint It Black did with Blacklisted, and I'll look at them and I'll have a look at one of the dates and have zero recollection of what this show was, or where it was, but I do clearly remember Norwich, and I have to imagine that it's because of the fact that we met you guys there. Maybe I wouldn't remember it so well if it wasn't for the fact that it was beginning of a now decades long friendship. The tour I remember being surprising and fun, I mean we've always done well in England, better than most places, and I have to imagine that has to be partially down to you and your support over the years.

(Tom) Ellis is another one I've been with since that tour, or maybe the next one. I think you were the one who connected us, because you were like "There's this great band, the Shitty Limits..." I always looked to Suspect Device to find out the cool new bands, and at the time it didn't get much cooler than Shitty Limits. I think you gave me a shirt, right?

T: Yeah, I did. That was in Newport. I gave you my shirt.

Andy: The shirt off your back. That's a real friend right there. I still have it. Another thing I wanted to touch on. One thing that I really like about what you guys have done over the years, and even when we met you had been doing it for a long time, like 20 years. One of the things that I think is under discussed; I'm all for youthful nihilism when it comes to punk stuff, and I'm all for bands who make a demo when they're 15 and then break up immediately, and I'm all for people like that saying "fuck anyone who's older than me, fuck any old bands, who gives a shit about any of this old stuff? What's important is what I'm doing right now." I think that's important, but I also do think it's important that there be kind of a push and pull between older generations and younger generations, because there's a lot of knowledge, like you said, Sean (Forbes) took you round and helped you learn how to put a record out, and I read your zine and learned a ton about, not just music history, but cultural history and networks of people, and that helped us as a band. So I think that it's ok if it's a little bit adversarial, a push and pull between young and old, and there needs to be older people who are still doing stuff, y'know, there needs to be narratives that include someone who's in their 50s or 60s still caring about punk, whatever that looks like. Maybe it doesn't mean touring for six weeks and putting out five records a year, or doing a zine every month, but it's important. I feel like Suspect Device, and you as a person, are one of the people that I think we all look to when we think of what that can look like.

Even now, releasing a new Paint It Black record, we've been a band for 20 years, we've never broken up, never had a reunion, or done a lot of things a lot of people do, we've definitely been less active than some bands, but I like the way that we have done things, and I'm really happy with that and I like the idea that people can look at how we've conducted ourselves as kind of a road map of how you can continue to be punk forever, and not just be like "I'm kind of old now, now I just watch TV." I think that's really important that there be people like you, or even someone like Ian Mackay, he still goes to shows he's still doing a label. That was something that was clear to me, and us, 20 years ago, and 20 years later, with every passing year I think it becomes more and more vital to have people like you remaining engaged to whatever degree you see fit.

T: I wish Paint It Black would do more some times, but I like that fact I'm still friends with you, and I'm still friends with Dan and Dave Wagenshuts, and Darren...

Andy: Yeah it's cool... I'm grateful that there's people like yourself and all our friends over in England, or all across the world really now, who are people that you've known for 20 years, or whatever, who are still a part of the texture of your life. But also things that I've done as a band member, as a member of a culture, it's very cool. For you, it sounds like you can go on holiday and you have people everywhere.

T: Yeah, and I like that.

Andy: Most people don't have that. Some people don't have friends at all, let alone someone in every continent who they can ring up and say "Hey, I'm in town, do you wanna hang?"

T: I think about that a lot. Because of the fanzine, and punk rock I can say to someone "I'm driving to Scotland, can I come and see you on the way up?" And it means a lot, because I'm not very outgoing, and I'm not sure if, without punk rock and the friends I've made, I'd have survived. I'm really grateful for that.

Andy: Do you ever wonder what your life would be like if you hadn't found it?

T: Yeah, I heard punk rock when I was very young, I was 11, and a year or so later I was buying punk records and two years after first hearing punk I was wearing a Sid Vicious t-shirt and a fake leather jacket. So, I have often wondered what I'd be like if I hadn't heard it, but I don't know what would have happened.

Andy: Everything in my life has stemmed from it, y'know. My job is I do concerts, that has fully stemmed out of the bands I've been in. I'm not cut out for a regular job, I have no idea what I would do. It's hard not to lapse into cliches when you talk about this stuff, but it's really wild to think about what our daily lives would be without it.

Andy: Let's talk about when you came to Philly.

T: We came twice.

Andy: When was the other time?

T: The first time we came was when Kid Dynamite played CBGBs.

Andy: Oh yeah, I was there.

T: And the second time was when you did the weekend of album release gigs (for New Lexicon).

Andy: How did you end up coming to the Kid Dynamite thing? Did it get announced and you thought "fuck it we'll get on a plane."?

T: I think I was up staying with Si when it was announced, and we jokingly said we should go. And by the time we got home the decision had been made to go. I was in contact with Dan, and mostly Dave, and Dave offered to put us up. There was meant to be a gig in New Jersey that was cancelled, Lifetime was going to play, and Paint It Black were going to play, then you must have put on a gig in Philly that 108 played and Lifetime. And I know we met you there as it's in the zine. Then we went to Baltimore to see None More Black, which I think was Dave's last gig with them, then we went to see Kid Dynamite. Oh, on the first day we were there we went to see None More Black at the Knitting

Factory (in New York). We went straight from the airport to the gig. That was the first time we came out.

Andy: That was a crazy week, I remember. I can't believe how many shows that happened while you were there. What luck.

T: Well the same thing happened the next time, with the two Paint It Black gigs, then there was a gig at Disgracelands, with The Unloveables and Static Radio, then we came to a Paint It Black practise.

Andy: Really? Where were we practising?

T: I think it was Josh's parent's house?

Andy: Wow, you went there? That's amazing.

T: Then there was Pissed Jeans somewhere, and you played with Mike McKee, in an Oi band.

Andy: Was that the show? Really, wow, we played that?

T: Was it Combat...

Andy: Yeah, Combat 215. I didn't remember we played that.

T: I was really struggling with tiredness, and was a bit grumpy.

Andy: That's crazy that you got to see that. We didn't do that very many times, but every time we did it was so fun. Although in the presence of some real Brits we probably should have been a little more nervous than we were.

T: I remember enjoying it, but talking to Mike Mckee and saying that some of the songs you played weren't Oi songs! You did some Stiff Little Fingers songs.

Andy: Yeah, he just wanted to do it, and he picked the songs. I can't remember what we did, but we probably did a bunch of Blitz, Cock Sparrer, but also 'Alternative Ulster' and probably 'Suspect Device'.

I remember you guys coming. Forgive me if this is repeating myself, but I remember thinking it was very validating to have some guys that we considered to be super legit, like yourselves, to come all the way from England to hang out and come to the gigs and stuff. I remember, at the time being really blown away that anyone would do that. It was like "Holy shit, the Suspect Device guy is here, that's so cool." It seemed like a crazy thing, but natural because you guys were our friends. It was really nice to have you there, because, y'know, you do this stuff because you want to foster some kind of connection between people, so a connection between England and the US, and one across not just geography, but generations, is pretty meaningful. That's the kind of stuff we care about, and have always cared about.

T: That's probably why I like Paint It Black so much, because you care about the same stuff I do. I love the music, but that fact that you're coming from the same place, you have the same idea about stuff, that's why it means so much.

Andy: You know when someone is kindred to you, it seems like it's not a big deal, but it's actually really important.

T: And that's why we want the book to have our friend's voices in it too.

As an aside, I remember one time Ceremony came to Southampton to play at The Joiners. I couldn't make the gig, but I did go into town during the day to meet up with Andy and we had a walk around town talking about music and gigs and friendship. He took me to meet the other guys in Ceremony before I had to go. It was a shame I couldn't go to the gig, but I'm pleased I was able to spend a bit of time with Andy while he was in town.

Gaz:

Issue #49 – Despite everything we were still waving the flag for Punk Rock and I was back in the saddle doing an interview with local Anarcho's – Social Parasites. They were lined up with Deny Everything, Whole In The Head and Small Arms Dealer. You can't say we've never brought you variety. This issue also marked the passing of Lance Hahn of J. Church and Sean Forbes of Hard Skin fame gave him a suitable and heart felt Punk Rock obituary. Looking back I think I was happy to see the back of 2007!

Issue #50 – This issue marked 25 years of the zine and we split it with #11 of Zonked from Brighton written by our mate Pete Zonked. Pete has now become as big a part of SD as I've ever been and that to me represents everything I ever wanted the zine to be. Tony holds it all together, but the collective is what I wanted to achieve and I think we have done that. By now I was living in Norfolk, but with the technology now available it was no barrier to communicating. This issue had Mike McKee, Higher Giant, The Disrupters who I've always liked and they are appropriately from Norwich, Ralf Vergeldt who put on gigs in Brighton, Union Town, No Choice and the fantastic Career Suicide! 60 pages made this a big issue.

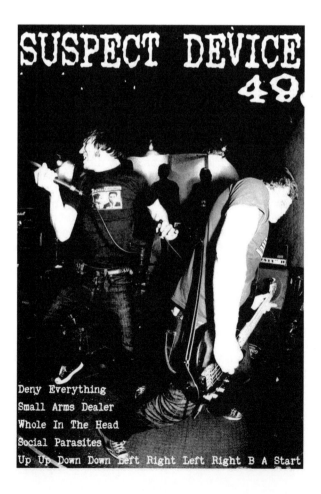

Tony Suspect - One Eye

The split issue came out in January 2009 and it was a full year before we got the next one out. But, I have a good excuse. Around the time we were writing the split issue, I had found that my deteriorating vision had nothing to do with age or extended computer use, it was because there was a tumour behind my right eye that was growing and pushing the eyeball forward. So while the sight in my left eye was still pretty good, my right eye was getting worse, quickly. They thought it was benign, but couldn't be sure, so I was booked in to Moorfields Eye hospital in London to have the tumour removed. I had to make several trips to Moorfileds in the year before the operation, but when the day came, mum and dad took me up there as Becca was at school, so Sarah had to be home for her. We got there very early, but I waited around all day and eventually had the operation quite late, around 5pm. This meant an unexpected over night stay in the hospital for me and it also meant that mum and dad had to either go and find somewhere to stay the night, or drive home and then back up in the morning to collect me, getting across London to Waterloo Station on my own that soon after the operation wouldn't have been a great idea.

I had to put on the usual hospital gown, but because I wasn't actually ill I could walk to the operating theatre, although the route was through the main waiting room, so I had to walk, wearing the fetching hospital gown and with a huge red arrow drawn on my forehead pointing at the eye that needed operating on, past all those sat waiting. The operating theatre was crowded with people, all masked up and when I got up on the operating table, a couple of people seemed to be talking to me, but I somehow couldn't really understand what they were saying. I was vaguely aware of a needle going into the back of my hand, more muffled voices and several faces peering down at me. And that was it.

When I came round I was back on the ward, I was awake but not quite with it. I wasn't in pain, but was aware of some pressure on my eye, which turned out to be from the heavy dressing.

Now, when I am given anaesthetic, or any strong pain killers for that matter, it messes with my head a bit and I get really spaced out. At one point during an MRI scan on my head (which had located the tumour behind my eye), they injected me with something about half way through, and I instantly started hallucinating, seeing a floating deathshead skull, a nazi soldier and a ghost, all bobbing around behind the doctors I could see in the room adjacent to the MRI scanner I was in.

Having just come round I was still in a strange, muddled world, and at some point, while still on the ward after the op, my sister called to see how I was and I apparently told her that I had no clean underwear. I have no recollection of this conversation, neither do I remember the countless number of incoherent texts I sent to people when I was back on the ward. Eventually, mum and dad went off to find some accommodation for the night and someone, a nurse or orderly (I was still spaced out so can't remember who), wheeled me to a private room in a wheelchair. When she stopped to book me in she said "This is Mr Whatley, he has eaten and passed water." I remember thinking "Have I? When did I do that?" My confused mind was still playing tricks on me through the night as at one point I was convinced a bearded doctor had entered and was floating round my room. It seemed more than just a dream.

Anyway, all was good the next morning, and after having the dressing removed and given eye drops and strong pain killers, we were on our way. I was back home before

Becca came in from school, she ran into the room shouting "daddy" then saw my bruised face and funny looking eye and immediately backed away saying "eewww."

So, SD#51 was put together slowly as I couldn't spend too much time in front of a computer screen as my vision wasn't great and I needed to not strain the eye while it recovered. I had to put the zine together in short five to ten minute sessions in front of a screen.
After three weeks off I went back to work, and before the first day was over they had to take me to the emergency eye unit at Southampton General Hospital as being back in an air conditioned room with banks of heat producing servers had dried my eye out so much I was in agony.

Si and me had more adventures together around this time. We saw The Stupids in Southampton, Strike Anywhere in Bournemouth, and in September we saw a few Paint It Black gigs when they came back to the UK. I saw them in Guildford without Si, then we went to Kingston together. We saw them a few more times, including Southampton, where Andy and Dan stayed at our house after the gig, and finally London, in a small basement venue that was hot and sweaty, where PiB were fantastic.

Si Briggs mentioned seeing Paint It Black in his column:
"Definitely didn't get to as many gigs this year but the ones I did get to were top quality. Got to see Paint It Black 5 times on their jaunt over here which is always a true pleasure, a truly awesome band, and really great people to boot. Getting to knock on the bedroom door and wake Dan Yemin and Andy Nelson up one morning is something that for some very strange reason makes me smile. Recently caught Strike Anywhere play a few dates over here, another band that is very special to me, and both these bands released absolutely top quality material this year too, nice."

I managed to get the issue finished and it featured The Shitty Limits, Boss Tuneage Records, Social Circkle, Anti You and another collaboration from Pete and me for an interview with our friend from Brighton, Allen Silburn, who had been in Sleep and Immolato Tomatoes.
After the split issue, Pete contributed a lot to SD#51 with plenty of his excellent live photos, including the one of The Shitty Limits that I used as the front cover.
There were also photos from the Limp Wrist gig in Brighton that I drove to with Mike Fox. The Scepters and Whole In The Head were both brilliant that night, but Limp Wrist were outstanding. It was a special night where everything that is great about DIY punk rock was in evidence: Friendship, inclusivity, fun and blistering music. I was so inspired that on the drive home I said to Mike the we should start a new band. Screwed Up Flyer had fizzled out some time previously, and I had began to think that my days of playing in a band were over. I was in my 40s and thought that ship had sailed. But, after that gig Mike and me decided to form what would become The Shorts.
Both Pete and me did a round up of the previous years best releases/gigs, not quite the Top 10 lists that we do now, but maybe the start of things to come.

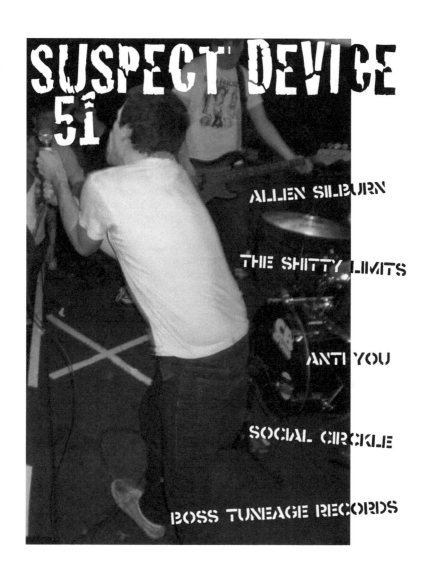

SUSPECT DEVICE
51

ALLEN SILBURN

THE SHITTY LIMITS

ANTI YOU

SOCIAL CIRCKLE

BOSS TUNEAGE RECORDS

Tony Suspect - Hey, We Are the Boys

Famously, punk rock has prided itself on there being no distinction between the band and the crowd, "I don't wanna be nobody's hero" and all that. It seems, from reading Ian Glasper's excellent Burning Britain book that some of the early 1980s punk bands were looking for managers, record deals and chart success, so it was heartening to find that meeting one member of one of our favourite bands from the early 1980s was down to earth, friendly and happy to chat.

I think it's fair to say that if Gaz and me were to list our favourite bands, then we'd both have Blitz right near the top, so when Si and me went to see Paint It Black in Manchester in August 2010 I was a bit surprised, and not a little excited, when Andy Nelson told me that Mackie form Blitz was coming to the gig. Andy asked if I knew what he looked like? I think the last time I'd seen a picture of Mackie at that point was on the Rose Of Victory 7", and I assumed he'd have changed in almost 30 years since that record came out. As it was, Mackie came up to talk to Andy and I was introduced to him as well. I don't think anyone from any band is better than anyone else, but fucking hell, I was talking to Andy Nelson and Mackie, two people who have played bass on some of my favourite records. Mackie was cool and we kept in touch, which is why we were able to have an interview with him in SD#52.

It had been almost another year between issues, but as always lots had been going on, and once again I found myself trying to complete another issue while off work after another problem with my eye: Nothing as drastic as the major surgery I had the previous January, but fluid had built up behind the scar tissue that was left by the tumour causing my vision to deteriorate again, so the hospital had decided that laser surgery was worth a try to remove the scar tissue, this time the procedure was done at Southampton General. This left me with a big red "splodge" obscuring the vision of my right eye, making reading and using a screen very difficult. There was some suggestion that if the laser treatment didn't work I'd end up having to have another major operation.

As it was, my vision didn't improve at all, but they didn't think that another major operation would be worth it and eventually I was discharged from both Southampton General and Moorfileds. The tumour was gone, it was benign, and there was nothing more they could do about the damage to the eye apart from hope it healed itself in time (it hasn't, and my vision is still deteriorating).

There was some good news in this issue, Andy Morris, who we had lost contact with for quite some time, got back in touch. He'd been having a really hard time but was now getting back on his feet and it was great to hear from him again. Of course I asked him if he wanted to get back involved with SD, which, thankfully, he did. There is also mention that I ran into David Stuart at a gig, and also that Stuart Armstrong had also got back in touch after a period of not hearing from him, There is also a column from Iain Ratcliffe, who was another to get back in touch. All of these people had been big parts of the Suspect Device story, and more importantly, good friends, and it was great to hear from them all again.

Speaking of old friends, Paul and Stu from Older Than Dirt had started a new band, and got Mike Fox to do some vocals for them, Paul was still living in Spain so this was an anglo/Spanish band, and it was good to be able to feature them in this issue.

Pete had contributed questions to the interview with Mackie, and also did an interview with Regulations from Sweden. Gaz did plan to include interviews with another couple of people from early 1980's UK bands, but neither Vice Squad's Shane Baldwin or Chron Gen's Glynn Barber got replies back to him. He did interview Septic Psychos though, and Si spoke to The World Concave.

As mentioned above, Paint It Black were over in the UK again that summer, so Si and me set out to see as many of their gigs as possible. First though, I caught them in Kingston, which is where I met Dave Stuart, and then Sarah, Becca and me headed up to the North East to do one of our favourite things, spending a couple of days with the Briggsies. As usual we had a good time, and it also allowed Si and me to nip over to Manchester to see PiB (and meet Mackie).

Si joined us for the train journey South, and as I had an appointment at Moorfields eye hospital, Si and me stopped off in London while Sarah and Becca carried on with their journey home.

Once discharged from the hospital, we made our way to Tunbridge Wells, for the next PiB gig. Si's wife, Paula, had booked a B&B place for us, it was cheap, but three miles out of town, so once at Tunbridge Wells train station we decided to get a cab to the B&B to to drop our bags off. We reasoned that a three mile trip couldn't be that expensive and would allow us to get our bearings.

The taxi driver was a maniac, he drove like an idiot randomly swearing at people. It seemed longer than three miles and the £11 fare was a bit of a shock. Still, it was good to be out of that car and although I took his phone number we had no intention of calling him to take us back to the venue.

Little did we know this was only the start of a crazy time in Tunbridge Wells.

This big house stood in front of us, and Si pushed open the door and strode on in, I followed and as I made sure the door was closed I heard a woman's voice greet Si. Then they came back round the corner and the woman greeted me with a look of shock on her face; remember that bit in the second Terminator film where Sarah Connor is escaping from the hospital and runs into the Terminator, and not realising he was on her side the film goes in to slow motion as she backs away with a look of terror on her face, that's similar to how I replay that moment when I think back at it now. All I remember her saying was "oh!" She then showed us to our room. Paula had booked a twin room with its own bathroom, so walking past a room and the woman saying "that's the bathroom" before leading us to the other end of a landing wasn't a good start. Then we walked onto a double room with one small double bed. For some reason my first reaction was to look for a wall socket so I could charge my phone, but Si was demanding the room that had been booked. I couldn't work out if he was being told that someone else was in that room, or that the room Paula had booked on the internet didn't in fact exist.

The woman asked us to wait while she sorted something out; a few minutes later she appeared and said it was sorted, the person currently in the room would have to move, but they were out at the moment, so if we wanted to get off back into town they'd move our bags into room 12 ready for when we got back.

Not forgetting our last taxi ride, and with the way back to town not being clear to either of us we asked if they could recommend a taxi. We called the number they gave us and a different guy arrived. This one didn't randomly swear at anyone and was interested in why we were in town, when Si mentioned we were going to see a punk band he thought for a moment and then said "I saw the Sex Pistols you know, 1977 it was, they were musically terrible but it was great."

Funny enough neither Si or me believed him, but we kept quiet as I think deep down we were fearing for our lives. This trip was cheaper, only £10! The driver asked what time we'd be finished, and we said we didn't know but probably around 11.30 pm; he gave us his number and said if we called he'd come and get us.

Stepping out of the cab, we saw Andy Nelson sat outside the venue and went and had a chat, then Ben (Hard Skin) and Josh (PiB) came out of the venue, they were off to get a coffee, and we wanted food so we walked with them a while. They went into a bistro while we wandered off to get some chips, stopping on the way to give someone completely wrong directions to the venue; we didn't do it on purpose, and I felt bad later, but it wasn't until the car drove off and turned the way we had suggested that we realised we'd been wrong, very wrong. But we'd never been to Tunbridge Wells before either.

On the way back to the venue we bumped into the rest of PiB and went with them to the bistro Josh and Ben were in. It seemed quite strange to be all sat in this fairly nice place drinking tea and talking about Hard Skin songs. Ben told me of their plans for their next album and that they were going to release two versions of it, one with different families singing instead of him and Sean.

The gig was strange too, it was in an old Public Toilet, which was cool, and although PiB played superbly, and it was obvious people were into them, and were singing along to all the songs, the reaction was very muted after each song. PiB gave everything though and both Si and me were excited even if no one else seemed to be. After the gig, we said our goodbyes and Si rang our friendly Sex Pistols fan for a lift back. He wasn't working that night(!) but someone else came. I don't remember any conversation on the way back, I just remember handing over another £10.

Then we were back outside the B&B, and it looked deserted. The front door was open though so we walked in and started up the stairs looking for room 12. We reached the top floor and hadn't spotted it. We walked down again and found no room number over 10. We walked up and down the stairs another couple of times, found our way into the kitchen and out the back door. We went back in and Si phoned, but got a fax machine. We were stood in the hallway of a B&B with no room 12, and our bags were nowhere to be seen. We went out into the kitchen again, then we went outside and then back in again. We tried calling a second time but only got the fax machine again. Out the back of the B&B was a house, it was fenced off and just looked like a normal house, we wondered if that was where the owners of the B&B lived, Si went up to the door, but instead of knocking he tried the handle, it opened, we stepped inside and some guy was there, sat in his pants watching TV. Si apologised and explained our predicament. He said the room was in the main B&B house, so we explained that it wasn't and he looked blankly at us before suddenly saying "Upstairs!" Now was room 12 upstairs, or was he ushering us up the stairs for other purposes?

We went up the stairs and saw a door with 12 on it, along with a note instructing someone (the guy in his pants?) to sleep on the sofa. The room didn't have it's own bathroom, but it did have a double bed and a small put up bed, there were two small towels and a kettle with tea bags and coffee. And our bags.

We made a hot drink and then went to bed; Si opted for the single one, so I jumped into the most uncomfortable double bed I've ever experienced.

The guy downstairs had the TV on loud, maybe it was his protest at being turfed out of his room. I put my ear plugs in and went to sleep.

Early next morning it was very noisy, lots of loud voices, loud TV and doors banging. My ear plugs couldn't keep the noise out so I put my earphones in and listened to punk rock to drown them out; it seemed to work as I dropped off to sleep for a while.

Si then went for a shower while I dozed, he came back clean but holding a towel that had blood on it, it wasn't his blood though. I roused myself and looked at the towel I'd been left with; it was small and a bit threadbare, but there was no blood, so I went and jumped in the shower.

Once washed and dressed we wanted to get out of there as quickly as possible. The house was now quiet, and deserted. We made our way back to the main B&B, which was also deserted. We looked for someone to pay, but there was no one around, so we buggered off.

We'd decided to walk it this time, but as we got to a bus stop a bus arrived with Rail Station on the front, so we jumped on quick and made our way back to Tunbridge Wells.

We needed breakfast and had seen a cafe, it offered a veggie breakfast, but not a vegan one, so I nipped into a branch of Holland & Barrett opposite because it was close and I knew H&B sold vegan spread. But the Holland & Barrett in Tunbridge Wells had no cold cabinet. Luckily, nearby we found a small fair trade shop that did have some vegan spread, and I felt better about giving my money to them rather than a big chain, so we were all set.

Once breakfasted we got on the next train and got out of Tunbridge Wells, and back to London. We headed to Rough Trade in West London and on the way, in Portobello Road we saw Bill Nighy stood having a chat with someone. Mr Nighy is probably a very nice man, but we hurried on to Rough Trade and got to chat to Sean Forbes, which was a win for us. While we were in Rough Trade, the Paint It Black guys arrived, and after a while Si and me sat outside with Josh Agran and talked nonsense, which was very funny. Paint It Black played at The Garage that night.

The back cover of SD#52 had a picture of Ari Up from The Slits, who had recently died. By the time we got to putting out SD#53, in October 2011, we had three more punk rock deaths to report. Pete Dimmock from Chron Gen and Chelsea, Redson from Brazilian legends Cólera and Poly Styrene.

The zine had some good varied content. Mackie had, by this time put a new band together, with him playing guitar and as Epic Problem had just put a demo out we interviewed him about that.

Mackie:
> "When I bumped into Tony at a paint it Black gig in Manchester, I told him about my new band at the time Epic Problem, Tony was a big Blitz fan and genuinely interested in hearing the new EP stuff.
> Tony asked me to do a few best of lists and an interview about the old days and new stuff, always happy to contribute to fanzines, they keep the scene going, online stuff is ok but a printed copy is great to have."

Gaz interviewed Destructors and Stuart Armstrong was back contributing to the zine by interviewing Crocodile God. I also contacted Section 13 after hearing their new release on Boss Tuneage, and after being blown away by Limp Wrist in Brighton I made contact with Martin Sorrondeguy and he was good enough to do an interview over a series of emails.

I was listening to Martin's bands a lot at this point, not just Crudos and Limp Wrist, but Needles, Tragatelo and the band that I was particularly taken with, N/N.

In my intro I mention that it was a new issue of Zonked! coming out that made me get my arse in gear to get this issue finished. Pete had planned to include a feature on people's first gigs in his lates issue, but that didn't make it, so he offered what he had to us, and with a few additions we put together a nice little feature.

Paul Vary also wrote an entertaining account of his trip to LA.

I'd been to some good gigs in 2011, two in particular have stuck with me. Both were at Sticky Mike's in Brighton. I had recently reviewed a Night Birds 7", and singer Brian had messaged me to say thanks. We became regular correspondents so when they came to the UK and had a gig in Brighton, I made the drive over. I got there early and had a good chat with Brian and Alex, from their label, Grave Mistake. I mentioned that I liked their song 'One Eye' because of my recent eye problems. Brian said that when he was a kid he'd tripped and fallen while carrying a pen and it had gone into his eye. It made me cringe, and I had to admit that he had a worse tale to tell about eye injuries than me. He did add my name into the lyrics of the song that night too, which was pretty cool, and the band were superb. The only downside to that gig was that Pete was away, so didn't make it. The other gig I really enjoyed was Punch. I'd become pretty obsessed with them, and again the chance to see them play was too good to pass up, so I was on the dreaded A27 again. Like the Night Birds, Punch were great.

To start with The Shorts were just Mike and me, so when we wanted to record a demo, we booked a studio session and recorded a few songs, him playing guitar and singing, me playing drums. We needed someone to play bass on the songs, so we asked Kev Borrett (Pilger), thankfully he agreed and so we went over to his house and he recorded bass straight onto my laptop. I mixed it all at home. Eventually, Neil Clelland (Intent/Pilger) joined us, to play guitar and then we were offered a gig, in Brighton. It was with Peter & The Test Tube Babies, at the Prince Albert and was a Fuck The Royal Wedding gig. We really wanted to play, so after a bit of begging, Kev agreed to stand in on bass. After that we were offered a second gig at the same venue, this time with The Stupids. Again, Kev stood in on bass for us.

We did some more recording, again with Kev helping out. One of the songs was called 'Bring Me The Skinned And Mutilated Corpse Of Bear Grylls', which I wrote the words to very quickly after seeing a brief bit of one of his supposed "survival" TV shows. During the short amount of time I was watching I saw him pick up a snake that was slithering away from him, and slit it down the middle with a big knife. This callous bit of animal abuse for a TV show appalled me and I scrubbed down some words. I felt it was a bit of a schoolboy rant so gave them to Mike and asked him to make them less simplistic, but all he did was add in extra profanities.

Kev didn't want to commit to The Shorts long term, so we asked Alan Marshall, who was at that point playing with Whole In The Head, to join us, and thankfully he was into it. Playing his first gig at The Hobbit. We recorded some more songs with Alan, and released the 'Hang Em Flog Em' 7"EP, which backed the songs we'd recorded with Alan with the ones Kev had recorded with us earlier. We released this record on SD.

Gaz:
Issue #51/52/53 – All of these issues have again escaped my own personal collection and again I don't really care! People own them and that's all that matters.

Tony Suspect - You're Nothing But a Fucking Bully

I had never experienced bullying at school. There was the odd nasty comment, plenty of piss taking, but no actual bullying, just the usual schoolboy nonsense. But when I was in my 40s I, along with plenty of others, was the subject of workplace bullying from a new manager. It seems that my crime was that I didn't have a degree, or any formal qualifications for the job I was doing. It didn't matter that in my most recent appraisal my line manager had said I was the best, most reliable and hard working member of the team, and suggested that I might like to consider becoming the team's supervisor, a role that was in the process of being created. I didn't want that, I was happy with the role I had and was content to carry on as I was, forging a "career" and progressing up the ladder has never interested me, which may also have gone against me. This new senior manager, who wasn't as yet my own manager, came in like a demented David Brent firing out bullshit corporate buzz words like a caricature of a corrupt capitalist from a lousy movie. In fact the very first thing I heard him say as he burst into an office full of people, some more senior than him, and throwing his coat over the back of a chair was "The jacket is off, let's role play."
Unfortunately this silly cartoon character proved to be a vile, misogynistic, homophobic bully who blazed through the department leaving a trail of broken people in his wake. I suffered because I just wanted to get on with my work and because I, like the rest of my team, didn't have a string of letters after my name or certificates on the wall, so I was deemed as "not good enough".
After a while this arsehole became our boss and the bullying got worse and worse until we ended up having to re-apply for our own jobs in a "restructure". In my interview he destroyed me, and I had a panic attack so all my focus was on not fleeing the room, rather than concentrating on the questions I was being asked, questions which were totally irrelevant to the job I was currently doing and designed to trip me up. I obviously didn't get my own job. When the news came that we weren't going to be keeping our jobs I wasn't surprised, but it made one of my team cry. The arsehole did all this with a smug grin on his face.
I was offered another job in the same department, one I didn't particularly want, but the prospect of finding work in the real world scared me and I was pretty shellshocked by the whole episode, so I took it. Things got worse when, like we were still in that lousy film, the bully became the manager for my new team, and the bullying continued. In the end he picked on the wrong person, they lodged a complaint which opened the floodgates and a staggering number of people came forward. I took my turn explaining everything to HR. He was put on gardening leave, and never came back.

Anyway, while all this was going on things at home, and in my punk rock world were going just fine, which helped hide the inner feelings of hopelessness and fear.
I started the web shop, the zine was still going strong and SD Records put something out for the first time in several years when we decided to release The Shorts 7".
I touch on the problems I'd been having in the "real world" in my intro to SD#54, but I didn't go into details, and I wasn't calling it bullying at that point. But, that aside it's a really packed issue. Gaz interviewed External Menace and The Domestics, Pete brought us Bloody Gears and we collaborated on the Violent Arrest interview. There was also Burnt Cross, Punch and Carol Hodge talking about joining up with Steve Ignorant and the Last Supper gig.

Among the good bands I saw around this time included another couple of trips to Brighton. First up was Porkeria at the Cowley Club. I was on holiday in Bulgaria when I got a text from Mike saying that The Shorts had been offered a gig in Brighton with this band I'd never heard of. It was the day after I got back from holiday, but it was a gig, and it was in Brighton so I was up for it. Porkeria were fantastic and I bought the album and 7" that night. The other gig was back as Sticky Mike's and it was Punch again. This time they were over with Negative Approach. Most people were excited about seeing NA, and they were good, "Can't Tell No One" is a perfect punk rock song, but I was there for Punch, with NA as an added bonus.

The Shorts also played in Southampton with Violent Arrest, who were stunningly good. A couple of old favourites who I didn't think I'd ever get to see live also came to Southampton. Anthrax and A-Heads were playing again, and both were pretty great. I'd recently been in contact with Gary Budd, from Anthrax too, so it was good to be able to say "hello."

In June 2013 we did another mini issue, calling it SD#54.25. The STE collective were putting on a gig to celebrate their 25th anniversary, so we thought we'd mark the occasion with an issue. It featured an interview with Rich Levene, and also had photos from STE gigs through the years and memories from people who'd played gigs for them, been to their gigs or were there at the start. People like Mike Fox, Neil Cox, Matt from Intent, Sean Forbes, Pete Zonked, Alan Marshall and Justin from The Vaccines as well as Gaz and me. The gig itself was fantastic, not only did some great bands play, including Violent Arrest, but the amount of friends, old and new, there made it very special. The Shorts also played, we'd asked Nath to stand in for Neil, who couldn't make it, then on the day Mike also couldn't make it, but instead of pulling out, because the three of us were there anyway, we decided to play a largely instrumental set. Photos from the day look like Abrazos played, but it was definitely The Shorts, Abrazos hadn't become a thing yet, although things were brewing on that front. Even better than the bands, was the occasion, it was great to catch up with Neil Cox, Punky Steve and Graham Sleightholme were over from Bristol, Pete and Ralf over from Brighton and of course Baz and John from Violent Arrest. There are a couple of cool photos of Graham and me doing our stalls, and Pete and me showing off current issues of Zonked and SD. It was a perfect day, full of great people, great bands and so much fun.

We were doing more and more stuff on our website, and building up the distro, so we were only really doing one full issue a year at this point, and we almost didn't make it in 2013, we started to work on it in November and managed to get SD#55 out in December. The cover had a couple of photos I'd taken of graffiti on a trip to Barcelona that summer, one was just a circle A drawn on a bus shelter, the other was on a wall near where we stayed which said Fuck The Mainstream. Over the top of that we put a picture of the Night Birds that Darren Bourne had taken at their Brighton gig. Night Birds were featured as well as an interview with Anti-Pasti drummer Kev Nixon as they had just reformed. Then two of my favourite bands at that time, No Statik and The Love Triangle, both very different bands in terms of sound and lyrics, but I loved each of them. I also reviewed the Las Otras album, a band that would, along with a couple of others, inspire me to write songs and record them at home.

My continuing internal struggles were mentioned in my column, but to try and combat them I had started a podcast. It was just an extension of the zine, I just wanted to play people songs by bands I loved as well as write about them.

At some point during 2014 Alan Marshall had decided to release a compilation EP on 2" vinyl. The EP was to feature bands from Southampton and Portsmouth all recording their second songs on the same day in the same studio. The Shorts had written a song called 'Strong & Proud', and I think we got to the studio first to set up and record first. I know that at some point during the day I went off to my parent's house, which was then near Planet Sounds where the recording was happening, to get something to eat. I came back to find that one of the bands had pulled out on the day, but Alan, being the organised man that he is, said he had a plan, he'd written three super short tributes to Napalm Death and Extreme Noise Terror, just in case. The only people left in the studio were Alan, Mike Fox and me. So Alan showed Mike what to play, and I did my usual one beat, on one of the songs anyway. The three songs were called 'Mega Cheese And Onion Breath', 'You Bought This, But Why?' and 'Gas Community Support Officer Bastard' and we grouped them all together under the title 'Grindcore Megamix'. Laying around in the studio was an old comedy book, I forget the title, but flicking through it we came across the phrase Baby Juggling, so we became Baby Jugglers.

Towards the end of 2014 we put out SD#56, which celebrated thirty years of doing SD. It had a feature running through the zine with various people answering set questions about their own punk rock journeys. However, the best bit of this issue, for me, was that we got to feature Las Otras. I'd loved their album, and 7", and had been watching YouTube clips of their gigs in Barcelona, which were ace. Then, they came to the UK and were playing Brighton. Initially The Shorts were offered a support slot, but Alan couldn't do it, so Mike and me went down anyway. I thought they were absolutely brilliant, I loved (and still love their stripped down, political punk. I'd also become a fan of Replica. We'd previously featured No Statik, and drummer B was also in Replica, so I got back in touch with him with another set of questions. B also sent over a couple of Martin Sorrondeguy's brilliant photos of Replica.
Also featured were The Pukes, The Dogtown Rebels and a Hard Skin tour report from Fat Bob.
I also mention my idea of doing a short film about the zine, and saying that I hoped to do it some day. I don't remember ever thinking about it again.
The cover is a photo Gaz took of some graffiti in Norwich saying "There Is No Authority But Yourself". The back cover had pictures of every SD cover up until that point.

In 2015 we resurrected the Baby Jugglers. Alan had written some more songs and we had practised a couple of them, and decided we should record. Nath brought his 4-track to the practise room and we recorded the ones we'd practised, along with 9 more that Alan showed us on the night, Mike's amp kept feeding back, and he couldn't stop it, but that just added to the noise. Nath took it away and worked his magic and it actually sounded great. We called it 'Musical Malfunction' and put it out on tape, and CDR, as well as having it available on bandcamp.

Around this time that I starting to write some songs, not for The Shorts, but just on my own. I'd worked out how to record my guitar onto my computer, and after an evening of listening to Rudimentary Peni and Wire and realising that their short songs may have been basic, but they sounded fantastic and really lifted my mood, taking my mind off the troubled thoughts I'd been having. So I decided to see if I could write some basic, short songs too. Obviously, not really being able to play guitar, none of them would be as good as, or sound anything like either of those bands, and because I was also listening to Las Otras, Crudos and N/N a lot there ended up being a hardcore edge to what I was trying to write. I was limited by the speed of the computerised drums I could use, and also my limitations on the guitar. But I was happy with the first song I wrote, so I scribbled down some lyrics and called the song 'Warmonger'. I then wrote a couple more, with more personal lyrics. I tried to play the bass bits on the guitar, not entirely successfully, and I did attempt to do some vocals, but hated my voice. I really wanted to get Gaz interested in doing vocals, and felt that it was really time we did some sort of band together, but now that he lived in Norfolk that was not really going to work, so I sat on the songs for a bit, periodically writing a few new riffs, and sets of lyrics when inspiration hit. The lyrics touched on my mental state which was suffering because of my work situation, but many were mainly just frustrated rants about the political climate and animal rights abuses.

Eventually I asked Alan if he'd add some bass, I took my laptop round to his house and he played along to the songs while I recorded it. After a few practises at Alan's house, we booked a practise room at Planet Sounds and did vocals by connecting a cheap microphone to the laptop. I didn't want to do vocals at all, but Alan convinced me that we should share vocals, and unfortunately for me, it worked, and our different vocal styles went well together. Initially I was calling the band Time Bomb, just because I had the idea that this would be Gaz and me and Time Bomb was a take on the name Suspect Device. I assumed there were probably countless bands with the name Time Bomb, but as the songs weren't for anyone other than me, and possibly Gaz, the name didn't matter at that point. So when Alan and me were thinking about doing a demo for other people to hear, we needed a name. Alan suggested Abrazos, and there wasn't much more discussion after that. Martin Sorrondeguy's lesser known band, N/N had become a bit of a template for us and 'Abrazos' was the title of one of their songs. We liked the idea that the name Abrazos sounded aggressive in our southern English accents, but it actually meant something much nicer as it's Spanish for hugs. We also liked the anti-war message of the image of the hugging couple Flux Of Pink Indians used under the quote "All The Arms We Need" and Abrazos went with that too. We put the finished demo up on bandcamp, it featured three of my early songs, one of which, 'Such A Pretty Face' (about animal experiments by the cosmetic industry), had some bits that Alan came up with to make it a much better song. Alan had also written lyrics to two of the songs.

We continued to practise, working on the songs I'd written on my own, and also new ones that Alan had written. The songs were a different style to those he was writing for Hack Job, obviously, and had to be kept simple because I was playing guitar and I still wasn't very proficient. Once or twice we booked a practise room, where we would practise the songs with me playing drums on one run through, and then guitar when we went through them again. This was because we'd decided to do a flexi disc. Boss Tuneage had released some flexis from new(ish) bands who hadn't yet released anything physically. I had asked Aston if he would consider Abrazos for a future release, but although he said he would have, he wasn't going to do any more at that point, so we decided to do our own. We booked a recording session at Planet Sounds, and were going to re-record the songs from the demo with another new one from Alan and three more of my earlier songs. We recorded the drums and bass first, and as Alan and me had been used to being the rhythm section when recording songs for The Shorts, when we got going on these songs we powered through them, playing them faster than they had been when we practised them at Alan's house, with me on guitar. But they sounded good and we were happy, however I then had to play guitar. I did I did struggle with the pace of the songs because I couldn't keep up with myself! But I got there eventually, and adding the vocals went smoothly, despite my continuing unease at hearing my voice. We sent off the songs to Aston who had agreed to help us get the flexi pressed up, we designed a simple folded cover that Alan got printed at his work, and when the flexes finally arrived, we had an evening folding the covers and stuffing them in plastic sleeves. Flexi's may not be everyone's favourite format, but they were cheap, and it felt good doing something a little different as neither of us had done a flexi before. It was a split release by SD and Alan's Peabrain label.

Alan:

Abrazos - The Tony has to be in two places at once years

Abrazos grew so naturally out of me and Tony being mates and the gentle implosion of The Shorts that I don't really remember how a lot of it actually came about (which I am aware is not especially helpful when writing about it for a book).

Let's start briefly with the end bit of The Shorts. After recording the second side of the Hang 'em and Flog 'em 7" (Kev played bass on the first side) we did a few gigs, which were always a lot of fun, but for one reason or another these became more sporadic until they kind of fizzled out. (In fact, there was even one where Nath stood in on guitar and Mike wasn't able to make it, so really that was the beginning of Abrazos although even we didn't know it at the time. I'm sure the audience probably deserve their money back for that one, it was definitely a seat of the pants type of set, but great fun).

There were no dramas or fallings out, The Shorts just kind of reached the end of the road. After that there was a hiatus where I wasn't really doing much musically, and then the inevitable itch to create something noisy began to kick in.

With impeccable timing Tony asked me at a gig (can't remember who we were watching) whether I would like to record some bass on a few tunes he had written, and they arrived by email, some with drum machine tracks, some just Tony playing the guitar riffs. They had a lovely Ramonesy, 80's hardcore feel and I took time to learn them by playing along to my phone. They were fun to play, had no frills, and the whole process was very chilled out. Once I knew them well enough we met up in the utility room of my house to run through the songs - Tony squeezed in by the dishwasher, me periodically smacking my bass head on the fridge freezer - until we had them working right, and then recorded them directly into Tony's laptop. No fills, no frills, just verse chorus, verse chorus bosh! A few retakes when the dog barked and we were done. Listening back it sounds raw of course, but I think it stands up. The vocals sound ferocious and there is a touch of Crass in there due to the drum machine style and limited means of production I think.

The sound of Abrazos is probably worth a mention at this point. We had no game plan (we still have no game plan other than making music we enjoy), and despite a broad overlap, Tony and I have very different influences at the heart of our punk rock universes. It was a joy for me to play something more hardcore influenced, but inevitably I bought some D-beat and added distortion to the party too. The blend (clash?) of styles, tied with political lyrics and a less anarcho-punk sound always intrigued us. The vocal mixture of Tony's rational arguments and my deranged fuck offery are one of the things I like best about Abrazos in general. It is evident in those early recordings in particular, although we haven't stopped doing the same thing – we wouldn't know how!

Still drawing from the list of songs I was originally sent, we started practicing again to record the next bunch as a self-titled flexi. Our choice to release a flexi (which I know some of you hate with a passion, but if its good enough for Heresy...) was driven half by finance and half by the fact that neither of us has ever done one. That seemed reason enough so we soldiered on.

We booked a few proper rehearsals this time as the recording date drew nearer and the door fridge was getting dented. And now came the interesting bit! It suddenly dawned on us that Tony needed to be in two places at once; 1) sat on a drum stool, and 2) foot on monitor dishing out guitar licks, so we had to practice every song twice and Tony had to switch gear from one instrument to the other. Add vocal duties into the mix and he was definitely working considerably harder than me on those evenings. The upshot was that the day of the recording was the first time we had actually heard what each song was going to sound like.

In the DIY style that exemplifies Suspect Device, Tony, and his approach to music, he pulled it off seamlessly. Almost. In a fit of pique the distortion pedal he was using decided to unravel dramatically during recording, with the guitar lead's jack plug stuck inside the socket and only bare wires linking the two together. Some of the songs were therefore recorded with me lying on the studio floor holding the cable in place like human Gaffa tape as Tony played frantically to complete everything before it finally gave up the ghost. The recording is certainly frantic and I think the adrenalin helped.

Gigs beckoned, so short of some kind of Brundlefly teleport or cloning machine antics, we needed a third cohort. Drummers are hard to come by, so Tony got back behind the kit and our good pal Nath stepped up for guitar duty. At this point Nath and I also started writing a few tunes and we used up the last of the original drum machine song ideas alongside all of us writing a bunch of new ones. Nath bought another set of influences to the band but is a perfect fit, and we were off at a pace, with the added novelty of knowing what we were making before we left the practice room!

When Covid levelled the world and silenced the music scene it was Abrazos that kept me busy. We experimented with making lockdown videos, playing bass standing in my vegetable patch and garden shed gurning at a phone screen, distance recording where we blasted tracks into iPhones and lined cupboards with pillows to create vocal booths. We even snuck off into the woods when you were only able to meet with one other person to record a Christmas hit – I know, fucking anarchists right! Like the worrier I am I was convinced we were going to get caught and need to scatter, as if 3 blokes all carrying drums and guitars just happened to be going for separate permitted walks at the same time (if only I had known then what we know now. Fuck you Boris!). Obviously, no such thing happened and we all had a well needed afternoon of band time keeping socially distant whilst trying to stop the camera falling off a log.

More recordings and a few more gigs have followed, and we are still doing what we do best over a 400 mile distance between Southampton and Stirling. I suspect we will, on and off, as long as the same things anger us and entertain us.

The thing that allows it all to work was/is our synchronicity, (possibly not always universally evident if you've ever seen us play live). Writing and recording with Abrazos has always been an easy, stress free, experience and the songs just seem to plop fully formed into our laps. Where there are changes to be made we all seem to instinctively know what is needed. That is a mark of great mates and DIY ethics. We kept it simple from the very first songs deliberately, and we don't think it needs anything else (if you think it does, start your own band and fill in the gaps). Punk has functioned like that forever - if it ain't broke don't fix it. If it is, try and hold it together like human Gaffa tape until it fucks up properly.

It was August 2015 by the time we got SD#57 out. Dan Roberson had offered to design a cover for us, and I gave him free reign to do what he liked, and I think what he came up with was a fantastic piece of artwork.
Two of my favourite bands at the time were Torso and Permanent Ruin, and I was happy that I was able to include both of them in this issue. Pete had seen Permanent Ruin in Paris, and so was able to provide some cool photos. Gaz had interviewed Healer Of Bastard and Stuart Armstrong had sent us one with The Number Ones. My intro was very brief, and my column was about the affect Endstand has had on my life. Pete wrote a piece about his adventures in Paris.
We sent a copy for Maximum RocknRoll to review and I remember being a bit fed up with what the reviewer said, not because I think everyone should love what we do, but I felt they missed the point of DIY zines. In fact the whole issue felt like MRR had changed and didn't really reflect the Worldwide DIY scene like they used to. It was all a bit sad.

SD#58 was another split with Zonked! It seems this wasn't the initial plan, but as we were both working on issues at the same time, and both Pete and me had contributed to each other's zines, it seemed like good idea. We didn't want to do just a half SD, half Zonked! issue, separating the two zines, so we completely amalgamated the content in one big zine.
I had an interview with Chroma from Barcelona, who featured Las Otras' drummer, Rebe, now playing guitar and signing, and I also interviewed Hack Job before even hearing them. But they were Alan's new band, and I wanted to support him. Before the issue came out, but after I'd done the interview, Mike and me went down to see them in Portsmouth, and thankfully I loved them. I didn't really know the other two, Jochen and Damo, at the time, but it wasn't long before they both became good friends. Gaz interviewed the excellent Dry Heaves as well as Army Of Shanks, a band I hadn't heard of, but that's what's great about us having slightly divergent tastes, I would never have thought to interview AoS, just as Gaz probably wouldn't have sought out Hack Job, or Chroma. But we both loved Dry Heaves. My friend Casey Jones sent a moving piece he'd written about the tribute gig for his friend, Sense Field singer Jon Bunch, who's recently died.

THE JON BUNCH BENEFIT CONCERT by Casey Jones
When I first learned of Jon's passing, I thought it was a hoax. One of those stupid rock 'n' roll publicity stunts carried out in poor taste. Bunch had recently started a new band, which had a bit of a party element to it so it made perfect sense. You know, sort of in that live fast die young vein but more tongue and cheek. I got the first text that morning and then another and

another in fairly rapid succession. I started to get really nervous and decided to call him so that just by answering his phone, he could immediately relieve this anxiety that was building up in my chest. No way it could be true. This is just a very tasteless ruse. My call went straight to voicemail - that ridiculous outgoing message that he's had for eons that simply states "Jaaaaaaahhhn!" with his voice audibly breaking through that shit-eating grin. His outgoing message always made me laugh but this time, I welled up because I knew instantly that it was all true. I don't know why. Calls have gone to voicemail before but this time it was different. I left my message and started sobbing before I could even get to the end of it then hung up and just cried by myself. I was confused those first couple days like we all had it wrong. Like somehow misinformation had permeated our social media accounts and that the real truth would come out soon. Have you ever said that you can't believe something to emphasise a point? Haven't we all? It's a common thing to say - "I can't believe this traffic" (yet I live in Southern California with millions of other people, I can't believe how hot it is (I live in Southern California - you get the point. The weird thing is, if you dissect it for a moment and think about whether you ever actually meant it, odds are you can't. This time was different. And although I don't think I actually said that to anyone. I remember having that feeling for several days. Disbelief. It remained to some extent until his memorial service almost two weeks later. How could anyone so vibrant, so colorful, and so incredibly nice just be gone, just like that.

So here's how the fund and the memorial show came together. First the fund. Back to the day I first received that horrible news. Me and some close friends from the scene started a private thread on Facebook. This is how it started - "Guys, I'd like to put something together for Jon. Actually, something to help out Jack hopefully. I haven't spoken to Cristina in awhile so I don't know what shape she's in financially to take care of Jack without support. Regardless, maybe something where people he was close to could play in tribute. Let me know what you think." (I chose to delete one small piece from the above for privacy reasons. Everyone was immediately on board, as this was the obvious thing to do. Then our friend Sven from Leipzig brought up the idea of a donations page, and Brett (Ignite) followed that up with the GoFundMe idea, Sven nominated me as the "finance guy" to set it all up and the fund page was live by that following evening. Before launching it, I wanted to first speak with a few of Jon's family members to see if Jack's education funding was a indeed even a hole that now needed filling. For all I knew, Jack had a billionaire uncle somewhere to cover his schooling and we would be told to direct the proceeds to save the sea otters or whatever. It didn't matter. The point was that we all wanted to do something and if the world was going to support it, it should be something that Jon's family thought important. As it happens, Jack doesn't have a billionaire uncle and so the fund was setup to help with his future education expenses and also at his family's request, funeral expenses and a music program for underprivileged youth. To date, it has raised almost $60,000 and I (and more importantly, Jon's family am grateful to every single person that has contributed. Next, the show. Chris Lisk and Joe Nelson were included in the original thread and instantly went to work to secure a venue and start reaching out to bands to see who would be interested in playing. Word spread like wildfire and although there may have been a few people that got in touch with us for self-interested reasons throughout the process, I genuinely believe that everyone involved was there to pay/play tribute to their friend. Bands started messaging us on an almost daily basis once word got out that we were putting on a benefit for Jon. Bands like Texas is the Reason, Red 5, and so many others that had played with Sense Field so much back in the day. Even Drumkan from Japan reached out. They had toured Japan with Sense Field and Further Seems Forever and came all the way from Japan on their own dime to play a 20 minute set in support. Amazing. In addition, singers like Popeye who Jon meant so much to and vice versa, contributed however they could even if the old band couldn't make it all the way back together. Lisk, whose had the most experience of any of us putting on something like this - he organised the Rev 25 shows back in 2012, which had just as many bands but over the course of four nights - got a hold of Efrem from Death by Stereo early on and locked in the Yost Theater in Santa Ana where he works booking bands. The owners were generous enough to allow us 100% of the ticket sale proceeds for the cause. Nelson knows pretty much every musician you can think of and he got to work reaching out to some of the bigger names to see whose schedules would allow them to join us. The support was overwhelming throughout but there were setbacks along the way, including a tragic stabbing resulting in the death of a young guy at one of the stages we had reserved. This happened about two weeks before Jon's show after we had sold nearly 1500 tickets and for awhile there we were uncertain whether the venue would even remain open since the police had been investigating. As it turned out, the officers determined that club security wasn't to blame and we were allowed to proceed.

All told, in the end we had 25 bands across three stages in one day! Even after paying for all of those plane tickets to get musicians from all over America out to California for a day, sound crew, catering, a fully-funded documentary and live recording, and everything else that goes into a massive undertaking such as this, the ticket sales and Revelation Records booth proceeds netted over $30,000 for the fund. Every single band played for free, including heavy hitters like Rocket from the Crypt and The Bronx...no one ever asked for a single dime. There were so many highlights for me, foremost being the first time that Ignite's original lineup has appeared onstage together since 1994. That set, albeit a short one, was amazing to play and I will never forget it. Having Scream come out and play was a highlight for me too. Pete Stahl has been doing this continually longer than any of us and Scream has always been one of my favorite bands. Jon loved them too. Pete didn't hesitate when we reached out to him about playing and ended up telling a very sweet story onstage that day about a letter he received from Bunch back in the 80's. I saw so many people that I haven't seen in years. Joe Nelson put it best when he wrote, I saw every single person I've ever known inside of 30 minutes. It was so special - probably the most special thing I've ever been involved in. I also have to say that the day was truly a happy one. From the beginning, it was always about everyone coming together to celebrate Jon and not some morose event to mourn the tragedy that brought us all together. The singers that came up for Sense Field's set all did an amazing job. Some standouts were Kenny from The Starting Line who until then I personally had never heard of but he has a fan for life in me now. So much energy and presence. Jeff Caudill from Gameface and Popeye from Farside gave heartfelt performances and Garrett from TITR absolutely crushed it singing Dreams. The list goes on and on. They all put their hearts and souls into it, not to mention all of the members of Sense Field who came together from all over the country and only practiced twice before the show. You never would have known it though. They were so incredibly tight, just like I remember them from back in their heyday, and together with the emotion and talent of all those singers, it made for one of the most amazing sets I've ever witnessed!

Next we have the aforementioned documentary and live CD underway. Also, Revelation has been so generous with their time and resources, including steadily facilitating auctions on eBay of items donated from all over the country. Such rare and unique items have been coming in. Ian from the Aquabats had all of his band mates sign his first guitar from when he was a kid and he donated it to the cause. We are also currently in the midst of planning an east coast show to be held at The Theater of Living Arts in Philadelphia on June 25 for everyone that couldn't make it to California last month. In addition to Sense Field, Further Seems Forever will be joining for this one, as well as several other bands. It is just one stage for one day but the goal is the same - to celebrate Jon's life and his music.

I miss Jon a lot. Right now as I think about it, I particularly miss his smile and the way he always called me by name several times throughout a conversation. That always made me feel like he was really interested in whatever we were talking about and like an affirmation of our friendship. But I also feel that staying busy with all of this activity related to him has kept us close in a way even though he's gone. Rodney (Sense Field) said he was bummed that Jon couldn't come to the show...that he knew Jon would have dug it so much. Those two were very close and I know he's still hurting over the loss of his friend. I hope somehow that Jon's been able to see all of this happening and that he did get to see the show for Rodney's sake. I hope Jon had his own set of unique highlights from that day while he sat smiling on whatever cloud he chose to watch from. Maybe he can even share them with us someday too. I obviously don't know what happens when we're gone but that really doesn't seem so far-fetched to me when I think of it."

On the Zonked! side of things were Immolato Tomatoes, the wonderful old Brighton band who'd recently had their demos released on CD by Boss Tuneage. He also spoke to Andy Turner and Simon Mooney after Boss Tuneage re-released the second Instigators album, 'Phoenix'. Plus Rotten Mind, Time Waster and a great interview with our friend Darren Bourne.

There was also a few mentions of the UK's referendum that had narrowly decided that leaving the EU would be a good thing. Not for any well thought out and reasoned ideal of leaving a vast capitalist juggernaut, but what was, really, thinly disguised xenophobia and racism built on a lie.

Gaz:
Issue #54 – Bloody hell it's October 2012! Violent Arrest on the cover and interviewed along with Punch, Burnt Cross, The Domestics, Bloody Gears, External Menace and the wonderful Carol Hodge talked about Steve Ignorant's Last Supper. Some great gig photographs in this issue too.

Issue #55 – Nope! Don't own a copy!

Issue #56 – Oh yes! Great cover picture and 30 years of the zine! This issue came out in October 2014 and for the cover picture I had to drive my Step Daughter - India into Norwich to take a picture of some graffiti I'd spotted. I've always been a Luddite, but she possessed to skills to email the picture to Tony. 'There Is No Authority But Yourself' read the graffiti sprayed on the fence in Waterloo Road and that kind of summed up our 30 years I thought as it was a Crass slogan. This issue brought you Las Otras, Replica, The Pukes, Dogtown Rebels, The No Marks and those legendary Oi boys – Hard Skin on Tour.

Issue #57 - It's August 2015 and this issue probably has our most 'arty' cover supplied by the much underrated Dan Roberson. Torso, The #1s, Permanent Ruin and Healer of Bastards featured. I took the back cover picture of MDC's set up on stage at the sadly long lost Owl Sanctuary venue in Norwich. I did once rate MDC as the worst band I'd ever seen when they supported the Dead Kennedys in Southampton. I think they were a complete shock to what 16 year old me was listening to at the time is my excuse! It goes without saying that founding member Dave Dictor now has my total respect.

Issue #58 – Hell's teeth! Another split issue with Zonked! Pete's half represented issue 13.5 for him. For our part in all this we interviewed the Dry Heaves, Chroma, Army of Skanks and Hack Job. In Pete's half were Rotten Mind, Immolato Tomatoes, Time Waster and Darren Bourne. You can't claim a lack of variety there in this June 2016 extravaganza!

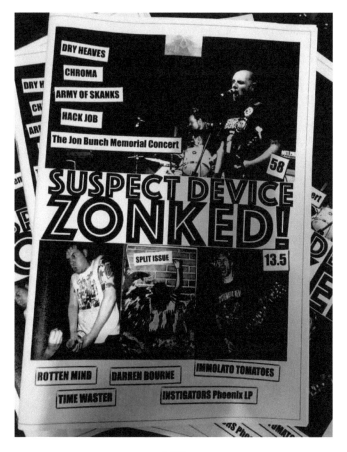

Make A Cup Of Tea, Put A Record On
The Suspect Device Podcasts

Tony:

One of the things that have kept Gaz and me doing the zine all these years is a desire to turn people on to the music we love, and to try and help the bands we admire in any small way we can. This was the reason I started the SD podcasts back in April 2013, calling it Make A Cup Of Tea, Put A Record On, after a line in 'Waking Up' by Elastica, a song I love and one of my favourite things to do.

I was shocked to discover that I started this ten years ago, in 2013, and it carried on almost every month until 2022. There's no real reason I have, temporarily, stopped doing them, it was just that I had other things occupying me, not least this book, and also the nagging feeling that others do the punk rock podcast/radio show much better than I do.

When I think about it, it was an odd thing for me to do, I may have had vague ideas of being a radio DJ when I was younger, but never had the confidence to actually pursue it, and I don't feel any more comfortable with this sort of stuff now. But, for some reason I decided to make a playlist of some of the songs I'd been listening to and talk about them, and then put it up on line.

I made a decision at the start that I only ever wanted to play songs from DIY releases.

The songs played in the first podcast were:

NEEDLES - Desesperación
THE SHIRKS - Motherhood Of The Wolf
EPIC PROBLEM - Choke
HASSLER - Apathy
THE GUTTERS - Work
HARD SKIN - Crack On Have A Booze
SLAVES - It's An Epidemic
SECT - Money
ANTHRAX - Monochrome Dream
PUNCH - Do It Yourself
BURNT CROSS - Break The Law Not The Poor
GLAM - Crisis Atomica
THE SHORTS - String The Bastards Up
NEEDLES - Servitudeg
STATE FUNERAL - State Funeral

When I posted the first one on the blogspot page for Make A Cup Of Tea, Put A Record On I said "In future, if this has a future, I'm thinking of asking people to submit 4 or 5 five songs they'd like me to feature." This shows an uncertain parallel with the first issue of the zine, and also the wish for collaboration. I carried on alone until September 2013 when I took my laptop over to Pete's house and we recorded an episode together. Despite feeling an idiot still, I enjoyed the collaboration much more than sitting alone and doing it. Pete would be a regular contributor from that point on, usually he'd just submit a set of songs for me to play, sometimes he'd send voice notes over with explanations of the songs. A couple of times Pete selected all the songs while I was away, leaving me to just put them all together and make it available.

Then, in May 2014 I got together with Alan and recorded an episode where we celebrated his 2"EP on Pea Brain with a set of songs under 30 seconds (apart from the first one which was called 'Short Attention Span' by Citizen's Patrol but was the longest song at 1 minute 42 seconds).

CITIZENS PATROL - Short Attention Span
WHOLE IN THE HEAD - A Brief History Of Working Class Resistance
DS-13 - DIY Killed By The Kids
F-MINUS - Rise To Power
NEEDLES - Not Losing Faith
COKE BUST - Another Fucking Problem

ADHD EP side 1 - Peabrain
BLACK ANCHOR - We Are Sick
JOYTHEIF - Neighbours
CHEMICAL THREAT - WCD

GO! - THE ABC Song
LAS OTRAS - Fronteras
VIOLENT ARREST - Watch Your Back
NIGHT BIRDS - No Spoilers

ADHD EP side 2 - Peabrain
THE SHORTS - Strong & Proud
SHOOTING FISH - Heartfelt Confessional
BABY JUGGLERS- Grindcore Megamix

LOS CRUDOS - Vas A Regresar
NAPALM DEATH - The Kill
IRON LUNG - Monolith
PROPAGANDHI - Superbowl Patriot XXXVI
BLOODBUZZ - A Brief Moment Of Darkness
PUNCH - Four Letters
PERMANENT RUIN - Solution
ANTI YOU - Big Man
DESCENDENTS - Coffee Mug
PAINT IT BLACK - D.F.W.
DROP DEAD - Requiem
HEALTH HAZARD - They
RIPCORD - Empty Faces
THE STUPIDS - The Pit
RUDIMENTARY PENI - The Psycho Squat
HERESY - Ghettoised
SEDITION - Nobody
NOFX - Whoa On The Whoas
THE ERGS - Johnny Rzeznick Needs His Ass Kicked
KID DYNAMITE - Sweet Shop Syndicate
GLAM - Cara De Mierda
GERIATRIC UNIT - All Tries Will Fail
DIS-TANK - All Fucked Up
RAD - We Got Lost
PILGER - Still The News Is Fit To Sing
CHINEAPPLE PUNX - I Need Religion
THE DAY MAN LOST - More Rocks To Throw At Cop
COMBAT WOUNDED VETERAN - Rocks In A Blender
LIMP WRIST - Back In The Days
WAT TYLER - Washing Machine
ELECTRO HIPPIES - Mega Armageddon Death

The Baby Jugglers track on the 2"EP wasn't planned, but when we recorded more songs and released a demo, I decided to play the whole thing in the podcast, in November 2015, calling it a Session!

I did a few more with Alan, one that included Damo and Jochen from Hack Job, and also with Nath when we got together virtually during lockdown. I don't find it easy being the one taking the lead, but I did enjoy these collaborations, because it's just talking about records with friends, and who doesn't love to do that? When Pete and Gaz both joined me it was a lot of fun, we all have slightly different tastes, but share a common journey to this point with plenty of common punk rock influences along the way.

Alan:
Invasion of the Podysnatchers
When I was a yoof I spent literally hours every week on my hands and knees pulling records out of the shelves in my room to play to my mates, or crouched in their rooms pawing through their record sleeves and doing the same. Sometimes it was slim pickings (I was surrounded by metal-heads and Echo and the Bunnymen fans), but many of my happiest times were whipping the needle off one favourite record half way through just to demonstrate how great the next one was like an over excited plate-spinner. That's the curve that moved me from Madness, to the Specials, to The Cockney Rejects, to The Exploited, To Conflict, to Extreme Noise Terror... and so on for the next 35 ish years. It simply wouldn't have happened without a captive audience of interested kids wanting to get into new stuff.
The knees aren't up to it any more, but I have a very visceral feeling that that is exactly what I'm doing all over again when I am asked to record a Have a Cup of Tea, Put a Record On podcast.
Tony has a simple, Peely inspired, way of selecting records for his podcast, seemingly with an ease and simplicity that I wish I could emulate. If it's new and exciting - it's in the playlist, if It's 40 years old and it's still exciting - it's also in the playlist. Records I have never heard followed by records I forgot I even owned. If it's DIY and punk (sometimes not even the later) it's fair game, and even just as a listener it feels like that experimental plate-spinning unfolding again.
As I have said elsewhere, Tony and my tastes meet in a broad swathe of bands in the middle. We both like all sorts of stuff from melodic jangly indie through bits of Goth, to some brutal hardcore stuff, and every now and then he finds something he knows is right up my street. A great example is the understated simplicity of Pinen from Barcelona, which he introduced me to a few years back, or the recent Prey – Unsafe LP not long before I write this, which made me purchase a copy of the vinyl before I got to the end of the first song, but there have been many gems I have picked up in conversation on and off the podcast. Cue note scribbling and online purchasing during teabreaks.
My approach on the other hand seems to be a compulsion to make the whole affair over-complicated. " We should both pick one track from each decade since we started buying records from the towns we live in" or "We should only pick records that have a member of the band from the record before in and see how far we get" or " Every record title should be an anagram of what we had for breakfast on the day it was released". That kind of thing. Tony (and Nath when we have recorded an Abrazos special) are very patient and just let me get on with it, and there is some kind of puzzle solving satisfaction with trying to find the right bunch of tunes, but it's the

simple act of hanging out playing records that makes it a joy to do. I usually also pick at least one bonkers grindcore track just because I know it pushes the playlist a bit (often for as much as 20 seconds).

One time, Tony suggested we try and record an episode as a more freeform conversation and just chat about music we like and he would drop in the tunes we discussed. The end result was great fun, but must have been a nightmare to edit as we went off on so many musical tangents. We had a shortlist of things to discuss but spent more time reminding ourselves of previous releases, or other bands we saw play with them at a gig in 1991 etc.

The podcast feels like an extension of Suspect Device's paper cousin, and largely achieves the same end only with music instead of print. It reaches far and wide covering old favourites and newcomers, bands with big names and, importantly, those with no platform and marginalised voices, which is what good DIY media should do. It carries the same spirit as the zine, and I always come away with a new avenue to explore.

Tony:
The ideas that Alan, and Pete, come up with are great fun, even if they do drive me crazy at times, but I can't help but get carried away with what's required.

Gaz also did other podcasts with me, as did Mike Fox and Stuart Armstrong, and both Graham Sleightholme and Darren Bourne have also contributed song suggestions at times.

Pete:
Collaborating and contributing to the 'Make a Cup of Tea…' podcasts are something I've enjoyed immensely over the years. There is nothing better than passing on cool tunes that've got you excited to a wider audience, hoping others gain equal pleasure. And being turned on to new sounds too.

Early on when I got involved in the podcasts (which was a whole new experience to me) I'd record voice files to go with my contributions, but I'm no fan of hearing my own voice, and think they work way better with Tony in vocal command. He will say that he lacks the self-confidence to be fronting them when in fact he's a dab hand at assembling the shows, and natural when it comes to presenting. He's been a real sport when I've come up with random program suggestions. The selection of 'Open Your Eyes' songs springs to mind, and Tony reminded me recently about my 'Running' themed show. So many choices! There was a latter-day set the two of us did of entirely all female fronted bands that came out great (and deserves a follow-on at some point) whilst the Year-End round up episode guarantees a neat diverse listen with many of the SD Gang chipping in. For the win.

Getting together on Zoom with Tony 'n Gaz to share stories and tunes is always highly entertaining. Much credit must go to Tony for recording, then editing, our laughs, rambling 'n banter into something cohesive for the loyal listener. He truly has The Patience of a Saint (pun intended) My pick though is the show where The SD Brothers discussed their early days of friendship/record buying, and darts. Priceless.

Oh, and here's a funny thing; Tony named the podcast after a line in an Elastica song, which was produced by a guy I was at school with and had originally turned me on to Crass. Passing it on. It's what it's all about. "Mister programmer, I got my hammer…"

Tony:

Pete has reminded me that the times we gave ourselves a theme made for a good list of songs, and I particularly enjoyed putting those ones together. Sometimes we just had one set of four or five songs with a particular theme, other times it was a whole podcast. I did like the female fronted podcast we did, we didn't make a big thing of it being all female fronted bands, we just put the songs together and put them out with no mention of the theme. The songs stood out on their own, and no one mentioned the fact that all the bands had female singers, and that's as it should be. Again, I like the collaboration of friends coming up with ideas and sharing music.

Gaz:

I'd like to make it clear that the idea of the Podcasts is entirely Tony's and even if I had thought of it – technically beyond my limited computer skills and even further beyond my ability to turn them into reality! As Pete rightly points out in his submission to this bit of the book – Tony's almost Saintly dedication and perseverance actually knows no bounds. I've alluded elsewhere in the book to the fact that the Podcasts, the fanzine and even the record label requires his drive behind our merry band of contributing slackers!

I've taken part in a few over the years now, but If it's one thing that doesn't sound good about the ones I've contributed to, it is the sound of my own voice on the recordings! I sound fuckin' awful and the only saving grace is the music that precedes and follows it.

I don't have any idea of our listening figures, but I hope he finds the energy to do more in the future. It does give a great platform to so many bands old and new, where people listening in may have heard of a band, but never heard. Even in these days of instant internet gratification you still have to have the seed planted. I guess that's my great hope for the legacy of these Podcasts and a tribute to Tony's passion – someone might look back one day and reminisce that they first heard a certain band on an SD Podcast! Not quite John Peel between 10pm and Midnight, but none the less - Job done!

Tony:

Everyone thinks their voice sounds terrible when you hear a recording, I certainly do, but when I listen to Gaz and Pete and everyone else who contributes, they just sound like the voices I know.

I also struggle with the technology, but have somehow been able to find a way, although I haven't done anything about making the show more accessible, which I probably should at some point.

We haven't done any for a while now, but I haven't called time on it altogether, and when they do come back I'd want them to always be more collaborative, maybe making them proper podcasts.

As I type, the last one we did was in October 2022, and was another idea that Pete and me had for a theme, this time all the songs were instrumentals.

Instigators - In One Ear...
Subhumans - Intro
Werecats - Toast
Neighborhood Brats - All Nazis Must Die
Dead Hero - Mtl Bta
Fugazi - Brendan #1
Culture Shock - Concentration Dub
Night Birds - Agent Zero
Self Abuse - Self Abuse (Intro)
2 Sick Monkeys - Superhero
Wat Tyler - Heavy Metal Vivisector
Agent Orange - Miserlu
Fuel - Untitled
Rose Of Victory - Overdrive
Ripcord - Intro
Instigators - ...Out The Other

I see these podcasts as an extension of the zine in that we give the music we love a little bit of exposure. We know it's not much, but it's something.
I have some ideas of how I'd like the podcasts to progress, but organising it all and making it happen feels too much for me, and the thought fills me with dread, but I still want to do it.

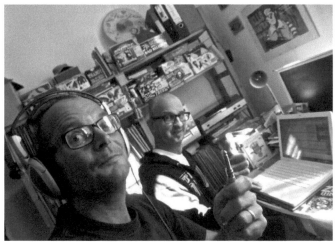

Pete and Tony recording an episode of the podcast at Zonked! HQ,
September 2013

Tony Suspect - All That I Can Give You Is...

It was over a year before our next issue, but we hadn't been slacking, there was a lot of SD related work going on. We were one of the labels who contributed to the release of the Hack Job / Hooked On Christ split 7", we had the Distro and the podcast and we'd setup a new Blogspot page to replace the website. Also, Si Briggs and me had another adventure. With our changing lives, our adventures had dried up, but Paint It Black were back in the UK, for one date, which actually turned into two sets on the same day at the same venue, one in the afternoon, the other in the evening. This was a no brainer, we were going to see Paint It Black, and we were going together. I met Si at Kings Cross station and after grabbing something to eat in a Vegan place near the station, we made our way to South East London for the gig at the DIY Space For London. It was a long journey and we walked the last couple of miles, going past Millwall's ground, The New Den, along the way. DIY Space was a cool place, it had a record shop, so that was obviously our first stop, it had a cafe, so we also got tea. It was great to catch up with the PiB guys again, we hadn't seen each other for several years, but they greeted us like the old friends we have become. Obviously their first set was brilliant, and we also got to see Petrol Girls be a force of nature, State Funeral also play two great sets and Nachthexen who I don't remember much about, but notes from the time suggest I enjoyed them.

Between sets we went looking for some food, and while some people went off to see Strike Anywhere in Camden that evening, but as much as we like Strike Anywhere, be had already decided that we were going to stay and see PiB's second set, which was again brilliant. Afterwards we were facing the prospect of a long walk back to the nearest tube to take us back to Waterloo, that was until Ben (Thatcher On Acid/Hard Skin), who was driving PiB, offered to drop us at the station, which was really nice of him. However, our friend Mike Doe, who had driven up for the evening set, offered to take us back to Southampton, despite him living in Portsmouth, which was really good of him.

It was a shame to miss Strike Anywhere, who also hadn't been over to the UK for many years, but our friendship with PiB had been forged by our trips to Philadelphia and the Pilger tour, so staying to see their two sets was what we were always going to do.

It was September 2017 before we got another issue done. For SD#59, Gaz had got a contact for Uproar and did an interview with them, while I decided to feature local bands as there were a few new(ish) ones playing gigs that I wanted to give some exposure to. Andy Morris was playing with Armoured Flu Unit with Nath, they are a great band and also featured and Danny from Haywire, and Iain Ball who'd once been in Exalt, who Gaz had interviewed in an early issue of SD. AFU were the band that I had initially interviewed, I then sent a set of standard questions to Horseflies, Latchstring and Kontakta, while Pete gave us State Funeral, which was good as I had really enjoyed them when they played with Paint It Black in London.

We were back with another mini issue in December 2017. SD#59.2017 was the first of our A5 Top Tens issue where Gaz, me and our friends selected our top ten records (and gigs, books and anything else) of 2017. The cover photo was a bit of graffiti I'd spotted on our walk to the PiB gig in London earlier that year that just said Police State 2017.

SUSPECT DEVICE
59.2011

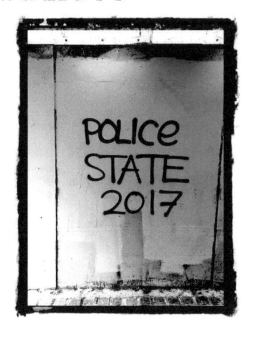

By July 2018 I was feeling energised again, small DIY gigs had started to be come a little more frequent in Southampton, thanks to Phil Hedges and Ben Marin putting bands on under their A Public Dis-Service Announcement banner. At one of these, at The Shooting Star, Rites, from the Netherlands played and were excellent, so I wanted to feature them in the zine. Also, Worst Witch had emerged over in Bristol and were fantastic, Alan wanted to interview them for us, which was not an offer we were going to turn down. I'd also been inspired by the Bratakus album, after reading a review that Nath did for the Louder Than War website. Their youthful enthusiasm, great lyrics and brilliant tunes really struck a chord. Two sisters who lived miles from anyone, meaning there weren't really any other people they could form a band with, so they did it on their own. I love that attitude, that's punk rock, you work with what you've got and the two of them had some wonderfully abrasive, yet melodic songs. I was really happy when they were up for answering some questions. Keeping it in the family their dad Angus Quinn (Sedition/Scatha) had started a new band with Brian Curran (Disaffect/Quarantine), like Bratakus they were a two-piece, but unlike the two sisters, living in the same house, Brian and Angus live several hours apart and only had one song on-line, but it was such a good song and I liked their approach, so I wanted them in the zine too. Plus, with Abrazos also being a duo at this point it was good to be able to feature bands who also only had two members. Gaz had interviewed Left For Dead, more old hands still producing new music, and James Domestic let us print a long report he'd written of the tour The Domestics did with Guilt Police in Europe. So SD#60 was a pretty packed issue.

The intro page featured another of example of Dan Roberson's brilliant artwork, he'd sent us another SD logo, which looked more like a banner.

Sadly, the back page has photos of Huckey (Target Of Demand/7 Sioux) and Steve Soto (Adolescents etc) who had both sadly died.

I'd been to some good gigs in the second half of the year, and when Gaz was down for one of his visits, we sat around drinking tea and decided that we should do another issue before the end of the year. SD#61 featured an interview Pete did with Rotten Foxes, who I'd seen with Pizza Tramp and Hack Job in Portsmouth, and I wanted to interview Natterers, who I'd driven down to Brighton to see. Their newly released album, 'Head In Threatening Attitude', was brilliant, and I didn't want to pass up the opportunity of seeing them live, so made plans to drive over to Brighton. Although the distance between Southampton and Brighton is only about 60 miles, it can be a difficult, long drive at times, and not wanting to miss the gig I left straight from work. It took me two and a half hours to get there. It was 7.30 when I arrived. I parked up, found the The Pipeline, then found that the gig wasn't starting until 9.00. I could have gone home after work, and then travelled up a little later avoiding the worst of the traffic. I had a walk around the sea front, before bumping into my friend Mike Doe. We went into the tiny pub, stayed downstairs until Pete arrived. It was worth all the hassle, the Pipeline is a tiny venue and it was so great to see Natterers in that space, they were superb. The drive home wasn't without incident, as the main road was closed, meaning a huge detour along the small coastal roads, adding about an hour to the journey.

Alan had discovered Trappist, and band featuring members of Infest, Spazz, Despise You and Crom who sang about DIY produced beer and wanted to interview them. We are always happy to feature interviews other people have done for us, and I really like the questions Alan asks. Not being into beer, and not being as big a fan of the past musical out put from the Trappist people as Alan is, his questions and the band's answers made me want to check them out. And when I did I found I quite liked them. The whole point of doing the zine is to turn people on to music they may not have heard, or may not realise they need to hear, so Alan definitely fulfilled the brief with this interview.

Mackie had started to do his own Blitz t-shirts to counter the amount of those produced, using his artwork, without asking for permission, so we did a little interview with him about this project.

We also put out another Top Ten mini issue in January 2019. SD#61.2018 rounded up our favourite things from 2018, with the cover picture being my old Epicenter Zone t-shirt showing a jukebox with the words "Where Punk Is Always In Style" on it.

Abrazos had done some more recording, and released a CDR featuring the rest of the songs I'd initially written, as well as new ones from Alan, and a cover of the N/N song we took our name from. The recording didn't go quite as smoothly as the first one, this is the recording where the jack of my guitar lead broke in my pedal, meaning I played half the songs with Alan laid on the floor holding the lead in place. Also, around this time, we decided we wanted to play some gigs, so we would need a proper guitarist as I wasn't good enough to play guitar in front of an audience, let alone try to do vocals as well. We hadn't got as far as talking about who'd we'd ask to join at this point. Then, one day early in 2019 Sarah was running a 10K in Winchester. While she was running I met Becca (who was at University in Winchester) and her Uni friend and we went to a cafe, where Sarah joined us for some vegan cake after she'd finished. While she ate and recovered from her run, an alert popped up on my phone telling me that Marc "Mates" Maitland had taken his own life. I remember feeling numb, and initially thinking I must have misread the message. After all I had been speaking to him, on Messenger, just a few days before this. We were talking about our new musical projects, sending each other new tracks we'd recorded. He had done some recording that Mackie had contributed to, and Abrazos had just put the CDR out. I happened to mention to Mates that Abrazos were thinking of playing some gigs, but we would need to find a guitarist. What he didn't tell me was that he was also messaging Nath that night, and had mentioned what I had said. I then got a message from Nath offering his services as Abrazos guitarist. There was really nothing we need to think about or discuss, if Nath wanted to join us then he was in. Most importantly Nath is a friend, that would have been enough on its own, luckily he is also a great guitarist who understood instantly what we wanted, and was able to make our stripped back, no frills songs sound exactly as I had always wanted them to sound.

I said in my intro to SD#62, that Abrazos were having a great time now that we were a trio, and we had Mates to thank for that. When typing that I thought about Mates and conflicting thoughts swirled around my brain, I was loving what Abrazos had become, but there were always the sad thoughts of Mates.

Despite the shocking news about Mates, there had been a lot to be happy about. I'd finally got to see The Skids, and they were fantastic. I went on my own something I am never truly at ease with, but I absolutely loved it, they were better than I could ever have hoped for. Gaz and me had taken a trip up to London to see Steve Ignorant's Slice Of Life at the 100 Club, with Rubella Ballet and The Cravats. We'd met up early to do a bit of record shopping before the gig, and while we were in All Ages Records in Camden it started raining, and it didn't stop. This wasn't just rain, this was torrential rain of the sort you see in movies and think "it doesn't really rain like that.", but it did on this day, and we got absolutely soaked. We ended up in a pub near the 100 Club; Gaz doesn't need too many excuses to go into a pub, but on this occasion we both just wanted somewhere warm to try and dry off. Our soggy clothes didn't stop us enjoying a fantastic gig with all three bands being on top form. At some point during the evening Gaz spoke to The Shend who was keen to do an interview, so we were able to feature them in issue 62.

DIY Gigs in Southampton and Portsmouth were more regular and the atmosphere at both was really great, the best it had been for quite some time. I had seen Rash Decision and Human Leather play fantastic gigs in Portsmouth, and both of them were happy to do an interview. With good interviews with The Cravats, Rash Decision and Human Leather we had enough to put an issue out, but then Jodie Faster came over from France and played at the Shooting Star in Southampton and blew my mind. I really wanted to have them in the zine too. Luckily, they did the interview in super quick time, once they got back home, so we were able to feature them as well.

The affect Jodie Faster had on me was similar to that both Endstand, Strike Anywhere and Limp Wrist had all had in previous years. This young band, from France, came to our town, played a small venue and were not only blisteringly good, but were funny, friendly and with the same political outlook as us, it was truly inspirational. I've seen them three or four times since and they continue to be nothing short of phenomenal. The other thing to be happy about was that Mike Head was contributing to SD again. It had been some years since he'd done anything for us, so it was good to have him involved again.

The front cover of SD#62 was a great Human Leather live shot, that the band supplied, with the back cover our little tribute to Mates.

Hack Job were planning another split 7", this time with Conquerer Worm, so again we offered to be one of the labels helping to get this released. I'd sent over some money and left it to Jochen Such to do all the arranging. This suited me just fine, we got to play a a part in helping our friends put music out without having to do too much hard work, sometimes it's nice to take a backseat. Although, while on a family holiday in Somerset, I found myself sat in a cafe in Weston-Super-Mare trying to get a decent 4G connection to enable me to email over the SD logo for the sleeve.

2019 was the year that Abrazos played our first four gigs. The first, in July, was at The Shooting Star in Southampton. Before we went on we were asked if we wanted to headline, above Tape It Shut and Rhi & The Relics, but it was our first gig, so we declined and went on first. It felt good to play our songs live and it was nice to have Gaz down to mark Abrazos' first live outing. My friend from work, Sam came along too, he's not really into punk, but came anyway. Since the gig I have introduced him to Hard Skin, and he has become hooked on them. Someone else form work came along too, but got there late and missed us.

We then played two gigs in September, at the Birdcage in Portsmouth with Pizza Tramp, Rash Decision, The SLM and Rotten Foxes, and then at the Cowley Club in Brighton with Butane Regulators and Nana. Both were a lot of fun.

In December of 2019 I was working on another Top Ten mini issue when Gaz sent me two interviews, with The Headsticks and Eastfield, so we decided to do two issues, the Top Ten A5 issue and a full A4 issue, and give the mini issue, SD#63.2019, away with SD#63. I had to get my arse in gear pretty quick. Thankfully Alan did a Pizza Tramp interview for us and Tomar Control over in Peru, who I'd recently become aware of, were happy to answer my questions via email, then when James Domestic offered us the use of an interview he'd done for Maximum Rock N Roll that was now not going to see the light of day, we had plenty of good content.

Both zines were ready for a special Xmas gig Abrazos played at Planet Sounds in Southampton with Kontakta and Werecats. It was a benefit for a refugee soup kitchen put on by Kontakta's bass player, Rich, and although it was a lowkey gig, it was a lovely, intimate evening full of friends, with a special atmosphere and it was a lot of fun.

Werecats asked not to play last due to one of them needing to get a train back to London after the gig, Kontakta didn't want to do it, so Abrazos ended up playing last, and we even played some new songs. I have enjoyed all our gigs, and I'm extremely grateful to everyone who's offered to put us on, but this one remains my favourite.

Before our next issue came out, the world ground to a halt. The news coming our way from the Far East saw me going from saying "It's probably no worse than the flu" to "Shit, this is really serious" in a matter of a few days.

Thankfully before we were all confined to our homes, Abrazos recorded some songs with Dave Sloan in Portsmouth. These songs would be released on a memory stick taped to the front of a lyric booklet (we added a 16 song live set recorded at our gig in Portsmouth, by Dave Sloan), and some of them would eventually come out on a split 7" with our friends Brain Anguish, released by SD and Angus's Screaming Babies Records.

There were also a couple more gigs to go to. King Of Pigs played a Sunday afternoon gig in Southampton, they played first, it was early, but they were fantastic, one of those bands you see and they totally blow you away. Self Abuse played their first ever gig in Southampton, and they were fantastic, and what was better was the Subhumans were playing too, and Gaz was there with me.

Then, Abrazos played our fifth gig. Geraldine and Rhys' birthday gig at The Joiners was a blast. I enjoyed playing, but then just as much I enjoyed catching up with friends. Marv Gadgie had come down from Boston (Lincs), Target Of Demand played and it was good to see Rainer and Mops again. Andy Nazer brought the C-30s, Dealing With Damage were great and then there was Dangerman and Lucky Malice. Dangerman had played here before so we knew we were going to like them, but Lucky Malice were new to a lot of us, but I think everyone left with a new favourite band. They were the smiliest band I've ever seen, but they also have important political points to make, and who doesn't like to sing along to a song that goes "no nazis, no nazis, we want no nazis in our streets"? Crispin came over for the gig, which was cool, and Michael and Cil from Werecats were there, plus loads of old faces from local gigs past and present. It was a fun day.

The Rezillos also played in Southampton again. Not as great as their previous visit to The Brook, but still good to see them again, and also good to see Alan and Soozin, Nath and Michelle there too.

Gaz:

Issue #59 & #59.2017 - If my maths is right, it looks like more than a year has passed between issues! I guess 70 proper issues in 40 years does not equate to us being prolific?! Anyway, I prefer steady! This September 2017 outing brought with it - Armoured Flu Unit, Horseflies, Latchstring, Uproar, Kontakta and State Funeral. It's a little known fact that Latchstring feature my godson Phil on the vocals and he's still promoting a few DIY gigs to this day. Issue 59.2017 was a round up of the year in a mini A5 style, which got loads of people to put their top ten of everything down to entertain others for the year 2017. Tony put a really camp picture of me under my contribution taken from such an angle that I look like I'm sporting a chin of Peter Test Tube proportions! They say the camera never lies! The digital age really does piss me off – back when we started this lark, hardly anyone had a camera. Now look at it – you can't escape them! Mind you! The flip side is that SD has had some ace band pictures over the last few years and you can take as many as you like I guess and don't have to save up to get a film developed! Remember those days?

Issue #60 & #61 – Over to Tony's bit!

Issue # 61.2018 – I don't have the main issue, but I have this December 2018 round up of the year, which contains a picture of me standing in a bush! Yes! I'm fully clothed!

Issue #62 – Easily the best thing about writing a zine has been the great people we've met over the years. The Shend of the Cravats has been no exception and Tony and me met him at the 100 Club in London after the Cravats had supported Steve Ignorants Slice of Life. He happily purchased a copy of SD at the gig and was very keen to be in it as he loved the fact that we wrote a paper zine. Quite sensibly we seized the opportunity. We surrounded The Cravats with Human Leather, Rash Decision and the mad Frenchmen who go by the name of Jodie Faster.

Issue #63 & #63.2019 - Basically this December 2019 Issue was a Bogoff (Buy one get one free - if you're not up with Supermarket analogies?). The main issue featured Eastfield, Tomar Control, Pizzatramp, The Headsticks and James Domestic, while the A5 mini issue was a round up of everyone's Top Ten of everything for 2019. When I say everyone, I mean anyone who contributes or can be bothered, of which I'm pleased to say there are a few.

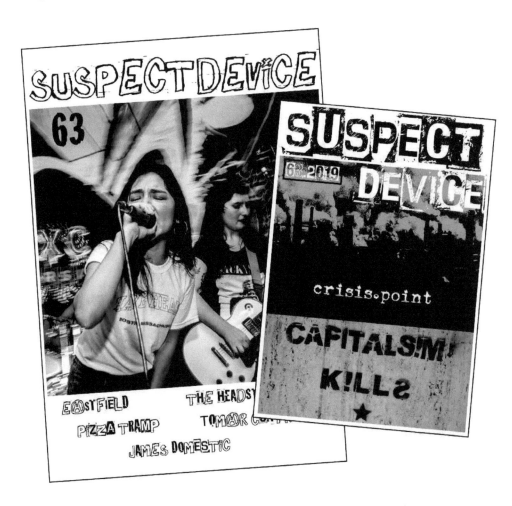

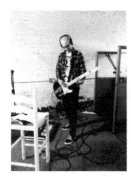

(Left) First Abrazos recording, Planet Sounds, Southampton.
(photo by Alan Marshall)

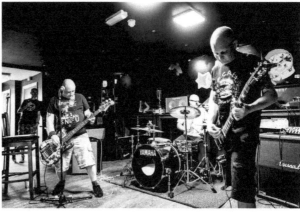

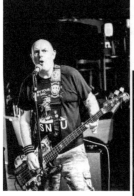

(Above) Gaz watches the first Abrazos gig.
(Left & below) First Abrazos gig, Shooting Star, Southampton
(photos by Dave Sloan)

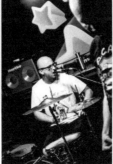

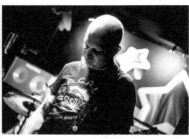

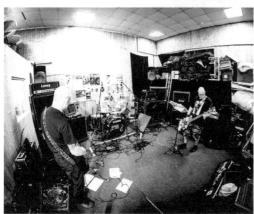

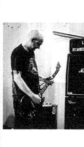

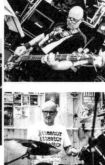

(Left & Above) Recording the Abrazos album
at The Fishtank, Portsmouth.
(Photos by Dave Sloan)

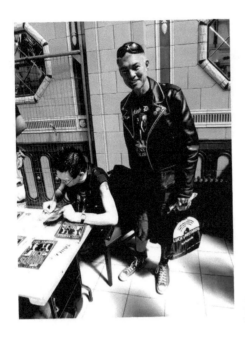

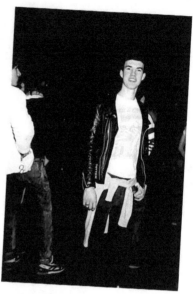

GAZ: (Above left) Gaz watches Shane Baldwin (Vice Squad) sign his book.
(Above right) Gaz at Basins, Portsmouth.
(Below) Clash City Rocker - Gaz tries to recreate the first Clash album cover on his own.

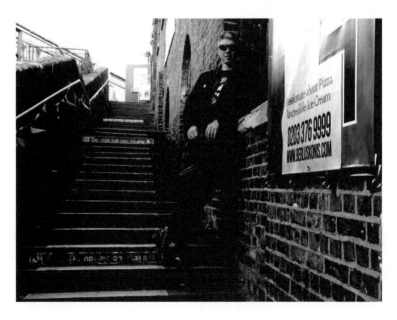

Here Comes The New Punk

As I said earlier, after Gaz and me had been into punk for a little while and were busily soaking up all that the early 1980s punk had to offer us, we didn't really know any other punks, we had each other, we had Sounds and we had John Peel. Up and down the country there were people paving their own paths which would eventually lead them to us, via DIY punk, and our zine. **(Tony)**

Pete Zonked! - I washed up on Planet Earth midsummer 1965, in Bermuda, where my newlywed parents had moved the previous year. Coincidentally, one of their early friends on the island were an English couple who'd recently had their first child, a boy too. In the early Eighties he was heavily involved in the Bradford Punk Scene (playing in Living Dead, promoting gigs) and still works in the Music Industry I believe. After Bermuda there was a stint living in England's Midlands (where my brother Tom came along) then Dad got a job teaching modern languages at an international school in Singapore. We were on the move again. Life in Singapore was great; warm weather all year round, fantastic food, and lots of travel 'n adventures.
Those years were very impactful on me growing up, shaping the person I became. We'd go swimming most days, either at Dad's school pool, or the Swiss Club, which we were able to join thanks to my Mum being a native of Toblerone-land. Tom and I were regularly in scrapes, getting injured and patched up. Poor Mum! Something not on my radar during those years was Western Popular Music, of the kind many of my peers in the UK would have been listening to. Being in a tight-knit melting pot of South-East Asian cultures meant there was always some kind of exotic music hitting the ears though. During Chinese New Year the Dragon Dance would come down our street, and you'd put a red envelope containing a couple of dollars in its mouth for good luck. Well, 'good luck' for whoever got the money!!! The Hindu Festival Thaipusam was the craziest; raucous devotional singing charged by dancing and the beating of drums as men in a trance-like-state pierced their skins with hooks and put skewers through their mouths and tongues. Quite a bit to take in! Dad thought it was brilliant we were exposed to all this. In Bali he sneaked me into a Cock Fight once. That's how he rolled. A few short years later the same man wouldn't let me go see Crass with some school mates because he didn't like the sound of it. Go figure. I never forgot that. Bali's traditional music is The Gamelan, a hypnotic orchestra of drums, gongs, flutes, and xylophones, I did like. Even now, whenever I hear the Gamelan, I'm taken right back. Dad recorded from the TV some themes songs of shows we kids liked, my favourites being 'Banana Splits' and 'Hawaii 5-0' (... guess The Dickies and Radio Birdman were digging those tunes too, hah) On a night out with my Texan friend Chris and his folks to the American Club I first saw Batman on a big screen. Biff! Bang! Pow! I loved it, and another cool theme tune! So yeah, no early Seventies Western Pop Music for me, and I can't thank my parents enough for that. They'd have never understood why. When Dad's contract in Singapore was up, he toyed with maybe going next to New Zealand, or Canada, but opted for South-East England. That's where we headed next. Another new start.

Here We Are In A New Age

When Dad got a new job teaching in East Sussex, we moved to a largish village about 15 miles north-east of Brighton. This semi-rural environment took some adjusting to after the cosmopolitan hustle 'n bustle of life in Singapore. And the weather. The first proper summer there was the fabled Scorcher of '76, giving me a completely unrealistic expectation of British summers. I'd soon learn. Those late '70's winters were harsh too from what I remember, lot of snow. I found it brutal. After outdoors PE I'd crawl back to the changing room unable to even untie my football boots laces I was so frozen. My hands in pain. The winter months remain a seasonal battle of wills for me. We had countryside across the road from our house, and being right by the school gave easy access to the playing fields, tennis courts, and playground for skateboarding. That was brilliant. These days it's all fenced off. Entry Verboten. Back then, being surrounded by lots of open space was a big-plus. I spent as much time as possible outdoors, somethings that's followed me thru my adult life.

There was no 'pop music' in our house, wasn't my parents' thing at all. Dads' records were mostly of the classical variety. Mum would occasionally stick in a tape of traditional Swiss folk music. The radio stayed tuned to BBC stations 3 + 4. My brother had a small black & white portable TV in his bedroom, and we'd started to tune in occasionally to Top of The Pops. Must have been more out of curiosity than anything because nothing we heard had any impact. Then, on an April evening in 1977, something clicked; a very catchy upbeat song being belted out by a bunch of odd-looking blokes. Their vibe was surly and mean. The chorus went "Go Buddy Go Buddy Go Buddy.. go go go". That got our attention. The band were called The Stranglers. A cool name. Days later a clued-up guy in my class questioned what music I liked. A week earlier I would have been stumped. "The Stranglers" I hesitantly replied. He told me there was a lad from his village, in another class in our year, who liked The Stranglers. This led to my meeting Martin Chapman; we hit it off straight away, becoming firm friends for the rest of our school days, and some beyond. His Dad owned musical instrument shops in the South-East, including one in London, where Martin would go some Saturday's, returning with new records, that I'd get to borrow/ tape. 'Rattus Norvegicus' was the starting point.

The term 'Punk' might have vaguely registered for me, but I was mainly digging the rowdy tunes with offensive words chucked in. Nice! The timing of this musical awakening did coincide with my gradually developing a mental claustrophobia to the place we were now living. I was out-of-sync with much of the narrow-minded populace, their limited horizons and trying to keep up with Joneses. In my decade living there I did make some very good friends but knew I'd be leaving. Home life could be tense at times, rising interest rates in the later '70's meant a battle making ends meet after the bills/mortgage were paid. I didn't help; my parents being regularly disappointed by my poor attitude to school, where I struggled to either understand what they were trying to teach me (maths, sciences) or barely motivated by most of the other subjects.

All the travel I'd experienced should have made Geography of interest, but we rarely got into studies of actual countries 'n cultures. The History being taught was the Norman's, Tudor's, etc. I was hungry for knowledge about what was going on NOW. The Vietnam War wasn't long over, there were liberation struggles in Southern Africa, turmoil in the Middle East, The Iranian Revolution, and why the fuck weren't we being taught anything about 'The Troubles' in Northern Ireland? So when Johnny Rotten sang about "the M.P.L.A, the U.D.A, the I.R.A".... that got my attention! Henry the Eighth, and the Battle of Hastings took a permanent backseat.

I was a very plain 'n ordinary kid, now sporting national health specs, but a rebelliousness (I didn't even realise was there) had been ignited, my young/fertile mind developing rudimentary opinions on things like religion, politics, and the importance of questioning authority. Hearing these unruly Punkers sticking two-fingers up to The Establishment was quite literally music to my ears. A sonic portal to somewhere way more exciting than the village confines...

In the spring/summer of '81, Britain was Burning, and I sat my exams in early June with little care given for the outcome. I was done with school, and it was done with me. A year at Technical College in Lewes followed on a Business Studies course. Although only a few miles away from my village Secondary it was worlds apart, with a way more diverse mix of students. I liked that, met some interesting people, soon falling back into larking about over academic improvement. An early conversation with my future girlfriend/wife revealed she'd idled thru the same course in Uxbridge. Whilst over in Southampton, Mr Tony Suspect himself, for want of anything better to do, was another distinguished scholar of this dole-dodging Diploma. My school mate Martin had started a photography course at Lewes, having now moved nearby with his parents, so we'd often chip off back to his attic room and play records. Martin's musical tastes were expanding. Syd Barrett's 'The Madcap Laughs' album was on his flash turntable a lot. That was too much for my Punk palette, where Dead Kennedy's, Subhumans, D.O.A., Partisans were rocking my world.

College ended. It was time to enter The Real World. Coaxed by The Job Centre I began work in a small supermarket. Having steady money for records, gigs, and socialising was fantastic, even though a lot of my co-workers were a grim bunch. After 18 months I had enough, finding another job in the Hardware Store at an Agricultural Merchants. Proved to be a big improvement; better hours, decent workmates, plenty of laughs. That suited me for a year-or-so. My teens were drawing in, and I knew I needed to properly move on, spread my wings, go see some more of the world again. That was my next step.

As for Martin, we'd made a pact at college to not go on a Youth Opportunities Program and be cheap labour for the Fucking Tories. But soon after I got the supermarket job Martin announced he was going on a YOP at a Printers in Lewes. It was a start-up, and the company expanded quickly. He worked hard, did very well for himself. A few years later, hitching back from my parents, I spotted Martin bombing past the other way in his Porsche Carrera. He'd always liked the finer things in life!

Welcome To 1984

It was in that most Punk of years – 1984 - that Suspect Device 'zine began coming to life, furthering Gaz 'n Tony's friendship, and igniting a D.I.Y. partnership they can't have ever imagined would remain strong 40 decades later.

The increasingly distant memories I have of that year are of my musical tastes evolving fast. I'd taken a deep dive into the sounds that inspired Punk; Iggy/Stooges, MC5, New York Dolls, Flamin' Groovies, Radio Birdman, Heartbreakers, etc. Lou Reed's 'Transformer' took a while to digest. Lacked unruly loud guitars... help! This journey of retro-discovery was aided greatly by two Brighton bands I'd started hanging out with; Tales from The Tubes and The Violet White who were both in hock to the Proto-Punk aesthetic. A bit older 'n more streetwise, they looked out for me at their gigs. The booze and cheap drugs didn't interest me as much as the wild energy happening in small backroom pub/club venues. Couldn't get enough of it. I'm still grateful to those guys for the friendship they showed this geeky kid. The Violet White self-released an album in '85, its back cover adorned with scrawly caricatures of the colourful characters who inhabited their crazed universe, including me testifying "Radio Birdman, etc... brilliant!!". Yeah, 'Birdman were a whole new exciting line of musical discovery, cracking the door ajar on The Down-Underground.

Maximum RocknRoll's comp. 'Welcome to 1984' was a crucial release that year. Punk on a global level truly fascinated me; my upbringing no doubt influenced that. I recall in the early-'80's a fair amount of prejudice/scepticism existed, even amongst some more right-on UK Punkers, to bands from overseas. Thankfully not everyone was so blinkered; in '82 I'd mail ordered a cassette comp. called 'Punk Is', from an Andy 'Shesk' Thompson in Hull. Amongst the (homegrown likes of Xpozez, Cult Maniax and Born B.C. were some rough quality contributions by bands from Finland, Italy, and Brazil. Honestly, that blew my mind. A total game changer. Suddenly, the current crop of UK bands didn't sound quite so edgy. Andy followed up with two further tapes on his Xcentrics Noise label featuring bands from even more countries, and cool artwork from a guy called Pushead. Massive Credit to Andy for connecting people across continents and opening our ears to international Punk. I'd count those cassettes as being as important to my own early musical development as The Stranglers, 'Pistols, Crass, and Dead Kennedy's.

Still living at my parents in The Sticks, mostly going to gigs on my own, apart from having my younger brother to inspire/indoctrinate I didn't know anyone else tuned into this music I was steadily unearthing. That would change in '84; answering an advert for a 'zine in nearby Uckfield led to a growing friendship with the inimitable Johnny 'Death Head', at that stage still in full-on Anarcho-mode, but getting hip to Early-Eighties American bands. And soon Radio Birdman, heh! Allen Silburn, then a well know face on the Brighton scene, reminded me a while back that the first time we chatted properly was at a Miners Strike Benefit gig in '84, where the stencilled 7SECONDS on my leather jacket had caught his eye. Allen was singing in Fatal Mistake, who I'd go see all the time. He was another early Hardcore enthusiast, going on to front Immolato Tomatoes and Sleep. Allen's good mate 'Little' Mark Holden became one of mine too. Friendships that have endured.

I was still buying Sounds music paper in '84, but increasingly D.I.Y. distro's and 'zine's were keeping me informed of the Cool Shit. Looking back, I remain in awe at the dynamism of it all; this crude, but highly functional subterranean network linking up compatibly minded folk, existing mostly off the radar of the mainstream world. It was so exciting; receiving a record by a band you'd only read about, trusting your limited funds had been well spent. Hoping that battered/reuse soaped-stamp envelope containing a 'zine was gonna make it thru without a postal charge. Getting wind of gigs, where the turn out might be weak, but the bands gave it their all. Amazing Times. February '84 at a D.O.A. gig in London I brought a copy of Black/White 'zine from its compiler Paul. Its strong focus on North American bands, plus some from Mainland Europe, gave further clues there were others out there in the UK with open minds to Punk from overseas. Incidentally, I was a bit late to the party with Maximum RocknRoll magazine, only scoring my first issue a few months previously. What I held in my hands was truly mind boggling.

A random 'zine I sent off for in '84 was Impact, from the Home Counties somewhere. Still very UK-centric it included a Top Ten by Jim Brooks from The Ejected, by way of recommendations for younger kids getting into Punk. I immediately thought of Ten of my own, scribbled them down on a handwritten A4 sheet that I posted to the 'zine address. A few weeks later the new issue arrived, featured my piece. I was elated. So yeah, 1984 was where my own 'zine contributing first started. It's plainly a habit... that sticks...

Alan Marshall - Bored Teenagers

For the first 12 years or so of my life the rattling tube trains of the Metropolitan line were the only clue that London lay less than thirty minutes away.

Living at the end of the line, well beyond the rank and file 1930s terraces, I was safely cosseted in a bucolic world of woodlands, rivers, and all-day bike adventures with friends. We weren't rich, but we certainly weren't poor either and the world seemed boundless. Think Enid Blyton but with Raleigh grifters, Anglo-Bubbly and Rucanor baseball boots and you won't be far off the mark.

This existence was green and exciting until I reached my teens, when slowly and imperceptibly the horizons began to close in and the fields and lanes started to tarnish. Village fetes and jam tarts began to feel small, boring and insignificant, and the pinging underground tracks leading out of town became a tantalising draw.

I've heard many people say that they didn't find punk, it found them, fully formed and ready to rock the boat, and that was my experience too. Almost as soon as I heard a distorted guitar it felt like something within me was quenched, a missing piece slotted in, and when it arrived in my life it came snarling and hyped up like an evil twin.

The seeds were there, I gravitated to pop hits such as Billy Idol's White Wedding, Adam Ant's Kings of the Wild Frontier and The Stranglers Golden Brown without really knowing that these were the publicly palatable blossoms of something altogether more ferocious underground. My first exposure to proper punk was small and unassuming, a single picture in a school book – a sex education book to be precise. Near the back, past the diagrams of bisected genitalia and emotionless bodily function, was a section about relationships and a small colour photo of a mohawked punk hairspraying his girlfriends backcombed hair. It was all there; studded jacket, check! Siouxsie eyeliner – check! Razorblade earring -check! It wasn't that I fancied her, or him, it just felt like a kind of empty void. Whatever I was looking at, I wanted that. And without knowing what I was seeing, I was in.

It wasn't long before the sliding doors whisked me and my mates away to the technicolour worlds of Camden and Kensington Markets and overpriced punk tat of Carnaby Street, pawing and haggling over cheap knock-off belts and t-shirts, but it was the record shops that really grabbed me. I consumed records, first the Oi! Scene which served as an accessible and convenient bridge from my Madness and Specials loving cropped hair years to an altogether noisier world. I discovered quickly that I preferred the spikey-topped Exploited, Toy Dolls and Black Flag (remind me again why they are on an Oi! Album!?) to the ploddy terrace chants of the 4skins and Gonads tracks and grew my hair, ripped my jeans and absorbed punk into my very soul.

Then out of the blue came a gift from the gods. My mum's friend had a son (Pete) who was a few years older than me and one of the gang of coolest kids in the village to my young eyes. He was going to University and appeared at our door with a cardboard box of records he was getting rid of. He knew I was into the Pistols and stuff and thought I might like some. I flicked through the black and white photocopied sleeves, selecting singles and LPs on instinct, not knowing most of the bands and plucking ones with the most eye-grabbing covers like a card trick. Those records were to open a whole world to me. Amongst others they included Subhumans, Rudimentary Peni, Amebix, Conflict, and MDC singles (I still regularly wake in a cold sweat wondering what stone cold classics I left randomly in the box!) My disquiet now had a direction. This would have been about 1985 and I was aware that I was a fraction too young. My very first attempt to go to a gig was Antisect in a pub in Euston somewhere, where we were roundly kicked out as soon as we walked through the door by the landlord for being underage, and had to listen through the beer-cellar hatch in an alley down the side of the bar. Anarcho punk was ebbing away following Crass throwing in their black towel in 1984 (I am ignoring the jazz that followed), but I bought and learned Conflict and Rudimentary Peni records by rote alongside 77 classics which already seemed like remote cornerstones of a towering genre. I drew no distinctions – for me, The Ungovernable Force lit the same anti-establishment fuse as Machine Gun Etiquette – it was all fuel for the long repressed fire and I relished it.

Dave 'Pox' Fox was also a few years older than us and had no aspirations of going to university. He did however have 2 possessions that were the coolest things I had ever encountered; 1 – a shock of half peroxide, half jet-black spiked hair, 2 – a beaten up shit-brown minivan.

We bonded over matching skeletal Exploited paintings on the back of our jackets, but moved on quickly when he excitedly played me a tape of Extreme Noise Terror / Chaos UK's Earslaughter in 1986. I had never heard anything so fast, raw or downright terrible in my life, and so began my love of snotty, distorted grindcore and crust (or stenchcore as it delightfully got labelled at the time. Gigs in dingy basements with numerous friends followed in regular succession now I had learned not to look quite as much like a rabbit in the headlights. Sometimes this involved travelling home squeezed in and rattling around in the back of Dave's van full of tools, other times loud and cider-drenched tube journeys accompanied by the dull hiss of ear damage (now a permanent feature for many of us I am sad to say). Bleay eyes scanning flyers and zines we had picked up at the gig in the rattling carriages through Harrow on the Hill and Rickmansworth.

Inevitably, I set out on a series of missions to recreate the sounds I heard in the squats and back rooms of grotty London pubs on my own turf, and formed numerous bands with fellow salvaged souls (generally formulated, fine tuned and disbanded in the horseshoe bar of the Iron Horse public house, with only rare appearances in front of bemused audiences. Taddish McRadish, WANK, Piss up a Stick, Lumphammer, all came and went in a hail of dropped plectrums, broken equipment and spilled special brew. Attitude over ability was firmly the order of the day but no one seemed to mind too much. I attempted to play guitar (albeit through a broken 30 watt bass combo) but around this time I was given a lovely red £40 bass by a member of one of these bands, which I still play today and has served me well in bands I will come on to later. Through sheer tenacity, and possibly because we could now drive to the heady concrete delights of High Wycombe, one of these bands eventually congealed into something people seemed to want to listen to, The Chineapple Punx. No less silly but slightly more structured, we actually got gigs, and turned up to them, and played a long series of sweaty shows to a seemingly endless stream of lunatics who enjoyed getting Brussel sprouts, chocolate milk and mashed potato flung at them by a talentless Tizwas reject dressed as a policeman in Y-fronts.

Then we did something amazing. We made a record of our own. Not a great one, but it was ours and we joined a band of brothers and sisters I once held beyond reach. I have made a few since, with lots of excellent friends, but that first one seemed like an impossible peak - self-financed, self-released and mostly traded for other records we wanted instead of sold.

By this time I had been involved with Animal Rights for a good few years, become vegan and navigated the world I felt out of step with through stalls at gigs, lyrics tucked inside record sleeves and articles photocopied to within an inch of their life in zines.

This continued blissfully for some time until I heard the distant rattling train rails again. It was time for a change.

Craig Burton - 1976! What was that all about?

I remember the long hot summer and Southampton winning the FA Cup, but that's it. I was only 11 years old, and football & cricket were my life! Music never featured, so I was oblivious of the chaos, change and furore going on outside my bubble in the arts and entertainment industry. Punk had arrived, but not at 104 Turner Crescent.

Fast forward a few years and I am now 16 years old and at Itchen college! New friends have taken me along with them to see Bad Manners. OMD & Slade on nights out and beer has started to feature regularly. I have also struck up a friendship with some spikey punk types (namely Biff, Badge, Sid & Simon as they are also in the college cricket team with me. They look different to the other students with their Studs, Leathers & badges and over the course of the year have introduced me to the likes of Stiff Little Fingers & The Damned. The turning point in my life comes though when The Exploited appear on Top of The Pops, that's when I see the light and am hooked.

My first proper punk gig is on my 17th Birthday in March 1982. It is a charity affair at St Mathews Hall and Biff has tipped me off it is on, and they are going to it. First band up is local Portsmouth act Ad Nauseum followed by DIRT. The atmosphere is electric, violent, dingy, and exciting! The dancing is frightening and looks like a punch up at a football match to begin with, then, slowly a pattern appears, and it becomes apparent that it is all friendly with lots of smiles and sweat. I don't join in on this occasion and just watch amazed at the bands & audience. I go home elated and punk music is now in my veins.

It is a little while before my next gig and its Ad Nauseam (again plus Polemic at the Canute Hotel. I have tagged along with Biff and the gang again and while not quite as raucous as the previous gig it is still a good night, cut a bit short due to the overzealous landlord getting het up.

Gigs now come thick & fast. The Anti Nowhere League, The Defects, SLF, Subhumans, the Banshees, Dead Kennedys, Peter & The Test Tube Babies, The Meteors etc and then at the end of 1983 Biff tells me that Simon's Band (Suicide Pact are playing at the joiners in Southampton! This must be the most anticipated gig so far and St Marys Street is full of punks drinking from bottles ages before the doors open. Once in and the band starts its chaos! A little stage, people dancing, falling and ending up on stage in huge heaps. The management turn the power off to restore order and away we go for it all to happen again. In the end the power is turned off full stop and we are all made to leave the room, before being let back in for the main band (I think they may have been called COLD but they couldn't compete with what had already gone on.

1984 has arrived and the world hasn't ended, what has happened though is that I have a job and am buying Bands demo tapes and fanzines through the post. The first one I received was a tape from DEVOID called 'Drunk on Punk' a DIY affair with hand made cover etc and I loved it and the music. More DIY fanzines and tapes arrive and I am now part of the 'Soap your stamps' brigade to save postage costs.

I have still not met too many other local punks at this stage, but I am travelling to the 100 Club in London for gigs and the hornpipe in Portsmouth to see the likes of the Adicts, Toy Dolls, King Kurt, Subhumans, Conflict, The Sears and Angelic Upstarts. It is the summer of 1984 and I am thinking that it's time I got more involved. I can't play an instrument or sing so the natural & cheap option is a fanzine to see if I can drum up any local interest.

So that's what I do, Issue one of 'The Beercan' is compiled, printed and ready to go. Looking back, it is a bit crap, with a crap cover, But it's an achievement to get it out and at the time I was chuffed to bits with it, much as I presume Tony & Gary were when their 1st issue came out!

The 1st issue was 100 copies and were sold via a few distro's I wrote to, via the national music papers in their ads section and also via Underground records (who's owners were great music fans). A few local people did notice as well, and Mike Fox lived near me and ordered one so I walked round to drop it off to him, but he was out! I had also noticed an advert for a local distro service in Eastleigh and I wrote to ask if they would take some to sell for me. This person was Rich Levene (of the S.T.E gig Promotor fame) and after a 3 or 4 hour walk to his house to drop them off to him, he was out as well! So, I put them through his door and walked home again.

I did finally meet Rich later that year at a Conflict/ Icons of Filth gig in Bournemouth and gave him and his mate Steve Burgess a lift back to Southampton, as I was driving. This was first contact and next gig Rich introduced me to Mike Fox, at last, as I was walking around the joiners with a carrier bag full of zines that I was trying to sell. The doors opened from then on with me meeting Netley Mark, PJ, Rut and at some point, Tony & Gary of Suspect Device fame. I also got to reconnect with two old school mates, Johnny Fry & Dave Freeman who I had lost contact with after school and who were now turning up in punk circles.

The next few years were very productive with more issues of, The Beercan, coming out, helping put on gigs and I even started selling records and other people's fanzines at gigs on a stall.

I only did six issues of the Beercan fanzine, and I was proud as punch when each issue came out and I felt that I was part of something happening at the time. I can only surmise of how Gary & Tony must feel after 40 years of producing their fanzine 'Suspect Device' That's a great achievement in anyone's book! I learnt a little more with each issue I produced but never got anywhere near to how polished and professional Suspect Device has ended up looking.

The main thing throughout all of this though is the sense of being part of something. The bands, the fanzine writers, stall holders at gigs and the promoters all got stuck in, helped each other, and created a great local scene. So much so that most of us are still friends 40+ years on and still attending gigs on a regular basis although the hair for most of us isn't so spikey and the leather jackets are long gone and the knees not quite as up for jumping around!

As a generation we have probably seen more changes in our lives than any other group of people. But underneath it all there is punk music, camaraderie and Suspect Device!

Golly

I think the DIY underground culture has been a massive influence on my life and has helped shape me into who I am today. It's the foundation of having the right morals and being the best possible version of yourself and always trying to do the right thing. It's given me the opportunity to meet so many amazing people over the years and build friendships all over the world and its been great to see some old faces when I have been out playing with Diaz Brothers. It was fantastic to see Tony at our gig just recently at the Hope and Anchor and I really appreciate his continued support. It's scary to think of how long ago it was when it all started and personally for me I'm thankful I was able to choose this path in life and have all of those incredible memories that the DIY scene and all of the people involved in it has given me. Here's to a few more.

Mike Fox:

I don't think I was aware at the time that the punk scene gave me so many opportunities to be creative. I am not saying that much of what I created was worthy of anyone's time and that really wasn't the point. The point was that anyone could do it, whatever it was. I did compilation tapes, zines and bands. I was part of the SHFC & STE, promoting bands and organising gigs. We created posters and we fly posted. The friends I made then inspired me to be more and to do more. My life changed for the better for being involved and I became a better person because of those friendships.

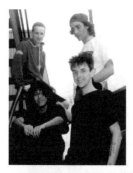
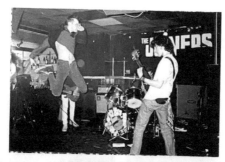

FUSION: Tony, Iain Ratcliffe, Paul Chambers, Shaun Hemsley

First gig, supporting Quicksand at The Joiners in Southampton

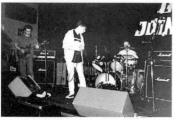
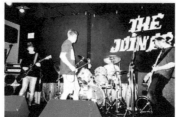

THIRST!: Steve Burgess, Jon Fry, Tony (Rob Callen out of shot)

THIRST! 2 :Rob Callen, Jon Fry, Tony, Phil Beavers

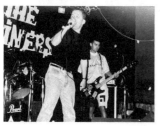
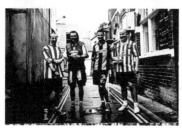

PORTISWOOD: Rut Harwood and Cov John (PJ and Tony out of shot)

PORTISWOOD 2:, Tony, PJ, Cov John, Mike Fox
(photo Pete Zonked!)

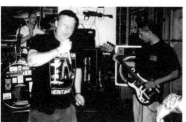
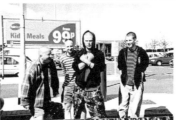

CHOKEWORD: Tony, Dan Roberson, Phil Hedges (Mike Fox out of shot)

On the way to Middlesbrough: Mike Fox, Tony, Dan Roberson, Phil Hedges
(Photo Tanya Hawkes)

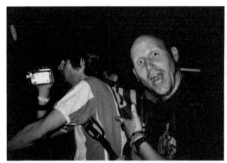

Si Briggs watching Paint It Black with Darren Walters

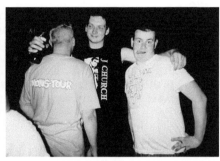

Mac (Travis Cut), Mike Head and Crispin Erridge

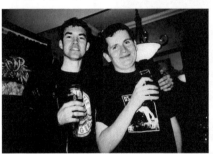

Gaz with Rich Levene

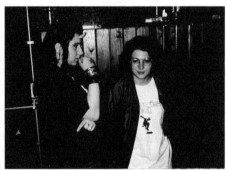

Mad and Em Watson

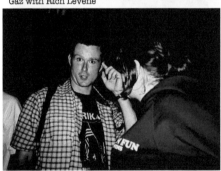

Dan Roberson

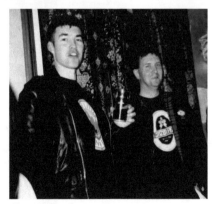

Gaz with Ian Canty

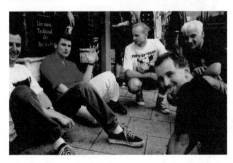

(Left) Chris Evans (Travis Cut), Neil Cox (Shutdown/ Diaz Brothers), Tony, Rut and David Stuart

...If We Can Do It, Anyone Can

Tanya Hawkes - A two-time contributor to Suspect Device.
One of my best memories is watching the lead singer of Life But How to Live It perform at The Joiners Arms when I was in my mid twenties. It cemented years of the punk and politics that was the backdrop to my life since I was fourteen. It's hard to know what came first - the politics, the music, the DIY culture - pushing the boundaries of class and feminist issues, however clumsily. I was a kid on a council estate, surviving in the benefits system, with all the difficulties and prejudices that come with that, and punk became my outlet for frustration and fun.

The punk bands I first fell in love with were Conflict and Stiff Little Fingers. I felt strongly enough at fourteen that I tattooed SLF on my arm with a needle and indian ink! It was like a switch flicked and a bunch of simmering feelings about injustice bubbled over as I played my new records, which read: 'pay no more than £2.99 - or similar! - on the covers. Everything about 'Time to See Who's Who,' and 'Inflammable Material, the angry lyrics, the animal rights, the powerlessness in the face of government policies that constantly ground down the lives of poor people on my estate, the Irish politics (I grew up part of Gloucester's Irish catholic community) - felt like coming home. I'd finally found people who felt like me! I was alone with my newfound music, though, and basically wandered around trying to meet other 'punks' for a while. I had no idea how to go to gigs, or where to find anywhere that punks hung out, other than the streets of Gloucester city centre, where I grew up.

Eventually, aged 17 I started to meet other punks in pubs and then my new found tribe and my friendship circle grew from there. I shared a house with a bunch of Cheltenham punks, discovered a more DIY punk culture, and an even more DIY political culture as we shared giros, 'skipped' our food, went hunt sabbing, rescued animals, fought the poll tax and listened to Napalm Death and Deviated Instinct, Culture Shock and Oi Polloi. We had no money, but we knew how to share and look after each other. Punks from all over the world came to stay at our little house at 143 Fairview Rd - from Minneapolis, Greece and Sweden. We travelled around Europe to gigs in squats and basements, sharing politics and food with like minded people, and closer to home at collectives like the Bradford 1 in 12 (I can practically still taste those fantastic vegan burgers!). Everywhere I went were people from mostly poor and working-class backgrounds, building solidarity with each other, and developing mutual aid-style politics. It was a time that forged deep friendships, some of which I still value now, thirty-odd years later.

By age twenty-one I left for Southampton to study History, and found a whole new group of punks and politics - the core of which revolved around the STE gigs and Suspect Device zine, which I wrote one or two pieces for. The STE scene was a life saver. I was struggling to fit in the new academic world I was in and the combination of Hamwic Housing Co-op for living and STE gigs for socialising brought the perfect combination of fun, music and collective action to help me through the years I lived in Southampton - and was probably one of the key reasons I stayed for 10 years.

I was a twenty something woman, usually going to STE gigs alone, or with friends. It felt safe and welcoming, mostly. The gigs themselves are a blur and I wish I'd documented more of them. I must have been to dozens over the 10 years I was there. Gigs I remember: Shutdown, Older than Dirt, Decadence Within, Culture Shock, Chokeword, and Life but how to live it, which was definitely the highlight for me. Suspect Device was a way to connect, learn about new bands - and now I realise to document the culture, music and politics as it evolved. The attitudes of Tony, Rich and others who helped organise the gigs and the zine filtered through. I'd never known a scene to have that blend of serious dedication mixed with fun and variety. It's only now that I look back and realise what a massive undertaking it must have been to organise: The zine with all its interviews and articles and the consistent dedication to finding and hosting great bands with a DIY ethos.

Punk shaped my life, there's no doubt about it. I'm now 52 and look less scruffy, wear less black than I did in my youth. I sometimes pull up an old track that takes me back to those days - Alternative Ulster by SLF, or The Ungovernable Force if I want to let off steam. I go back to Ugly by Life But How to Live It, still taken aback by the complexity of the music. More than anything it's the politics that has stayed with me. Someone once wrote that punks are 'good people pretending to be antisocial' and I often think of that when I see older punks helping out at the unofficial food bank in my town and in the housing coops, or the younger punks in the their late teens/twenties wearing Oi Polloi T-shirts, alongside pink hair and LGBTQ badges and organising anti-fascist demos. Zines have evolved. I heard some younger punks talking about zines recently - online and colourful, but no less punk! It's great to see punk evolving in this way - more women, more transgender people, intersecting with Black Lives Matter, renters unions, anti-austerity and disability groups. The people living on the margins, collectively organising to protect their communities are still, it seems, led by punks.

Nath Haywire - DIY, SD and Me

Tony wanted folks to write about how they got involved with DIY. But first, a few words about our sponsor. Suspect Device is always a good read. The enjoyment I get from it is enhanced because I have known most of the folks who write for it, some for over 30 years. This means that before I read a review or an interview I check who contributed it so I can read it in their voice. It makes those words come alive. So here are a few stories about how SD has impacted my life for the better.

SD quenches your thirst

The first time I met Gaz was when me and my mate Russ travelled up from Weymouth to see Joyce McKinney Experience at the Joiners in 1989. We drank cider on the train journey and were met by Mike Fox for a few more drinks and then on to the gig. Gaz was mates with John Anderson who played bass in Haywire, a band I would join a month later, so hearing people from Weymouth were in the area he came up and introduced himself by buying me a pint. That's the sort of friendly welcome that goes straight to a young skint punk's heart!

I was an SD salesman

In the early 90s I was running a distro and having bought a copy of Suspect Device at some gig or other Haywire had played at the Joiners, I contacted Tony and took some copies to sell. My zine and 7 inch distro stopped after a police raid and I decided asking for it back was a bit too risky as some of the other material they also took could have resulted in conspiracy charges (at the time when Green Anarchist and ALF Supporters Group folks were being hailed through the courts).

SD saved my life

In the mid 90s, a few of us went to a big World Day for Laboratory Animals march in Brighton, smashed some stuff up, stayed overnight then hitched to London to see Oi Polloi. They had a day off the next day, and would eventually need to get to Bath so we offered to make them dinner, sleep on floors and party in our shared punk house in Broadlands Road, Southampton. Danny and I got a lift to Bath and en route we showed them how we had "Freed The Henge" a couple of months earlier while sabbing a fox hunt in the area. We just jumped the fence. Unfortunately in the process I slipped and impaled myself on a big spike, going an inch or 2 into the back of my leg. Although we stemmed the bleeding, I was having trouble walking and the prospect of hitching home seemed really difficult and inadvisable as I needed proper treatment. Then who should pop up at the gig but Gaz Suspect and his wife Helen. Gaz gave us a lift home and saved the day.

I was a secret SD editor

In the late 90s along with my mate Dave Carr, I used to do stalls at local punk gigs. We sold huge amounts of badges, a fair few records and hardly any of the books and magazines that were our real motivation, but the badges subsidised the literature so it could be cheap. We spent a lot of time with our wares next to Tony and the SD stall. Sometimes having a laugh with each other behind the stalls provided more amusement than the bands. On one occasion, Mates (RIP) - drummer in Blocko at the time - arrived to play a gig and seeing a shaven headed handsome fellow put 2+2 together and came up with 45 RPM. "Hello Tony" he beamed and grinned at me. My sarcastic response to the equally hairless Mates about how me and Tony looked the same was enough to put him straight, but for a few minutes I was an editor of Suspect Device. It was an embarrassing anecdote I would recycle many times if Blocko were playing down our way or Mates was doing the door at a gig in London. "Hello, my name's Tony". Mates eventually played a part in me joining Abrazos, I'm guessing so he could have all the Tonys in one place where he could keep an eye on them.

SD Cabs

In recent years I have bagged lifts to a gig here and there out of town with Tony. Mostly Portsmouth but as far as London. "SD Cabs" provides a wonderful service - we always have a laugh and get to discuss new records or bands we've heard. Invariably Tony refuses constructions towards fuel, even though he comes out of his way to pick me up. The best road trips are when Gaz is down as well. I just sit in the back and marvel at the memories being dredged up alongside the gossip about new record and bands. All the SD talent in one car is a big risk to take in case a rival zine editor like Welly attempts some sort of kidnapping but it's been okay so far.

Getting high on the SD supply

Throughout the 2000s, Tony has been a constant presence at local DIY punk gigs, usually with his distro in tow, and I've scored a fair few great records from him. I've also enjoyed watching him play in Pilger, Screwed Up Flyer and The Shorts. I even played guest guitar for The Shorts once but that's another story. SD has always been supportive of bands I've been in and now I play in Abrazos so it's fair to say that SD has played a supportive, positive role in my ongoing DIY punk rollercoaster journey.

Iain Ratcliffe

The first record I ever bought was 'Young Parisians' by Adam and the Ants at the ripe old age of 9 from a small record store next to my sweet shop in Eastleigh. I started my punk spiral somewhat early but it took until my mid to late teens to awaken to the underground and the US/International scenes/sounds that were my introduction to the south coast punk scene. I had been listening to the more mainstream bands such as the Skids, Public Image Limited and Killing Joke when an old childhood BMX friend mentioned that he had been playing on a 5-a-side football team with this guy Steve - who had crazy blond hair and played in a Southampton punk band called 'Corporate Grave'. The friend suggested I come along one weekend night and that is where I met Steve EMI. I watched the game and later went for food where we became instant friends. Steve was a very likeable guy, and I soon realised he surrounded himself with good people. Within a week I had seen his band 'Corporate Grave' play a show in Woolston and met many of the Southampton scene there. Previously, I had been teaching myself to play guitar, on this real PoS guitar I had acquired through a mail order catalogue, Steve on hearing this, excitedly invited me over for 'lessons' which became the start of many a night at his house repeatedly picking up the record needle and dropping it to catch and emulate the latest riff from some new Dischord release. To better complete my homework, he lent me his immaculate white Fender which was usually tucked away in a case in a corner closet as he preferred to play his beaten and abused Les Paul copy.

Through Steve I met Tony Suspect, Rich et al. and embedded myself in that local scene, going to most, if not all the shows, and creating long lasting friendships that are still going today. We would also venture further afield, once taking a long weekend trip to Holland for some Fugazi shows as they were playing with a great band we knew from Hoorn called The Vernon Walters. Myself, a friend Geoff, and Steve packed our backpacks and headed out on the ferry. We hit up the squat/record label/record distributers De Konkurrent and hung there for a few days. One time during our perusing of their wares the door bell rang and we were told to go downstairs to answer it, starstruck, we were greeted by Andy Kerr and Rob Wright from NoMeansNo. It was a short trip but as Geoff's brother was living there at the time, he had the wheels to convey us to the shows and a place to stay. We took in the Hoorn show and managed to also take in the other Fugazi show at the Melkweg in Amsterdam. These are kind of memories that stick with you for life.

It wasn't long until I was immersed, and decided it was time to get a jam band together in my parents' garage with Geoff playing drums and Steve EMI on bass. The first song learned and 'performed' to the lawnmower and the stepladder was 'Tequila' by The Champs shortly followed by 'Wet Spots' by Channel 3. This soon led to more involvement in the STE Collective (Southampton, Totton and Eastleigh - although I lived closer to Winchester) and the commencement of my first real band. I don't remember the actual first moment I met Tony Suspect but it must have been at one of the early STE shows, possibly the Scream or Soulside gigs at the West Indian Club. Tony was in-between musical projects and Steve was still committed to Corporate Grave, so we reached out to Paul and Sean from the recently broken up 'Hate That Smile'. It was a little bit of a complication finding and arranging practices somewhere that made sense as Shaun and Paul were in Dorset, me near Winchester and Tony in Southampton but we managed to get some writing and practicing sessions together before our first gig. For inexplicable reasons I had suggested the name Fusion, as in 'a combination of many things' and it seemed to stick. In hindsight not the best name, not very descriptive and the association with jazz seemed counter intuitive. As STE had a steady stream of touring bands coming through it wasn't too hard to book a support slot when we were ready. It didn't take too long, and if my memory serves me well, our first real show was supporting, coincidently, one of my favorite bands at the time. Quicksand, the NYC post-hardcore supergroup were coming through on their first EU tour and we were just about ready, a set worth of songs, somewhat practiced and committed to memory. In fact that night we had more songs ready to play than Quicksand did. We went onto play a few support slots with other visiting touring bands until I left for the US and didn't end up coming back. There has been some recent talk of a reunion show, but as we are now divided by even more miles than Dorset and Hampshire with me still in California, Paul in Glastonbury, Tony in Southampton and Shaun in Thailand.

In the Summer of 1991 I moved to the US so Fusion and my involvement in STE was over. But my contributions to Suspect Device had just begun. Initially I had planned it to be just a 6 month traveling vacation across North America to see friends, meet people and ride my BMX bike but it eventually became my home. I settled first in Southern California, then later moving up to the city of San Francisco which I still call home. Thanks to friends I had met through the touring bands at the STE shows in the UK, I already had a welcoming community across the continent. I met up with members of Quicksand, NOFX etc., but through one group's show that STE had produced, Samiam, I became particularly ensconced. At that time they were mainly based in the East Bay area of the SF Bay and my ongoing friendship with all members led me to find work, more like minded friends and taking off on tour with them multiple times.

Being in the city also allowed me access to the city's very vibrant and eclectic music scene at the time. Most of my early city nights were consumed with getting out and seeing bands so writing about that afterwards became my pastime. My first foray was an interview with California punk band JFA (Jodie Foster's Army) for Suspect Device and I have continued to write for SD since. Suspect Device has been the glue that holds a scene together. Not everyone can be in a band or lead a political movement but most people have an opinion, a voice and stories to tell with ideas to make this world a better place to live and zines like Suspect Device are a community's cohesive tool. I am still excited to get the latest copy with news from the UK's south coast scene. Long live the Zine.

Si Brigs - My Life in SD

It was a long time ago now and I have a terrible memory but I can distinctly remember meeting Tony for the first time, I had been pen pals/tape trading with David Stuart for a while, no idea how that came about, I must have come across one of his Cambridge zines somewhere I guess? Anyway, at some point The Descendents announced they were playing some UK shows in the year of our lord 1997. and so Paula, my wife, and I got tickets for the Leeds show and also the London show, which were quite far apart I seem to remember, think they went to Europe in between? David kindly offered to put us up for the night for the London show and so we arranged to meet him beforehand at a pub down the road from the venue. It was the first time meeting David and so I was a bit nervous, mainly because I was, and still am, quite socially inadequate but he's a very cool guy and he was with other friends and so it all went fairly swimmingly. One of the other friends that he introduced me too was a chap called Tony, who at the time was and probably still is, as socially awkward as myself. We were sat near this Tony chap and so we both tried our best at making conversation, I remember him apologising as he said he wasn't even that fussed with The Descendents, words of sacrilege I'm sure you'll agree, but he seemed a nice chap and so I eventually forgave him. At some point in the evening we must have swapped details, which was postal addresses and landline phone numbers at that point in time. And that, as they say, is history.

We have been very good pals ever since I am most happy to say.

At some point in our relationship Tony asked me if I would do a column for Suspect Device zine which, I'm not going to lie, I was over the fucking moon with, and felt deeply honoured, and then that also led to some reviewing, and as I tend to listen to stuff that's more poppier and melodic than Tony's, and Gary's tastes, it worked out well I think. I also interviewed some bands for the zine, though I haven't done that for quite a while, after quickly running out of questions that were remotely interesting.

As our friendship blossomed, Tony and I also got up to quite a few adventures together, some truly amazing times, some of the very best times of my life. Thinking of them always makes me feel amazingly happy.

Over the years we have travelled many miles watching bands together, Strike Anywhere was a band we both really liked and still do, and we saw them in various places in the U.K. and even flew to Amsterdam to see them. I can remember we met up with Big Lloyd who often roadies for them, or also just travels to see them, and then also the band, before the gig and had something to eat with Thomas, the singer. We watched the amazing show, they are an awesome live band, getting name checked, and then we wandered round Amsterdam late into the night before going back to the airport to fly home. Also, as you know, Tony loves Kid Dynamite, as do I, and through SD became friends with a few of them which led us to a few other amazing adventures including actually seeing them play in New York at CBGB's!!!! Still can't really believe that happened. And we went to the Paint It Black "New Lexicon" record release weekend in Philadelphia at The First Unitarian Church, again truly amazing, and both times we stayed with members of the band. Before that Tony's band at the time, Pilger did a 5 date UK tour with Paint It Black and Tony invited me along as a "roadie", 5 dates with a good bit of travelling and that again was another unbelievable experience that would never have happened if not for Suspect Device zine.

I've been very lucky, and though our travels have slowed down somewhat I still like to believe we have a few more in us. And I even still do the occasional SD review!

Em Watson

There's no doubt that Suspect Device was the first fanzine I ever saw and eagerly purchased. I don't have a head for details, especially 35 years on but it was definitely at a gig, at The Joiners Arms pub in Southampton and at the 'distro' stand. Because that was what you did back then.

I first started attending gigs with my schoolfriend Mad in the late 80s and we were very fortunate that during those formative years we lived in a town where there was a thriving DIY punk scene already, waiting for us to discover it. We took the indie/ grunge route (as opposed to the thrash/metal one) and our main gateway would have been the national music press (especially Sounds, although I bought them all weekly), John Peel's radio show, of course, and trips to Underground Records shop. All these roads ultimately led to The Joiners and the STE gig collective. We were in!

However, as welcoming as the local scene was, being young, inexperienced and socially awkward, I needed an extra push to be able to put names to faces and connect with people. For me, that is where fanzines were an essential part of the scene. On the surface, their purpose was to publicise and inform about music that was too underground for the major press, through band interviews and album reviews but really it was about bringing people together. In this internet age of social media, it seems bonkers that you had to photocopy and distribute pages by hand. The columns, where people opened up their feelings and personalities were my favourite part. I can't remember exactly what I contributed to Suspect Device zine but I do remember the feeling of being a part of something in the DIY community. The more fanzines that you read, the more you heard about others and the ritual of sending off an SAE (stamped addressed envelope) in the post, accompanied with a polite note and sellotaped pound coin evolved into a culture of lengthy letter writing to punk penpals across the country. All these things helped to ease the isolation of times between gigs, especially living on the outskirts of the action. Inspired by Suspect Device and admittedly as a way to meet the bands we liked, Mad and I made our first fanzine, cut and pasting in the garden during one of the long Summers of youth with endless time on your hands. Since then I have made other fanzines (slightly less silly) over the years, although none with regularity and am still proud of them all.

So 35 ish years on, I'm 50 and I love how diverse the age of the punk scene has become with original gig goers still there and not growing old gracefully. My musical tastes have changed and evolved but although my life no longer revolves around the punk scene it is still and has always been a constant. In the last year, I have seen great acts such as Hagar The Womb, Ye Nuns, Top Left Club, Civic, Rough Guts, Electric Cowboy Club, Young Francis Hi Fi, Flash and Special Interest. It is still there for when I need to let off some steam and be reminded that there is always an alternative to society's general nonsense and the daily grind.

Andy Morris

I first encountered Suspect Device whilst playing in a band called Suss. Must have been around 1995 or so? I picked up a zine at a gig somewhere and I think I wrote to (Tony) after devouring every word in it. I hadn't realised there was an active and vibrant scene in Southampton and it was just wonderful to actually discover it. We supported 999 at the Joiners and that's where I met a few of the people involved in the DIY scene and we were interviewed by SD at that gig (though it was never used due to the massive egos of a couple of folk in that band (I remember apologising to you the next day)! But you sent me tapes introducing me to a lot of bands I'd never heard of - The Bouncing Souls, Broccoli, Serpico, Rhythm Collision and many many more. I still have those early tapes and dug them out recently.

As mentioned, Suss were interviewed in that abortive attempt. But after a while after getting to know Tony and Gaz at countless gigs I ended up writing for the zine and reviewing releases. Got to hear some great bands doing that (but also a fair bit of rubbish). And it was Tony who suggested that TV21 play at a STE festival (one of my favourite ever gigs).

The DIY scene was massively important to me. Living in a small town, our local scene died away with most people moving on in life to other places and things. It was a breath of fresh air after a good few years of nothing, for me to discover this underground punk scene in Southampton , and from there, across the country. I bought into it 100% at the time. Couldn't get enough of the music, the gigs and the books and zines. Suspect Device zine has always remained top of the pile for me. That's not to say other zines weren't any good, quite the opposite, but it was the first one I came across. And I got to be involved with it for a few years. Proud of that and it's a good memory I have even now.

I've always been quite political in my thinking and always been on the punk side of the political spectrum. The DIY culture taught me a lot about inclusion, acceptance, challenging the status quo and so on. It was great to see gigs that were self policed and where aggressive and bigoted behaviour wasn't tolerated (some off the horror shows in the early 80s where violence and intolerance were the norm almost spring readily to mind). But, unlike a lot of the old punks of my age, I haven't turned into my parents and voted for the right wing and think immigrant boats should be sunk. I still love the music and still hunt out new bands when I can. I love the fact that everyone tries to keep the prices down as much as they possibly can so it remains accessible and there are always gigs going on (albeit, since the pandemic I've not made it out to too many shows).

So, overall, I'm proud to have been involved in Suspect Device, even though it was a very small part. But it was such fun. And as I've said, it taught me so much and introduced me to so many great and like minded people some great bands and music. Thanks for allowing me to be a part of it and long may Suspect Device continue.

David Stuart, Cambridge January 2024
From 90's hardcore punk emo records and fanzines FB group - 25th December 2023
"Nostalgic heavy post- It's so easy now to access new music but pre internet you had to work for it. Whilst I try to avoid "it was better in my day" nostalgia I can't help but feel the rewards were so much greater and the excitement when you discovered something new so much more. Finding new music was hard, especially when you didn't have many friends who shared the same tastes in music. I used to love getting stuff through the post, fanzines, LPs , flyers etc. One time when I ordered a bunch of fanzines a couple of mix tapes were chucked in free. I will never lose the thrill of listening to these for the first time. I didn't ask for them and never met the sender, but they blew my 15 year-old mind, and for that I'll be eternally grateful. I'm a lot less tribal now in the music I listen to, but in my raw heart it will always be punk and hardcore that lights the biggest flame.
I think the sender was called Dave and from Cambridge......he might or might not have been something to do with the Suspect Device fanzine from Southampton, but my memories are hazy. If you recognise the handwriting, and it was you, thank you!" – Oliver Tate

It's the little things that can bring out the broader smiles.

When I was involved with Suspect Device in the early to late 90s, I had found a new punk rock family with Tony, Gary and the gang. I found myself traveling down to Southampton on a fairly regular basis, I was interviewing bands for the fanzine and writing pages of material for each issue. I was enjoying music, gigs and friendships to the max. But my favourite pastime was writing, writing about music, about life and about my take on things. Just writing out what was spinning around in my wooden noggin. There are great writers and truly awful writers across every element of "music journalism", but I only ever cared for the honest ones and knowledge meant very little if it came across as sermonised or belittling.
After a few of my own self-published fanzines, SD is where I grew as a writer and let the boundaries expand somewhat. I learned to just write from the gut, and when an idea took a bite, I'd let it run the line out and not try to reel it on in. Cue several pages of half-assed ideas, numerous typos and several trains of thought that often collided into a true wreck of the English language! But I'd then work through those "notes" the next day, take the little specks of gold washing around in the muddy pan of utter crapola and come up with something amusing, interesting and sounding like me, the person you could run into at a gig, in a record store. Never a keyboard warrior and never an actor. I have seen "big" fanzine personalities out on the wild, have witnessed the complete contradiction of their fanzine persona and was a little disappointed with that. With Suspect Device, everyone I met was the same person I knew from their written word.
I contributed a fair old number of pages to SD over a relatively short period of time. I started with record reviews, a column, some live reviews and then I started interviewing bands again and eventually, I just built my own pages and sent them "good to go" for adding to the zine print run. So, I would be sending anything from six to twelve pages over each issue and over the time I interviewed many people including Tim Armstrong, Ben Weasel, Dave Smalley, Mike Magrann, The Descendents, The

Queers, Weston, Stephen Egerton and many more. I was fully addicted to fanzine work and fully committed to Suspect Device. I'd hook up with Tony for London gigs and these would be days out, shopping, playing football and hanging out until the gig cometh. Some great memories and some wonderful friendships were forged. They were truly great days...

One day, I decided to stop being part of Suspect Device. I felt I'd done what I could do and had a fear of repeating myself and becoming half-assed with things. So, I took on a new challenge with a magazine called Fracture that was becoming a big thing, and as well as contributing, I also shipped out 1,000's copies across Europe and the USA via my job at Southern Records. I jumped ship, maybe that wasn't a cool thing to do and maybe I could have done it better, I don't think I thought too much about it at the time, but as years passed, I did become very embarrassed with my actions and ultimately, I drifted from some solid friends. I don't do regrets, but I do accept my mistakes and poor decision making.

I did jump onto the good ship Suspect Device a few more times over the years, but I never could go back to those most fantastic days of the 90s.

In the late 90s, Tony published a book written by him and myself, called "From Inside as Well", which I was very proud of and extremely honoured to be a part of. We always pondered a second volume, or a revamped edition over the years, but it never happened. Who the fuck would be interested in that twenty odd years after the fact? All I ever wanted to do with punk rock was spread the word, if I heard an amazing band, I wanted to tell the world about it. Now it is a social media link, but back in the day it was fanzines and mix tapes. The biggest thrill is turning someone onto a band, and then that person ends up loving the band too, and hopefully does the same. Spread it!

I may be really poor at that now, but Suspect Device is still going strong and spreading the punk rock word. Supporting new bands, new writers, new labels and promoting friendships across this scene. Tony, Gaz and crew deserve medals for time served and duties undertaken fighting the good fight under the punk rock banner. I was proud to be involved for a little while and walk the walk with these fine folk.

Alan Marshall - Something to Prove

I moved primarily to start an archaeology degree, really just to see if I could do it, but I wanted new challenges and felt a bit burnt out from years of hunt sabbing and settling for the wrong work life balance. My girlfriend at the time (now wife of some 16 years – where did that go!) was the catalyst. She had just finished her degree and suggested I spend 3 years in abject poverty, drinking too much.

I settled on Winchester/Southampton after a hippy in a Hawaiian shirt showed my round on the open day and then turned out to be a professor. I knew some people on the south coast through bands – Haywire had been regulars at punks picnics and national hunt hits alike and we often saw each other, and Dan from the next village along to mine was, by chance, in Chokeword with Tony Suspect.

Others I knew through other protests and animal rights demos, and yet others who I came to visit after they moved to the sunny south coast – not least Rob, stalwart veteran of all the above and author of the marvellous Drunk on a Bike zine, which I had scribbled a few bits for in the past.

I am pretty sure I first encountered Suspect Device on one of these visits, buying a copy or two from the purple sanctuary of October Books, at that time on Onslow Road.

But it wasn't until I moved closer to town and began to see Tony (and occasionally Gaz) at gigs that we got chatting, often over a box of LPs.

There seemed to be a plethora of gigs over the next 7 or 8 years at the Joiners and the King Alf, and I was introduced to all manner of new sounds and lovely people who quickly became close friends (not to mention seeing the likes of Tragedy tear the roof off one of the smallest rooms you could actually stage a gig in) . A handful of those gigs I was lucky enough to play with Whole In The Head, dusting off that trusty £40 bass and getting a lovely raucous reception wherever we went. We played far and wide and got to see the hard shoulder of many international motorways and autobahns waiting for tow trucks.

When WITH finished I played for a while with Like Grenades, crowbarring crust-driven bass lines into essentially non-crust tunes, before Tony asked if I would like to play bass for The Shorts. It was great to play some classic hardcore and more gigs and recordings followed. Around the same time (I think) I started to scribble some record reviews and interviews for SD. I have always gravitated to the noisy end of the spectrum; give me the Damned over the Buzzcocks, Disorder over Vice Squad, Rudimentary Peni over Omega Tribe any day, so the regular Swedish crust releases and Russian grindcore outfits naturally fell in my camp and saved Tony's ears a battering. A match made in heaven.

Hip Hop famously has its founding 4 elements (Breakdance, Djs, MCing and graffiti) and I feel that punk has its own take on the idea – DIY gigs, Vinyl collecting, Activism and Zines.

When done right, the elements merge into one another so seamlessly they appear to be a whole and provide enough space to nurture a huge family of like-minded creative people, who on the whole, have your back, share your dislike of authority, and get off their arses and do something about it. These are the people who pick you up when you slip on spilt beer in the pit, who are happy to chinwag endlessly about different pressings of a 30 year old record everyone else has forgotten about even if they knew about it in the first place, who wait for you in a cold van long into the evening outside a police station after being arrested sabbing, and who chronicle our scene and broadcast our news. This is what I found and left in the rose gardens of the home counties, and what I found when I arrived in Southampton in 2001 and ever since.

Zines were always important through the years I have reduced to a blipvert above (honourable mention the Gadgie and Bald Cactus in particular). They felt, and still feel, like Chartist pamphlets, World War II spy missives or occult tomes. They are secret, vital and ours. Traded under the counter wrapped around TKD mix tapes or swapped for pound coins Sellotaped to cardboard with soaped stamps on the front.

Over the years Tony and Gaz have given me the opportunity to interview a handful of cracking bands – Pizza Tramp, Worst Witch, Trappist and Bitterman to name a few and it has been an absolute delight. I don't know Gaz as well as I should due to simple geography, but Tony breathes and eats music (and little else), forever turning me on to new music I would probably never stumble across otherwise.

I do not possess the patience to produce a zine alone (anyone who bought my short-lived 2" square zine Peabrain knows that well enough) but it is a sheer joy to play a very tiny part in the annals of SD every now and then. And just as much pleasure to read each inky issue which I have not had a hand in. Suspect Device is always a great treat and it is a gift to create stuff with such genuinely generous, enthusiastic music lovers.

Mike Doe

I first met Tony sometime in the late 80's at either the West Indian Club or the Joiners Arms in Southampton. I've never kept a diary so dates etc are hazy. Not sure how or when I first became acquainted with Gaz but my earliest memory is of him shouting "a song for Totton" at any band who played in Southampton.

Tony and I would often see each other at various gigs in and around Southampton and we soon became firm friends. We would often chat about all things punk while I was buying a copy of SD. A friendship that I'm proud to say continues to this day.

Back in pre internet times, zines were our information superhighway. They contained record and tape reviews. Reviews of other zines. Interviews with bands, gig promoters, activists alongside opinions and articles that would try to educate the reader on things happening in the world that the mainstream press would ignore through fear of alienating their financial backers. All the things we now take for granted because they are available at the click of a mouse.

The thing about zines that set them apart from mainstream publications was the DIY nature of them. Most zines were put together using typewritten pages that were then pasted together with black and white photos and then photocopied on mass usually in someone's workplace office after hours. They were written by people who genuinely cared about the music and articles they featured in their zines. They were not going to sugarcoat their reviews and opinions to appease some major label record company or the current flavour of the month band.

The UK has long been a hotbed of zines. Notable publications included Attitude Problem, Riot, Problem Child, Zonked, Artcore, Ripping Thrash, Tadpole and Armed with Anger to name a few but the one I always made sure I picked up was Suspect Device.

Over the years I have had the honour of being asked to contribute to the SD in various forms. My favourite being the annual top ten list than usually features in the end of year issue. One time I put together a playlist of songs that spelt out Suspect Device which Tony then used for an episode of the SD Podcast much to my surprise and delight.

It's great to see SD still going strong, issue 71 has just been published and I'm told its currently the longest running zine in the world? Not that Tony and Gaz would care. One of the things I love about reading SD is the complete lack of ego in the writing. In an age where physical media is slowly becoming a museum piece it's encouraging that SD is helping keep the DIY zine flag flying for all us dinosaurs who still want to read something on paper. Tony and Gaz I salute your efforts and look forward to many more issues of SD that I can make a cup of tea and listen to a record while reading it.

Paul Samain

One of the best things of the scene was how quickly anyone or any band are accepted. There is no snobbery or hierarchy, there is minimal management and actually it was a case of just putting on a gig and people would just turn up. Most bands would be willing to play, there was no "you have to guarantee 20 tickets to play" like other scenes. What also become apparent was the reputation of the SCHC scene nationally. Bands would come from all over to play in Southampton, and friendships were formed which allowed SCHC bands to play in other scenes. There were many scenes and fanzines about, but Suspect Device seemed to have the biggest reputation across the UK. I learnt very quickly, I didn't hate other bands or music, in fact I started to respect other bands. Although I may not appreciate their music, it doesn't mean you have to hate the band. Until you are in a scene such as this you do not realise how many variations of punk rock there is. Me personally I was either into the old school scene with Exploited or GBH or the American hardcore scene such as Biohazard, Madball or Life of Agony. The SCHC scene bought in everything and everyone no matter the backgrounds or music styles.

Towards the end (of Intent) Matt moved to Brighton to continue his studies and it didn't feel right to just replace him, so we invited Dave (a mutual friend) and Dan from Circus Act to play guitar. We formed 'Burn Stuff' short for 'I Used to Burn Stuff'. Although we played a handful of gigs the band fizzled out due to other commitments. Stew and Neil did play for other bands on the scene but eventually Neil joined Mike, Tony and Kevin (all ex Pilger) to form 'Screwed Up Flyer'. I joined them originally on guitar but then moved to bass when Kevin left and again we had a few gigs before we lost the rehearsal room and the band fizzled out. Neil stuck with Mike and Tony to form 'The Shorts', Stew did sing on occasions for other bands but I drifted out of the scene and joined 'Shades of Indigo'. Whilst writing this I am unaware of any of us playing at all at the moment, I know Matt is still playing guitar with his son and I am still playing drums at home but no one is committed to any projects.

For me personally what stood out the most was the quality of the bands. I was so used to the commercial music industry you never appreciate the DIY scene until you are part of it. I loved watching bands such as Pilger, No Substance, Circus Act and Jets v Sharks. The fanzine was key to introducing these bands as well as other bands nationally and internationally. The scene was strong enough that someone could put a band on from anywhere and there would be enough support from the scene to make it worth while putting the gig on for them. Even the scene itself was amazing, how many gigs have you seen people hanging from air duct pipes in the ceiling or crawling between guitarists legs on the stage. Also it was never about the money, no one was in it to make money, all they wanted to do was cover the cost of the gig and no one getting hurt. There was no fans in the scene, everyone became friends and was there no matter who was playing. The fanzine was the glue for the scene and brought it all together. Not only did they review albums and gigs, they also allowed anyone to contribute whether it be music, politics, ethics or a story. Thanks to the way it was distributed most scenes in the country had a say, but it definitely put SCHC scene on the map. Suspect Device would also pay for bands to produce CDs / vinyl and would create split EPs. Again it was never about the money, as long as it paid for itself. Tony would even turn up at gigs with 100s of CDs for sale, and through that I was introduced to some older bands I would never have listened to. I remember just giving Tony a tenner and telling him to pick CDs he think I would like, and although he knew I was a metal head at heart he knew what bands I would like because he was so knowledgeable about his punk music. Personally I always thought the zine was well edited and published, and always allowed people to have a say. It was jammed with CD, band and gig reviews and it was always a heart warming feeling to read other people's views on your own bands. There was never any controversy with it and in fact it opened an area for conversation and debate.

There were other DIY labels in the scene (Red Crayon springs to mind) but the zine never excluded anyone, there was no such thing as competition it was always just about the music and the people and everyone supporting each other. I had the privilege of covering Tony when Pilger went on tour with 'Paint It Black' (another band Tony really got me into that I would have never known of if not). We played the Underworld in Camden, and I took my full kit knowing I wouldn't need all of my toms. I remember the sound engineer micing up one of my rack toms for me to say "I wouldn't bother with that one, it is just for show" and Mike laughing at me. Eventually I joined

Mike and Tony in Screwed Up Flyer, and it was my first time in front of the drum kit. We didn't play too many gigs, but I do remember buying a wireless receiver for the bass, so I could jump around in the crowd more.

I personally fizzled out of the scene, and ended up in a project that wanted to be more semi professional. It was different having to sell tickets to be able to play, it wasn't about building up a fan base, it was more about who in the band had the most friends. I cannot count how many gigs I paid for my share of the tickets and ended up not selling them, so in affect I was paying for myself to play. There was nowhere we could get band or CD reviews as easily as we could with Suspect Device, and most of the band felt there was an image to upkeep. After 5 years I think the band realised it had no future and without even discussing it we just ceased. I do miss the SCHC scene and everything it brings to the music industry. You will never make your millions in the scene, in fact if you can cover the costs you would be happy. The one thing you will make though is long friendships which looking back is more important than anything else. I am really proud of all the recordings I have been on, but I do still listen to my Intent and Screwed Up Flyer songs and it does bring back happy memories (I would also listen to 'Burn Stuff' but I am not sure we ever recorded anything). None of this would have been possible for me if it wasn't for Matt, Stew and Neil knowing of the SCHC scene and Suspect Device fanzine. What next for me? Tony has now put me back in contact with another band who were looking for a drummer, so watch this space, I am excited to see what this brings.

Matt Coleman

I was aware of STE and local stuff in the late 90s when friends were in punk bands (Unmarked and Cervical Smears), I was at Uni in Southampton and went to many STE then OOMF gigs. When Intent started (2002?) we played a few gigs with friends bands and sent out a demo that got us some OOMF gigs, we got to know people and we got involved. The rest of the guys, Stew was in Older than Dirt so involved earlier, Neil was a regular punk gig goer but not into the Soton scene, Paul liked some punk bands but was more into metal with a capital M but all embraced the DIY punk community we found.

When Intent got involved in the scene in the mid 2000s we were older than most of the bands playing out but it was a great community, Pilger, Jets Vs Sharks and No Substance stand out as great people and bands but there are so many more. One zine criticised us for having a bar code on the first demo but that was soon forgiven and became a running joke!

As for fave gigs there are so many memories coming back. One in Basingstoke where people knew the songs and went so crazy I couldn't sing as the mic stand was bashed about, they sang along and stuff which was a great experience. The double positive release show was great as a lot of people came out. We went all the way to Stoke to play to 5 people as we were put on at 3.00pm during an England game. Neils stag was a good un, I got to play guitar solos for Neil Karaoke and it was amazing seeing him as a front man. My 30th was a good one, wearing wigs and we played some metal songs, I got crowd surfed out the venue across the road and back again. One of my favorite gigs was with Stew watching Paul and Neil playing with Pilger at the underworld, so nice to see them up on a big stage supporting PiB, that was special.

OOMF gigs were great and saw some amazing bands. Rooster once told me we sounded terrible but had so much fun on stage he would put us on whatever bill we wanted. Me and Neil stood outside the door of the HorseShoe in Pompey for ages as we were both too nervous to open door. We needed Stew or Paul for things like that....

Got up to some mischief I don't want to share...... was a great time with awesome people.

(Suspect Device) my personal favorite all time zine. Tony and Gaz are great people and always supported us. We will always be grateful for the label putting out the 'Double Posi' release and the last recordings for the cover CD. Playing Suspect Device at the SD anniversary gig was a nice moment for us. If you ever saw Tony stand on a chair behind the distro table to see the band you knew they were a good one. Thanks for everything Suspect Device xx

Andy Nazer

When Tony asked me if I wanted to contribute a few words for the book about the Suspect Device last Sept, of course I said yes, but unfortunately over the last few months I've been somewhat poorly, so these words have been chucked down relatively swiftly.

What struck me tho' was the last time I contributed [to the piece on the History of Dorset DIY Punk Rock], it was back in 2007 - 17 years ago...where did all that time disappear to?!

Since that last piece, around 2011 I moved some 30 miles across Dorset to Dorchester, not much going on Punk Rock wise, but I did hook up with Paul Curran [part of the early Dorchester punk scene with Shock To The System] and help him with his PCBs recording project contributing various instruments and backing vocals.

Self Abuse continue to exist and finally got to play in Southampton in Jan 2020, supporting Subhumans at the 1865 just before the lockdown kicked in. At last! Only took 38 years for Self Abuse to play in Southampton! It was great to play to quite a chunk of old Soton punks from back in the day who used to traipse all the way to Bournemouth to see us.

Alas we were also due to play again with Subhumans at the end of last year [2023] at the 1865 but we had to cancel due to illness.

In other SA news, Jarvis/Roger has decided to hang up his guitar and retire from the band, we wish him all the best and we'll be venturing on as a trio from now on.

C-30s [the other band I'm in with Dom from SA and Sonic on bass] have also continued to play and a couple of the highlights are when we played the Anvil in Bournemouth last year and a bunch of Soton suspects [pun intended!] came over for the gig...along with a certain Rut [play a song for Totton!] Harwood who was visiting from his now home in the USA. Also when we played the STE all-dayer at the Joiners a few years back, which featured Dangerman! Lucky Malice and Dealing With Damage amongst many others.

Can I just say a big well done to Tony & Gaz for their dedication to Suspect Device!

All Individuals But With a Common Bond...

Nath Haywire - DIY, how and why?

Tony actually asked me to write about how I got involved in the DIY punk scene, so I suppose I ought to get to the point. It's a weird question really. I mean, what counts as involvement? First DIY release or zine you bought? First time you Did It Yourself? Or is it about the inspiration that led you to participate in the DIY scene.

Punk has always been about DIY, right from the early days. It wasn't some late development or strategic shift, it was there from the word go, even though some people may snootily look down their nose on the first wave of punk. So my first DIY punk activity, in 1978 probably, would have involved scraping the existing face off a small badge, cutting out letters from newspapers or magazines and sellotaping the words onto the shiny badge face. For extra effect I was able to blag some bright yellow tape from my Dad. I successfully made DIY "Sex Pistols", "Sham 69" "X ray Spex" and "Sid Vicious" badges and even did a fine job of recreating the PiL logo in a similar fashion. Despite actually having "proper" X ray Spex and Sex Pistols badges the size of a small dinner plate. Of course then Crass came along and DIY took on another level.

The first DIY gig I got involved with was a collectively organised effort. A bunch of mates in Weymouth, including Danny (Haywire, Armoured Flu Unit), Gary and Noel, who all live in Southampton these days, had squatted an old hospital building at 43 Dorchester Road, known to us all as simply 43. There was a Nissan hut out the back which had been a workshop of some kind. It was possible to lock off access to the rest of the building but allow access to that space...perfect for a gig! Local Dorset bands Haywire, Victims and SOS played. My involvement was minimal other than helping clear out the gig space and redecorate it with pages of Class War stuck up with flour and water (AKA flyposter "glue")..I did get to provide extra vocals for SOS when they played Discharge's Decontrol - my first DIY punk performance. Within 3 months I would get to (attempt to!) play drums, and then guitar, for SOS - the first DIY band I joined. Not the last. To Be Continued.

At the age of 16 I wrote off to Endangered Musik after buying the Antisect and Oi Polloi singles they had released. Somehow this led to me being put in touch with some fella who was helping organise tours for bands. He was from Birmingham and his name was Daz Russell. You may have heard of him. This would lead to the first international DIY band I helped promote. NV Boys came from Holland and I suggested we get them to play 43. The answer was yes. Having hooked up a band, my other contribution was in the refreshments department. 5 or 6 of us each made 40 pints of homebrew, which we sold at 10p a pint. Everyone got back the money it cost them to make the brew, and a few pints free. We also scrubbed a sack of potatoes (quite possibly liberated) and sold jacket spuds for 5p, lovingly wrapped in a leaf from Yellow Pages. No-one let on that it had been lying on the toilet floor as a replacement for big roll for 6 months so was probably more yellow than anyone bargained for.

Listening to John Peel, I wrote to the likes of Active Minds. I started trading tapes and even releasing them, eventually running a tape and zine distro and then selling releases from labels like Words Of Warning. There was no single inspiration, it just sort of snowballed cos it seemed the logical next step. DIY culture meant mates supporting you by buying distro stock and you providing them new records they might not otherwise hear, or saving them a couple of quid.

Promoting gigs, releasing records, writing a zine, doing artwork or layout for records, it all just seemed like the obvious thing to do. This can-do attitude and punk politics led me to other activities and organising which put some of these skills to good use in the fight for animal and human liberation.

So, how I got involved with DIY in truth was really I just took the challenge or invite seriously. You don't need to ask permission. There is no gatekeeper but yourself.

Ashley Colman: (DIY) was/is my world. Fanzines and the punk scene are still the cool thing to me, and i'm inspired- enthused by a great record or read of a zine still to the tender years I am now.
The impact is in the whole way I try to present myself as a person, and giving a shit, along with trying to fight everything that represents mainstream politics. Also, the music and people involved in the scene will ensure that one day sanity will prevail?

Dan Roberson: (The DIY punk scene) was everything to be honest, from the age of 14/15 I was hooked, me and a couple of school mates would nervously attend local punk gigs, my mate Rob wrote a zine called Barpth/drunk on a bike, he was instrumental in getting us in to interview bands (two 15 year old school kid's interviewing Angus from the Rythymites was a happy memory), the older punks were on the whole really welcoming and we were introduced to a world of music/gigs and politics.
We would also head into London to see the odd 'bigger bands' like the Ramones and Fugazi, but I think my life took a serious turn when I first saw the Blaggers... no turning back.
By 16 I was heavily involved in anti fascist and animal rights activism, which went hand in hand with the soundtrack.
Now as I write this I've been living for 20 years in Wales, I'm not so much involved with the scene these days, I'm a keen observer from afar. Thankfully the internet allows me to maintain old friendships and to keep abreast of what's happening.
My life has been shaped by underground culture, I'm a 48 year old straight edge veggie punk who has just stuck an anti monarchy poster on my front gate (today is the coronation).

Jochen Such: (The DIY punk scene has been) very important to me finding myself when I was younger. Me and Rob started The SLM when we were about 16, just jamming and that I defo could hardly play the drums and Rob was a good guitarist and we just wanted to play NOFX and Pixies songs at the time. After discovering the Horseshoe pub and going to gigs at the Wedgewood Rooms in Pompey. That gigs were happing in Pompey opened my mind, and was like there are people that loved doing this sort of stuff like me. I was given a Zine back then (I forget the name) but it had lots of good reviews of local bands in it. That was it, I was hooked on Punk. Now, years later I have been in many bands: The SLM, Hackjob and EDwood to name some, put on shows and even tried my own DIY label... Cheers fanzines
(The DIY/underground culture) Made me come out my shell. From this kid that grew up out of town and then moved into Portsmouth and over time, meeting more and more people that loved the same stuff as me. Made some of my best friends this way,

also touring over the UK and Europe, met some lovely people that I still keep in contact with today, and I never would have been to these places and seen the stuff I had if it were not for the punk DIY scene. Also gave me a great mindset for life, openness, everyone is welcome... don't be a dick! Best thing i ever did / got in to! I think the scene is really good, Hastings and Manchester, I always see things happening, Pompey is ok, I have a new job and with my hours it is hard to do what I used to do. but have things lined up.

Lloyd Chambers:
(Fanzines) were certainly the "internet" of the day, one of the few ways to provide connections for people like myself to join the dots without the aid of a smartphone and explore the wider world of music in its many forms... "DIY" was the only logical way at the time for me to devour shared knowledge and musical loves by actually getting off my backside and finding it, via gigs and radio and tapes and flyers and records and zines. Living so close to London when Mega City Four and Snuff and Senseless Things seemed to be playing every week was extremely fortunate and it absolutely fired me up. Used to work my early postman shift, go to bed for a bit, off to gigs 'til late, last train back, bed for a bit and do it all again. I then started travelling around this country hunting down gigs in different towns with different scenes and different local bands, all of which I loved and could never get enough of. It became my whole life, and eventually I ended up packing in my job and going off to work for Mega City Four in September 1990. They encapsulated everything about music and bands and camaraderie and shared good times in sweaty backrooms that I loved.

Mackie:
The fanzines and DIY scene are one of the most positive things to come out of the punk explosion, it allows anyone to get involved, be creative and add their side of things to what's going on. DIY networks can sort gigs and put like minded people in touch for the good of the scene in general.
Punk rock has shaped my life entirely, little did I know it would have the lasting effect it did when i was just a spotty 'erbert getting into The Clash. It shaped my political outlook and told me to question things and feeling different and wanting to do things in music with little skill was/is possible.

Paul Fox:
The DIY punk was everything to me, it was my life, my passion, I was forever writing to new people, sending off for cassette demos, tape trading, going to gigs, many out of town, hitch hiking or catch a bus or train, meeting new people or putting faves to names of people I'd written too, people just like me, instant friendships were struck up and strange faraway towns became familiar and friendly, a network of friends just kept getting bigger, sometimes it was a leap of faith, arranging to meet a person you'd only written too, in the 80's this was our only source of information, there was no one to do it for us so we did it ourselves, learning of gigs near and far, becoming involved in issues learnt from lyrics, learning of injustices and becoming angry, standing against the perpetrators and having a voice, a voice that in those times, was an actual threat, our anger and action DID make a difference, DID make people think, DID make individuals question authority, people became involved in many issues we thought was wrong, animal rights, nuclear disarmament, apartied, racism, sexism, homophobia, capitalism! The youth were angry and we weren't going away, the government had to implement new bills to combat our unrest, all because of listening

to lyrics from a band with people in exactly the same as me, we were United and strong. I started my own fanzine which was called 'Ignorance of the Unborn' and ran for 3 issues, selling at cost price or any profits going to animal rights organisations. That era of the DIY punk scene was such a special time to be involved and will doubtfully never be repeated.

To this day I hold those majority of values dear, always question injustice and stand up for the weak, it's ingrained into me, I'm still angry and will continue to be so while there is still breath in my body. I'm still attending gigs and support the underground DIY punk community.

Steve Lee:

The only way you could find out about new music, any non-mainstream music really, was through friends, through tape trading and through fanzines. You learnt which opinions you could trust and often went blind into buying albums, something that was quite a big outlay at the time. During the late 1980s and early 1990s there was a real network of zines, labels and distros that seemed to keep the scene going, actually, along with gig promoters and, of course, the bands, they WERE the scene.

I don't think the scene was terribly insular by choice, I just think it was quite small. Everyone you spoke to, no matter where in the country, always seemed to have mutual friends and acquaintances. Communication was via phone calls and letters, people meeting up at gigs, talking to bands, stopping at each other's houses, trading tapes and zine, the same names always cropped up when you were talking about who you knew, what you read and which bands you listened to.

During the early 20th Century there seemed to suddenly be more money around for advertising and promotion and there were more and more releases coming out. While this was obviously a good thing for almost everyone involved I started to get totally jaded by the amount of mediocre music that was getting pushed and swamped by stuff to review for my zine, a lot of it totally uninspiring. Likewise, gigs started to become bigger and, again, while this was usually beneficial for bands you started having to turn up early and queue to ensure you got into some gigs, loads of bell ends started to show up, venues like Leeds Duchess started having bouncers on the door, it just seemed like that feeling of everyone being in the same boat was ebbing away and, in some cases, the 'us and them' divide between bands and audiences started to become a factor.

(The impact the DIY/underground culture had on (my) life was) immeasurable. I really think it's shaped the way I look at almost everything in life. Most people you see utterly fawn to anyone in 'authority' and lap-up any shit they're told whilst looking down on anyone 'lower' than themselves but I genuinely think the diy / underground culture has given me a strong sense of egalitarianism and the confidence to question authority.

I still get such a massive kick from hearing a fantastic new band, attend a killer gig or read an inspiring interview with someone involved with the underground scene. My hearing and wallet have suffered over the years but it remains an absolute joy to meet new people at gigs and bump into old mates I've made across the decades.

There are people I initially met through doing my zine and going to gigs over thirty years ago who've remained great friends, many from other parts of the country and even though I don't see them as often as I'd like, it's always great to meet up from time to time.

I think it's pretty safe to say the only people who've stuck with the diy scene for all this time are the decent ones and the vast majority of the bellends and chancers have slunk away.

Negative impacts? Honestly, I can't think of any.

Dave Wagenschutz:
Funny how punk has evolved. I was a "metal kid" for the longest time. Still love the music but I grew away from the community when I sobered up. Is that cliché? The "punk" bands in the Midwest and the ones that traveled thru became my everything. Going to shows and booking shows in St. Louis. Traveling to Louisville and Indianapolis. Similar passions and priorities. I had found my people. I sit here in Philadelphia today, married 22 years, two teenagers and one on the cusp – all because I packed up my life and took a chance on a group of fellas I'd never met. In 1992, Lifetime needed a drummer and I did not need another excuse to move to the east coast. I'd say that this community changed everything for me.

Dave Sloan:
When starting out with my first band back around 2010 I was fairly wide eyed at what is actually going on within the local music scene, though I had been going to gigs since the late 90s, I never knew what the DIY scene was. Most of the gigs I had been to before playing in bands were just bigger shows for the big bands I'd gotten into growing up. The music scene to me up until that point was just simply buying a ticket, waiting in line and staying out of everyone's way whilst the show played out.

It wasn't until gigging life happened that I started chatting with other like minded bands, just so happens that I lucked out that my musical tastes led me into the world of Punk. What always seemed like a hugely competitive "industry" was blown away when I started playing with other punk bands. Everyone we played with, baring the occasional band or two, were great to hang out with and the sense of community exploded right in front of me. I've made lifelong friends through the Punk scene and although I've always had an open, sharing the knowledge, remove the barriers kind of ideology, I never knew that the music scene could align so perfectly with the way I want the world to be.

I'd be remiss if I didn't mention the impact of Southsea DIY to my future in music, a local DIY scene that a friend and I happened upon that put on punk bands from all around the country, bands such as You, Me and the Atom Bomb, Chillerton, Attack Vipers, Bangers, The Arteries and... there are too many to mention, chances are if you went to punk gigs at least around the south coast in the last decade you know all these bands. Our first show that we went to was filled with so many like minded people, if they weren't in bands, they were promoting bands, putting them up when they were on tour, feeding them, running the sound, or even just looking after the merch desk for them whilst they played. Everyone was in it together and eager to help out in any way they could.

The merch table was packed with cds, t-shirts, flyers and even small booklets/folds containing reviews/poetry/upcoming shows (later I put 2 and 2 together and realised these are "zines").

I wanted to be a part of this!

I've been involved in the local music scene in Portsmouth in various capacities since probably 2008 playing in various bands - Shooting Fish, BloodBuzz, DeadSet and Bitterman.

I've been running a low-fi community driven DIY Studio / Practice Space (known as The Fishtank) in Portsmouth since 2010 and have recorded quite a few local bands. Born out of wanting to "Do It Yourself" and being obsessively technical about wanting to learn all the facets of making music, we managed to luck into an industrial unit to use for recording our own crazy band ideas then completely organically we grew the place into a community space for some local bands that were struggling to pay for practice space time and half decent recordings.

It's still mind blowing how fast technology has changed since starting that adventure, considering bands these days have access to a lot of recording equipment in their own homes. Back even just a decade ago, we had to string together multiple mixing desks and some janky computer equipment just to record a small drum kit with the cheapest mics we could afford.

Nowadays we mostly cater to friends-of-friends bands looking for a step up from their home grown Demo tracks, we specialise in a that authentic "recorded on a budget" / "untreated garage" sound that works pretty well for most DIY Punk bands. Get in, get it down in a weekend style recordings where there is no "time is money" style ethic. We do what we can with a band in the time frame that suits everyone and we polish until its done.

Outside of the "studio" I'm also involved in the Charlie's Big Ray Gun Records Label and Portsmouth Punk Promotions teams, helping run local gigs and releasing music. Although sadly that has been struggling to recover a bit since the pandemic and the general cost of living taking a huge toll on everyone, we still have the occasional show going on and mercifully a new breed of promoters have sprung up in the last year or so and it feels like things are getting back on track.

You'll often find me behind a camera at gigs taking photos which I'll release on social media platforms and share with bands for their own promotion, if anything it shows others that might not go to gigs what they are missing out on.

Then finally, one of the last remaining aspects of the music scene, outside of writing zines of course... Music videos! Way back in 2018, I made it a point to start recording live bands, mainly to help with promoting gigs but also as a way to document my own band(s) history, built a website called https://cbrg.tv which, at the time of writing, has over 150 videos online, bands from all over the country and even a few from outside our little island have their full sets available on there, if you've played at a Portsmouth Punk Promotion gig since 2018, chances are you are on there :P

This led on to producing full music videos for bands, as is the common thread here, super tight budget "lets see what we can do in a weekend" style projects that always surprise me on how well they turn out. As with all DIY efforts, you learn on the fly and improve each iteration.

I guess this has become a bit of a ramble about how much you can actually do within this amazing DIY scene, you don't have to have a talent/skill to get involved, this community nurtures those that want to get involved, if there is something you fancy trying, just have a go. I promise you that you are welcome.

Janne Tamminen (Endstand): Oh, (the DIY punk scene) was very, very important to me as a person and also for the band. Without the whole scene the band wouldn't have gotten anywhere! It was the only way for us to be able to release records, tour and have our name spread via fanzines. Mainstream music world showed no interest in us at that time - a long time that also happened a bit for some strange reason, bit I think we maintained our integrity till the very end.

At that time I spent pretty much all my time with DIY punk; I had my own label, booked shows and tours for my friends and wrote letters around the globe with other active people in the scene. It was a great hobby keeping me busy while being unemployed.

It was a culture that took all my time. By doing all the things I did, I learned a lot from life in general. And by touring with Endstand and also with some friends' bands, I learned the basics of how that world works and later more professional bands and agencies started to use my services and all the sudden that all became a full time world. I never dreamed of touring the world as a tour manager for one of the biggest bands coming from our country, but that happened. My intention wasn't to work on the commercial side of the music business, but along the years I ended up doing so. But with my background, I think I treat people with greater respect and also see the whole music business from a different perspective than the guys with their blazers on do, haha! I'm still happy to get to work with music, really.

And what comes to friendships, I'm still in touch with people around the world I wouldn't have met without this culture. It's safe to say that DIY / punk rock culture made me what I am today and for that I'm forever grateful!

Matt Coleman:
(Did the DIY scene have an effect on your life) Massively, it made me change what I did for a living, how I consume and eat. Really positive changes that I still hold to this day, huge impact and am very grateful it happened.

Andy Morris:
The DIY scene was massively important to me. Living in a small town, our local scene died away with most people moving on in life to other places and things. It was a breath of fresh air after a good few years of nothing, for me to discover this underground punk scene in Southampton , and from there, across the country. I bought into it 100% at the time. Couldn't get enough off the music, the gigs and the books and zines. Suspect Device zine has always remained top of the pile for me. That's not to say other zines weren't any good, quite the opposite, but it was the first one I came across. And I got to be involved with it for a few years. Proud of that and it's a good memory I have even now.

I've always been quite political in my thinking and always been on the punk side of the political spectrum. The DIY culture taught me a lot about inclusion, acceptance, challenging the status quo and so on. It was great to see gigs that were self policed and where aggressive and bigoted behaviour wasn't tolerated (some off the horror shows in the early 80s where violence and intolerance were the norm almost spring readily to mind). But, unlike a lot of the old punks of my age, I haven't turned into my parents and voted for the right wing and think immigrant boats should be sunk). I still love the music and still hunt out new bands when I can. I love the fact that everyone tries to keep the prices down as much as they possibly can so it remains accessible and there are always gigs going on (albeit, since the pandemic I've not made it out to too many shows).

Geraldine Lawrence

I'd probably started going down the Joiners late 87/88, a lot. I was down the Joiners until early 91. I saw Flick Spatula quite a lot, I don't think I went to any STE gigs.
I got into Culture Shock, and the Instigators, but I used to go out clubbing as well, so I didn't spend loads of money buying records and I was buying clothes, out clubbing and drinking all the time and playing snooker. So I didn't accumulate many records really, there were loads of distro lists I'd written off for, but never got round to send off for all the things I wanted.
I used to go and see rock bands and I was allowed to go up to London on my own to go to big gigs, but my mum wouldn't let me go up to London on my own to go to the pub gigs at like 17, 18. So I was banned from going to that last Culture Shock gig, much to my eternal disgust. I kind of got a bit lost musically, really and nothing really interested me that much.
I went to Glastonbury on my own, I went to Reading on my own. So, I was trying to get more back into music, and I went to Red Hot Chilli Peppers in Hyde Park, which was good, but I thought, I know what I'm missing, what I really want to do is be back Joiners side, like . small stuff. So I looked around the Internet and found Jets Versus Sharks and You, Me And The Atom Bomb and Circus Act, and I had a CD that I'd made-up with Through These Eyes and all other local bands on and, the first gig I went to was Agnostic Front, Jets Versus Sharks and No Substance at Nexus. It was in the summer, and I thought, well, I don't know who's gonna be in there, like how old, I don't know what they're gonna look like, and I walked past the door like, four times before I struck up the courage. So I went in and I spoke to Stew from Intent and Joey. And and then I'd go and see Jets whenever they were playing, and Joe would always talk to me. So I started going to a lot of gigs. Then when I came out then in 2005, then I started going to quite a lot of gigs again.

Golly:

I always remember being at school as a 14 year old doing what 14 year old kids did back then and then punk rock hit me and totally changed everything and how I saw the world.It was exciting and dangerous and blew my mind. As the initial punk explosion faded along with bands like the Sex Pistols and the Clash I found myself being drawn to the more political side of punk and bands like Crass really influenced me and how I thought so I decided to form a band called Hex who you could say were heavily influenced by the likes of Crass and Conflict and other bands who spoke about the more political side of punk. We played some gigs supporting the likes of Conflict at the Hope and Anchor in London and released a single on Words of Warning records. I then joined HDQ in 1985 as the vocalist and toured non stop around the UK and Europe releasing a few albums and this was when I first really became aware of Suspect Device fanzine as Tony was a big fan of the stuff we were doing and the fanzine was very supportive too. One of the things that I remember was that Suspect Device was always one of the best most professional looking fanzines back then and was always honest when it came to reviews etc.

Pete Zonked:

Despite Punk's early days battlecry to pick up musical arms and 'involve yourself', regardless of your ability, my rudimentary attempts at learning an instrument went nowhere. I lacked patience, and any aptitude. It was my brother who'd been gifted with The Rhythm. Strumming or drumming along to songs came very naturally to him.

Somewhere, possibly, exists a tape of our short lived shed-band Disaster, with Tom banging on hard objects and me attempting to sing, including a cover of 'Change It' by The Alternative. One of the more listenable tunes on Bullshit Detector Vol.1. - an album that truly pushed the boundaries of musical competency, but...

So yeah, I was drawn, quite literally, to the creative aspect of Punk, with art used as a tool of mockery and subversion. Conceiving music had proved to be beyond me, but I could doodle, make stencils, cut 'n paste collages, and even string a few words together (still working on that one, hah) It was fun, and a way to express myself. Many years (well, ok - decades) down the line I'm still a firm advocate of D.I.Y. Punk as a place to get involved, no matter your perceived capacity, or confidence levels, and where the sprit of cooperation, encouragement, and creativity remain key. It's about making things happen without being driven by a profit motive, and an alternative to just acting as a subservient consumer of others Products and Services. Really, is it any wonder the Right-Wing drones have launched a Culture War against people who challenge The Establishment, and want to retain an element of independence and free-thinking in their lives. The blinkered haters want to crush what they can't control. Which means it's a threat to them; and that's all the justification we should need to carry trying to Stay Free of their nonsense.

"Me and You, We're gonna fight the narrow minds. Make our own rules.... Live your Life... I'll Live Mine".... (7Seconds)

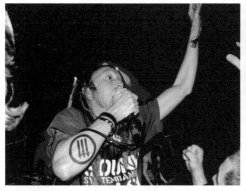

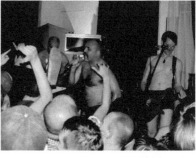

Above: LIMP WRIST, Brighton
Left: STRIKE ANYWHERE, Bournemouth
Below: PAINT IT BLACK, London

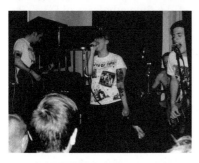

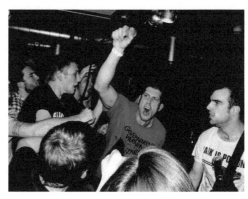

Above: SCEPTRES, Brighton
Below: WHOLE IN THE HEAD, Brighton

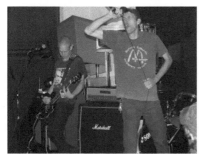

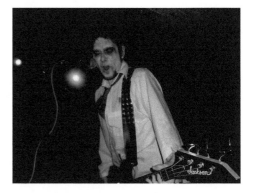

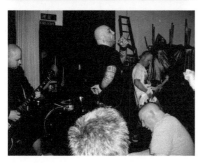

Above: INTENT, Halloween gig at the Totton Youth Club

Left: GERIATRIC UNIT, Brighton

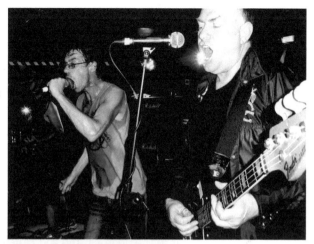

Subhumans at Sticky Mike's
Frog Bar, Brighton
(Photo by Pete Zonked!)

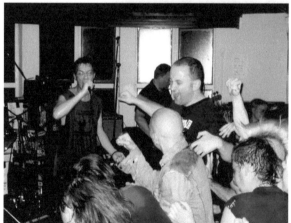

Nath and Rut get involved at
a Subhumans gig in
Bournemouth

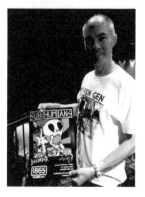

(Left) Gaz nabs a poster
before seeing the
Subhumans at the 1865
in Southampton.

(Right) Tony shows off a
Subhumans poster Gaz
sent him.

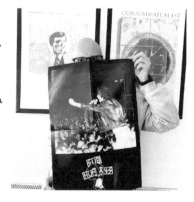

Tony Suspect - You Give Me Disease

2020: Around the time the death toll attributed to Covid-19 was starting to make headlines, but before anyone in the UK wore a mask or stayed home or even mentioned the word "pandemic", the stress of having to live with my dad, who had dementia, put my mum in hospital, with a suspected stroke. Thankfully it turned out not to be a stroke, but she was still confined to hospital for two or three weeks. As it was not safe to leave my dad on his own, my sister and me took turns staying with him, but eventually we had to go back to work, and the only option we had was to put him into a home as we couldn't be there 24/7 for him. It was tough when we took him to the home and had to leave without him, as he had no idea what was going on. It was also his birthday.

While all this was going on I was starting to have palpitations, quite strong ones, some of which left me feeling dizzy and disorientated. After one morning at work when they had been particularly bad, I had to stop while walking through the town centre as it felt like my heart was going to burst and the world started spinning. I got back to work and the same thing happened, I was sat at my desk and again felt like I was having a heart attack. It was time I went to the doctors, and so I called them straight away, something that is very unusual for me.

Over then next couple of weeks I had several visits to the doctors, I had blood tests, an ECG, and lots of questions about lifestyle (No, I don't smoke, or drink, or take drugs). Eventually I was sent to the hospital and was fitted with an ECG that I had to wear for 24 hours, keeping a diary of any palpitations. These 24 hours included a day at work, which provided plenty of entries in the palpitation diary, and then an Abrazos practise where I didn't have any. I never had any at Abrazos practices. All the tests indicated that my heart was healthy, and so the doctor suggested that the palpitations were being caused by stress and anxiety, which made sense and explained why thrashing the drums with my Abrazos chums never caused me any problems, that was my stress relief.

Not long after all that, the government reluctantly decided to take the Covid pandemic seriously and enforced a nationwide Lockdown.

It took a little while to get used to working from home, and at first I wasn't happy with it at all, but the need to be creative was strong, and to fill the gap left by not being able to get together with Nath and Alan and bash out Abrazos songs, we were soon working on new songs, writing separately and sending ideas through via email and WeTransfer. This wasn't perfect, but it kept us connected and creative. One plus was, I was still working, but wasn't spending any money, so I could afford to get myself an electronic drum kit, which helped with the song writing. I also started on a new issue of the zine. In time, Pete and me also did an e-zine, using photos we'd taken and adding relevant lines from songs. It was a simple idea that kept us busy and in touch, and I enjoyed it greatly. Walks in the forest gave plenty of opportunity for photos, plus with Becca working throughout the lockdown, I would often be in a deserted town centre waiting to pick her up, so again plenty of photo-ops in an eerily deserted town centre, both on sunny mornings and dark late evenings. I'd often be stood in the centre of town very late with only the scurrying rats for company. I'd always have the project in mind so would be taking photos, usually with song lyrics already waiting for a photo opportunity to present itself. We called the zine Put These Words To Music, which doesn't make much sense if you think too much about it (so I suggest you don't), but we love 7Seconds and their positive message, and this was a positive way of staying creative, staying connected and using what we had to entertain ourselves and keep our minds active.

Pete

"The Pandemic, remember that? Of course, you fucking do! As the reality of The Lockdown kicked in Tony and I were bouncing some 'creative ideas' around, to keep ourselves amused 'n productive. They landed at an on-line 'zine pairing photos with some matching lyrics. In our excitable minds it was a genius concept! My eyes are continuously tuned to their surroundings, am habitually snapping images, whilst having a head crammed with song lines... so, yes... this was the perfect project to get stuck into. People across the land were learning to make bread, larging it on Zoom parties, and inventorying their toilet roll stock... but myself and Tony were trawling back thru our photo archives, remembering better times, accumulating new shots, and using our imaginations for lyrical inspiration. Tony came up with the 'zine name, pulled from a song by 7SECONDS, a band we both have a lot of love for. With a stack of (virtual) pages accumulated between us, a front 'n back cover constructed, and an intro banged out, Tony worked his magic collating the whole lot into a single PDF then uploaded the finished product to share with our mates on social media, etc. I know, totally cutting-edge use of Technology... a Brand New ZineAge, hah! People dug it, which was super cool, but that was outweighed by the fun I had collaborating with Tony. We ran to 4 issues in the end which was magnificent. Who knows, we may return one day!"

There was also a Messenger group created by friends in Brighton that I was included in and that was a great help in helping in feeling less isolated. It was also another demonstration of the wonderful punk rock community that I have been able to surround myself with.

In May 2020 we finished putting a SD#64 together. The last three gigs I went to before Lockdown had inspired my choice of interviews; Lucky Malice, King Of Pigs and Werecats. We also featured Ättestor, a new band from Brighton that our friend Darren Bourne had joined. Gaz arranged for a contact of his to interview Menstrual Cramps, Punka and IDestroy, and Pete had contacted Chain Cult. Nath did a review of a gig him and Alan had gone to in Belfast, and Gaz resurrected our Great Forgotten Album feature with a piece on some great compilations. We got it printed as soon as we were able.

As lockdown went on, the weather was hot, and work was tough, but when I wasn't suffering palpitations at work, and getting the stress sweats, Sarah and me would enjoy waking in the New Forest. With just a fifteen minute walk from our house bringing us to trees and heathland, ponies and cows. With no people about the animals came out and we regularly saw deer, buzzards, voles, and more birds than we'd seen for a long time, and a highlight was seeing a big buzzard perch on a tree branch right in front of us. It flew off quite quickly, but it was an uplifting moment. So we didn't mind lockdown too much, generally, although work was very stressful and it was hard not being able to see mum, who, thankfully, had come home from hospital just before lockdown hit. It was good that she was home, although without dad there she was on her own, luckily my sister lives within walking distance so could pop by to see her through her patio doors during her permitted "daily exercise." Also, not being able to practise with Abrazos was a downer as those couple of hours in an evening making a noise with Alan and Nath was a way to forget work issues, as well as being great fun. I'd often not feel like going out to practise after a shitty day at work, but when I got there I loved it and really benefitted from being in that little room making a noise. Again, a good example of punk rock and the friendships it has brought me being a real life saver.

To make up for not being able to practise, we started making Abrazos videos, filming ourselves in our respective homes miming away to our songs, which I then edited together. To start with I felt a bit silly miming along to our songs, on my own in my little room, but once I got used to it, it was good fun. After a while we got our friends involved too. It was another good way to keep us active and creative, and also to keep us in contact with our friends. Eventually we started writing new songs, and as lockdown was relaxed in the autumn, we were able to write and practise some new songs, and we also booked into The Fishtank in Portsmouth with Dave Sloan to record 8 of these new songs. Then the week before we were due to record, another national lockdown was announced.

At the time Nath wrote:

"In January 2020, Abrazos spent 3 hours or so recording with the amazing Dave Sloan (Bitterman guitarist, genius sound engineer and all round technical wizz) at the Fishtank in Portsmouth. We released that initially as a limited USB stick & zine and the tracks will be coming out on a split 7" with Brain Anguish in the next few months. We were so pleased with Dave's work we booked ourselves up to record another 8 songs on 7 November 2020. We had a couple of months between lockdowns in which we were able to practice and we were all geared up to lay down these songs and then on 31 October, a national lockdown was announced starting on 5th November. We were gutted! But we hoped that maybe in December we would be able to do the recording. Of course, during December we couldn't even practice, let alone record, as the tier we were in didn't permit it. Then a full national lockdown was announced starting on Boxing Day.

Although as a band we'd kept up communication and made some videos, we got to thinking that by the time we got back together we might have forgotten half of the songs. It's worth pointing here that we would often forget between practices that we had changed a song until someone deciphered some scribbles one of us had made the fortnight before.

Spurred on by this thought, Tony went out and bought an electronic drum kit. Actually he didn't go out, cos no-one was allowed to go out. He ordered an electronic kit. And he was able to record himself on his computer. This was a game changer!! I had already been recording some music from home for a couple of projects so started thinking about how we could pull together something "just for us to listen to".

Initially Tony found the electronic snare a little difficult as it was so bouncy he was hitting it twice every time, but with perseverance he managed to get his traditional "one beat" back on track.

Luckily we had some ropey mobile phone recordings of songs from practices so Tony had something to play along with in his headphones. The only problem we had was that the high-hats were too loud. Other than that, we knew we were in business.

For vocals we figured as long as the song was playing in headphones, Tony could just sing at his phone. But it didn't quite work out quite right, so he bought a special lead enabling him to plug a microphone into his computer. But it bounced off the wall with a bit of echo, so Tony had to go and sing in a cupboard.

Tony laid down the drums and vocals for 6 of the 8 songs we had originally decided to record and sent them over to me.

I lined the drum tracks up with the practice recording and then made sure the vocals were lined up.....well, sort of. Then I set up my guitar amp in the bedroom/office at home, putting it through an old PA speaker I have lying around, and laid down some guitar. My beloved SM58 microphone ran into a 4 track mixer which was connected to the PC and that was that sorted. I couldn't crank it up to proper volume due to the neighbours as we live in a terrace.

So far so good. We had drums, half the vocals and some guitar. We still had a problem with the hi-hats being louder than they would be on a real drumkit. Normally when you record you have separate track for the snare, the kick drum, the hi-hats, each tom and the cymbals, so it's a simple matter of pushing a fader down. We had our drums all mixed into one track so we had to improvise. I created 3 duplicates of the drum track and then on one I boosted all the low frequencies, on another I boosted the mid frequencies around where the snare sound lives, and the third was left as is. Mixing the three together we were able to bump up the snare and kick drum enough so that the hi-hats sounded okay. Not ideal, but we can live with it.

Nearly there....our final hurdle was how to record the bass and Alan's vocals. Alan also has a microphone but his computer has no inputs. In "normal" times I would take my laptop and mixer round, we could take a direct line from his bass and also a microphone on the speaker and that would be the job done. But then if it was normal times we would have been with Dave at the Fishtank doing it all in 3 hours rather than creating snippets of songs and sending them across the internet to each other! So we tried an experiment.

Alan plugged some headphones in with the existing drums and guitar, set up his trusty iphone in front of the bass speaker in the garage, hit record and blasted away. And it worked! Well, sort of. Cos, ya see, these smartphones are really clever and when you are recording something too loud, so that it doesn't distort, it reduces the volume. Which meant the first half a second of each song was massively loud, then over the next 2 seconds got progressively quieter until it reached a constant level.

We used the same technique for Alan's vocals. Except to cut out the echo and bounce, he created a wall of pillows to soak up the noise. We had the same problem as with the bass. LOUD AS FUCK at the start and then settling down to normal a few seconds in.

I tried using a compressor and a limiter but they took a lot of the life out of the recording. There was only one thing for it. The digital equivalent of getting out the scissors and sticky tape. I manually went through the first few seconds of each song (or when there was a break!) splitting it up and then reducing volumes until everything was roughly okay.

And there we had it. Except I had put some of the vocals in the wrong place, but once we had that ironed out, and with about 4 rounds of sending songs backwards and forwards to get the sound right, we produced a demo.

This demo is nowhere near the quality that Dave has done for us in the past, so we will make a trip back to the Fishtank to do these songs "proper"" but I have heard worse released on vinyl (I'm personally thinking of labels like Touch and

Go!). It's urgent (that will be the sound of us all shitting ourselves as we hit record and quickly pick up a plectrum or drumstick). It's raw (that will be the limitations of low tech recording somehow working in our favour). We hope that these songs will ensure people stay interested in Abrazos so when we get back to gigs and records we aren't forgotten. For us it means we will have something to help our ancient brains remember what our own songs sound like, and also despite a few ball aches, it has been fun. It's helped us stay creative and positive among a period of boredom and groundhog day repetition. It's kept us connected. And for me it has kept me motivated when a work only existence could have put me into a pit of depression.

So what was the point of this ramble? I've compressed hours of staring at a computer, hours of Tony hitting a snare in a million different ways and the frustrations of Alan trying to get a good recording level on a mobile phone just to convince you that it's possible. If you want something bad enough you can make it happen. It's worth giving it a try! Even if you have to use a mobile phone instead of proper microphones you can still create something listenable (we think). Isn't that what the DIY spirit is about?"

We put the 6 songs up on Bandcamp under the title of 'Old Men Shouting At Phones In Cupboards', and Nath did some Bad Brains influenced art for it.

Abrazos were able to briefly get together, when the restrictions were relaxed again just before Xmas 2020. On one of Sarah and my Lockdown walks I noticed that a fallen tree, with upturned roots looked like a bass drum, and with various stumps that were laying around I made what looked like a drum kit. As were were allowed to meet up in outdoor spaces we decided to record another video where I would use this woodland drum kit. We had recorded a song called 'Let It Snow', which isn't a Christmas song, but we wore Xmas jumpers, and filmed ourselves messing around in the forest. While we were there a herd of deer ran by, very close to us. They came out of nowhere and it took me a while to get my phone out to video them. Nath would eventually add a snow affect to the video and some Xmas trimmings, including sleigh bells over the footage of the deer running off through the trees. The finished video was put up on line just before Xmas.

We also used this time to put SD#65 together. Gaz sent me a Breakout interview and Pete had done one with Japanese band Daiei Spray, so I got my act together and contacted Danger!Man and after I heard the Sickness album, I knew instantly that I had to make contact to ask about an interview. Thankfully Nick was up for it and it was done in super quick time. I was also very happy to be able to feature Diaz Brothers; Golly and Neil Cox are old friends, my love for HDQ and Shutdown is well documented, and I absolutely loved the Diaz Brothers album, it was melodic, but full of driving punk rock songs with moving, heartfelt lyrics, I found listening to it an emotional experience, so I really wanted to have them in the zine. Thankfully Golly and Neil got their answers back to me very quickly.

Art has played a big part in spreading the punk rock word since the late 1970s, and in this issue Alan wrote a great piece on punk rock's long standing use of cut and paste artwork for record sleeves, logos, posters and much more. The impact of this style is now seen in many areas of the media, often to advertise companies who's ethics and practices couldn't be further from punk rock's ideals. Alan called his piece Running

With Scissors, and illustrated it with examples of art. The piece is reprinted below, without the accompanying artwork.

RUNNING WITH SCISSORS
PUNK'S LOVE OF CUT AND PASTE ART

Neatly predicted by Adam and The Ants in Zerox, surely nothing has been as ubiquitous in punk since its very beginning as cut and paste artwork (with the exception perhaps of the humble safety pin – which is basically cut and paste in its own sartorial way if you think about it).

From the simple necessity of early zines like Sniffin' Glue and the stylised art-school elegance of Jamie Reid's jubilee queen, to the deliberate badging of a thousand Dis-band 7" covers, and garage-styled pop such as The Briefs, not only does cut and paste represent the very ethos of punk – literally picking up a pair of scissors and running with them – but it has come to represent many aspects of the whole scene.

It is at once; slap-dash yet creative, a re-hash of the old and boring presented in a new way, an homage to pinching other peoples art, cheap, cheeky, seedy, sinister, and most importantly of all irreverent.

It is not so surprising then, that as graphics and technology have moved apace from the rattling drum of a Mimeograph (printing in any colour as long as it's purple) to computer software which can recreate pretty much anything but probably take much longer than actually reaching for the Prittstick, we as punks have stuck with recreating something which looks like it took no time or skill at all.

From the very start, cut and paste meant being able to work outside the capitalist media. It delivers instant results without censorship or judgement from the unlucky print worker asked to run off 200 copies. And vitally it means you really can say what the fuck you like!

Dadaists knew this back in the 1920's of course (see Raoul Hausmann's The Art Critic for a direct descendant of the Buzzcocks' - Orgasm Addict sleeve, or the Stations of the Crass fold out poster). Punks merely picked up the idea of sneering at authority by tearing up traditional media, and writ it large for a new generation.

Also, rather handily, it is perfect for mimicking ransom notes and other underworld missives, which fit right in, whether you are after the misguided 1970's shock value of Cambridge Rapist T-shirts, or the ominous millennium V for Vendetta anarchist approach.

I thought it might be interesting to look at a few examples which have made me sit up and take notice over the years, and think about why cut and paste

has outlived razor blades and bondage trousers and seen white t-shirts supplanted by black ones to truly define punk rock identity.
These are purely personal musings. I am sure there are hundreds of better examples which pop into your own heads. I actively encourage you to go and have a rummage.

Photocopiers were a fairly new invention in the 1970's and early 80's - at least ones that were available to people in the punk scene - so there were really only 3 ways to create art; draw it yourself (with mixed results – yes, I am talking to you Disorder), Letraset – the fiddliest possible way to create anything (I was alright with Spiderman transfers, but bugger me that stuff was hard to use - an honourable mention to Deep Wound who are the only band I can think of who actually achieved a good enough result with Letraset to use it for their logo), or lastly, nick it from school library books, newspapers or your mum's Woman's Own and Gloy it to something else with one of those little plastic spreaders.

Before being repurposed for records and their sleeves there came gig posters and flyers, and there are loads of examples of early punk gigs using porn, newspaper print, and cut up band photos to lure punters through the door, way before the bands ever committed anything to vinyl.
So by the time picture sleeves were needed it is no coincidence that 3 of the big 4 punk band's first singles include cut and paste art somewhere on the sleeve – The Damned's New Rose, Sex Pistols' Anarchy in the UK, and The Clash's White Riot. Only the Buzzcocks' Spiral Scratch defers cut up art for later releases like the aforementioned Orgasm Addict.
By the arrival of Never Mind the Bollocks, cut and paste was an adopted language ready to be stylised, and despite the graphic design makeover, post-Bollocks it appears everywhere!
999 - Emergency, The Tubes – White punks on Dope, The Adverts – Gary Gilmore's eyes, Killing Joke – Wardance etc. etc. In fact the more I looked for examples, the more I noticed.

By the 80's, punks had settled into a more or less distinct uniform, and good old cut and paste lent an equally unmistakable shorthand to what sounds you could expect inside the record sleeves.
70's Albums such as Sham 69's That's Life are a riot of information and energy, which visually reminds me of a youthful stance somewhere between school art class and the Daily Star world of building site canteens. The same idea is picked up later on one of my favourites, Angelic Upstarts' Teenage Warning, which just reeks of post-pubescent angst and the stark black, white and Day-glo world of hanging about up the park with a bunch of 'erberts. Their single Who Killed Liddle Towers is even starker. Simply a white sleeve with cut out letters glued on, taking the approach to its reductive limit.

Punk and disorderly III – The Final Solution is another great example, with more cut and paste than you can shake a studded stick at. It is used with such wanton abandon that it doesn't even matter that one spikey-topped geezer appears at least 3 times in the same scene and the armed police look like they are going to miss the whole line of them. As a 14-year-old whippersnapper it meant I knew exactly what I was getting inside and that was the point.

It is impossible to delve far into cut and paste without mentioning Crass and Gee Vaucher of course. Crass took the same glued together scattergun approach as many of the first wave bands, but through an agit-prop art school lens. Their use of collage is darker, less about pop-art imagery and more about sloganeering and the subversive language of Dadaism. Sometimes this takes the form of simple essays, like the packed Financial Times style cover to You're Already Dead. Other times it is wonderfully surreal, like the cover of Feeding of the 5000 – copying cut and paste but with the sublime painting of Gee reproducing the scissored landscape in oils. The cover is bought into sharp relief by another single pasted image of a desiccated hand torn and caught on barbed wire inside.

Anarchists all over followed suit and spawned a new black and white copy culture to replace the neon of the Pistols. Comps like We Don't Want your Fucking War and Discharge's Why 12" disposed of the fragmented ransom note approach and let the pictures sell the story. Brutalised victims of war, torn from library books and exhibited as a call to arms (or more accurately a call to put arms down for good).

There are other examples which need you to delve deep inside to get the true cut and paste hit. The Dead Kennedys' Fresh Fruit for Rotting Vegetables recreates their manic and unhinged soundscape on a poster which is so crammed with detail that the lyrics are almost pulled under by the weight of deranged advertising and Jock yearbook mug-shots. But it was always the encircling eyes that added the (literally and figuratively) sinister edge for me. The Dead Kennedys use of collage to offset the straight American heartland against its disfigured underbelly is something they would return to again and again with the marvellous Winston Smith at the helm - most notably for me in the lyric booklet of Give Me Convenience or Give Me Death which inspired a scree of art zines in the late 80's and 90's.

Later in the 80's both The Stupids' Peruvian Vacation, and Doctor and the Crippens' Fired from the Circus and Rhapanadosis used a very similar poster collage method full of cartoons, horror movies and adverts to peg their skewiff views of the world. You don't get that with an Mp3 download!
 I spent hours pouring over Fired from the Circus in particular, and many more recreating elaborate local gig posters so dense you literally could not see which bands were actually playing.

As punk and metal became more entwined as the decade drew on, some bands swapped their scissors for brushes and started to reproduce the lurid metal covers preferred by NWOBHM bands. Not so early Napalm Death; they stuck to their artistic guns, at least partly. Scum, and From Enslavement to Obliteration both feature painted versions of stylised cut and paste art, the pasted company logos on the former and the repetition of shattered images - a visual representation of Mick Harris' seismic drumming - linking back to their roots as a straight up punk band in visual shorthand.

Painted covers by Death, Cannibal Corpse etc. always put me off to be honest, but give me a good black and white Doom gatefold (Doomed from the Start leaps to mind) and I'm in!

By a convoluted route it is interesting to note the Discharge approach of butchered corpses being reanimated by combining the fractal images of Napalm's FETO and splatter movie influences on Carcass' Reek of Purification. Images of the dead, yep, but warped into pure flesh-crawling shock value that has been aped by a million goregrind bands since. As the first band to do it, Carcass get away with it for novelty value, but for my money it can get a bit boring and uninventive, reproducing splattered heads for the sheer hell of it.

By the time we get to D-beat bands such as Disclose, Honnor SS and Framtid, there is a very deliberate ritual being played with. Their covers repeat imagery like a mantra with Discharge firmly in the pantheon of gods being adored. This is punk looking back at itself, without the influence of Dada and Pop art, using the shorthand purely to show its place in the family tree.
It is impossible to pick favourites but the sheer audacity of ripping and pasting Discharge's classic logo into your own has to go to Disclose.

The examples I have chosen here are just a few of the bands I like to listen to (it gave me an excuse to dig out some old favourites, and writing this gave me something to do while I listened). There are as many branches on the family tree as there are punks of course. Inherited punk DNA means that cut and paste formed part of the artwork of the Grunge and Riot Girl movements for example – Bikini Kill in particular made great use of it in lyric booklets and zines, and Garage bands like The Spits and The Briefs use it as often as they do 1950's sci-fi (well maybe nearly as much), but even bands as distanced from punk as Carter the Unstoppable Sex Machine (to pick a random example) make use of cut and paste in their logo, using punk's visual heritage to promise something more raw than your average synth-pop combo can deliver.

Cut and paste is alive and well. It is always my tool of choice when I get to make posters or record covers (ok, maybe one of three – but don't get me started on stencils or over-contrasted photocopies, we could be here all week). So healthy is the link between ransom note lettering and disaffected youth in fact that punk is now being used as a marketing tool to short-cut any actual rebellion.
The fact that companies like McDonalds, Subway and Brewdog nick punk's scrapbook approach to, generally quite badly, inject a bit of 'yoof' appeal into their products should come as no surprise.
Punk is defined by image as much as any other sub-culture and it is good currency.
But for every advertising exec. who owns a Clash T-shirt they can no longer get into, there are a dozen vibrant new uses for cut and paste's well-worn rough edges within the scene.

One recent band's album worth a final mention is Teething's We Will Regret This Someday. This brings the Sham 69 newspaper shredding method right up to date. Not for simplicity's sake anymore, but masterfully thought through and with a huge nod to a punk movement with pedigree which predates the guys in Teething even being born. There are many other examples I am sure, but it strikes straight to the heart of the matter. A cheap, cheeky, seedy, sinister and irreverent shorthand for the music inside.

It is fitting that the image cut and paste projects is so intrinsically linked with the punk movement - we can filter out the corporate bullshit like we always did. Ignoring the media is what brought us here in the first place.
Who cares that that image occasionally says, 'Give me the money'.
More importantly, in the hands of the right people, it still more often says, 'Fuck you, I'll do it myself!'

In true cut and paste style, Pete Zonked's collages have become a regular feature on our back covers.

Pete:
Right from my early days of being drawn to Punk, I was fascinated by the artwork. Jamie Reid's ground-breaking 'Pistols designs immediately captured my imagination. They were clever and provocative. That was cool. I learned his style had its roots in something called 'Dadaism'. I wouldn't have had a fucking clue! I do have a dusty memory of getting a bollocking from a teacher for having a messy textbook... being sternly told to 'cover it up'. I swiped a full page Buzzcocks advert from an NME in the library, neatly crafting parts of it as my new cover. The bad reaction when I pulled it out at his next class was perfect; I knew this was a way to have some fun!

When Crass records started entering my life, I'd spend ages poring over the fold out sleeves; a ton of thought and effort went into making something way more informative 'n visual than the industry-standard front 'n back cover format. It was mesmerising. The 'Pistols parody poster in the Crass/Poison Girls split 7" was brilliant. Gee Vaucher, and soon after Dead Kennedy's artist Winston Smith, became big inspirations in the collage department for me. Nick Blinko's manic drawings caught my eye too, spurring on the doodling I seemed to have been doing, forever... and ever.

My collages start with a blank A4 sheet, sharpened pencil, and a couple of black gel pens. Then the doodling begins, working on different shapes 'n fills. There's really nothing very thought-out taking place at this stage, but I know soon enough if I'm happy with how things are developing. On I go, spending a bit of time in the evenings furthering the page-fill, listening to music, and generally zoning out from the world. It's very therapeutic. Filling up the A4 can take me weeks depending on the effort I put in, and by the time I've finished there's a good chance I know what the overlay subject is going to be.

Once the thread of an idea is in my head I start to play around with the imagery. I've got a couple of folders with old cuttings, newspaper articles and magazines to dip into, as well as searching for suitable images online to print out. Assembling the collage I'm in classic cut 'n paste territory, with Scissors 'n Pritt-Stick as trusty assistants. In this Technological Age, where internet artists like Cold War Steve produce fantastic on-line work, my approach is like me; Very Dated. Whatever, I still get a kick out of watching my constructions forming. Although it's not lost on me, as I start overlaying content, I'm basically now covering up a largish percentage of the doodles I've spent many hours on. Which is nuts, I guess. I've no doubt Artificial Intelligence programs would analyse in horror my laborious design technique.

In my eyes, the theme of the end-product is clear, because I'm not smart enough to be too cryptic. I like to inject a level of humour too, which hopefully comes thru. But who knows! The regular back covers on Suspect Device have been a brilliant opportunity to keep my creative gears turning. Thanks again guys!

We managed to get SD#65 printed before the end of the year, using the brief relaxation of lockdown restrictions to collect the zines and post out copies. It included the top ten lists for 2020, this time incorporated into the zine, rather than being a separate mini issue. Several of the lists mentioned the Lockdown inspired creativity in the shape of live streams, DIY videos and home recording.

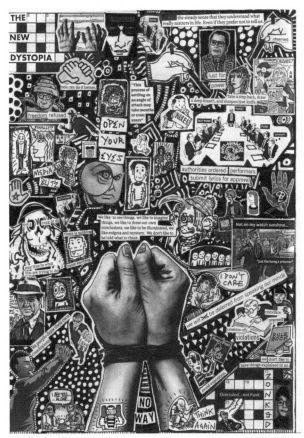

Pete Zonked's collage that appeared on the back cover of SD#70

On Boxing Day 2020 another full national lockdown was announced.

2021 was one hell of a year. A lockdown in winter wasn't as much fun as a lockdown in summer, our walks weren't as good, or as frequent, due to bad weather, and with work being so stressful I was suffering with palpitations more and more. When we eventually started to come out of lockdown, my dad died. His health had been worsening over the previous months, and despite the lockdown restrictions, we had been able to visit once a week, sitting outside in the cold talking to him through open doors, but with a clear plastic screen between us. He didn't understand it and we could see him becoming more and more frail as each week passed. He died just as we were allowed to gather indoors, but the first time we were allowed into his care home was on the night he died. He didn't want a funeral, but we had a wake for him, and Gaz came down for it, which I was very grateful for. It was hot and Gaz turned up in shorts and a Chron Gen t-shirt, dad would have approved I think, he always liked Gaz. I wore a No Sweat produced Food Not Bombs t-shirt because the last conversation I had with dad was about this shirt, he didn't understand it, but it was the last time he directly spoke to me. Funny enough it was a black shirt, which I seldom wear.

Within a month an uncle and an aunt (two of dad's siblings) had also died. Then, as we prepared for a Sumer break in Somerset, my mum fell while walking back from the shops and broke her femur and smashed her knee cap, meaning she had a six week stay in hospital and a big operation.

During all this, as has so often has been the case, punk rock was the beacon I could look to in the dark moments. Abrazos finally got to record, but the 8 songs we had planned to record initially had increased to 21, with new songs written and some old ones being re-done with Nath, as he hadn't played on the previous versions. So while in 2020 we had planned to record an EP, we were now going to record an album. We recorded 21 songs back to back with no break. The idea was to play each song twice and just go through them all. Which is what we did, in fact we'd gone through half of them (twice each), thinking we were recording, but Dave assumed we were still warming up, so we had to start again. Towards the end of the recording we each, independently, thought we were slowing down, so we sped up. We hadn't actually been playing slower, so some of the songs were played faster than we had intended, including a couple we had put in to slow things down a touch, to give a little variety. But, the finished recording sounded so good, it was raw and fast and we were all really happy, if tired. The album is fast and raw and sounds exactly like I'd always wanted these songs to sound.

Nath's notes on the album sleeve gave a rundown of the day:

"(the album) was recorded by the inimitable Dave Sloan (Bitterman) at the Fishtank in Portsmouth. We arrived at 2pm, started slowly setting up, micing up the gear and by 10pm all the music and the vocals had been done. We recorded the music live then overdubbed the vocals. This might sound easy, but because we are so used to the singing we managed to fuck up some of the songs with as many as 4 takes required. No second guitar. We wanted something raw and immediate. And we feel that is what we've got."

We re-recorded one song that we'd recorded for the memory stick/split EP, but this time we asked Bratakus to sing on a new version of 'Halfcore'. Their vocals were ferocious and really added something different to both the song, and the album. I was blown away that they took the time to do this for us and so happy with how great their vocals sounded on the song.

Despite lockdowns and restrictions, we had released the split 7" with Brain Anguish, recorded an album and even got to play a gig, in Plymouth, despite Alan having moved up to Scotland.

When gigs started up again, I got to see Hack Job, Austerity, Bus Station Loonies, Pizza Tramp, Rash Decision and the mighty Jodie Faster live.

I also went up to London to see Diaz Brothers, Dealing With Damage, The Charlemagnes and Dinosaur Skull. I was especially excited about this gig because I really wanted to see Cil and Michael's new band Dinosaur Skull, and also because I was desperate to see Diaz Brothers. Both bands were great, and it was good to see so many good friends there, not least my travelling companions. I went up with Mike Doe and Pete and we met Gaz there. It was a great night. Gaz came back with us and we had a fun journey home through London, seeing the sights and having a good laugh. Our trip home saw us go down to Brighton to drop Pete off and then back to Mike's in Portsmouth where my car was parked. Gaz and me then drove back to Southampton. Within days, three of us had tested positive for Covid. Gaz somehow didn't get it. I was really ill, for 12 days I was incapacitated, and because I couldn't properly sleep in bed, I would force myself to the sofa where day time TV caused me to finally get a bit of sleep. When I did start to feel better, the fatigue that followed it was indescribable, and once that had subsided the brain fog replaced it. For a few weeks after that I struggled on walks in the forest and frequently had to stop to rest. It took a long, long time to finally feel 100% better. On these forest walks Sarah and me discussed me going part time. I was 55 and able to draw some of my pension, and working less seemed like a good way to deal with the stress and anxiety that was causing the palpitations. We also started to seriously think about getting a dog. We had talked about it during he first lockdown, but it wouldn't have been practical when we were both back to working full time again. But now I was working at home most of the time, and if I was to cut my working hours down it would be worth investigating.

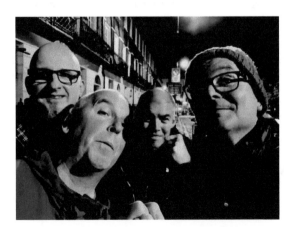

Tony, Mike Doe, Gaz, Pete Zonked! After the Diaz Brothers gig in London and before the drive home in the Covid wagon.

Despite all this we were able to produce two issues of the zine. To start with Gary Budd asked us to let him give away a copy of the zine with the new Anthrax album, 'Serfs Out', so we decided to do a special issue dedicated to Anthrax, GYO Records and also featuring Hagar The Womb because not only have Gaz and me always loved them, but at the time Steph was a member of both Anthrax and Hagar as well as being half of Grow Your Own Records.

Being huge fans of both Anthrax and Grow Your Own Records we were thrilled to be able to do this. We did 100 copies of the zine which even had a bit of colour on the cover. They were all given out with initial copies of the album.

Gary Budd:

"My interest in fanzines dates back to before we formed Anthrax, and Gary (Oscar), Fod and Rob Challice started Enigma fanzine in 1980.
When we reformed the band and got back into the scene, we put out our retrospective compilation album, One Last Drop. On the cover we included links to lots of fanzines and distros that we liked, and Suspect Device was one of the first fanzines we thought of. Tony and Suspect Device have always been very supportive of Anthrax and our label Grow Your Own Records, and the fanzine is very well put together with good content. So when we came to release our latest album, Serfs Out, we thought it would be a nice touch to give away a copy of Suspect Device with the first 100 copies sold. We were surprised when we received the issue that it was purely about Anthrax, which was lovely."

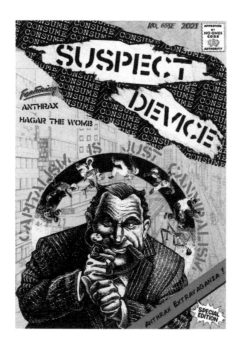

Not long after we finished the special issue for the Anthrax album, we started work on SD#66. I had dowloaded some stuff by a Peruvian band called Las Ratapunks, and loved their stripped down punk sound. Then most of these songs were then released as a 7"EP. Kibou Records were releasing it in the UK, so after buying the record, I dropped them some questions, which they answered very quickly considering they were doing the interview in English. I did offer to get the questions translated, but they said they were happy with English. Stuart Armstrong sent us an interview with Slalom D, Pete did an in depth interview with Rich Levene and Alan did a great interview with Chris Wheelie Wilshire (Bus Station Loonies/CDS/etc etc). I also sent some questions to Disstraxx. Pete suggested doing a piece on 7 Seconds' debut album, 'The Crew', which had just been remastered and rereleased by Trust Records, and featured a booklet with photos and anecdotes from the band and people around them at the time. Pete, me, Gaz and Mike Doe had ordered the album together and along with David Stuart, Graham Sleightholme and Mel Hughes we wrote pieces on the album and what it meant to us when we first heard it, as well as our thoughts on the new reissue.

Graham also wrote a piece on obscure punk rock singles, which had me scouring the internet for the bands and records I hadn't heard before. The piece is reproduced below:

People laugh at me cos I like weird music

From the off, punk threw open the doors to anyone brave, daft or creative enough to have a go. Talent wasn't necessary. DIY record and tape labels sprung up, budget recordings bypassed traditional music channels and labels. Fanzines supplanted the role of the music weeklies (NME / Melody Maker). This meant that whilst a lot of bigger punk bands (Pistols, Clash, Damned etc) realistically followed standard rock structures as a trajectory to popularity (managers, big labels, press shoots). Others used the opportunity to go off in other directions with different goals.

Inevitably what became tagged "DIY punk" or "Xerox music" was a tough sell. The average person (including punks), wrote this new scene off as untalented rubbish; it didn't settle on one sound . Many of the bands actually didn't want fame or adulation outside their own bedrooms. Some hardly gigged, some didn't. Some wouldn't do mainstream interviews. Navigating your way through the hundreds of oddball bands who might of only released tapes, had two songs on a compilation LP or released one poorly distributed EP is hard work. For some context a lot of punks consider CRASS as a band / label to be one of the ideological founders of escaping the mainstream major labels, releasing your own music on your own label, keeping costs down, and giving bands autonomy. Most of the records here were ahead of that curve but they didn't club together around one label.

I'm no expert but here's a few bands which I think deserve a bit of attention. I've covered a few I think you'll know to give the article some sort of grounding and also i've stuck to vinyl releases. Doing that I've cut out a huge chunk of whats out there. Also I stuck to UK releases but if you like whats on offer below there is a wealth of this stuff waiting for you. Some good places to track down more of the same stuff would be via the MESSTHETICS series which did lots of CDR releases and really did uncover some truly wonderful bands (and some utter nonsense). I mean who doesn't want to hear THE SPUNKY ONIONS?

Also Johan Kugelberg did a brilliant top 100 DIY releases article which can be found online. Finally, I have to mention BUZZCOCKS for their inspirational self released EP which influenced TVPs and others to have a go, such as SWELL MAPS, MEKONS, THE FALL, THE NORMAL, SUBWAY SECT, KLEENEX, METAL URBAIN and Rough Trade for being adventurous to release records which might not sell.

Desperate Bicycles - The Medium Was Tedium / Dont back the Front 7" 1977 (refill)

Releasing their 1st EP in April 77, and this one in July 77, on their own label, Desperate Bicycles are rightly considered the begining of the 'Do It Yourself' punk scene. "it was easy, it was cheap...go and do it" and "xerox music's here to stay" were hard to ignore. The use of an organ was probably a bit much for some punks but the inept charm and sublime lyrics really do take this to the top of the pile. They didn't do interviews and don't want to do reissues.

Television Personalities - Where's Bill Grundy now? EP 1978 (kings road)

Released in '78 this band is probably well known for the song 'Part time Punks' A scathing early attack on poseurs on the Kings Road. Basic and stripped down musically, this is an inept classic. A lot of the early punk bands were attacking authority. TVPs were laughing at those punks blindly following the fashions of the day without questions. Nods to two other great bands in the lyrics of 'part time punks' - O'LEVEL and SWELL MAPS was a nice touch, Both deserve a listen. Importantly TVPs also printed all the pressing information details on the back sleeve, pushing along the Desperate Bicycles manifesto a bit more. TVPs have carried on in one way or another up until today.

Gerry and the Holograms - Meet the Dissidents 7" 1979 (absurd records)

Described as Avant New Wave...it's keyboard and echoed vocals...it's very weird and has an electronic drone. Fans of industrial sounds might get a kick out of this, or people who just laugh in the face of common sense. Released on the aptly titled 'Absurd Records' label from Manchester. The 2nd EP was glued inside the sleeve as some sort of anti-music stance. It probably still sounds better than that 2nd Flux of Pink Indians LP.

Various - Weird Noise EP 1979 (fuck off records)

Released on a label which for the most part put out tapes. This 5 band compilation is inept and as budget as it gets. The bands, THE SELLOUTS, DANNY & THE DRESSMAKERS, The 012, The DOOR AND THE WINDOW and INSTANT AUTOMATONS turn in songs which are painfully bad and unliftingly hilarious in equal measure. The 012 with 'Fish from Tahiti' is incredible. However, Danny and the Dressmakers deserve a special mention. They were exclusively on tape but were one of the few bands to play live. Considering their disdain for tunes and structure, combined with songs like "Come on baby lite my shite" and a four and a half hour tape release of their "set", the mind boggles at how they went down with audiences.

The Petticoats - Normal 7" 1980 (bla-bla-bla)

Self released on her own Bla-Bla-Bla label, and also responsible for all the instruments; this one woman ramshackle endeavour is thrown together with enthusiasm oozing out. A fantastic wild screech part way through the title song to accompany the lyrics about the banality of modern life is great . There's a hint of KLEENEX in there for a comparison. These songs aside there was an appearance on the obscure 'Scaling Triangles' Comp LP.

Puritan Guitars - £100 in 15 minutes EP 1980 (riverside records)

Clang clang clang guitars with someone shouting the song title and "rock n roll" over the top of the metronomic drone. You are not here for the tunes. Originally it was thought the title was about how expensive and long the record took to record but apparently its about a drinks bill at a Rough Trade records party. They didn't get signed. Listen to this and guess why. Self released oddness I picked up on a whim.

Instant Automatons - Peter Paints his Fence EP 1980 (deleted records)

The only record from the time by this duo. The 6 songs on here are free flowing punk, folksy, free festival sort of takes on life and its oddness, being often bleak and sarcastic. The song 'People laugh at me cos I like weird music' places itself alongside DESPERATE BICYCLES and TVPs for their vision of doing things differently. They advertised in the music weeklies at the time that if you sent them a blank tape with enough postage, they'd send your tape back with an album on it. Pushing against conventional ideas was part and parcel of this small scene. Its also probably why it never gained much traction as it was hardly marketable. Protag later turned up in ZOUNDS and ALTERNATIVE TV along with being a mainstay of the 1in12 Club following his ideals through until his death.

The Prats - 1990s EP 1980 (Rough Trade)

This Scottish band formed in 1978 and aged between 12 and 14 this lot shows what can happen when you encourage anyone to have a go. These four songs are kids with very little talent but an endearing charm. The song 'Nothing' in all its 1 minute 8 seconds of glory has a kid who hasn't yet lost his voice shouting "nothing to do, sit here and be bored" with a solo which made 'Boredom' by Buzzcocks sound professional. It probably didn't sell very well and the artwork seemingly has nothing to do with the songs.

Graham Sleightholme

Gaz:

Issue #64 – A mighty issue appearing in May 2020. Lucky Malice, iDestroy, Werecats, Punka, Attestor, Chain Cult, King of Pigs and the wonderful and intimidating all at the same time - Menstrual Cramps. Ha! They scared a few fat old Skinheads at Rebellion when I saw them there that's for sure!

Issue #65 – Two huge issues in a year? Us? Yup! This came out in December 2020 with Breakout, Dangerman, Sickness, Daiei Spray and the Diaz Brothers, who feature none other than the guy who avoids me at darts – Neil Cox! Great band as much as I hate to admit it. We didn't go for a top ten mini issue this year either and combined it with this one.

Issue #65 SE - This was a Special Edition given out with the release of the Anthrax LP – Serfs Out. Only about 100 exist and I'm pleased to report they sold out very quickly. We interviewed Anthrax and Hagar The Womb for this one and apart from a few memories from various contributors it was a complete one off. No reviews or any of the other zine content you'd expect. A young lad called 'Fred' did a great job on the cover and apart from anything else it was a privilege to be asked to do it. I'd really like to do others if I'm honest.

Issue #66 – I actually didn't think I owned a copy of this, but it turns out I do! Anyway, we've nearly fallen through another year and this November 2021 issue brought with it Las Ratapunks, Chris Wheelie Whilshire of Bus Station Loonies fame, Slalom D, Disstraxx and the mighty Mr Rich Levene. I basically went missing in action this issue and apart from an intro the contribution I made was limited.

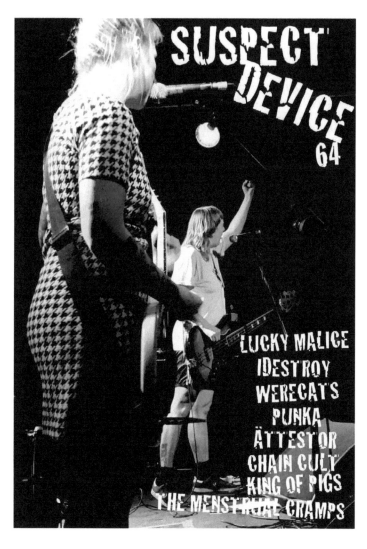

Tony Suspect - Onwards and Upwards

Our 2021 Top Ten issue wasn't a hard copy, it was a PDF that people could download for free. Because of everything that had been going on in the past 12 months, we gave it the number SD#Sixty Sick and the cover picture was a positive Covid Test.

Gaz added a little bit about my dad before his top ten:

> I want to mention one other late great legend of the Oche, who whether he liked it or not, played darts to Blitz and the Upstarts with a beer in his hand. I raise my glass to Tony's Dad – Dave. Many a sociable evening spent at the former SDHQ of 'Brynton' listening to now classic Punk albums, drinking a couple of homebrews and throwing darts. Cheers Dave.

Despite managing to record an album and having Alan come down from Scotland so Abrazos could play a gig in Plymouth towards the end of the year, both of which I greatly enjoyed, 2021 was a worse year, for me, than 2020. But. the Xmas break was the first one for as long as I can remember where I felt really relaxed and as the New Year beckoned I wasn't left with a feeling of dread that another year of full time work lay ahead of me. That dark tunnel of previous years, where I couldn't see any sort of light, was gone. I was embarking on a change, and was now a part time worker, supplementing my reduction in wages with a payout from my pension. I had taken 80% of a pension I had been paying into for over 30 years, with a lump-sum too, so as I was still working three days a week I actually wasn't much worse off, financially, but the weight that had lifted off my shoulders was worth more than money.

Then, on January 9th 2022, Sarah, Becca and me headed off to Swindon to collect a dog that had been rescued from the streets of Bosnia (where she was due to be put down) by a charity and offered for adoption. She had initially been due in England before Xmas, but a problem with the transport meant that the charity delayed the journey. Hard for us to take as we were excited for her arrival, but it was done in the best interests and wellbeing of the dogs, so we couldn't really complain.

We got to Swindon easily, but finding kennels was a bit tricky, but we finally found them, feeling a little nervous and not knowing quite what to expect. We knew our dog was gentle and calm, and we had seen a picture of her, and some video, but I felt the same sense of worry that I felt just before Becca was born. I was excited, but fearful that I wouldn't know what to do or be able to cope with being responsible for another living being. After we pulled up at the gate things moved quickly, we told the kennel staff the name of the dog we had come to collect, and our name, and before we knew it they brought her out, placed her in the travel crate and we were on our way home. Becca sat in the back with her and gave her a treat and Alice (the name the shelter had given her that we didn't see any reason to change) took the treat and settled down for the journey home.

Very quickly we realised that Alice was perfect and along with my reduced hours, having Alice around proved to be a huge benefit. At the time of writing, over 2 years on, I haven't had a single bout of palpitations. Even getting Covid a second time couldn't dampen my spirits, although to be fair I wasn't as ill as I had been first time round, just a few days on the sofa feeling bit shit, with Alice keeping me company.

My new found contentment, and still feeling the spirit of creativity from the Lockdown times, I came up with an idea for another project for us. For punkers of a certain age, the 7" record is the perfect format for listening to punk rock. When us old buggers started buying records, the 7" was king, which was good as it was all we could afford. Of course punk bands are still releasing 7"EPs and the format has endured. With this in mind, in February 2022 we did a one-off, e-zine simply called the Suspect Device 7" Issue. Over 28 pages Gaz, Pete and me, along with our friends and contributors wrote about 7" records that have meant something or hold cherished memories for us at some point in our lives. I suspect this was another project that came out of a conversation Pete and me had one day, and we ran with it. It was a fun thing to put together, and I enjoyed reading everyone's pieces.

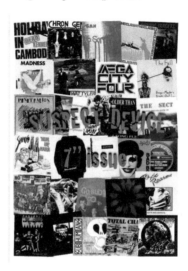

There were also some good gigs happening as well. Stuart Armstrong had offered me a ticket for Stiff Little Fingers, The Professionals and TV Smith in Bournemouth, although on the day he couldn't go as he was ill, so my mate Ade Howarth took his ticket. We thought we'd got there in plenty of time, but still missed TV Smith, which was a shame and I felt bad, so I made sure I bought something from his merch table. I'd never seen The Professionals before, but had been a fan since their first 7" came out in 1980. There was no Steve Jones, but they were still great, and I can't pretend it wasn't nice to see Paul Cook playing drums. SLF were good, in fact their songs sounded very good, but somehow there was a spark missing and I didn't enjoy them as much as I wanted to. Still it was a good gig, and because he couldn't go, Stuart had asked me to save my ticket stub for him, so I decided to see if I could get Paul Cook to sign it. I'm not really interested in autographs, but I knew Stuart would like it. Paul Cook was happy to sign, which was good of him as it seemed everyone wanted to speak to him as he stood behind he merch table. After he had signed the ticket, he left to go to the back stage area, and the young security girl on the entrance to the band area asked for his ID. She may well have been the only person in the venue to not know who he was or that he had been in a band that were part of the reason we were all in that venue that night, and that includes the other bands playing. It made me laugh as I thought about it, but, being the down to earth bloke he seems to be he happily showed his Backstage Pass without complaint.

Great DIY gigs were still going on in Portsmouth pretty regularly, and we got to see The Domestics, Armoured Flu Unit and The SLM, while in Southampton we had Rash Decision, Misfortune Cookie and Bitterman. Then, on my birthday, the Subhumans came back to Southampton. I may have got a little emotional when they played 'Evolution'. It is probably my favourite Subhumans song, and the EP did a lot to shape my view on the world, particularly when it came to animal rights, and boycotting companies who profited from cruelty. I had been given a Free The MBR Beagles hoodie for my birthday and I was wearing it as they played that song. It felt like a special moment, and I couldn't have asked for a better birthday present.

Also on my birthday we released the Abrazos album. Because of the problems with getting records pressed, we had been waiting a long time for the records to arrive, but it was worth the wait, and I still think it's the best release that I have been part of, for a lot of reasons.

As the summer hotted up Pete, Mike Doe and me headed up to London again to see Career Suicide. Gaz couldn't make it, unfortunately, something that he was gutted about as he'd also had to miss Career Suicide when they played Southampton, some years before. Again, they were superb and I loved the fact that I was seeing them with Mike and Pete. We'd even had another eventful journey up to London with the M25 coming to a standstill when someone had jumped from a motorway bridge.

In June we put out SD#67, and it's an issue I really like. I was so happy to have Dinosaur Skull in the zine, as well as Dogma, who's album on GYO had been a real favourite for both Gaz and me. Pete interviewed Ben from Raising Hell zine. A new issue of Raising Hell had just come out and Amorphous Pieces had compiled (almost) every early issue of Raising Hell in a superb book, so to accompany Pete's interview and because Sned also did punk rock jigsaws that I had enjoyed doing over the lockdowns, and a wonderful book on The Garage in Newcastle, I sent him some questions too. Gaz had Post Mortem, Surgery Without Research and Slow Faction which gave this issue an eclectic and interesting range of interviews. We also ran a piece from Graham Sleightholme about the sad death of Calvin Sewell from Grand Collapse. We had wanted to mark his passing, and as Graham had worked with him, and knew him well, I asked if he'd write something. What he wrote included memories and anecdotes and was very moving. When I read it I knew I had done the right thing asking Graham to write it, it told you everything you needed to know about Calvin and why he would be so missed, not only by those who knew him, but everyone who was aware of his talent and contribution to the DIY punk scene.

Calvin Sewell - 1985 - 2022 - Singer of GRAND COLLAPSE

Earlier this year the DIY punk community lost a friend and major player in our collective punk culture. Tony asked me to put some words down, so here I go.

I didn't know Calvin until he got a job in my office. He was "Stig from the Icons of Filths son". We would sit next to each other for 10 of the next 12 years sharing the idle banter of an office, along with an unhealthy amount of chat about punk rock, politics and sport. After a while you just get under each others skin. You talk about growing up, friends, relationships, family and most importantly 'were hash browns better than potato smiles?'

During this time I watched Cal form the band he fronted, GRAND COLLAPSE. The band we all know him for. His only band. He seemed to have an energy and enthusiasm for Grand Collapse which I've rarely seen in others. Driven to surround himself with friends and political allies for his band mates, it wasn't going to be an 18 month project with 1 EP and 7 gigs. It wasn't about getting hyped or on the right label. No, it was for the long haul. 10 years on; three albums, two EPs, a tour of the USA plus gigs across Europe and the UK, they'd certainly put the graft in. Cal was a natural at singing. Early on some of us older punks would tell him he looked like his dad when he was on stage. The way he held the mic, the spiky hair, the absolute conviction of the delivery. Cal wasn't for singing regurgitated Discharge haikus or Oppressed verse chorus verse rants (although we laughed about how that would be easier) he was singing well crafted songs, from the heart. They can be read apart from the music.

Politics played a huge part here and vicious tirades against Hunters, Politicians and the state of society were all dealt with. Cal wasn't singing these from a distance either. He got out there sabbing and confronted the EDL on the streets. There are many anecdotes of his rumbles. Cal's songs also delved into personal experiences of loss and despair. His life experiences were intense and desperately sad at times. His dad died when he was still a teen and he had lost his brother in awful circumstances. The ability to turn these moments and situations into songs was a brave and emotional move.

On the flip to the above, whenever Calvin went away for a tour or just a long weekend of gigs, our office would usually joke on what he would forget to take or bring back. Inevitably he would have to admit to leaving a coat on a plane, losing his phone, yet another credit card (6 in a year!) or missing his flight home. It was comedy gold. The party and the ensuing carnage was all part of life. London band GOOD THROB wrote the song 'acid house' after staying at Calvins house one night. I told him about the song and the lyrics (go read them) "It wasn't that bad " he shrugged. He'd sometimes roll into work looking absolutely bedraggled after a weekend, but after a plate of hash browns or a pot noodle he'd be back on track and chatting about Cardiff City, MMA or Rugby. As work went, Cal wasn't in favour of it, even though it was a workers co-op (no bosses) and we are a veggie / vegan outfit. He was however good at his job and his intelligence shone. Sometimes we would laugh that a bunch of punks and freaks were running a massive enterprise.

Calvin suffered a heart attack two months after an operation on his heart. That far into recovery and for someone so young and strong. it really wasn't expected. A lot of us cried at the pub the next day. Lots of hugs and tears together really did help. The funeral was obviously tough but was beautifully done, in both his native Welsh and English language. Conducted in a humanist manner, with the the lyrics to Icons of Filths 'fucked up state' being read aloud. Tunes by The Clash, Flying Pickets, Propagandhi and Phil Collins (fuck, we laughed) all tied in with the grief of what was happening. A post funeral drink up led to people having to queue to get in the pub. It was brilliant to see and meet people who had travelled from across the country to pay their respects. Friendships strengthened and new ones made. I hope my words do the lanky twat some justice, I welled up twice writing this, looking at his beaming grin staring at me from a recent photo of him holding up 'Empty Plinths' LP outside our work the day it was delivered.

Graham Sleightholme

With Alan up in Scotland, Abrazos made another video, and again we got our friends involved to help out for the song Strength In Numbers. It was fun to put together, and nice to have contributions from some of our favourite people.

As much as I liked issue 67, it cost us quite a bit to get printed, so we had to charge more and I felt uncomfortable asking people to pay over £4 for the zine, so I thought it would be a good idea to start doing more regular, smaller issues. So in November 2022 we had SD#68 done. Mackie had released a new single under the name Rose Of Victory, Gaz and me always liked their original 7" released in 1983 and as Mackie was now a mate we wanted to give him the chance to talk about this new release.

Our little dog is as gentle as dogs get, and she likes nothing more than a doze on a comfy sofa and a belly rub, but as she got used to her new home she became territorial, so anyone walking past the house got a good barking, and she had taken to attacking anything that came through the letterbox. This was all very funny when junk mail or bills got chewed up, but when she first took a bite out of a Damned book I'd ordered, and then put a hole in the Rose Of Victory sleeves (and a Dinosaur Skull t-shirt), things got serious, and we had to put a post box on the wall outside.

Gaz's mate Matthew Worley gave us an interview he'd done with Paul Wellings and I wanted to feature Hastings band Comeback Clit. The cover featured some graffiti Gaz took a photo of saying Co-operation Not Competition, which kind of sums up DIY punk and the way we've always felt about SD. My one regret is, despite countless checks, and both Gaz and Pete also signing it off, there was a spelling mistake on the cover where the E was missed out of Comeback. I still feel bad, and annoyed with myself when I think about it or see the cover.

But there is good stuff in this issue, Graham's report from the Static Shock Fest is good and there's a photo I took of Zero Again at The Hobbit in Southampton. I liked the two singles they had out at that point, but live they were phenomenal, so much power and such great songs. I spent a bit of time talking to Ian Glasper. We talked about the Zero Again album that they were preparing to start recording, but mostly about his Subhumans book. It was pretty much done and, knowing my love for the Subhumans, he took me to his car to show me the first draft of the book that Earth Island had put together in a proper cover. It wasn't the finished article, just one of a few copies that they had put together for Ian and the band. I was able to flick through briefly, but it looked astonishing. Ian later offered to get a PDF copy to me for an advanced review. I usually don't like reading books digitally, I find it harder to concentrate on the words, but as it was a book that Ian had written, and because it was about the Subhumans I started to read it on my phone and I couldn't stop. It was a great read, and although I have loved the Subhumans since the early 1980s I found that the book just reinforced what a special band they are and I came away loving them even more. I liked the fact that they weren't from a big city or trying to be cool, they just made punk their own, I could see some parallels with how Gaz and me got into punk living on the edge of the New Forest, like many others all over the country, we were removed from any big city influences, but punk rock had stuck a chord and we started to do our own thing.

I got straight on with the next issue, aiming to get it printed in early January, featuring our now annual Top Ten lists.

But before the year was out I took a trip up to Scotland to stay with Alan and go to see Bratakus and Burning Flag in Glasgow. It was in a small venue, that had a good, diverse, friendly crowd and Bratakus were fantastic. It was good to spend some time with Alan and we also got to catch up with Brian Curran and Bratakus. Alan also convinced me to buy a boxset version of Adam & The Ants' 'Kings Of The Wild Frontier' album. It was fairly inexpensive for what it was and I am a sucker for extra live discs and info booklets, all of which this edition had.

Crispin got me a ticket for the Ruts DC gig in Southampton. I probably wouldn't have gone on my own, but I was grateful to him for the ticket as they were superb. Also, it was good to see TV Smith after missing him early in the year in Bournemouth.

Just before Xmas 2022 I'd gone to see Bitterman in Southampton, Alan had already done an interview with them for us and I wanted to get some photos to use with the interview. It had been a cold month, but this night was freezing, and the venue, which had been moved at the last minute, wasn't any warmer than it was out in the street. It was so cold and as I watched Bitterman my feet felt like blocks of ice, despite the two pairs of socks I was wearing inside my big boots, so I stayed in one position. I was able to get some good pictures, even though I was just using my phone, and one looked good enough for the front cover. I had to leave after a couple of songs by the band that followed. I wan't particularly into their music, and it was so cold, I just wanted to be home with a nice cup of tea.

We were able to get SD#69 out in January 2023.

Gaz interviewed young band The Human Error, who include the sons of Welshy from External Menace, and Pete did a great interview with Dealing with Damage. The added 2022 Top Ten lists meant is was another bigger issue and I think I'd already quietly shelved my plan of more regular but smaller issues.

The first few months of 2023 were a busy time, but in a good way. The best of the best kicked things off, and I drove down to Portsmouth with Nath and Ady to see the Subhumans. It was in a venue none of us had been to before. We parked up and had a look down a narrow ally and wondered if we were going to walk into a drug deal, but it turned out that it was the venue, which was a brewery. I had a chat with Dick, who was quite happy with the review I'd done of Ian Glasper's book. Of course the Subhumans were great, as they always are, and it was good too see some younger people there getting into their songs.

Then F. Emasculata played in Southampton and were superb, and a couple of days later Mike Doe asked if I wanted to go to Brighton on a Wednesday night to see Motive and Churchgoers. I hadn't heard of either of them, but Motive sounded good on Bandcamp, so I was in. To be honest the main reason I took Mike up on his offer was because I knew it would be fun to go to a gig with him, and also because Pete was going as were Ralf and Darren, and that seemed like the best reason to go to a gig. As it turned out, just being there with good friends was enough, Churchgoers were ok, I liked the fact that they were youngsters and playing noisy hardcore, then Motive played and were absolutely fantastic. The sound wasn't great in the Cowley Club, but that didn't matter to Motive as they powered through a set that sounded like Chaos UK from 1982. In fact as the set went on I added Disorder to my comparison, it was quite something for a bunch of teenagers. They were great and I knew then I wanted to feature them in the zine.

Despite not being able to get together, Abrazos had been writing songs, much like we did during Lockdown. When we had enough songs we were happy with, Nath and me had proper practise to run through the songs. I recorded them on my phone and then sent the rough recordings to Alan. The plan was for Nath and me to record guitar, drums and half the vocals with Dave Sloan in Portsmouth and Alan was going to record bass and his vocals up in Scotland with Rat (Statement).

A week later Sarah and me drove up to Scotland to stay with Alan and Soozin, stopping in Middlesbrough to pay the Briggsies a visit. It was a long old drive, and Middlesbrough isn't really on the quickest route, but we couldn't go that far North and not nip over to Middlesbrough. It was a nice way to break the journey up, and we paid a visit to Dan Briggs' Coffee Shop, Off The Ground. It was a thoroughly relaxing and lovely way to spend some time. As ever we were well looked after and, refreshed, we started on the road to Scotland the next morning. Driving across the Pennines was interesting, we went from driving in sunshine with the temperature gauge showing 15 degrees, to suddenly, dense fog and 3 degrees. It slowed us up for a little while.

We had a great time in Scotland, visiting Lochs, seeing mountains and having a brief trip to Glasgow. Alan and me also sat down and went through the songs sorting out who would do what with the vocals. The eventual 9 hour drive home, mainly due to a closed road near Oxford, couldn't ruin the good time we'd had.

Before the end of February I was at my 4th gig of the year. Rut and Lisa were over and there was a C-30s gig in Bournemouth. Gaz was down and I drove over with Crispin, picking up Stuart Armstrong on the way.

By this time I had started on SD#70, but the gigs kept coming. The next one was one I'd been looking forward to for some time. Despite me not liking big venues, Gaz and me went to see Killing Joke play their first two albums at The Royal Albert Hall in London. It had been 40 years since we'd first seen them together, at the University in Southampton. It felt strange going to such a venue to see Killing Joke play those songs, but it was also good to be there with Gaz. Obviously we approached London from opposite directions. I messaged him as I got on the tube at Richmond and we decided to meet at tube station in Kensginton. I had a much shorter journey there, so was expecting a bit of a wait. As I got off the tube I had just messaged Gaz again, to let him know I was there, when another tube pulled in and he got off right next to where I was standing. We had a wander around London, without getting wet this time, although some random girl asked Gaz if she could have his Crass beanie. Our tickets were the cheapest we could get, so we were up high, but right at the front looking down on the stage. The staff there offered us "better seats", for free, lower down, but at the back of a row of seats. We declined and were able to see the band perfectly, despite the altitude. The event finished in time for Gaz to make his tube back to his car, on the way he took a photo of an empty tube carriage which he sent me saying "This would make a good zine cover."

Nath and me then went down to Portsmouth in March to record our bits for the Abrazos EP, that SD was going to release, thanks to an offer of money from Stuart Armstrong, and Gaz's super salesman skills on eBay, as he got rid of most of my CD collection, we had discovered we could get a picture disc done, and as it was a format that none of us had done before we decided to go for it. In discussions about what the picture would be, Alan mentioned he liked the idea of paying homage to a classic album. I remembered that Nath and me had discussed, some time previously, recreating the cover of 'Germ Free Adolescents' by X-Ray Spex. Nath then went to work creating what I think is a masterpiece, we each took pictures of ourselves pretending we were in test tubes and he expertly recreated that iconic sleeve.

The recording was made easy by Dave Sloan again, but it didn't feel quite right recording without Alan there. We were happy with what we'd done, but it wasn't as an enjoyable experience as recording the album had been, and I think Alan suffered more doing his stuff up in Scotland on his own. When all the recording was done, Dave stapled it all together and it all sounded good, and thanks to his mixing mastery you wouldn't know it was recorded in two different locations, but as a band experience it was a little lacking, and the songs lack a little bit of the energy that comes from us all being in the same room. Next time we record we will be together, as that's what makes Abrazos so much fun, it feels effortless and we can bounce ideas around meaning songs come together much quicker, and the result has more of a raw, urgent quality.

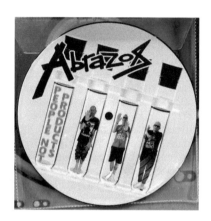

Work was also progressing on the zine, but I still had time to go and see Steve Ignorant's band playing Crass songs, supported by Omega Tribe, which proved to be another fantastic gig with both bands being excellent. I know some people don't agree with him doing this, but he doesn't pretend it is Crass, and the songs are given a new lease of life with the addition of Carol Hodge's vocals and a hard hitting drummer. Each to their own, but it is fantastic hearing those songs live and loud.
The gigs continued, with The Damned and Nightingales triumphing over the Southampton Guildhall's terrible sound and both putting on great performances. Dinosaur Skull were also fantastic at The Hobbit on Easter Sunday. It was good to see Cil and Michael again, and of course we mainly talked about our dogs. Bad Breeding were very good not long after that and then there was another brilliant gig to go to in Portsmouth. Gaz had come down to see The Restarts, and I drove up with him, Nath and Ady. Uncivilised played their usual energetic set, before a new band to all of us, Sin Nadie Al Mando, from Colombia, played and were absolutely fantastic, they blew everyone away with their hardcore influenced punk sound. It was another of those gigs where an unknown band became everyone's new favourite. I had seen Restarts before, many years ago, but I hadn't really kept up with them, so it was good to get reacquainted as they were great. It was one of those special nights, with great bands and great friends.

In June 2023 we put out SD#70. Gaz interviewed The Samples and GBH's first drummer, Wilf. I got Motive in the zine and spoke to Ian Glasper about the forthcoming Zero Again album. He'd sent me an MP3 copy to review and it was so good I wanted to get some thoughts on it to put alongside the album ad that David Gamage sent me as Engineer were doing the CD version. I would have liked to have done a more in-depth Zero Again interview, but time and space were limited, and so I decided to focus on the album.

Mike Head submitted a short interview with Clobber, which had appeared originally on his Musings Of An Old Punk Facebook page, and Marv Gadgie did a report of the Manchester Punk Festival.

Gaz and me then did a little Subhumans feature as I reprinted my review of Ian Glasper's book, and Gaz reviewed the Pirate's Press released boxset.

The cover was the shot of an empty tube carriage Gaz took as he made his way out of London after the Killing Joke gig.

Casey Jones:
"Tony continued sending me SD issues for a bit and still sends me whatever he records. From Pilger to Abrazos, I remain a huge fan and if I ever get the stones to finally put together that 2nd issue of my old fanzine 40 years too late, Abrazos will be my first (new) interview! It's no small feat that you continue banging out new Suspect Device issues all these years later. I see that the latest Issue #70 has Wilf from GBH again. (Funny side note: A few of the GBH guys heckled us at an Ignite show in Birmingham in '95 or '96 and ended up hanging out with us after the show. We even talked Jock into coming to London with us but had to turn the bus around on the way there when he phoned his wife and she told him to get back home. Great times!) Anyway, what a cool scene it is to have someone from SD Issue #2 still around for another interview. Here's to 70 more!"

My year of going to 25 gigs was rounded off by Diaz Brothers, Prey, Cockney Rejects, Subhumans again, Hakan, Fords Fuzz Inferno/Scoundrels, the absolutely brilliant Chain Whip and was rounded off in brilliant fashion with Ruts DC at The Joiners. The band were brilliant, and being there with good friends made it even more memorable.

We did manage to get one more issue done in 2023. In fact SD#71 was pretty much finished by the end of November, but we had a couple more reviews to add in, and then Iain Ratcliffe said he'd interviewed Scott McCloud from SoulSide, Girls Against Boys etc after going to see SoulSide in San Francisco, and asked if we wanted it for the zine. So I said yes, and Iain had photos too. That day I got an old box out of the loft space, it was full of old SD stuff, and on top was a set list from SoulSide's gig at the West Indian club in 1989. So that interview joined those I'd done with Marla Watson, who's excellent photo book had just come out on Earth Island, Alan's new band Collision Course, Scene Report Records and Anarka & Poppy. Pete had got in touch with Parallel Worlds and Alan interviewed his old High Wycombe chums in Prey.

With the zine complete, I held off sending it to the printers straight away as Prey were playing in Southampton on December 10th, and I wanted to take a couple of photos to go in the interview. I finished the zine that night and sent it off. As ever I sent Gaz and Pete a PDF copy, and Pete got back to me to point out an error in my layout of one of the interviews. I quickly corrected that and sent a panicked text to Stuart Armstrong (who, as he always does, was sorting out the printing) asking if it was too late to change the submitted zine for a new version. Luckily he managed to sort it so the issue that he drove over with on December 14th was the correct one.

Gaz:

Issue #67 – Good Lord! After issue 66 I appear to have gone mad in June 2022! Slow Faction, Post Mortem and Surgery Without Research interviews all done by me! Dogma, Dinosaur Skull, Raising Hell Fanzine and Amorphous Press helped bring all the Punk factions to the middle.

Issue #68 – Almost getting up to date! The picture on the cover I took while going to an office meeting in the Jubilee Pub with Steve, Jona and Matt. Good job it was on the way too or I'd have walked straight past it on the way back! Cooperation Not Competition read the graffiti on the wall and who am I to argue that? Comeback Clit, Rose of Victory and Paul Wellings made up this November 2022 issue.

Issue #69 – Just two months on for the last issue and 2023 starts with us on fine form. Young punks The Human Error, Bitterman and Dealing With Damage along with the Top tens of 2022 make this a packed issue.

Issue #70 – This May 2023 issue has a great picture of an empty Underground tube carriage on the cover – not sure who took it?!! Like his style though. As importantly the contents. Clobberer, Motive, Zero Again, The Samples and original GBH drummer – Wilf all feature. Big round up of the Manchester Punk Festival too.

Issue #71 - As I type this for the book its actually our latest issue and apart from a few reviews it's one I did not really contribute to. I thank our loyal army of regular contributors for making me look good once again. Great diversity of interviews though with Scene Report Records, Parallel Worlds, Maria Watson, Prey, Anarka & Poppy, Scott McCloud of Soulside and Collision Course all featured. I was also very pleased with the great print job on this issue too. No point in so much hard work going into a zine if it's hard to read.

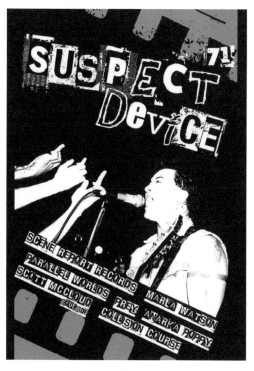

Tony: Committed For Life

And that's us up to date. The new Abrazos EP, which was expertly stapled together by Dave Sloan, has just come out, the most recent Suspect Device Records release, and the picture disc, with wrap around colour sleeve look great. We have also contributed to the release of the Bomba X LP that came out towards the end of 2023. Bomba X are based in Mallorca and feature our friend Paul Vary (Old Than Dirt).
Gaz came down to Southampton to see the Subhumans in December 2023 and on the drive to and from the gig we plotted the next issue, which we will start putting together early in 2024, 40 years after we started putting the first issue together.

To paraphrase 7 Seconds - 40 years and we're still going wrong.

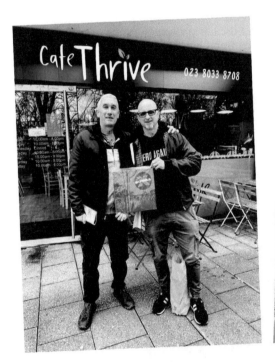 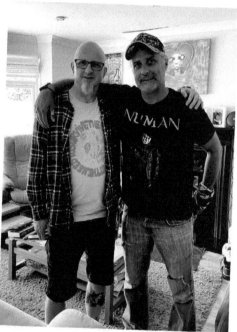

(Left) Paul Vary and Tony with the Bomba X LP (photo by Stuart Woodward)
(right) Tony and Iain Ratcliffe (photo by Carolyn Larson)

Extra Track

Neither Gaz or me do the zine for any monetary gain, or any kind of recognition, we don't think we're special or better than anyone else, we do it because we love doing a zine and we love DIY punk rock. Also, we still get the buzz of excitement when we hear a new record or see a new band and we want to tell everyone about it. We've never asked for free stuff, and are always very grateful to anyone who takes the time to send us their record or zine for review. It doesn't happen very often these days, which is understandable given the cost, and we are happy to pay for music, to support the bands, labels and individuals who work hard to bring us the music we love.

Suspect Device zine has benefitted greatly from the DIY punk scene, especially locally, it was a support network for us. I've made friends that are closer and more important to me than anyone I met at school (Gaz aside of course), the fact that a lot of them live a long way away is irrelevant. Also, I always wanted to be in a band, and the DIY scene let me do that, despite the fact I cannot really play drums very well, and my song lyrics are still little more than schoolboy rants. Since the age of 19 I have played in bands with people who's talent blows my mind, I've played on records, and done more than I could have ever imagined when I first started buying records back in 1978. And now, in my late 50s I am in a band that I love, playing music that excites me with two people who astound me, not only because of their musical genius, but because they accept my contribution, want to play music with me and know how to make my vision for the band a reality.

I remember around the time we were starting the zine, Gaz saying that we probably wouldn't be into punk when we were old men, well here we still are and we have no plans to stop any time soon.
(Tony - February 2024)

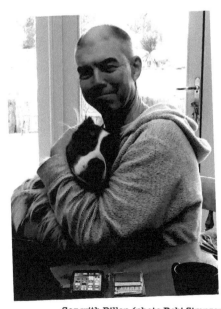 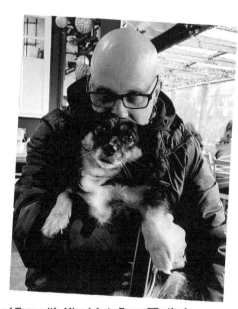

Gaz with Dillon (photo Debi Simpson) and Tony with Alice (photo Becca Whatley)

HANX

Suspect Device has always been about friendship and co-operation, all we have ever wanted to do was to help in any small way we can, and we are very grateful that these fine people have helped us write this book. Thank you to everyone who spoke to us, answered our questions, supplied photos, did artwork and continues to help and support us, we wouldn't be here without you all.

Stuart Armstrong, Si Briggs, Gary Budd, Craig Burton, Lloyd Chambers, Paul Chambers, Neil Clelland, Ashley Coleman, Matt Coleman, Neil Cox, Mike Doe, Crispin Erridge, Sean Forbes, Mike Fox, Paul Fox, Marv Gadgie, David (Golly) Golledge, Nath Haywire, Casey Jones, Tanya Hawks, Mike Head, Steve Ignorant and Jona, Geraldine Lawrence, Steve Lee, Rich Levene, Alan Marshall, Neil (Mackie) Mclennan, Andy Morris, Andy Nazer, Andy Nelson, Iain Ratcliffe, Paul Samain, Graham Sleightholme, Dave Sloan, Jochen Such, Janne Tamminen, Andy Thompson, Andy Turner, Em Watson, David (Stuart) Wilshire, Ralf Vergeldt, Dave Wagenschutz, Stewart Watt, Matt Worley.

Special thanks to Dan Roberson for his exceptional artwork and being so generous and letting us benefit from his talent.
Also to Pete Zonked! for proof reading and also for his constant friendship, encouragement and contributions, both to the book and the zine.

There are many people who do not appear in this book, but have contributed to the zine throughout the last 40 years. Thanks, you are also part of this story, and we are grateful for all contributions.

Of course, we have to thank David Gamage at Earth Island for believing in us and encouraging us to write this book. I hope we didn't let you down.

Most of the photographs in this book were taken by either Gaz or Tony. We have done our best to credit any that we didn't take, but unfortunately we have long forgotten who took some of the photos, sorry.

Gaz thanks: I don't think it's unreasonable to start this thanks list with me saying that none of this would exist without my oldest mucker Tony and his 40 years of drive and dedication to the cause of Punk Rock! His undying spirit and patience with me are worthy of some sort of long service medal if such a thing exists? However, he'll be the first to say that we've not done it for anything other than for the hell of it and it's what we've always done. Let's face it mate, we've only ever lost money, but the compensation and rewards have been that we've had and will continue to have a lot of fun doing it and we've met loads of people we love and respect along the way.

Next I'll thank my partner Debi as she just does not get it. Grow up, move on etc.. Had it all.. What's the alternative I say? Love ya! My parents bless em' - Both in their 80's now, but still shout 'Banned From The Pubs' for a laugh! Ha!

Special thanks to Matt Worley, Steve & Jona - The Office crowd for the interview in the book and getting it transcribed. Not to mention all the lifts to the pub!

Finally I'm going to give everyone I can think of that I know a mention for their friendship, time spent at the bar together and gone to a gig with, while Suspect Device Fanzine has been in existence. In no particular order - Pete Zonked, Crispin, Stu Armstrong, Rich, Craig, Dave, Rob, Rut & Lisa, Ady, Chris, Roger, Spud & Becky, Ken & Michelle, Digger, Mike Fox, Bren, Rooster, PJ, Biff, Cov John, Netley Mark, Hearn, Punky and Graham over in Bristol, Jesse Eastfield, Badger, Mark Slaughter, Clara, Chris, Jack, Sid, Phil Hedges, Welshy and his boys, Shend, Mike, Both Bods! Andy Nazer and Dave of Self Abuse, Alan, Nath & Michelle, Danny, Saul - Ayyyyeeewire! Stu and Paul of Older Than Dirt, Neil Shutdown, Alan of Immolato Tomatoes, Kev Nixon, Chris Damage, Sean Forbes, Pig, Fred, Steve DIY, All the Norwich and Pompey Punks I always talk to but can't remember your names, Paul at Soundclash Records in the Fine City, All the bands we've ever interviewed, Our loyal followers on eBay who support the zine and finally any band that's ever done a song for Totton! Immortality guaranteed for them! Hopefully that's most people!

...and finally! Thank You to Earth Island for giving us this opportunity to write a best seller and organising all the book signings in Waterstones. (Made that bit up!)

Tony thanks: Sarah and Becca for putting up with me and living in a house full of records (and record mailers), books, zines and piles of SD stuff. My sister, Jane, nephew Josh and nieces Sam and Lahnee for allowing me to rope them into various SD/Abrazos activities over the years. Pete Zonked! for the reasons mentioned above, Alan and Nath for their friendship, contributions and helping to make Abrazos a reality. Also, huge thanks to Gaz for being with me throughout all of this, he may like to tell people that I do everything for SD, but in truth, without him SD wouldn't be what it is.

RIP

Some people who have featured in this story or our local scene didn't make it this far, but are always in our thoughts: Steve Burgess, Simon Gregory, Lance Hahn, Dickie Hammond, Wiz, Shane Baldwin, Allen Adams, Dave Freeman, Mark 'Mates' Maitland, Marcus Howells, Harald 'Huckey' Renner, Calvin Sewell.

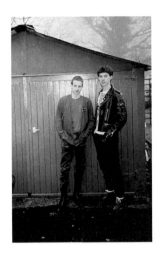 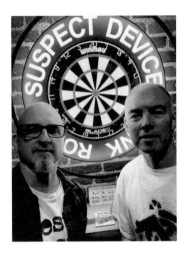

Gaz Suspect and Tony Suspect met on their first day of school aged 5, so have been friends for over 50 years. This friendship was solidified in their teenage years by a mutual love of going to football and punk rock. Going to football meant facing the weekly dangers of opposition supporters, violent police and Tony's grandad's driving, but they came through it all relatively unscathed. Cycle rides between their respective houses meant running the gauntlet of unlit country roads, scary woods and the threat of seeing Tony's grandad's car coming towards them. Gaz's dad could never understand why they both bought the same records, while Tony's dad introduced Gaz to darts and home brewed beer.

Tony doesn't play darts or drink beer.

They have been through most of the ups and downs life throws at you and survived due in part to this friendship and punk rock.

Gaz now lives in Norfolk and Tony lives in the New Forest.

Tony has been in several bands - Obvious Action, Fusion, Thirst!, Portiswood, Chokeword, Pilger, Screwed Up Flyer, The Shorts and is currently in Abrazos.

Gaz hasn't been in any bands because he has no rhythm, no sense of timing and can't generally remember what day of the week it is let alone lyrics.

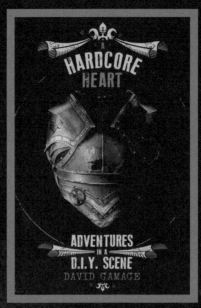

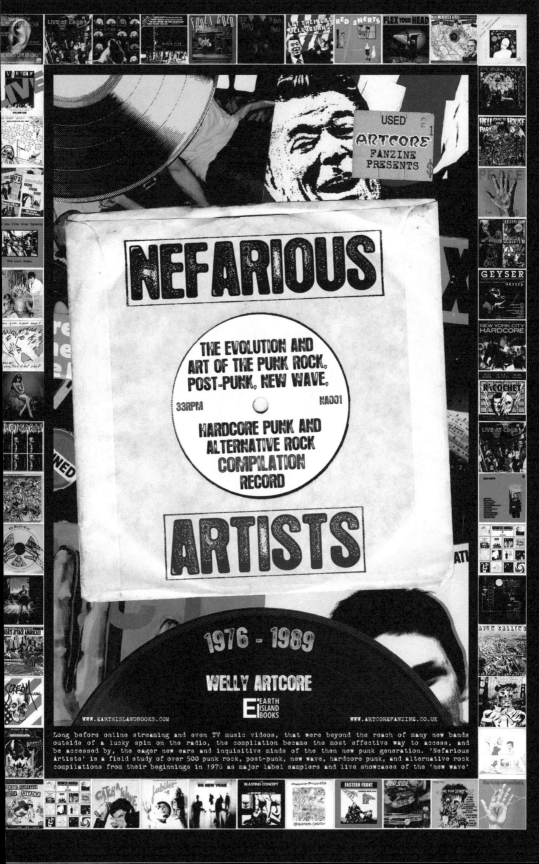

USED
Artcore
FANZINE
PRESENTS

NEFARIOUS

THE EVOLUTION AND
ART OF THE PUNK ROCK,
POST-PUNK, NEW WAVE,

33RPM   NA001

HARDCORE PUNK AND
ALTERNATIVE ROCK
COMPILATION
RECORD

ARTISTS

1976 - 1989

WELLY ARTCORE

E EARTH
  ISLAND
  BOOKS

WWW.EARTHISLANDBOOKS.COM   WWW.ARTCOREFANZINE.CO.UK

Long before online streaming and even TV music videos, that were beyond the reach of many new bands outside of a lucky spin on the radio, the compilation became the most effective way to access, and be accessed by, the eager new ears and inquisitive minds of the then new punk generation. 'Nefarious Artists' is a field study of over 500 punk rock, post-punk, new wave, hardcore punk, and alternative rock compilations from their beginnings in 1976 as major label samplers and live showcases of the 'new wave'

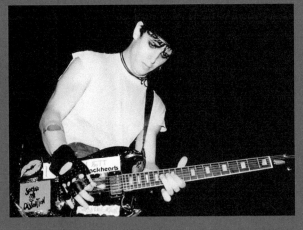
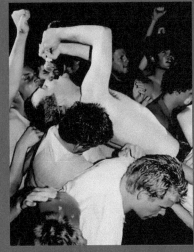
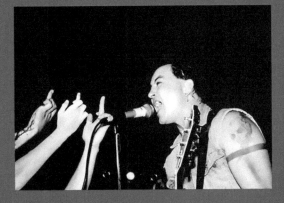
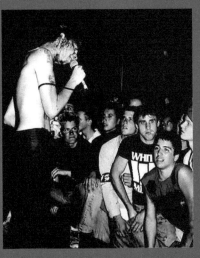

MY PUNK ROCK LIFE:
THE PHOTOGRAPHY
OF MARLA WATSON

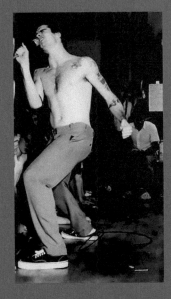
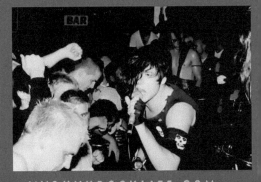

MYPUNKROCKLIFE.COM
EARTHISLANDBOOKS.COM

EARTH ISLAND BOOKS

PUNK ROCK LIFE PRESS